"*Complicated Fun* is a great rock book that works the same way as a great rock song. Find the right voices, lead with a riff, spit some truth, then watch everything explode. The result? Punk messing with punk, and birthing indie rock."

—MARLON JAMES, AUTHOR OF *A BRIEF HISTORY OF SEVEN KILLINGS*

"Cyn Collins's indispensable and incredibly entertaining history puts the reader inside the record store, at the club, and in the practice space with the music geeks who brought one of America's greatest music scenes to life. The only thing this book is missing is the music—you've gotta buy that separately."

—MARK BAUMGARTEN, AUTHOR OF *LOVE ROCK REVOLUTION: K RECORDS AND THE RISE OF INDEPENDENT MUSIC*

"In 1984, Minnesota music owned the world. While it may seem like it exploded out of nowhere, such a vibrant scene doesn't happen overnight. *Complicated Fun* tells the story of the pioneers, misfits, punks, and musical mavericks who paved the way for what became the most original and exciting music scene of that era. Cyn Collins does a fantastic job coaxing the stories from the people who lived it. This is a tale that needed to be told about bands that need to be heard."

—KEVIN COLE, KEXP-FM RADIO IN SEATTLE, FORMER DJ AT FIRST AVENUE/7TH STREET ENTRY

"A comprehensive, intensively reported tribute to a creative scene that is too often overlooked by rock historians, written by someone who cares deeply about the music and the people making it."

—MELISSA MAERZ, MUSIC WRITER AND SENIOR PRODUCER FOR *VICE NEWS TONIGHT*

"Occasionally, genius flows from geographically isolated communities. The Minneapolis music scene in the early '80s is an excellent model and shows how the passions of an inspired community can lead to broad cultural influence. *Complicated Fun* faithfully examines this story through detailed commentary from many of the scenesters and artists that made Minneapolis happen. This is a must read for fans of punk/indie culture."

—BRUCE PAVITT, AUTHOR OF *SUB POP USA* AND *EXPERIENCING NIRVANA*

"'You had to be there.' Well, no, you didn't! Laden with earnest, firsthand anecdotes of a window in time when the Minnesota punk and indie music scene created itself, Cyn Collins's book is fun to read and perhaps instructive for anyone who wants to change the world themselves."

—CHRIS OSGOOD, SINGER/SONGWRITER/GUITARIST FOR THE SUICIDE COMMANDOS

"Cyn Collins's oral history of Twin Cities punk and indie rock depicts the iconic events and people with the cheerful one-upmanship of tales told around the campfire. More remarkably, it also uncovers the parts played by lesser knowns, like the Commandos' explosives expert Linda Hultquist, the after-show party host Jody Kurilla, and the barely recorded but essential NNB. Best of all, *Complicated Fun* shows how a vital and nurturing network erupted from a few dedicated music lovers, illuminating how hungry people were (are) to create—not just music, but community. So, what are you waiting for?"

—TERRI SUTTON, FREELANCE WRITER AND FORMER *CITY PAGES* ARTS EDITOR

"To this day, the so-called counterculture has always been my family—the punk movement is more infiltrated with rogue intellectuals, as opposed to derelicts, than people think. Say what you will, but they're smart people, and they're great mentors—my mentors."

—DAVE PIRNER, SINGER/SONGWRITER/GUITARIST FOR SOUL ASYLUM

"In *Complicated Fun*, you can almost hear the voices of the players from the fertile late '70s/early '80s Minneapolis music scene. Memory is a strange beast, but the wide scope of interviewees ensures that this is a fair summary and a damn good documentation of the era."

—PETER JESPERSON, MUSIC INDUSTRY PROFESSIONAL AND COFOUNDER OF TWIN/TONE RECORDS

"Cyn Collins has diligently collected prodigious stories from the memories of musicians and fans who experienced the greatest moments of Twin Cities music history."

—LORI BARBERO, DRUMMER/SINGER/SONGWRITER FOR BABES IN TOYLAND

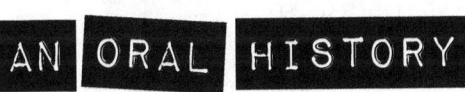

AN ORAL HISTORY

CYN COLLINS

MINNESOTA HISTORICAL SOCIETY PRESS

Text copyright © 2017 by Cyn Collins. Other materials copyright © 2017 by the Minnesota Historical Society. All rights reserved. No part of this book may be used or reproduced in any manner whatsoever without written permission except in the case of brief quotations embodied in critical articles and reviews. For information, write to the Minnesota Historical Society Press, 345 Kellogg Blvd. W., St. Paul, MN 55102-1906.

Credits for photographs and illustrations are included with the individual image captions.

www.mnhspress.org

The Minnesota Historical Society Press is a member of the Association of American University Presses.

Book design and composition by Ryan Scheife at Mayfly Design, and typeset in the Whitman typeface.

Manufactured in the United States of America

10 9 8 7 6 5 4 3 2 1

∞ The paper used in this publication meets the minimum requirements of the American National Standard for Information Sciences—Permanence for Printed Library Materials, ANSI Z39.48-1984.

International Standard Book Number
ISBN: 978-1-68134-032-6 (paper)
ISBN: 978-1-68134-033-3 (e-book)

Library of Congress Cataloging-in-Publication Data
Names: Collins, Cyn, interviewer.
Title: Complicated fun : the birth of Minneapolis punk and indie rock, 1974–1984, an oral history / [interviews by] Cyn Collins.
Description: St. Paul, MN : Minnesota Historical Society Press, [2017] | Includes index.
Identifiers: LCCN 2017001266 | ISBN 9781681340326 (pbk. : alk. paper) | ISBN 9781681340333 (ebook)
Subjects: LCSH: Rock music—Minnesota—Minneapolis—1971-1980—History and criticism. | Rock music—Minnesota—Minneapolis—1981-1990—History and criticism. | Rock musicians—Minnesota—Minneapolis—Interviews.
Classification: LCC ML3534.3 .C66 2017 | DDC 781.6609776/579—dc23
LC record available at https://lccn.loc.gov/2017001266

This and other Minnesota Historical Society Press books are available from popular e-book vendors.

In loving memory of my brother, Toby

*In memory of Monty Lee Wilkes,
loved by many in this music community and beyond*

CONTENTS

Preface ix

Introduction 1

PART 01

No Scene and No Place to Play: 1974–1977

1 Inspirations from Afar: New York, London, Detroit, and Elsewhere 9

2 The Godfathers of Minneapolis Punk: The Suicide Commandos 23

3 Before the Longhorn: Barns, Ballrooms, and the Blitz Bar 44

4 This Has Got to Be a Joke: The Hypstrz, the Mighty Mofos, and the Batson Brothers 55

5 Clubhouse for Music Fanatics: Oar Folkjokeopus Record Store 67

6 Sinister Forces: Curtiss A and Bob "Slim" Dunlap 87

7 We Do What We Like: Flamingo and Flamin' Oh's 102

PART 02

"Wham! It's a Scene!": 1977–1979

8 Punk Rock Gets a New Home: Jay's Longhorn 123

9 New World: NNB 152

10 Party Underground: The Podany and the Modesto 172

11 Ladies and Gentlemen, the Suburbs! 184

12 Local Wax: Twin/Tone Records 211

13 The Wallets Take It—to Minneapolis: The Art Rock Scene 231

14 New-No-Now Wave: M-80 Festival   *251*

15 New York City Exodus: Minneapolis Musicians Move to the Big Apple   *260*

PART 03

The Next Wave: 1979–1984

16 New Day Rising: Hüsker Dü   *271*

17 The Scene Goes On: Duffy's, Goofy's Upper Deck, and 7th Street Entry   *288*

18 Raised in the City: The Replacements   *314*

Epilogue: Kids Do Follow: National Acclaim and a New Next Generation   *327*

Cast of Characters   *347*

Acknowledgments   *355*

Index   *359*

PREFACE

My discovery of the Minneapolis music scene happened in a small independent record store in a small college town in South Dakota in the early 1980s. The knowledgeable clerk told me the best records to get in punk and alternative "college rock." During my college years, I bought all the Suburbs, Hüsker Dü, Replacements, Soul Asylum, and Prince records I could.

And then, the Suburbs performed one night in the college cafeteria. Tables and chairs were moved aside to make room for dancing. The band played tight, funky punk, crazy cool compositions. I'd never heard anything like it before. My friends and I were blown away. These five guys were all over the map—crazy keys, stellar guitar, and great rhythms making us wild to dance. Beej Chaney was a riveting front man, menacing and hilarious at the same time. And the funny, weird, interesting lyrics! "I like cows. And they like me. Hey. Move over." Their cool, aloof attitudes while singing droll songs to a funky beat fit my warped humor and my artistic bent as an eighteen-year-old. My friends and I laughed and danced the entire time. That was it. I was hooked. A carload of us would drive an hour to Sioux Falls or Sioux City to see the Suburbs whenever they came through. They remain a favorite to this day.

The Replacements performed there, too, and again, I'd never seen anything like them—colorfully dressed in striped pants, jumping around, singing and careening wildly. They looked like a circus but sounded so good. I saw the Phones there, with their cool new wave songs and look. The Flamin' Oh's reminded me of other favorite bands of mine, the Rolling Stones and the Cars.

I was eager to see this great live music more than the every few months I could in a small college town like Vermillion, which was practically a music desert. When I graduated, I moved to Minneapolis to pursue a creative career. I was excited about the opportunities to experience more of this music.

I hit the ground running, going to First Avenue, 7th Street Entry, the Uptown Bar, and underground shows near nightly, seeing tons of bands I loved, such as Soul Asylum, Babes in Toyland, Run Westy Run, the Jayhawks,

Arcwelder, Cows, and so many more—too many to mention. It was a whirlwind of fun. I felt so lucky to see live music whenever I wanted. I formed lasting friendships with people who were into the scene and similar music, feeling camaraderie and joy around what we were experiencing.

I soon began writing live music reviews and band profiles, which led to my writing the book *West Bank Boogie*, about Minneapolis's West Bank blues and R&B scene. I continued to be inspired by and write about the punk and original rock scene in various publications as well, and in 2010, I began my weekly radio show on KFAI, *Spin with Cyn*.

Through writing and my radio show, I had the opportunity to share underground, indie, and punk music, much of it local, with a wide audience of fellow fans. For years I wanted to share stories of the foundation of Minneapolis's punk and independent rock scene. I went to shows and learned more about some of these earliest bands—the Suicide Commandos, the Suburbs, Flamin' Oh's, the Hypstrz, Mighty Mofos, and Curtiss A.

In 2011, with KFAI and Ampers public radio network, I produced an hour-long documentary on the early Minneapolis scene. Talking with the artists for the documentary, I found that the youthful spirit, humor, and passion that had inspired them decades earlier remained strong, and despite some heartbreaking stories of dashed dreams of signing with a major label, these musicians persevered, never compromising their music. Many of the musicians in this book continue to perform, and some, such as the Suicide Commandos and the Suburbs, are working on new records just as I am putting this book together. To me, that illustrates the determination and tenacious spirit of the artists and support network of the Twin Cities music scene.

These pioneering musicians—whose music stands the test of time and is as relevant today as it ever was—deserve to have their stories, and their music, heard. I wanted to share stories of the beginnings of the scene through the words of musicians, engineers, tastemakers, journalists, DJs, and fans who were there making it happen, incubating it from birth, supporting it until it exploded into a thriving scene. These mavericks were truly punk rock, daring to create and perform their own music in their own way when there were no places to play in the Cities. It is an incredible story of how a vibrant community of hundreds of bands and dozens of venues emerged out of a handful of bands and pretty much one venue, Jay's Longhorn bar.

Interviews for this book were revelatory, as people told interesting, candid, and funny stories of their musical discovery, their experiences on the road, the struggles to get gigs and recording contracts, the slowly growing audiences, and the thrill of seeing fellow young musicians doing the same, as well as the waves that followed in further establishing Minneapolis as an important music hub. In the process of researching and talking to people for this book, I discovered and came to love many more bands, such as NNB, whose music was remarkably ahead of its time—dark, ominous, mysterious, with incredible guitar work and rhythms. "Slack" is one of my favorite singles of all time.

I learned of the complex interconnectivity (some might call it incestuousness) among the musicians of the Twin Cities in the late 1970s and early '80s. It seems that, at some point, most of the musicians played with most of the other musicians, either onstage or in the recording studio. They would leap up and join each other in the middle of a concert. They would form new collaborations, and individual musicians would often jump from band to band. Folks like punk pioneer Chris Osgood connected many people and projects, helping to get the scene going with a network of friends that got together to form bands, including many of his own. There was so much camaraderie and fun in that early, close-knit scene. And I learned—by talking to these men and women and attending their shows, reunions, and benefits—how much the connectivity, friendships, and mutual love have endured. These friendships forged the scene, and the support network is beautiful and inspiring.

There were many surprises and moving moments during my research. Interviewees, photographers, and collectors shared boxes of posters, photos, publications, and memorabilia from these early years, telling stories as we perused them. It was like going through a time portal, viewing thousands of photographs of these musicians as young men and women, performing wildly to enrapt audiences and occasionally goofing off. Curt Almsted, a visual artist as well as a musician, has the most amazing scrapbooks, works of art in themselves. And the walls of Dale T. Nelson's basement were covered with hundreds of posters, flyers, photos, ticket stubs, and buttons from the glory days of punk and indie rock. Others like Chris Osgood, Dave Ahl, Dick Champ, and Johnny Rey dug deep into their attics and storage spaces to uncover boxes of photos and memorabilia, some of which they themselves had not seen for decades.

Artifacts like the New York Dolls poster from Utopia House—where Chris Osgood and Dave Ahl lived when the Suicide Commandos were just getting started—were uncovered. I heard rare singles and early unreleased music, as well as live recordings from the Longhorn and elsewhere. Combing through music publications and 'zines, not only from the Twin Cities but from around the country, illuminated for me the impact of events such as the M-80 New-No-Now Wave festival and the release of *Big Hits of Mid-America Volume Three* on the national music scene. It brought to life for me the exhilaration and local pride that must have surrounded our artists as they first pursued their musical passions.

Sadly, several key people passed on during the writing of this book. The loss of Prince in April 2016 was devastatingly sad and had a deep impact on the Twin Cities and beyond, as people came together to grieve, dance, and share their love of him and his music. We also lost world-renowned front-of-house sound man Monty Lee Wilkes, a devastating blow to his family and many friends, including musicians, fellow sound guys, and crews who worked with him over the years. Monty did sound for several of the bands in this book, including Johnny Rey and the Reaction, the Suburbs, Curtiss A, the Replacements, Soul Asylum, and Prince, and he worked the board for many years at First Avenue. It was a special treat to hang out with Monty as he shared stories and graciously agreed to be interviewed for this book. He was brilliant, funny, and deeply passionate about the bands and people he worked with, and it meant a lot for him to be a part of this project. I was also fortunate to have interviewed the Suburbs' lead guitarist, Bruce Allen, at Nye's Polonaise Room about a year before he passed in 2009. These losses, and others, were very sad for me and fueled my drive to write this book.

Words can't begin to express how extraordinary a thrill it has been to interview artists whose music I have so deeply enjoyed and been inspired by over the years—enjoyment and inspiration that have only been strengthened in the process. I am grateful and excited to share their poignant and insightful stories of adventure, discovery, and challenges in building a punk and indie rock scene in Minneapolis. Memories of events and conversations from three or four decades ago may be cloudy, however, and one individual's memory may differ from others'. But this is their story, told in their words, recounting this important piece of Minnesota music history as they remember it—or as they choose to remember it.

Regrettably, not everybody who had stories to tell could be in the book, and many stories didn't make it in. There are people I missed or didn't have the opportunity to interview. I am grateful for all the contributions, including those that ended up on the proverbial editing-room floor. The punk and indie rock scene in Minneapolis is a story that I hope people will continue to share and build on.

Many of the artists and musicians featured in this book continue to perform on stages large and small, inspiring new generations of musicians and music lovers. It made my heart swell to see, just days after we lost our beloved Prince, Bob Mould and Chris Osgood share the First Avenue stage, with Bob introducing Chris as the man who taught him guitar and gave him the go-ahead to start a band, which would be Hüsker Dü—one of the greatest bands from our scene or anywhere. Osgood and the Suicide Commandos performed that night before the headlining Mould, and opening the bill was the great up-and-coming punk band Fury Things, another local three piece and one directly influenced by Hüsker Dü.

For the first encore of the night, the Commandos' Chris Osgood, Dave Ahl, and Steve Almaas joined Mould and his band onstage for a rendition of the iconic and timeless Suicide Commandos song "Complicated Fun"—as everything came full circle on that legendary stage.

"Complicated Fun" has also been the theme song of my weekly radio show, KFAI's *Spin with Cyn*, since its beginnings in 2010. I am forever grateful to the Suicide Commandos: this title speaks eloquently to this book's themes and the spirit that permeated the Twin Cities music scene of the late '70s and early '80s.

INTRODUCTION

In the mid-1970s, a few daring musicians from the Twin Cities—inspired by a musical revolution taking place in cities like New York, London, and Detroit—aspired to perform their own original indie rock and punk music. But the local scene was dominated by classic rock cover bands, hair bands, and blues bands. There were no places for these upstart musicians to play.

Many of these artists had come of age on Minneapolis's West Bank blues scene and in the garage bands of the 1960s, including such bands as the Del Counts, the Litter, the Trashmen, and, later, Skogie and the Flaming Pachucos. As teenagers, this next generation attended shows when they could, learned to play instruments, and, eventually, began performing alongside the established garage rock and blues acts. But as Top 40 music dominated the airwaves and the opportunities to experience the new and innovative music emerging from other cities were few and far between, these young musicians set out to forge their own path, developing their own bold style of music that defied categorization but later came to be labeled "punk" or "new wave" or "indie rock."

Pivotal performances by the New York Dolls at the Minnesota State Fair in 1974 and by the Ramones at Kelly's Pub in St. Paul in 1977 brought epiphanies in the hearts and minds of these young Twin Citians. They identified with the music, and as soon as they heard it, they knew that was "it"— music that was fast and loud; performances that were wild and outlandish; and musicians who were not exactly virtuosos at the art form but had a passion and an energy that carried them through. A match was struck; the torch was lit.

With an exciting new brand of music being created in other markets, but no radio station in the Twin Cities willing to play anything beyond the Top 40 hits, it was left to the record stores to bring the music to local fans. Led by Oar Folkjokeopus and its staff of dedicated music lovers, a handful of record stores began carrying imports and albums from independent labels. Releases from artists like David Bowie, Roxy Music, and Mott the Hoople introduced Minnesotans to innovative sounds coming from England in the early 1970s, and later in the decade London sent punk-inspired music from the likes of the Damned, the Sex Pistols, and the Clash. New York's innovative art scene produced a rich array of new styles and sounds, from the New York Dolls to Patti Smith, Talking Heads, Blondie, and the Ramones. Meanwhile, out of the Midwest, Detroit's Iggy Pop and the MC5 and Cleveland's Dead Boys represented the same rebellious spirit that fellow musicians from Minnesota were craving. The tastemakers at Oar Folk, Wax Museum, Electric Fetus, Hot Licks, and Northern Lights record stores shared these new musical experiences with adventurous fans eager for the next new thing, and the stores became gathering places where tunes and ideas were exchanged and relationships formed.

Soon, these young men, and a few young women—drawn together by a shared interest in the new edgy independent music—began to form their own bands here in the Twin Cities. In addition to performing cover versions of punk songs and playing louder and faster versions of other rock hits, they were writing their own original music. Bands such as the Suicide Commandos, Spooks featuring Curt Almsted (Curtiss A), Flamingo (originally Prodigy), the Hypstrz, the Suburbs, Fingerprints, and NNB would perform at parties or whatever venue would have them, playing in front of small, and occasionally hostile, audiences. They honed their instrumental, writing, and performance skills by practicing for hours on end and performing wherever they could—in high schools, rural ballrooms, dilapidated spaces, and dive bars in the suburbs and out of town.

These young musicians knew what they wanted to play and how they wanted to play it, and they went full speed ahead. But it was a slow build to gain audiences and media attention. Most people in the Twin Cities hadn't heard music like this before. Some loved it; others hated it. The scene grew gradually by word of mouth among friends, early fans, a few journalists, and community radio, such as KFAI.

In early 1977, local music writer Andy Schwartz hosted a gathering of musicians and tastemakers to discuss how to spread the word about the growing scene and, most importantly, find a place where these bands could play. A few months later, young entrepreneur and music enthusiast Jay Berine purchased the Longhorn Bar and Restaurant in downtown Minneapolis. Almost immediately, Jay's Longhorn opened its doors to live original rock and punk music, and bands like Flamingo, the Suburbs, and the Suicide Commandos took the stage in front of eager, and slowly growing, crowds. By the end of 1977, the Longhorn stage was *the* Twin Cities destination for traveling national and international punk, indie rock, no wave, and new wave bands. It went on to host such acts as Blondie, Talking Heads, Iggy Pop, Elvis Costello, the B-52s, the Only Ones, the Dead Boys, the Plasmatics, and Grace Jones. The Longhorn would also become one of the first venues where Hüsker Dü and the Replacements performed. Jay's Longhorn bar is a cornerstone in the foundation of Minneapolis punk and indie rock.

Within a few years, the primordial proto-punk scene rapidly expanded to include dozens of musicians performing indie rock, punk, new wave, no wave, art rock, and more. Minneapolis was on a parallel path with the few other scenes cropping up across the United States and England. Small but cohesive, the local scene comprised a tightly knit group of artistically inclined folks attending shows and hanging out at record stores and art and clothing shops like Rock-It Cards and March 4th. After parties and concerts held in alternative spaces—art galleries, warehouses, and people's apartments—played an integral part in forging these friendships and connections and in musical discovery.

The neighborhood around Lyndale Avenue and 26th Street was a major hub of the Minneapolis scene, with Oar Folk record store located on one corner and the CC Tap, a popular hangout, on another. Just a couple miles to the northwest, in Bryn Mawr, another cornerstone, the Twin/Tone record label was founded in 1977 by a trio of guys with the skills necessary to build and sustain an independent label. Paul Stark was a recording engineer with a savvy business mind. Charley Hallman supplied funding and enthusiasm for the bands. Peter Jesperson, who was also the manager at Oar Folk, did talent scouting and distribution through his record store channels. Within the first few years, Twin/Tone produced and released records by such local acts as the Suburbs, Curtiss A, Fingerprints, the Suicide Commandos, the Hypstrz, the Overtones, and, by 1981, the Replacements.

The triumvirate of Oar Folkjokeopus record store, Jay's Longhorn bar, and the Twin/Tone label worked synergistically to make Minneapolis one of the most original, viable, and vital music scenes in the world. "The Longhorn was the marketing wing. Oar Folk was the sales wing. Twin/Tone was the generating-the-stuff ring," observed Stark. "They all helped each other out. You need the triangle there, or you don't succeed."

This essential coming together of forward-looking record stores, a dedicated venue, and an independent record label not only helped to elevate

Chan Poling and Beej Chaney of the Suburbs performing at Jay's Longhorn bar, 1978. PHOTO BY PAUL LUNDGREN

local artists, but also elevated Minneapolis as an exciting and relevant music destination that could attract touring acts. Internationally renowned musicians came to the Twin Cities to perform and, in the process, were introduced to our own musicians. The local bands would soon be touring with these bands and playing in legendary clubs such as CBGB, Max's Kansas City, Peppermint Lounge, DC's 9:30 Club, the Rat in Boston, and more.

In September 1979, the Marathon '80: New-No-Now Wave Festival—better known as M-80 and billed as "a preview to rock in the '80s"—signaled another turning point for the Minneapolis scene. Organized by Walker Art Center and held at the University of Minnesota Field House, M-80 was the first major rock festival in the Twin Cities, and it featured some of the best no wave and art rock bands in the world, as well as a solid diet of hometown acts. In addition to expanding Minneapolis's exposure, the festival also marked a crossroads for many local musicians. Foreseeing a change heading into the 1980s, as no wave was transitioning into new wave, many Twin Cities musicians, artists, and journalists left for New York City, attracted by that city's much larger and thriving arts, music, and alternative scene. Several Minneapolis bands broke up around this time.

"The new wave is the old wave" sang Chris Osgood in the Suicide Commandos' signature punk rock anthem, "Complicated Fun." By the turn of the decade, bands were going even farther out than their pioneering predecessors in defying the mainstream, incorporating elements of performance art, punk, jazz, funk, noise, and complex arrangements. Bands such as the Wallets, Things That Fall Down, 2i, Fine Art, Têtes Noires, Urban Guerrillas, and Warheads employed over-the-top theatrics, absurdist humor, even abrasive or confrontational aspects in their performances, which drew mixed reactions while challenging and intriguing audiences. The Minneapolis scene was spreading beyond punk to encompass an even more diverse array of creative musical output. More hardcore acts were setting their own paths, distinct from the punks and indie and art rockers.

The scene exploded in the '80s. Bands such as Hüsker Dü, the Replacements, and Soul Asylum (originally known as Loud Fast Rules) took off, inspired to make their own defiant, nonconformist imprint. They brought their indomitable spirit and passion for performing loud, fast music with humor and high energy to unsuspecting audiences. With a strong DIY ethic, they persisted through obstacles in getting gigs and label support and through occasionally hostile crowds. But they also found deep support in a community that had been established by the Suicide Commandos, Curtiss A, Flamingo, the Suburbs, the Wallets, Hypstrz, NNB, and others: a solid network of audiences, music journalists, record stores, independent radio, and venues. Many up-and-coming bands performed on bills and toured with their predecessors, and the "elder statesmen" of Minneapolis punk—most of whom were still in their twenties or thirties—helped the newcomers record and release their music. Although Jay's Longhorn, after changing hands and becoming Zoogie's, had faded from the scene, new clubs and bars emerged in its wake to host punk, indie rock, new wave, and hard rock acts. Duffy's, Goofy's Upper Deck, and First Avenue and 7th Street Entry became the new gathering places for musicians and fans yearning to hear and see something different.

By the middle of the decade, Minneapolis was becoming widely recognized for its vibrant and diverse music scene, one rich with talented, category-defying bands that fused punk with funk, art with soul, and funk with rock and pop—the latter most notably and beautifully by Prince, who had catapulted himself to global renown in the late 1970s. As Prince, Hüsker Dü, and the Replacements signed on with major recording labels, local label Twin/Tone was attracting wider attention with its expanding portfolio of established and up-and-coming artists. Twin/Tone had released nearly forty records by the end of 1984—the same year that saw the releases of the Replacements' *Let It Be,* Hüsker Dü's innovative *Zen Arcade* on the California-based SST label, and Prince's album and film *Purple Rain,* which put Minneapolis and the now-famous First Avenue firmly on the international radar screen. Over the course of the decade, more and more Twin Cities acts made the leap from local darlings to international stars. After recording three albums and one EP with Twin/Tone, Soul Asylum was signed by A&M Records in 1988. Babes in Toyland made the jump from Twin/Tone to Reprise Records after two studio albums. The Jayhawks followed up their Twin/Tone release *Blue Earth* by signing with Rick Rubin's American Recordings label.

But before Hüsker Dü, the Replacements, Soul Asylum, Babes in Toyland, and the Jayhawks—not to mention hundreds of other talented and successful local musicians—it took a small group of young, creative, and audacious artists to build the foundation of punk and indie rock on which the Twin Cities could propel itself to the forefront. Their dedication—combined with that of a small but enthusiastic group of fans and support from local music journalists, DJs, record stores, and independent radio stations—allowed future waves to believe that they could forge a successful musical career out of the Twin Cities. Indeed, musicians from other parts of the country began coming to Minneapolis and St. Paul to partake in the vibrant scene and follow its path to success and recognition.

This is the story of the birth of Minneapolis punk and indie rock, as told through the voices of those who were there and made it happen: the musicians, the DJs, the record store workers, the venue owners and bookers, the producers and sound engineers, the band managers, the music journalists and photographers, the road and stage crews, and the friends and fans.

PART 01

01

INSPIRATIONS FROM AFAR: NEW YORK, LONDON, DETROIT, AND ELSEWHERE

During the early and mid-1970s, live music in the Twin Cities was largely limited to rock cover bands and the West Bank blues scene. Most radio stations played only Top 40 music. But in other parts of the world, artists were exploring new directions of musical discovery with the emergence of glam, punk, and new wave. This innovative, underground music from London, New York, Detroit, and elsewhere was making its way to curious fans in Minnesota through British music publications and select record stores, inspiring a few daring souls to pursue their own musical exploration. Appearances by the New York Dolls at the state fair and by the Ramones at Kelly's Pub—along with landmark record releases by those bands as well as David Bowie, Patti Smith, Iggy Pop, the MC5, and others—further sparked the drive to build a scene to support new, original music in Minnesota.

CHAN POLING: In the Twin Cities, there was blues, folk, hard rock, and a fusion jazz scene. We'd grown up in the late '60s and early '70s listening to really the heyday of FM radio. We had Led Zeppelin and the Beatles, Neil Young, and the West Coast rock. But by the mid-'70s, it sounds cliché, but it got really corporate. The hits of that time, at least in the rock world, were Foreigner and REO Speedwagon, that kind of stuff. So it got pretty schmaltzy and corny, in my mind. You know, I'm a teenager, I wanted to rock!

MARTIN KELLER: At the time, the dominant local bands were the Lamont Cranston Band, Willie Murphy and the Bees, Doug Maynard Band—the West Bank scene, and the Coffeehouse Extemporé folk music scene— Bill Hinkley and Judy Larson, Pop Wagner, Dakota Dave Hull, and Sean Blackburn. It was a West Bank scene until the punk movement struck in

Minneapolis, and then it was largely a downtown phenomenon, heavily influenced by south Minneapolis movers and shakers.

MICHAEL HALLIDAY: I followed that coffeehouse, West Bank scene. My older sister, Candi, went out with one of the guys. She had to drag me around to certain venues and it was fun. Back then, the drinking age was eighteen. So in high school I could go to bars. Not the best in the world for a young kid, but they changed it shortly after that to twenty-one.

It was the beginning of the scene back then, really. Even with the Longhorn, there were very few bands that came out and played all original songs. That was our onset thought: "We don't wanna play covers."

BOB DUNLAP: There weren't too many bands that were all that interesting. It was a time when bands were solo oriented—big, long guitar solos, organ solos, and sax solos. And every band in town kind of had a similar sound. There weren't many bands deviating from the norm, because if you stayed within the norm, you could get work. So there weren't many players who had a terribly adventurous spirit, it seemed to me. There were a few, but the bands that formed the original music scene all kind of deviated from the norm. And that appealed to me. I wasn't interested in being in a jam band. And it was so boring playing covers every night, just not a happy ending for anybody who had a creative interest.

CHRIS OSGOOD: In high school we would do gigs with the Cranstons and the Lake Street Stink Band. We were immersed in the West Bank scene. Dave Ahl and I used to go down to the Triangle Bar, the Flame, the Cabooze, and the Joint, and see all those bands play.

I admired people like Willie Murphy and good players in that genre. Willie Murphy was my hero. I cut my teeth on Albert King and Freddie King. I was in awe of Roy Alstad. We loved Lamont Cranston. We looked up to the Hayes brothers as real musicians who played all the time.

WAYNE HASTI: Local bands made a real impression on me—cover bands, but eclectic. Real rocking in the '60s, real guitar oriented, fast playing. My friend had the Trashmen record and I liked it. He bought the Beatles' "I Want to Hold Your Hand" and told me to come over and listen to it. I said, "Yeah, this is good, but it isn't as good as the Trashmen."

I came home that night and turned on the transistor radio for the first time in my life and started listening to music. I was nine years old.

ROBB HENRY: Peter Jesperson and I went to grade school together. We were both total Beatlemaniacs. In high school, our friendship got back together through music, around 1967, '68. There was a crowd of us that started to hang around together. Peter and I, Kevin Glynn, and a few other people who were musically inclined or huge music fans used to get together over at Peter's house. He would have record listening parties every Thursday night. He'd play what he thought would be a good soundtrack for our evening. He had a turntable behind a curtain. He'd disappear behind the curtain, and then some incredible sound would come on. I remember hearing Pink Floyd, Ten Years After, Procol Harum, Neil Young. He was always playing stuff that I didn't necessarily recognize. Sometimes he'd play really wacky things he knew would surprise us.

He's always liked being a DJ. He's good at it! I remember when he first started to play Bowie really early on. He was going, "This guy's going to be a big star." I didn't get it right off the bat. But Peter always had this sense about certain artists that were cool to see.

PETER JESPERSON: I was a record hound from the time I was a little kid. I was one of those guys that, like so many, was struck by lightning when the Beatles arrived in 1964.

My first job in the music business was distributing the British rock weekly, the *New Musical Express (NME)*. In 1972, I was in my senior year of high school. My father worked for a publishing company based in Toronto, and they had an opportunity to distribute the *NME* in the US. At that time the only British rock paper that was widely distributed here was *Melody Maker*. The *NME* was its closest competitor in England. They were going to test market it in major cities like New York and LA. They gave some sample issues to my dad and asked his opinion. He said he'd run it by me. I instantly loved it, thought it was hipper than *Melody Maker* at the time. So they selected me to distribute it in Minneapolis–St. Paul. The first issue I distributed had a flexi disc taped to the cover with excerpts from the upcoming Rolling Stones album, *Exile on Main St!*

I always had a lot of records and a good stereo, so lots of other fellow music nuts and musicians hung around my house in Minnetonka and listened to music. People like Robb Henry, Paul Sylvester, Kevin Glynn, and Mike Owens—and later, folks like Dick Champ, Rusty Jones, and Jim Tollefsrud, among others—became part of that tradition of getting together, listening to and raving about our favorite records. Once Oar Folkjokeopus record store opened, we all naturally gravitated there. The whole scene kinda developed around the record store. And I was lucky to get hired there in 1973.

Skogie and the Flaming Pachucos were really the first spark in that time period that led to the music scene we are talking about. Skogie was the first significant one because they made a 45 with a nice picture sleeve and wrote some original material. There could have been other people, but they are the first that came across my radar. Thumbs Up would be second, but Thumbs Up was a cover band, so that was a little different. What was interesting about them was they weren't whoring themselves like a lot of the cover bands by playing Top 40 material. They had that crazy hybrid of Curt's obsession with American soul music and the British invasion. It was like Wilson Pickett meets the Beatles. That gave them a sound that wasn't a commercial pitch to make money.

Poster for Skogie and the Flaming Pachucos, May 1972. Courtesy of Dick Champ

The Suicide Commandos would be third. Flamingo was about the same time. The Commandos were definitely part of a new movement, something that we hadn't really seen before—really short, fast bursts of rock 'n' roll that became known as punk rock. We didn't have a name for it at the time. But it was really smart, sometimes funny stuff. So they were definitely part of the new breed, whereas this other group, Flamingo, were a little more traditional and a little bit more of a Stones-y sort of thing.

CHRIS OSGOOD: A lot of what we were going to see and what we were hearing on the radio was inspirational to the Commandos, because we didn't like a lot of it. New York Dolls notwithstanding, whom we loved. Dave Ahl and I were at that show at the state fair, September 1, 1974. A lot of people have come to think that was the beginning of a new chapter, the Dolls coming to town and people like us thinking about the possibilities.

CURT ALMSTED: To me, that New York Dolls show was the beginning of punk rock in the Bowery Boys way—boys from the Bowery trying to out-Stones the Stones.

DAVE FOLEY: I took my girlfriend, Sandra, and her friend Nancy to see the New York Dolls at the state fair. They were totally freaked out, they had never seen anybody look like that and play music. From what I understand, the city of St. Paul passed this ordinance about dressing in drag onstage, so the Dolls couldn't dress as wild as they wanted to. So they showed up late on purpose and said, "We have to shut down the show early, because we know you farmers have to go home and shine your tractors."

They were standing in a beer tent after the show. They looked really extreme compared to the people around them. I go, "Come on, there's the New York Dolls. Let's go talk to them."

I say, "Hey guys, you want a drink?" I go get a bunch of beers and Nancy is just staring at Johnny Thunders. He's trying to talk to her and her eyes are just glued on him. She acts like she doesn't even understand English anymore. His hair was really white and really long and wild and cut like somebody cut it with a razor. They had their high heels and dresses on and makeup and were smoking cigarettes. It completely flipped Sandra and Nancy out. They had never met anybody like that. There was nobody doing that kind of thing.

DAVE AHL: We were aware of the New York Dolls and knew they were going to be at the Minnesota State Fair. Chris and I both really wanted to go.

To start the show, David Johansen comes out and asks, "Who won the pie-eating contest?" Then, *Blang!* They start doing their whole Dolls thing. With all due respect, I was amazed at how terrible they were. They were really not good musicians. It never occurred to me you could be a really poor player and really compelling at the same time. I wormed my way

New York Dolls poster from Utopia House. COURTESY OF THE SUICIDE COMMANDOS

backstage, got everybody's autograph, and talked to everybody in the band. The most talkative were David Johansen and Sylvain Sylvain. We made friends with them. We related to everything they did.

CHRIS OSGOOD: We were in the right place at the right time to pick up a lot of those signals. The same with the first Clash record. We were on our way to *our* thing. That was really great, but we were doing it already. We loved them, but there is no way we were going to cover the Clash. When the Sex Pistols came along, we just thought it was funny. The Sex Pistols were not much better players than the New York Dolls. But they were so cool at the same time. It floored me because they were such shitty players, but the music was so important.

The message is greater than the capacity to deliver it. I was smitten by the Dolls. I just went, "How can you guys play so bad and get a recording contract?" They told us how they did it. Then we did it ourselves.

The Dolls were our heroes because they made this music that was so rocking. To this day, when I hear "Personality Crisis" or other Dolls songs, I just go, "Fuck, that's it. That is the whole deal."

MARK TREHUS: I saw that New York Dolls show. I went with several of my high school chums. The band was outrageously campy. My friends' blue collar brains couldn't get past the makeup and high heels. "What a bunch of faggots!" I just smiled and nodded and thought to myself, "These guys are fucking *great!*"

As great as the Dolls and the MC5 were, the big one for me was seeing Patti Smith at the Guthrie Theater. This was after *Horses*. Here was this hypnotically seductive, androgynous babe casting a spell, forging poetry and rock and roll in a fashion that had never been heard before. There's that famous line from Jon Landau about seeing Springsteen and declaring, "I have seen the future of rock and roll." Patti Smith at the Guthrie was that moment for me.

MARK FREEMAN: We listened to the Modern Lovers and I was like, "Oh my god. What is happening here?" It was amazing. Television was great. Pere Ubu was just the ultimate. That first Talking Heads album, *Talking Heads: 77*. Everyone was young and nobody knew what was going on, which was so cool. Everything was so much its own thing. There wasn't enough of it for people to be ripping each other off yet. And so everything you saw was like little mushrooms popping up out of nowhere after a rainstorm. It was just an amazing time. I go out now and look at stuff on YouTube and stuff like that, and I know it's still going on, but I'm not sure there are concentrated places for it to happen like there used to be.

CHAN POLING: We're reading magazines and listening to records. We had Peter Jesperson and Andrew Schwartz and Tim Holmes, tastemakers. All of a sudden, it came to me: David Bowie was kind of the scene. He was a respected pop artist but really had an edge to him, really had an underground cachet of coolness. He was hanging out with the Andy Warhol gang in New

York. My older brother was always in tune with the artists and that New York scene, like the Velvet Underground. And these guys were precursors to this new kind of music coming up. Out of New York, you'd hear Television, Talking Heads, and the Ramones, of course. I also read about this notorious band in England called the Sex Pistols. We'd have rock mags and we could see the safety-pin clothes, and the torn stuff, and the spiky hair, and all that was really—you have to understand—*completely* new, completely unseen before. To see Johnny Rotten with his hair all hacked off and Sid Vicious with chains, that was *really* badass. It was really dangerous, exciting, sexy. When I heard the Sex Pistols, I thought, "Well, I'm done studying classical music here at Cal Arts. This is the new music."

I left LA, ended up back in Minneapolis. I was saying, "I want to do music like *this*," to my friends, most specifically to my good friend Chris Osgood, who had the Suicide Commandos. I had been living away for a few years, so I'd never seen them or heard them play. But I knew the sensibility; I knew they were kind of channeling the Ramones and that kind of stuff. I loved that.

TIM HOLMES: You were always listening for the next thing. I remember the Stooges making a big impact, the Patti Smith *Horses* record, and the Ramones record. Because of the Velvet Underground, New York was *the* place. I think it was viewed as a musical cultural center. Then there was CBGB.

There was this sense that there's a place where new bands are happening. I remember hearing the Modern Lovers album and *Horses* and knowing that these aren't bands you hear on the radio. So, if you found other people that were hearing these bands that weren't on the radio, then you had a certain camaraderie.

DICK CHAMP: It wouldn't be very hard to make friends because people were so excited about this music that was so absolutely contrary to what you might hear on the radio. When I look back to try to find milestones, one would be the day I met Peter Jesperson at a Lou Reed show at the St. Paul Civic Center, January of '73. I was in the front row with Jim Tollefsrud and Rusty Jones, and Peter was seated behind us. We overheard him talking about David Bowie—and we were like, "Wow! You know about Bowie, too?" He lived at his parents' place in the middle of nowhere, in what is now the Ridgedale shopping center. We'd go and listen to records, a total trip. Those are some of my fondest memories.

In large part, the people who gravitated to that scene were clustered around the bands that eventually took the stage at a place like the Longhorn. Many of us were really from the ashes of glam rock, followers of the whole British scene and some of the associated phenomena here in the States—things like the New York Dolls and a resurgent Iggy Pop by way of *Raw Power*. We had our world at Oar Folkjokeopus record store. So, you had that record store scene colliding with, welcoming, and joining with the very few bands that were actually playing original music at the time. Of course I'd be talking about Curt Almsted and his outfit Thumbs Up, Robert Wilkinson's band Prodigy, and the Suicide Commandos. Then there were the people who hung around with those bands, too. It was fun to go out to hear live music and see your friends. That's basically what the beginnings of that scene were.

I was in there with my little gang, people like Rusty and Jim, both of whom were in the original lineup of NNB with me and Mark Freeman, and a million other ensembles that followed through the years. Rusty, Jim, and I started playing music together around January of '75. We already had a kind of do-it-yourself philosophy that's a cliché now but was such a big part of it then. From day one, there was a real sense of intentionality and nonconformity to what we tried to do. Playing music certainly wasn't a career choice. Ha! Total joke! Anyway, all of us had discovered all this amazing music. It was only natural that the enthusiasm and energy would manifest itself in creating a band.

JOHNNY REY: As bands like Flamingo, the Suburbs, and the Suicide Commandos began playing together, we got to know each other better. It coalesced then. I think the music, and later having the same place to play, is what brought us together. We would say, "Oh, you like this and I like that. You should listen to this or that." It was so small at first because most of the country's listening to the Eagles and stuff like that. We were into David Bowie and Roxy Music and Mott the Hoople, in the early '70s before there's any Longhorn. I think it was artistic-type people that were into that. My friends and I loved that kind of music. You'd start seeing the same people at the clubs and start chatting about an album. And next thing you know, you're friends, because you have the common appreciation of this certain music.

KEVIN COLE: It was a weird time in music. There wasn't a lot of great music making its way to the general public. Top 40 radio had gotten pretty soft and FM radio was starting to get a little too "progressive" and denim-clad. I started working at my college radio station. It was a bit on the progressive side but provided an opportunity to explore and discover bands you couldn't hear anywhere else—but you had to dig for it.

When I first heard the Ramones, I purged my record collection. I kind of regret that now, but at the time I got rid of all the progressive rock and stuff like Lynyrd Skynyrd. After hearing the Ramones, those other bands no longer seemed relevant to me. I always was exploring imports and anything that looked interesting. So I heard the Ramones, and I was like, "That's it!"

JODY KURILLA: I was sixteen but I had a fake ID, so I would see all the blues bands and everything happening at the Cabooze. Then, when I found the first Ramones record, my world changed. It was all over after that. I remember getting that record and going into the basement of my suburban house with my best friend Ellen to listen to it. The two of us were like high school kids, jumping up and down. "Oh my god!" And that was the end. And the beginning!

BILL BATSON: You measured everything before and after you saw the Ramones. We changed our presentation as the Hypstrz after that night at Kelly's Pub in St. Paul. "Faster! Come on! Go! Go! GO! GO!"

ERNIE BATSON: The first Hypstrz show was the same weekend that the first Ramones show happened in town. Six of us went and saw them at Kelly's Pub the second night of their stint. Some of our good friends saw them the first night and came back the second night. It was a very good crowd both nights.

We'd heard the record, but seeing the Ramones was revelatory—not just for us, but for a lot of people. You hear the Ramones albums and it's all *[fast]* "Boom! Boom! Boom! Boom!" But live, it's even quicker! The Ramones had a great sense of humor, a real joy in what they were doing—a good time had by people who liked to have a good time.

TIM HOLMES: The Ramones were key to the whole thing. They were the great American punk band. At the time it seemed like this really radical, dangerous music, but it's so friendly compared to bands that really do assault and confront the audience. There are branches of punk like the hardcore stuff. The

Inspirations from Afar | 19

Ticket stub for the Ramones show at Kelly's Pub, with Berlin and the Suicide Commandos. COURTESY OF JOHNNY REY

Ramones weren't that. Those are pop songs. They weren't fucking around, but they weren't trying to crack heads open.

The Ramones performing at Kelly's Pub in St. Paul, July 1, 1977. PHOTO BY MICHAEL MARKOS

MARK FREEMAN: Max Miller was this old guy who had this office called 2M. He sold cutouts. I went there a *lot*. I bought a lot of really cool cutouts. I went there one day, and there is a copy of the Ramones' first album. It was this beautiful thing. I bought it and the first Modern Lovers' album. I went to Oar Folkjokeopus, where Andy Schwartz was working. Andy said, "What have you got?" He pulls the Ramones out of my bag, and he loses his mind. "Where did you get this? *We* can't even get this. Can I buy it from you? I'll give you anything for this. Can I play it?" I said, "Yeah, put it on." He put it on and that was *it*. I was like, "The whole world is alive again!" I felt like it was a dreary time in rock music. Suddenly it was like, "Oh my god, there is still hope!"

TIM HOLMES: I think there was a parallel development all over the world. It was happening in England, too. It was time for the next generation.

STEVE ALMAAS: At the Blitz Bar, we met Curtiss A, who had Thumbs Up. Then we met Robert Wilkinson, who had Prodigy, which later became Flamingo. We made friends with these guys. That was a four-set-a-night cover band scene we first got into, although even before we started Suicide Commandos, Chris was writing songs. I was very impressed by that, and that made me want to try to write. Being a three piece and liking '60s music, we naturally fell into the proto-punk thing a lot of other people were doing in other places.

MARTIN KELLER: It was a very organic development. Peter Jesperson at Oar Folk was one of the drivers. The Suicide Commandos were pioneers, probably on a parallel course with the Ramones in New York, and the whole punk explosion in England with the Sex Pistols and later the Clash, and all the great bands that came out of the UK. I think there were little micro punk or new wave scenes like this around the country, a reaction to the music culture, which had become pretty decadent. The days of free-form radio were pretty much over. There weren't a lot of venues, other than small, developing public radio outfits like KFAI and KMOJ, and to some extent KBEM. I think it was a reaction to a sense that rock music had lost its spirit. The Commandos and the bands that grew out of that whole period pretty much reinvented it.

TERRY KATZMAN: A lot of the local bands really wanted to prove something. Everything had to be done yourself. That made for a more dynamic experience for everybody.

The embryonic stage—you've got the big six, the A-team: the Commandos, the Suburbs, Fingerprints, Curtiss A, Flamingo, and NNB. Then we had the next tier—not down, but we had Smart Alex, Wilma and the Wilbers. I think it was the big six that really coalesced the scene. Curt Almsted was punk before anybody ever thought about it. You had bands that were more in the punk rock theme. You had bands that were really just rock bands, but they fueled on it, and they were elevated because of it. Fingerprints would be a good example of that, because they were a regular rock band, but they managed to make it more dangerous.

In the beginning, the new wavers would go see Flamingo, and the punk people would go see the Commandos. But in the end, both wavers and punkers fell in love with both groups.

JEFF BUSWELL: Until the Suicide Commandos, the only punk rock band I had seen was the New York Dolls at the state fair. When I saw the Commandos, I started thinking, "Okay! There's some new stuff going on here." I liked Todd Rundgren, Bowie, Roxy Music, because they were different than everything else. But it was pushed on the back burner to enjoy the new stuff. There was such an explosion in the late '70s.

ROBERT WILKINSON: 1977 was a pivotal year, when punk exploded and Patti Smith came out with her music and everything—it was happening other places in the world, and it happened here, too. It was a very electrifying time and the energy was palpable, it was in the air. People knew there was a big change coming.

Andy Schwartz and some local people had a meeting. We were all looking for, "What can we do to find our place? Where can we set up camp?"

TIM HOLMES: Andy Schwartz was working at the local paper. He had a meeting at his house to discuss how to establish a Twin Cities rock scene, finding places for bands to play and publicizing it. Everyone wanted a place to hang out and hear bands.

ANDY SCHWARTZ: I was inspired to write about the Suicide Commandos because there were almost no bands in the Twin Cities that performed original songs. Twin Cities live music was almost completely dominated by cover bands, except for West Bank folk and blues. I saw there wasn't any place for these new bands to play. I thought if the members of Television could convince Hilly Kristal to let them play at CBGB, then maybe some of the Minneapolis musicians can convince a bar owner in the Twin Cities to let them play.

I thought it was a unifying event. It made the musicians understand they had a collective goal and their collective strength was greater than that of any individual or any one band. When the doors are closed you make your own door.

CURT ALMSTED: Andy Schwartz had a meeting at his house. That was really a catalyst. We wanted to play somewhere. I remember Flamingo, the Commandos, and Skogie and the Flaming Pachucos were there. Andy was trying to think of a place we could turn into a clubhouse.

DICK CHAMP: Yeah, that was a big deal. It was a very Minnesota-type gathering at Andy's place. There's confusion about the exact date of that get-together, but common sense places it around six months before the June '77 opening of the Longhorn. Andy had the vision that there was a better chance of making something happen if we did it collectively. This is kind of funny in a way, because even though there was a gathering of all these different tribes, if you will, around these bands, it was still pretty competitive. You still wanted to be the best. But Schwartz got us together.

My recollection is that Andy developed a friendship with Jay Berine. Andy and I would on occasion have a cheap lunch with Jay at the Longhorn restaurant. But the meeting was fully represented by members of the bands that would later take the stage at the Longhorn. Curt was there with some of his guys. The Suicide Commandos, Bob Wilkinson, probably Johnny Rey. Members of Spitfire, Karen Haglof and Jan King's band, an all-gal group that morphed into the Wad. I think Tim Holmes was there, too. I showed up with drummer Jim Tollefsrud.

KAREN HAGLOF: I started to play music in about '75. Schon Productions would get us mainly cover music gigs in the five-state area and up in Canada. Jan King and I had the idea we should write songs and have our own music. We did a couple with Spitfire. I think we might have demised right before the Longhorn. Jan and I tried to form a songwriting partnership at the same time because of Robin Helgeson. She knew all about the Commandos. She was always the one who was hip on the "there's this great band we got to go see, the Commandos. They're these great guys. They play the coolest music. We should do something like that." She was the impetus for a lot of that.

I was coming out of a whole cover band land, trying to replicate note for note a Jimmy Page solo or Keith Richards's chunky guitar style. Then you see people that are doing an original thing. It was an entry into a whole different language and a whole different group of people focused on a whole different thing. Making it more your own is great when you're nineteen and playing cover songs. Trying to do original music—it seemed like this is a place it could happen.

JODY RAY: It was a pivotal time. I never experienced such a defined music scene as back then. Punk and new wave were coming out and looked really strong. There were a lot of different things going on, but it was such a huge family. Everybody was there for the same reason. Our scene and our band and a few other bands and performers were the ones that truly first put Minneapolis on the rock and roll map.

People wanted to come to Minneapolis and play. The word got out at that time—we were starting to be labeled the "Mini-Apple."

02

THE GODFATHERS OF MINNEAPOLIS PUNK: THE SUICIDE COMMANDOS

The Suicide Commandos—Chris Osgood on guitar, Steve Almaas on bass, and Dave Ahl on drums—are widely considered the godfathers of the Minneapolis punk and indie rock scene. Formed in the mid-1970s, the Commandos were often audacious in getting gigs, and in 1976 they convinced Hilly Kristal of the not-yet-legendary CBGB in New York City to give them a shot. The Commandos returned home inspired by the experience, and they helped pave the way for other Twin Cities bands to write, perform, and record their own original music and to take the budding Minneapolis punk and indie rock sound around the country. All three Commandos write songs and perform vocals, and their performances are fiery, fun, and filled with humor. The Suicide Commandos thrived through adversity, firings, and occasional threats of violence to become the first from the nascent Twin Cities scene to sign a record deal, and they broke ground touring to the few other cities that had independent music scenes at the time.

KEVIN COLE: The Suicide Commandos—well really, they're considered the granddaddies of the whole Minneapolis music scene. They were incredibly exciting and super fun. I'd go to every Suicide Commandos show. Watching the Suicide Commandos was incredibly entertaining. It was a rush of adrenaline.

CHRIS OSGOOD: The Suicide Commandos started in the summer of '75. Dave Ahl and I were watching the *Mel Jass Matinee Movie* one day, a movie called *Suicide Commando*. We looked at each other and said, "That's an exciting name for a band." That summer we started to audition bass players.

DAVE AHL: When we got to Steve Almaas, the second guy we auditioned, we said, "Steve, you're it." He was friends with Bruce Allen and Michael Halliday, Jeff Waryan and Linda Hultquist from Lindbergh High School, people we were friends with. And he was a like-minded guy.

STEVE ALMAAS: I met Chris and Dave while I was in high school. They were a couple of grades ahead of me. They went to Minnetonka and I went to Hopkins Lindbergh. They were dating girls that went to my school.

They lived in an old farmhouse, Utopia House. Everybody ended up over there for parties. We ended up jamming a little.

I went off to the University of Minnesota for a year. I got a call from those guys about starting a band where we would all dress up like insects. Not the most exciting idea I'd ever heard. That one didn't happen. But the next year, I'd had enough of college, and Chris and Dave invited me over and said, "We want to keep it a three piece so we can make the most money."

DAVE AHL: We decided to be a three-person band instead of a four-person band because we thought if we get paid $150 to play, fiscally that would be better. We could live on that for a week until we got the next gig. It was a hardscrabble existence, but it was great. It was really fun. It is a young man's job to do something like that.

CHRIS OSGOOD: We just didn't know how hard it was going to be...

The first rock show I ever saw, I went with Dave. We were in ninth grade. We saw the Doors in October 1969—we were hippies before we were punks. The second show was a month later. The Steve Miller Band was playing at the Guthrie Theater. The opening band was the Bonzo Dog Doo-Dah Band from England.

The Bonzo Dog Doo-Dah Band rocked our world. They were so funny. It was revelatory. I never realized that music could be that clever. They were dubbed the "English Mothers of Invention," but I saw the Mothers a couple of times, and they were never as clever as the Bonzo Dog band. The whole thing was a circus onstage. It was eye-opening. We became instant fans.

Music was different after that night. I realized it could be hilarious and clever, and it wasn't about wizards and Led Zeppelin-y stuff. We started writing songs about things we thought were interesting, things that amused us.

Everything they did opened our eyes to: "Rock 'n' roll can be funny." You can do whatever you want with it.

The New York Dolls at the state fair and Bonzo Dog were pivotal moments that defined what the Commandos were going to be. The others were Iggy and MC5. When we heard Detroit rock and roll, I said, "That's it." Dave and I went to the show at the Met Center. Iggy and the Stooges, SRC, the Amboy Dukes, and some others; Grand Funk Railroad was the headliner. That was 1970. It was a remarkable show. Iggy and those silver lamé gloves, diving into the audience. He was fearless. The music was so relentless and so powerful. We just went, "Wow."

DAVE AHL: Our first band was the Head Blues Band. We got gigs playing at our own junior high school and at parties.

CHRIS OSGOOD: Dave, Henry Neils, and I were Head Blues Band. It was between eighth and ninth grade. We started to play a lot. I really liked power trio bands. In high school, we were joined by our friend Carol Flaig, the lead singer of Sue Veneer and the Mementos. Then, E.I.E.I.O. was Dave, me, Henry, and Danny Anderson, before Utopia House. We played a week of gigs in Rapid City, South Dakota. That was the first time I'd ever gone to play a gig out of town and stayed. Guys came from the Ellsworth Air Force Base to see us. A lot of other people were speeding their brains out. They gave us some speed, and we played all our sets really fast.

I moved in with Dave at Utopia House during the summer of 1975, right after I came back from college, and we formed the Suicide Commandos. Dave's room and my room were upstairs in this old farmhouse. That's where we practiced and auditioned Steve.

STEVE ALMAAS: My parents lived three miles away. I was hanging out over at Utopia House every day. The first year was really the golden age of it, where we met and got it going.

Chris and Dave weren't like anybody I'd ever met. Even being just a couple of years older, they seemed worldly to me. They were into music like the New York Dolls, Iggy and the Stooges, Amboy Dukes, and the MC5—stuff that nobody else was listening to.

We started rehearsing, and we learned ZZ Top songs. Dave had been to

England and had Roxy Music and pub rock albums. We were learning songs off of those. We wrote original material together. After that, we managed to get a job in downtown Minneapolis at the Blitz Bar.

PAUL STARK: One night, the guitar player from Straight Up, Mark "Bucky" Lundeen, and I had the night off, and we looked at a *Sweet Potato* for bands to go see. The two weirdest names were Suicide Commandos and Minnesota Barking Ducks. We decided we'd see the Suicide Commandos at the Blitz Bar. I recognized Chris from having recorded him in my studio when he was in high school. Soon, Straight Up hired the Suicide Commandos as one of their pre-acts.

DAVE AHL: It was very much a slow build for the Commandos.

We were opening for Straight Up, which featured Tom Murray of the Litter and Xeno, the original singer from Cheap Trick. That's how we met Paul Stark. He was Straight Up's manager and their technical, sound, and lighting guy. Paul did their special effects, like laser beams and smoke stuff and everything that passed for high production value in those days.

We spent a lot of time driving on Straight Up's bus. We would meet those guys at Paul's p. david studios, which became Blackberry Way studio six years later. We'd throw our Commando amps and drums in the big bus and take off for wherever.

CHRIS OSGOOD: Eventually the cognoscenti found out about us. The Blitz Bar was lit by black lights, and anybody that had soda or tonic in their drink, their drink glowed. Each time we played there I could see more and more glowing drinks on the tables. We couldn't see the people. I could always tell when Tim Holmes came to see us because he would always order a gin and tonic, and it would glow in the black lights. I would go, "Wow. Tim Holmes is here."

TIM HOLMES: The Suicide Commandos were a band that had originals right off the bat. The covers they chose were from records I liked, and the original songs were good. They were stripped down and they were high energy. I don't think I would've called it punk rock at that point. They just seemed like they were a really good Minnesota rock band. They played whatever the hell they liked, and their sets were enormously funny and entertaining.

They were only a three piece, so each person really had to carry his weight. All three of the Commandos could really play well, and there was energy to what they were doing. The songs were a little complicated. They had individual segmented parts that fit together.

DAVE AHL: Around that time we aligned ourselves with Schon Productions. Randy Levy and Sue McLean became our booking agents. We became Sue's prom band, playing proms and little taverns and resorts.

CHRIS OSGOOD: Sue came down to see us at the Blitz Bar. We invited two other booking agencies in town, Marsh and Alpha Productions. The guy from Alpha Productions said to us after our set, "I wouldn't touch you with a ten-foot pole." He and the Marsh guy walked out. Sue goes, "Yeah, I'll start booking you right away."

Shortly after, I got a job working for Sue. Randy was doing the big shows, and Sue was booking clubs, fraternities, colleges, and things that paid well. I booked high schools and resorts and things that paid really poorly.

We had a stable of five or six bands that charged between $200 and $500. It was my job to pitch those bands. I would always pitch the Commandos last and say, "For $150, you can get this band, the Suicide Commandos. They'll play your high school, and they'll be great! Kids love 'em." Kids *did* love us, but principals hated us. The principal, not knowing anything about the music, would always make the decision based on economics. "I can get this band for cheaper. They'll probably be fine."

Afterwards, they were always mad. "You're way too loud. We don't like this." I would say, "Don't complain to me. Talk to the booking agent, Chris, on Monday. He has the same name. Complain to him." So I'd go in on Mondays and hold the phone away from my ear while the principal yelled at me. I would say, "I am so sorry. I'm gonna kick that band's ass. That bad Chris. I've talked with him over and over and over again, and told him they can't be that loud. They're never going to get away with that again." We wouldn't—until the next weekend.

BOB DeBOER: The last time I saw the Suicide Commandos was in October 1977. It was our homecoming dance at Murray Junior/Senior High. I have to be honest: as a fifteen-year-old in 1977 I was into heavy metal, folk, prog rock, jazz, fusion. I had no idea what the fuck was going on when the

Suicide Commandos played. People were standing around looking totally shell-shocked. Some people might've started moving their bodies, but they weren't sure how to feel. That was my impression of it.

The Commandos were loud. Before this, I had been looking for crazy-ass guitar with a heavy blues-rock bass line, like Led Zeppelin. These guys changed the game for me.

CHRIS OSGOOD: Eventually we quit doing the high schools and the resorts, and started to do college stuff, like Stabstock down in Northfield. We started working our way up to bigger venues, bigger gigs. We played a lot at Coffman Union at the University of Minnesota. By that time, we had some notoriety, so Sue and Randy were letting us open for shows when people were coming to town. We were getting to be the opening band of the State Theatre. That's when things really started to ramp up for us.

STEVE ALMAAS: Randy would give the Suicide Commandos a leg up whenever he could. He gave us a lot of opening spots at those State Theatre shows. We played with Cheap Trick, Iggy, Patti Smith.

CHRIS OSGOOD: The first time we played Uncle Sam's [before it was First Avenue] was with the Dwight Twilley Band. We knew they were gonna close with their hit "I'm on Fire," so we opened with it, thinking that would be the perfect thing to bookend the night. Their hit was our first song, which we thought was funny at the time.

The place was packed because it was Dwight Twilley. Jack Cunningham saw us play that night. He thought, "I'm gonna get the Suicide Commandos to play at my bar." We became the house band at Prior Place, in Prior Lake. Prior Place was a big entertainment complex, with a bowling alley and a big bar and a little bar.

We played at the cocktail lounge there through the winter and into the summer. We had to play four forty-five-minute sets a night. Then we graduated from the little lounge to the big lounge—and, consequently, got bigger audiences, and more angry audiences. That's where people first hung around to beat us up after shows. Sometimes people would go, "Wow. This is so cool." But mostly, it was, "Fuck these guys."

We were doing our thing before we heard the Ramones. Don Holzschuh brought over the Ramones' first record. We listened to it, and we just fell over laughing because we went, "This is us!" We had this thing in common with the Ramones, but we weren't trying to chase it down. It happened naturally.

DAVE AHL: That first Ramones record is just exquisite. It's like a comic book put to music. It wasn't called punk rock. It didn't have a name, what we were doing. We were calling it different things like over-minimalist or...

CHRIS OSGOOD: ... or, because we had already played at CBGB, "New York rock."

When we were doing a lot of shows opening for Straight Up, we were introduced—by Straight Up—as "from New York City," because what we were doing was being done by New York bands like the Ramones, Johnny Thunders, Talking Heads, and Blondie. It was part disclaimer that "this is something new you haven't heard before," and part hokum and serious résumé padding on their part. I always thought Straight Up was being semi-apologetic for our new sound by saying: "These guys are from New York." But we didn't care; we were on their bus and they were paying us to play. Those gigs were always fun.

We played with the Ramones at Kelly's Pub in St. Paul in '77. Tim Holmes and I and a couple other people had decided that we just *had* to get the Ramones to the Twin Cities. But there was no place for them to play. It must have been Tim who found Kelly's Pub.

We were the opening act, then Berlin, and then the Ramones the first night. The second night we got kicked up to the middle act and Berlin was the opening act.

DAVE AHL: We were super excited to play with the Ramones. It was a great time. I remember going to Oar Folkjokeopus the next day to the Ramones' autograph session. They were very kind and it was just a great day.

DANNY AMIS: The first time I ever snuck into a bar underage was when the Ramones played at Kelly's Pub. That was the first time I'd ever seen the Suicide Commandos. I was blown away by them. Besides being a great band, they really affected me that night. Growing up, I never thought about playing music professionally, because I thought only people from New York or LA did stuff like that. Then, to see guys up there from Minnetonka, playing original music and in a really cool band, really inspired me.

Dave Ahl of the Suicide Commandos at Kelly's Pub in St. Paul, opening for the Ramones, July 1, 1977. PHOTO BY MICHAEL MARKOS

GRAHAM HALLMAN: My dad [Charley Hallman, cofounder of Twin/Tone] thought the Commandos were by far the best live band in the Twin Cities. They gave it their all live and were certainly punk—like the Ramones, but even better musicians.

MARK TREHUS: On August 16, 1977, I saw the Dictators at Kelly's Pub. It was the day Elvis died. The Suicide Commandos were the warm-up act. They were a seismic revelation. Their originals and their choices in cover songs utterly blew my mind—songs I loved but I thought nobody else knew or *cared* about. I couldn't believe that a live, in-the-flesh rock and roll band was playing my secret jukebox.

DICK CHAMP: The Suicide Commandos were nothing if not hilarious. Their covers—they would switch the lyrics to all kinds of silly things. Once you got to know the band, you were waiting for that one line they would change.

There was a lot of humor in that scene. Funny stuff was always happening, all kinds of pranks. Most of us were very consciously testing the waters, to see what we could get away with. Everything outside the inner circle of what is now considered the original Minneapolis punk rock scene was so painfully boring.

CHRIS OSGOOD: I got shocked wearing a silver football helmet that had a 110-volt lightbulb mounted on the top of it that Linda Hultquist's brother Chuck designed. It looked like an idea bulb. I would don it for songs where I was going to be playing a solo. Linda, who ran our lights, could control it from our light panel. She would turn it on and blink it while I was doing my solo. After a few shows, it shorted out, so every time she hit the button to turn the lightbulb on, I was getting a shock in the back of my neck.

We also learned how to electrically detonate explosions. At the end of the night, Dave would sing Arthur Brown's "Fire" to close the set. He would go, "I am the god of hellfire, and I bring you fire!"—with the reverb cranked. Right before he sang "fire!" Steve and I would launch ourselves forward. We'd be flying through the air, and the two flash pots would go off beneath us. We would go flying into the audience, full tilt, on the wings of these explosions.

LINDA HULTQUIST: In the early days, it was a system my brother Chuck built. It was two wooden boxes and three hundred-watt bulbs in each. It featured under lights that showed up on the amps and one under Dave's drums. Chuck built me a box that controlled the lights. The box contained a very important red button that ignited the flash pots at the crucial point after Dave's saying, "I am the god of hellfire, and I bring you [explosion sound]," and there would be two huge stinking explosions. Dave used to put on welder's goggles before the song started. It was very dramatic. We used black powder, which you could just buy at the Frontiersman on Highway 12.

The flash pots were the beginning of the explosion craze that I went through. You'd take the extension cord with the filament and you put that down into the gunpowder. Then you pack it down with paper towels or Kleenex, put the cap on, and tape it, because the harder gunpowder is compressed, the bigger the explosion. I *loved* the explosions.

CHRIS OSGOOD: Linda would plant explosives in the yard at Utopia House before our Friday night parties. Then, over the course of the evening, there'd be three or four explosions. Often, it would be packed. We'd have our bigger, one- or two-hundred-person parties out on the lawn. Often they wouldn't get done until noon on Monday. Those were very famous parties.

STEVE ALMAAS: Bicentennial year, Fourth of July, we had an exceptionally good party out there. We put a TV in the yard and had the New York bicentennial celebration on, where they had all the big ships in the harbor and the fireworks going off. In celebration, we blew up the television. I remember this beautiful mushroom cloud going up into the sky.

A lot of good parties out there.

CHRIS OSGOOD: In between our two bedrooms upstairs, we turned the hallway into a nightclub we called Top O' Utopia. That's where we would have our after parties. When we got done playing some club or ballroom, we'd retire to Top O' Utopia to have a drink before we crashed. It had a really cool Sputnik chandelier and our big New York Dolls poster on a wall. We put Mylar up on all the walls.

For a year and a half or two years, our rent was thirty bucks a month. The last two years we lived there, we had no heat or running water.

DICK CHAMP: One of the places where friendships were forged was Utopia, the dilapidated house where the Suicide Commandos lived and rehearsed.

It was like a condemned building. It was eventually immortalized in the Chuck Statler video for "Burn It Down." But before that happened, it was just a place to go and drink, hang out, and sometimes a band, even the Suicide Commandos, would play while you were partying. That's where I first met Mark Freeman. But I didn't really talk to him. I was just watching him and I thought he was crazy. There actually were a lot of crazy people running around that Utopia place. Good crazy, I suppose, but crazy nonetheless.

MARK FREEMAN: It was a great place to hang out. And weird. We were blowing up TV sets.

CINDY BLUM: It was Utopia. It was "anything goes" there. It was this great house where everybody hung out and rehearsed and listened to records and partied.

ROBERT WILKINSON: The Commandos let us rehearse out there. That was so cool. Always loved the Commandos. There was a lot of love for the members of other bands.

CHRIS OSGOOD: Utopia period was lean and mean and trips to New York. Dave would hock his tools, and we'd hop in the van and go play CBGB.

DAVE AHL: Our van got stolen while we were playing at Max's Kansas City in New York. We went in, brought drums, guitars, and amps up. We left our PA, luggage, and everything else in the van. It was right before Christmas. We were going to leave that night to play with Devo in Ohio. We had to cancel the Devo gigs. We had to deal with the cops, who were very disinterested. "Yeah, a car is stolen in New York City. What are we going to do about that?" We had to find our own ways back.

CHRIS OSGOOD: Later we threw ourselves a benefit at the Guild of Performing Arts, which was one block down from the Cedar Cultural Center. A young photographer named Matt Quast took a bunch of pictures of us playing. Chuck Statler found out about us because Matt was a member of Chuck's filmmaking crew. They went on to make a lot of rock videos.

They made a film of Devo. Shortly after that, they started to do stuff for Elvis Costello, and a lot of people after that. The four of them—Chuck

Statler, Matt Quast, Dale Cooper, and John Harvey—wound up traveling the world making these movies that turned into MTV.

It was integral to making Minneapolis one of the linchpins in the whole scene internationally. That's why Elvis Costello and others developed a fondness for coming here. They knew Chuck. They knew some other people.

CHUCK STATLER: The first video I did was "In the Beginning Was the End" for Devo. The second video I did was "Burn It Down."

After Devo, I came back to Minneapolis and was really enthusiastic about putting more bands on film. I probably talked to the Suburbs, to Flamingo, to Suicide Commandos. Nobody wanted to do it. It's understandable, because it was pre-MTV. Then Chris Osgood called me out of the blue. "They're going to burn our house down, and we have a song 'Burn It Down,' and you wanted to do a video. What more do we need?"

CHRIS OSGOOD: Chuck said to us, "I'd like to make a little movie of you playing." Our Utopia House had been condemned, and it was going to be burned. We said, "Come on out and shoot that. That'll be a backdrop and we'll play a song." I very quickly wrote a song called "Burn It Down," and that became the song we played in the driveway as our house burned down behind us.

DAVE AHL: There were embers falling and melting holes in my drumhead.

CHUCK STATLER: A lot of people think it's not really happening in the same time and space as the band is playing. It's only by virtue of the fact that everything's black, and there's enough distance between the foreground element, the band, and the background that it really looks like it's just a background plate. Which is too bad.

The band set up in the driveway, and the house is in the background. The house was elevated because there was a grade to the property. It was a night shoot, so we were running a generator, and we had just a couple lights. It was bare bones. It really was *Little Rascals* style. And it was, for many years.

DAVE AHL: We were on Blank Records, which was a subsidiary of PolyGram, and we wanted them to do something with this movie and maybe help pay for it and use it for promotion.

CHRIS OSGOOD: They said, "Why would we want a movie of you playing?" Chuck wanted to sell it to them for $500, and they wouldn't pay for it.

In October 1977, three things had happened in very rapid succession: We played with Iggy Pop at the State Theatre, Utopia House burned down, and we got signed to Blank Records—all within ten days, at the most. That was a lot going on for a young band.

Much later on, Chuck Statler became the fourth Commando in a deal we did with a record company in New York called Anthology that wanted to release some Commando material. I said, "By the way, we have this video you can sell as a part of the package." We cut Chuck in for one-fourth of the profits on that. I remember proudly sending him a check for, gosh, it must have been the high side of $29. I included a note saying, "You realize now it's more glory than it is actual income, and social standing."

CHUCK STATLER: I've only ever experienced getting residual checks twice: Devo the first, and Commandos the second. By the third it's probably MTV, and then everything else went a different direction. I appreciated that the Commandos and Devo considered me.

TIM HOLMES: I remember when the Commandos started going to New York. That was a big deal: a band from our little town going there.

CHRIS OSGOOD: The first couple of CBGB gigs were in summer. We had no air conditioning in our van, so we always drove in across the George Washington Bridge with the windows open. The whole place smelled like hot piss.

We got our first booking on May 31, 1976. We were on our way to the gig, and we called there, "Our van is dying." With a bit of grumbling, Hilly Kristal, the club's manager, sent us one of his moving vans to pick up our equipment and bring it to CBGB. When we finally got there, David Byrne was there changing the strings on his guitar. He was articulate and soft spoken and wished us well. I visited with him for about twenty minutes as we were waiting for them to clear out, so we could load in. Talking Heads were still a trio—it was David and Chris Frantz and Tina Weymouth. Cheetah Chrome, from the Dead Boys, was running around. We were excited to see people we'd read about in magazines.

STEVE ALMAAS: Playing at CBGB that first time was like playing a local bar. That New York scene was a pretty small scene then, too. When we first played there, it was just a little stage in the corner. We had artist friends that were already living in New York—John King and Duncan Hannah and Steve Kramer. They came to our first gig there. Then some of Chris's Hampshire College friends from New York. So, we fell in with this arty crowd. Really interesting people to meet.

CHRIS OSGOOD: Wayne County, who was DJ'ing there then at Max's Kansas City, was very supportive. When we played at CBGB early on, the people that hung out at the club were the Ramones, the Dead Boys, Johnny Thunders and Richard Lloyd, Blondie, and bands like that.

August was a good time to get a booking in New York, because a lot of the local bands knew their constituencies and fans were out of town. So, you called up all your friends: "Would everybody please come down?" They did and were very supportive. Word of mouth could happen really quickly in New York. The hipsters would find out that you might be a fun band to see. It was like, "You ought to go see these guys." So we're grateful for that.

We played at CBGB five, six, seven, eight times. By the time we had done a number of shows there, the last two with Pere Ubu, we sold out. That was nice to go from twenty or thirty people to four or five hundred.

We had befriended Pere Ubu very early on and learned from them because they were releasing their own singles. We thought, if Pere Ubu can do it, we can do it. So we did. We got some help from Paul Stark and pressed the first couple of records.

We always played Pirate's Cove in Cleveland on the way out or back, or both, from playing the East Coast. That's where we met Pere Ubu. Ubu was happening, and they could get us on a bill with them in Cleveland. We would do Pirate's Cove, and then Hampshire College in Massachusetts, and then CBGB in New York, and a couple of other places. Eventually the Rat in Boston and then down to DC. That became a little circuit for us. We always knew we could get a gig at Hampshire. Hampshire College financed the syndicate. It would pay two hundred bucks and that would be our gas money to get to CBGB.

We'd keep adding clubs. Going west, it was Denver, then Los Angeles and San Francisco. Very long stretches. We had a couple of fun trips out west.

Playing in LA, we had a deal with Bomp Records and Greg Shaw. One of the reasons we went to Los Angeles was to get paid money we were owed. We had to drive out there and shake him down. He gave us a check for five hundred bucks. I took the check right to his bank to cash it, which we always did in those days. Back then when you got a check from a club, fifty-fifty it was good.

In Hollywood, we played at the Whiskey a Go Go in 1978, and we were very excited about that because we played with the Weirdos. We were interviewed by Rodney Bingenheimer, who was a big part of the LA scene.

We played the Aviator, in a suburb of Denver, opening for our friends, the Jonny III. The people went wild. The joint was jumping to the point where things were bouncing off the stage. When we were done, the place was ruined. People tore the upholstery and ripped the whole place to shreds and smashed all the chairs. The owner was crying. That place was ruined because of punk rock.

Handbill, showing Steve Almaas with Iggy Pop, for Suicide Commandos concert with Pere Ubu at Bookie's Club 870 in Detroit, March 25, 1978. COURTESY OF THE SUICIDE COMMANDOS, PHOTO OF STEVE ALMAAS AND IGGY POP BY CINDY BLUM

DAVE AHL: It was Denver when Peter Mensch brought Steven Tyler to see us. Peter Mensch was one of the two guys at Blank Records.

It was interesting to talk to Steven Tyler. He seemed to enjoy the show. His advice to us as up-and-coming musicians was: play frat parties. Get gigs, make money, and get experience.

CHRIS OSGOOD: When we were touring, we plopped ourselves on people's couches. You had to get organized in the morning again and find each other. We often had that planned. "We're all going to meet at such and such a place at ten o'clock in the morning." It was a different kind of communicating, much more fraught with the possibility of missing a call.

When we lost our recording contract with Blank, I found out on a pay phone in Winnemucca, Nevada. We were driving back from San Francisco, and we stopped at a pay phone to make some calls. I learned that we'd lost our contract. Pere Ubu had, too. It was the end of Blank Records. So there we are in Winnemucca, Nevada, at the Dairy Queen. I remember walking back to the guys and saying, "Guess what?"

We were grateful—I'm sure every band was in those days—to get to use somebody else's money to make a record. That hardly ever happens anymore. Record companies aren't banks, but they used to be.

BRUCE PAVITT: It was very exciting to see bands in the late '70s put records out by themselves, and it was a very exciting time. The Suicide Commandos were ahead of the curve, and I have a lot of respect for those bands who were going against the grain of popular culture at that time and before there was momentum and organization. I'm sure they got a few beer bottles thrown at them.

CHRIS OSGOOD: We completed our *Suicide Commandos Make a Record* by January 1, 1978, and it got released the first week of February. We were touring with Pere Ubu by the end of February or the first week of March. That's how quickly things happened in those days. There was no slack. We got signed, we got guaranteed the money, we went into the recording studio. We recorded it in two weeks, mastered it, and boom-boom-boom-boom.

It was a whole new thing for us. We were so happy to feel like we were a breakout band from the Twin Cities. We liked our scene. We were, I hope, as supportive as we could be of all our pals. To be able to do that was something we were happy about, of course.

We had the record signing party at Oar Folk. We had twin black and gold Honda 175s we bought from Dave's brother John. We wanted to be like the Monkees on TV, riding those minibikes. Steve was on the back of one of our bikes. We rode right in the front door of Oar Folk and took our motorcycles up and down. And then we parked them in the store and signed records. It was pretty cool.

STEVE ALMAAS: Writing songs and performing them was really important to me. If I had favorite Suicide Commandos songs I wrote, I think "I Need a Torch," "Attacking the Beat," and "I'll Wait" are good punk rock songs. It's frighteningly hard to do something that simple, sometimes.

The Suicide Commandos' *Make a Record* release party at Oar Folkjokeopus, February 1978.
PHOTO BY DANNY AMIS

The Suicide Commandos at Jay's Longhorn bar. PHOTO BY DANNY AMIS

DAVE AHL: We did everything we could do to find places to play, to try to convince radio stations to play our self-released singles.

CHRIS OSGOOD: We took our first single to the radio station in Sioux City, and they played it. We went down as a band and marched right into their offices, no appointment. "We're here. We have our new single. Listen to it. Are you going to play it?" And they indulged us.

DAVE AHL: They were probably just amused enough to throw it into rotation.

CHRIS OSGOOD: That's my life formula: people have been just amused enough by anything that I try and do, whether it's a single or a bottle of wine or whatever it happens to be. So, probably a few things in our lives were lucky breaks, because we were impetuous, we were fearless. We didn't know we couldn't do it. *Rolling Stone* called us beleaguered outsiders. The last sentence in their review for *Suicide Commandos Make a Record* was, "These guys are a band to love." We've been grateful for that ever since.

Humor and audience participation is still the most important thing for us. We learned from Skogie we could do that. Terry Katzman said the Commandos would control the crowd like a schoolteacher controlled her unruly pupils. People, for some weird reason, went along with whatever we were doing.

DAVE AHL: It was a friendly crowd, and it was *our* crowd. We loved them and they loved us.

STEVE ALMAAS: We loved what we were doing. We really enjoyed each other's company. The thing about the Suicide Commandos was it happened so fast. It was three years. We got in, we learned a lot, we made a noise, and we got out. It's satisfying to me that the Commandos did what we could do right then. Playing our own material was *huge* to me. We still played a lot of other material, but the bands that came after us didn't have to.

CHRIS OSGOOD: The night that we broke up, I knew I was going to smash my guitar—not my good guitar, but another guitar—and probably there'd be some mayhem. I turned around and Dave had his welder's goggles on, and he was sawing through one of his cymbals with a diamond-tipped saw. We would often push over our amplifiers.

We broke up in November of '78 and finished recording in December. Steve moved to New York shortly thereafter. Dave and I started working on our other projects.

TERRY KATZMAN: The Suicide Commandos were doing punk rock before anybody else was doing it. I have recordings of their very early performances. They were doing Alex Harvey and Iggy and New York Dolls. Nobody was doing that. So they were hip before it was hip.

Once they started moving into writing their own material and recording singles—"Emission Control" and "Monster Au Go Go" and "Mark, He's a Terror"—they were set off on their own. They took pop music and put it through the meat grinder. It came out on the other end as their own. The speed at which they played was amazing to witness. They played fourteen songs, probably, in thirty-five minutes.

How they interpreted rock and roll and their devil-may-care attitude, bringing so many influences into their sound, influenced a bunch of other bands to do the same thing. The influence carried on, because clearly from Suicide Commandos to Hüsker Dü—a three piece really shows off the merit and strength of a band because there's no two guitar players to hide behind. It's one guitar player. That's what made Chris Osgood special, that's what made Bob Mould special.

KEVIN BOWE: The Commandos are such nice people. Each of them has a very quirky sense of humor. A lot of artists I work with are what I call cultivated eccentrics. They want you to think they're different and weird, but really they're not at all. But the Commandos really *are* different and weird. Look at Chris. He's a weird dude and I love that. Dave is, too. The things they think are funny, they're just not typical, and you can hear those little tweaks in their music. "We don't like you 'cause you aren't any fun." Who writes "Guitar chords that sound real cool," or rhymes "cool" with "ooh"? It's just weird. These days in indie rock there's a lot of guys who are like, "I'm really different," and you do a record with them and go, "You're not different at all! You're just like the jocks I went to high school with." Not only the Commandos, but a lot of people from that era really were different. You had to be different to do this kind of music back then because the mainstream was the mainstream and punk was punk.

CURT ALMSTED: The Suicide Commandos were punk rock even more so than the Ramones—just like, "Wham!" There's no veneer. I love those guys.

CHRISSIE DUNLAP: Loud, fast, and furious fun! Once you saw and heard the Suicide Commandos, music was changed. So yeah, they were the first real punk rock band in Minneapolis and the leaders of the pack for that genre.

PETER JESPERSON: It can't be overstated, the Suicide Commandos really cut a path where there hadn't been one before, and they had real ambition. There were a lot of local bands that were really good, that were doing good work, but the Commandos always felt like they were looking to make a name for themselves and to get outside of the Twin Cities. They got to New York before anyone else, they got to LA before anybody else, and they were so hugely important. I think that there are a lot of us—me included—who may not be doing what we're doing now without the Commandos.

They influenced bands that probably weren't even fans. They were so important to the scene. It's like, people who claim to not like the Beatles are still benefiting from what the Beatles did. That rings true for the Commandos as well.

TONY PUCCI: Suicide Commandos for me were really influential. That was a door opening for me big time. To hear local stuff on par with some of the things from England and New York, it was "wow." They were a big influence. Chris still is a big influence.

PAT WOODS: Absolutely, for me, too. I loved them. They were doing their own material, they were doing rocked up versions of '60s songs that I had grown up with. "You can do that to a song?" I loved that about the Hypstrz, too—playing everything faster and harder. It was very satisfying.

MARK TREHUS: The Suicide Commandos changed my life forever. Chris Osgood taught me you could love rock and roll *and* find a way to make a living from it if you were dedicated enough and believed hard enough.

Handbill for a "Seven Day Bender" by the Suicide Commandos at the Longhorn, circa 1978. COURTESY OF DICK CHAMP

KEVIN COLE: You can't overstate how important the Suicide Commandos were to the development and creation of the Twin Cities punk, new wave, independent music scene. The whole scene—think Hüsker Dü, the Replacements, the Suburbs, Soul Asylum, and every punky, garage rock band that came out of Minneapolis–St. Paul. The Suicide Commandos were my favorite band. Hell, they were everyone's favorite band! Prior to them, you had cover bands playing Top 40 or future classic rock. The Suicide Commandos came along playing original songs that were fast, short, dangerous, snotty, fun, and smart. Well, at least semi-smart. The Suicide Commandos reclaimed rock and roll for the rest of us.

03

BEFORE THE LONGHORN: BARNS, BALLROOMS, AND THE BLITZ BAR

As more and more Twin Cities musicians began forming bands and exploring the new sounds of punk and indie rock, there was still a dearth of places for them to perform in front of live audiences. Jay's Longhorn bar would not become a rock music venue until June 1977. So in the beginning, bands like the Suicide Commandos, the Hypstrz, Flamingo, and Curt Almsted's groups had to travel to play at suburban and rural ballrooms, small-town bars, barn parties, and even high schools. And the response was not always welcoming.

The Blitz Bar, located kitty-corner from the Longhorn in downtown Minneapolis, hosted bands for a brief period, providing a small but growing base of fans, music journalists, and other artists with the opportunity to experience the city's burgeoning rock and punk scene. These early gigs further incited the bands' desire to have a regular place to play.

DAVE FOLEY: There was no place for bands to play in Minneapolis. First Avenue [known first as the Depot, and then Uncle Sam's] used to have big bands like Joe Cocker and those kind of guys. The bar scenes were into blues bands and rock bands like Crow. There was nothing to do.

I used to have parties in my loft. This guy would bring over guys in bands. One night was Albert King's band. Elvin Bishop played in the loft. These guys would come over after the Cabooze and play. We would have people hanging out.

There was nobody in downtown living in buildings except for me and a couple of my friends. There was a meat packing area, outdoor fruit markets, and a couple of bars that had blues bands, like the Jet-A-Way Lounge.

People got hip to the idea of getting into lofts, so they would knock on my door and ask, "You got any space?" I would say, "No, go away." So it started to get more and more popular.

Before the Longhorn | 45

Exterior of the Blitz Bar at 5th Street and Hennepin Avenue in Minneapolis, 1976. PHOTO BY DANNY AMIS

JAY BERINE: I of course enjoyed drinking and going to bars and having the kind of fun young people like to have. We would go downtown. We would go to the outlying suburbs for bars. Pretty much none of them had live music in those days. What live music there was, there was nothing original—it was all cover bands. We referred to them as Holiday Inn bands. We made fun of them, because many of them were not very good musicians and we really didn't care for the songs they played.

DICK CHAMP: It's hard to imagine because it's been so sugarcoated and Disneyfied, but downtown Minneapolis was a very rough-and-tumble place then.

I don't remember about the Blitz being particularly dangerous, but it's conceivable. I saw the Suicide Commandos there. They played downstairs, and the strip club was at the main level. So if you didn't like the band, there was a second option there. *[laughs]* We just thought it was outrageous! Definitely the kind of humor of the time, and we appreciated the juxtaposition of punk rock downstairs and cocktails and strippers upstairs. It was part of the fun of that early period.

KAREN HAGLOF: The Blitz Bar in downtown Minneapolis felt like a real dive bar, like a scary bar I wouldn't go into if I weren't going to see the

Suicide Commandos. It definitely felt on the down low. Before this era I used to see plenty of bands at the suburban clubs. I'd hear bands that did covers of the Doobie Brothers, or disco or disco-rock fusion, which was pretty glitzy. A different type of band, you would see there at the Blitz.

CINDY BLUM: The staircase outside the building went down to a door where you'd enter into the basement. It was a narrow, dimly lit stairway with a single lightbulb, Edward Hopperesque. Inside, it was an unassuming place. Very small, with low ceilings, mostly stage and dance floor, a few tables around the dance floor. I remember dancing till the end of the night. I saw Prodigy there, and the Suicide Commandos. It was always full when they were playing. It was about a hundred capacity.

MARK FREEMAN: The Blitz Bar was pretty short-lived. It came right before everyone started going across the street to the Longhorn. The Blitz was a dump; a tiny little dive, flat black inside. It was one of those places that had a lot of potential. A lot of my favorite bars have been dumps.

CHRIS OSGOOD: There were bullet holes in the Blitz Bar stall door. Somebody had died sitting on the toilet, shot there. They were pretty disgusting bathrooms. So we would go across the street to the Longhorn, when it was a jazz place, where they had nice bathrooms. Little did we know that we'd be getting a lot of use out of those bathrooms about a year and a half later.

TIM HOLMES: I don't remember the Blitz lasting very long, and I don't remember seeing any bands there other than the Suicide Commandos.

CURT ALMSTED: I know I played the Blitz Bar at least once, with Thumbs Up. The Commandos played there. We went there to see them, and that was a fun scene. It was a little different than we were used to. It was a little more raw and raucous. I probably liked it more than any of the guys I was playing with did, but still it was fun.

ROBERT WILKINSON: When Flamingo formed in 1977 we used to play the Blitz Bar. Curtiss A had Thumbs Up, and the Suicide Commandos and Flamingo would play the Blitz. That's pretty much where it started.

CHRIS OSGOOD: The owner of the Blitz loved us. He was a very nice guy. After our shows, he and I would go from cash register to cash register, and the band would get a third of what was in each register. There was no, "You're getting a hundred fifty bucks" or "You're getting five hundred bucks." It was a third of three tills. What a weird way of getting paid. We didn't know. But I never felt that we got screwed.

The guy that hired us at the Blitz Bar was murdered, for owing a debt to somebody. That was the end of our gigs at the Blitz.

Handbill promoting live music at the Blitz Bar, including the Suicide Commandos, Skogie, and Lamont Cranston, among others, November 1975.
COURTESY OF THE SUICIDE COMMANDOS

DAVE AHL: Every weekend we drove to some small Minnesota or Iowa or Wisconsin town. We had a map on the kitchen wall at Utopia House, and we'd stick a pin in every little town we played in. I'll be driving around outstate nowadays, and I'll say: "Oh, I played there." It's this little hole in the wall bar by the side of the road. The Hollyhock Ballroom or the Shamrock Ballroom—so many of them.

LINDA HULTQUIST: There were ballrooms all over in small towns. That was the place to go. Lots of different kinds of bands played there then.

CHRIS OSGOOD: Every different kind of band, from polkas to psychedelic. Big dance bands like Jules Herman. It was as far north as Grand Rapids, as far east as Rice Lake, Wisconsin, as far south as northern Iowa.

Before the Commandos, when Dave Ahl, Henry Neils, Carol Flaig, and I were Sue Veneer and the Mementos, we played a lot at Proch's Popular Ballroom, in popular Ellsworth, Wisconsin. We would open for bands like Flash Cadillac and the Continental Kids. I remember getting sage advice from these people, who had to have been twenty-one or twenty-two at the time. They'd really been around the block. It was also the beginning of us playing ballrooms. It was completely a thing then.

JOHNNY REY: From '70 to '75, it was all ballrooms. Bands hardly had any place to play in town. At the Union Bar they'd have the Explodo Boys and Willie and the Bees. Then we started playing our kind of stuff.

ROBERT WILKINSON: I remember playing ballrooms where more of the cover bands used to play. We'd play like MC5 and a lot of original music. We got a mixed reaction back then. But things started changing over time, '76, '77—that's when things kind of exploded with original music.

ERNIE BATSON: The ballrooms began hosting rock bands beginning in the '60s at least, maybe the '50s. The Trashmen played a lot of the same ballrooms that were around when we were playing. Most of them had lights but none of them had PAs, so you brought your own PA in. The ballrooms all looked alike. Big square buildings, big dance floor.

BILL BATSON: Wood booths all around. The good ones had a spring dance floor that moved. A lot of them had wadded-up horse hair underneath. That's what the spring was.

ERNIE BATSON: At a party hall at Trollhaugen, we were on a stage that was ten feet above the dance floor. It was tiny. We were just staring down at the dancers. We've done lots of things like that.

Mostly we were playing ballrooms up north, '74 or '75, in the punk rock version of the Hypstrz. We only did three sets with that band, up in Duluth or in a ballroom. That was pulling out all the stops, playing everything we knew that would fit: Eddie Cochran, Chuck Berry, the Trashmen.

We were still being booked by an agency, I think it was Peak Productions. Everyone booked with various agencies back then. We did a stint with Alpha and at least one long stint with Marsh Productions, where we first met Bill Pluta, our case manager, basically. I remember the first time we met him: we are all dressed up in our leathers and greased hair and he's got monster hair, gold lamé hot pants, and a gold lamé vest.

BILL BATSON: And platform boots. He looked like Ziggy Stardust.

ERNIE BATSON: We did the Horseshoe Lake Ballroom, in Browerville by Alexandria. The first time we played there, we pull up in the middle of the afternoon and the owner comes out and says, "Hey guys! Good to see you. It's been a long drive. Do you want something to eat? I've got some hot dogs, pop, and stuff." At the end of the night, "You guys had eight hot dogs and the water. We have to deduct that from your pay." After that we refused anything from them.

BILL BATSON: What about going out to Tilton Ballroom in South Dakota, just south of Sioux Falls? It was totally dead for the first set. But the second set all of a sudden the Sioux Nation came in, basically. They were all Sioux and were gorgeous as hell. Beautiful people. I'm like "Holy crap!" That was a fun time. They danced and they loved it.

It was a long drive back, though. That was one of the White Castle nights. We would buy White Castles on the way to the gig in the morning, and it's still on the dashboard when we go home the next morning.

ERNIE BATSON: We would also play up at Williams North in Duluth. It would be three nights in a row, bring our own PA and lights in for that. It was a supper club. Those were wild nights.

The supper clubs were way up north, so we stayed at a motel right across the street from Williams North, the Flamette, run by this lady who had five or six Chihuahuas. It was a great place.

BILL BATSON: Each room was a double room. The front room had a bed in it, and there would be a back room with a bed. Party in the front and sleep in the back. So we would fill the front room with beer cans after three nights. "We don't need any towels or anything. We're fine!"

ERNIE BATSON: We would all run and get in the van and wait for Bill to pay and then he would come running out before they started cleaning.

I think the last time we played there, Flamin' Oh's were up there a couple weeks later. They said the owners were asking, "Do you guys know a band called the Hypstrz?" We had left a really bad mess. They were like, "No. We've heard of them, but we don't know them."

CHRIS OSGOOD: Playing resorts up north, we knew, after doing two or three of those, we were gonna get fired in one or two nights. So we would tell our girlfriends, "Yeah, we'll be home on Friday or Saturday night." The usual booking was to play Thursday through Sunday.

We'd negotiate an out to the contract and head back down. That happened two or three times. We usually wound up settling for cases of beer and bottles of whiskey. Sometimes more—whatever it took to get rid of us.

STEVE ALMAAS: We definitely were not above enjoying getting up people's noses, just playing too loud and fast. Sometimes you could really feed off that energy. It would be great. But sometimes it was a drag, too. We'd get fired.

LINDA HULTQUIST: These guys were not *trying* to piss people off, really.

CHRIS OSGOOD: Well, sometimes we were. Like when I was baiting those guys down in Prior Place. When they started throwing stuff at us.

LINDA HULTQUIST: You were just playing music they didn't understand.

CHRIS OSGOOD: It was sort of a typical thing that the people that stuck around wanted to beat us up, because their girlfriends were intrigued by us.
   One time on our way to a gig, we call the bar and say, "Our car died on 35." They sent out a fleet of four or five station wagons to haul us and our gear to the gig. We announce halfway through the night that we need a place to sleep. A farm kid steps up. He was this nice, shy kid. He went out to the bar when his parents had gone away for the weekend.

DAVE AHL: We slept on the living room floor, and in the morning he made us this wonderful farm breakfast, with fresh milk, right from the cow.

LINDA HULTQUIST: He was not like some rock and roll kid at all. And to have him take us home and let us sleep there...

DAVE AHL: "Bring a punk rock band home!" *[laughs]*

CHRIS OSGOOD: That was one of the times Cindy Blum showed up to save us. Cindy was driving her car, a white 1962 Impala with a red interior. It was really a beautiful car.
   She also came to get us from Mankato one time. It was me and Dave and Steve. We had opened for the Babys at the Cobblestone Ballroom by Lake Okoboji, Storm Lake, Iowa. It was probably one of the biggest audiences we played for. Going home, we all crammed in the front seat of my mom's station wagon. I'm driving down the hill into Mankato, and I go: "Wow! There's my mom's wheel, rolling along next to the car." The wheel had come right off the car. We spent the night at the Happy Chef and waited for the sun to come up.
   We played down in Owatonna; there was a place called the Cedar Inn. Then we played at a biker party and a pig roast down there. All those bikers were really high on speed.

LINDA HULTQUIST: It was ophthalmological-quality cocaine, the kind that they put in your eye for eye surgery. It looked like a little ice cube. I remember that gig as being really weird, slightly threatening. But a lot of these things were.

CHRIS OSGOOD: We didn't do any of that speed. It was spooky because these guys were like outlaws. Altamont had happened. You weren't sure if they were going to come after you with pool cues at the end of the night.

One time, we played up in Hugo on a flatbed truck in the middle of nowhere. These guys, again, were high on speed and so they didn't want us to quit. They just kept passing the hat and coming up with another fifty bucks. Then we would do another set. Then another fifty bucks, and we'd play another set.

I think the bouncer at the Cedar Inn was the connection to those bikers, and that's how we got that gig. He was a gentle giant kind of a guy. He'd put me on his shoulders. Master and Blaster—it was right out of *Road Warrior*. Here you are swaying around on the back of this giant and playing. I got picked up from time to time. I was quite a bit skinnier then, so I was able to be manhandled.

STEVE ALMAAS: At the biker party near Hugo, they were not ready for us to end. Seven sets. In a cornfield. With a gasoline-fueled generator. With amphetamine-crazed drunken bikers.

BRUCE ALLEN: We played a biker party near Farmington. It was put on by DC [Dann Carlson]. We played in this big barn. They weren't throwing hundreds at us to keep playing, however.

CHRIS OSGOOD: There was a barn near Highway 100 and Brooklyn Center. It was a big farm. Jeff Buswell came to see us. He couldn't see the band. He was used to band members being taller. His comment to me afterwards was that Steve and I were as tall as Dave was sitting down. I remember going back and that was the first time I saw Fingerprints, playing that barn.

BRUCE ALLEN: That was the first time I saw Fingerprints. That's kind of where they made their debut. They did cool covers like Iggy Pop's "Lust for Life." Then things got much more urban.

JODY KURILLA: The barn parties! That barn party is still going on. One of the first barn parties was the Hypstrz and the Suburbs. I remember how much fun that was. It was an inspirational hootenanny like no other.

The Hypstrz performing on a flatbed truck at a barn party in Rosemount, Minnesota, summer 1978. PHOTO BY PAUL LUNDGREN

BILL BATSON: With Dann Carlson, we did a couple farm parties, a flatbed-truck kind of thing. Those are what started us on our trip—on our way!

JOHN HAGA: Dann Carlson and Kurt Nelson had a barn party down in Farmington. The Hypstrz on a flatbed trailer. That was the first barn party we did. You lean forward on an audience and it freaks them out a little bit. We kind of scared people.

KURT NELSON: Dann Carlson was getting into promoting shows. We almost got the Clash here. We promoted some cool shows. We had Destroy All Monsters, which was Ron Asheton of the Stooges with Michael Davis of MC5. Dann was promoting a lot of early Suburbs shows. Had a lot of barn parties with the Suburbs and the Hypstrz back then.

HUGO KLAERS: The barn parties were our first exposure to the Hypstrz. We played at Elko Speedway, too, later.

KURT NELSON: Dann might have made it as a promoter, but we got a show together at Elko Speedway, and it was a debacle. He had Mitch Ryder,

Dwight Twilley. My band Simba was one of the few bands that played, Flamingo played, and Eric Burdon of the Animals, I think. It was a big show. They were even giving away a hot-rod car. Then the show was rained out. It was a *huge* loss. They had rain insurance, but the insurance went by how much it rained at the airport. They didn't get an inch of rain at the airport. It rained a *whole* lot more in Elko. So it wasn't covered. That pretty much was the end of all Dann's promotion work. We promoted the hell out of it. It was on the radio. We made our own commercials. We were going around to all the parks in Minneapolis, handing out flyers, which were little comic books that Dann wrote and printed up.

The Suburbs didn't get to play. Beej Chaney was on acid and bummed as hell, sitting in the rain crying.

Dann did great up until the debacle we couldn't get back up out of. We had another party where no one got to play, in this empty warehouse downtown. There were a thousand people in there and sixty kegs. The cops shut it down before we even got to start.

But yeah, some of these barn parties were incredible successes. A thousand people. And these are people that had no idea who the Suburbs or the Hypstrz were.

The Suburbs—*(left to right)* Hugo Klaers, Bruce Allen, Beej Chaney, and Michael Halliday—at a barn party in Farmington, September 16, 1978. PHOTO BY PAUL LUNDGREN

04

THIS HAS GOT TO BE A JOKE: THE HYPSTRZ, THE MIGHTY MOFOS, AND THE BATSON BROTHERS

Beginning in the early 1970s, brothers Bill and Ernie Batson formed a series of bands—King Kustom and the Cruisers, the Hypstrz, the Mighty Mofos—that exemplified the furiously fast and aggressive aesthetic of the new musical movements and layered it on top of 1960s garage, surf, and psychedelic rock, as well as their own punk-inspired originals. The Hypstrz were one of the first local bands to take the main stage at First Avenue (then known as Uncle Sam's), where they opened for the Ramones. Their *Hypstrization!* album, recorded live at Jay's Longhorn in April 1979, was a pivotal release in bringing national attention to the Twin Cities scene. Over the years, the Batsons and their bandmates performed countless shows with other foundational bands, including the Suicide Commandos and the Suburbs, and their raw power and high-octane intensity inspired other musicians, from the early '80s through today. They are revered as one of Minneapolis's best live rock and roll bands.

ERNIE BATSON: We started in the basement at the Dupay house.

BILL BATSON: When I was fifteen, I joined a band that turned into King Kustom and the Cruisers. I met Randy Weiss. He was in eighth grade and I was in ninth grade. I met Joe Dupay. Mark Paquin started singing. We started with five songs, for our first ten rehearsals. Ernie joined later.

We started going out every Sunday to the Friars Club, which is a dinner theater. Every Sunday they would do Butch Greaser & the Hoods, "Back to the Fifties." They let me in because I was dressed up and I was six feet tall. We all went greased and drank pitchers of 3.2 beer.

ERNIE BATSON: I started in May or June, 1974. They had been going since '72. They decided they wanted a second guitar player. I could barely play guitar, but I said, "I'll do it!" My first guitar was a $25 acoustic my folks got me. After a year, they got me a Yamaha classical guitar. You guys were practicing in our basement and I went down and played Joe's Telecaster and I thought, "Wow, that's really cool sounding." My folks bought me a Telecaster. They were very, very supportive of our efforts.

Joe had an extra amp. For sixty bucks or so, we got that huge Fender speaker bottom. Then we got a Vox Super Beatle. I used to carry it up the stairs into my bedroom and play up there, and then carry it down in time for shows. I was so glad when I finally got a smaller amp.

By then the guys had gotten a loan from friends to get a PA. We were learning tons of songs to play lots of shows, so we could pay off the PA loan. That went until 1976, and then we started woodshedding for the Hypstrz, practicing and coming up with what we wanted to do.

BILL BATSON: That's how I learned how to scream. I listened to Paul Revere & the Raiders and James Brown. I couldn't match that. Mark Lindsay from Paul Revere & the Raiders is the best screamer. I heard the Sonics' "The Witch" and "Psycho." Those had great screams. I was inspired because I had Ernie, my brother. He had records. I didn't. We grew up on the Monkees and stuff like that.

JOHN HAGA: I hung out in a music store on Hennepin called Knut Koupeé, in 1973 or '74, when it first opened. Next to Knut Koupeé was a musician's referral service. Zippy Caplan, who was in the Litter, ran that. He was one of the greatest guitar players in the Twin Cities in the '60s.

One day I'm sitting there after school—my senior year, fall of '75—and these two guys in leather jackets, big, hulking figures, come in. It's Bill and Ernie. "We need a drummer." I'm like, "Okay, I got a bunch of drummers. What kind of stuff do you play?" "We play stomp '50s." I'm thinking, I can play drums with these guys. "When do you need a drummer?" "Right away." Bill is in my face out of the gate. I said, "I can do it." "Oh *can* you?" I said, "Sure!" He says, "You have to audition."

We went out to the Snail Lake Supper Club in Shoreview. They're all greased up, they're wearing leather jackets and they change into Hawaiian shirts when they do the surf. It's King Kustom and the Cruisers and they're playing Eddie Cochran, Gene Vincent, Beach Boys, Little Richard. Bill Haley & His Comets was their high point, where they all did moves together.

I even greased up for the gig because I was so excited. They call "Peggy Sue." Peggy Sue is paradiddles, but most people fake it out. Then they call "Wipe Out." If you could play both those busy drum songs back to back, you were in. I thought that was an amazing way to test somebody's stamina, because it's all about stamina when you're playing with those guys.

King Kustom played ballrooms, bowling alleys, lounges. Monday nights we played the Burnsville Bowl week after week. We'd go to Duluth and play Williams; we kept going to the Snail Lake Supper Club. We played all the time. We each made $17.50 a night. We played around for a year and a half.

There was a '60s cover band called Eddie Hurricane. They did really cool pop stuff—Dave Clark Five, Paul Revere & the Raiders, Gary Lewis and the Playboys, the Animals. We said, "We're doing '60s stuff from Soma in King Kustom. Why don't we just beef it up?"

BILL BATSON: We were watching a curve. There were a lot of '50s cover bands making money. We were making *okay* money as King Kustom, but we're at the bottom of the totem pole. So, "Hey, let's do '60s bands." We liked all these local '60s bands: the Trashmen, the Del Counts. We were doing those.

As King Kustom we had maybe two hundred songs. We did a complete surf set. We pretty much dropped all those into the original Hypstrz.

ERNIE BATSON: The Hypstrz started out as a '60s cover band. In the first version of the Hypstrz, Joe Dupay, the lead guitar player in King Kustom, became the bass player. Rick Reller, this navy vet, played lead guitar. I took on lead guitar, too. John Haga played drums. We were doing ballrooms and bowling alleys, the same as we did in King Kustom. But we were a '60s band, so I combed my hair down. We all got suits. The suits came about as a result of wanting to look like the bands nationwide. The Beach Boys wore suits, the Astronauts wore suits. The Astronauts were a big influence for us.

We went down to Foreman & Clark's shop downtown on 5th and Hennepin to get matching suits. We told the guy what we were looking for. He goes, "Let's go in the back room." He was so happy. He had all these sharkskin suits that had been sitting around since the '60s.

After about a year or so, Bill and I wanted to become more punk rock.

The Hypstrz at Jay's Longhorn bar, 1978. Photo by Paul Lundgren

Joe and Rick left the band and we brought Randy Weiss back on bass. The punk rock version of the Hypstrz started at a New Year's Eve show. We made some money at it.

JOHN HAGA: Ernie dug up new material—Eddie & the Hot Rods, the Ramones, Sex Pistols, the Damned. He got excited about, "We should do 'Wooly Bully' like *this*." Instead of Sam the Sham and the Pharaohs' version, we did Eddie & the Hot Rods' version, which was sped up, dumbed down, and more forceful.

Pretty soon we morphed into the Hypstrz as most people know it. We were still wearing our '60s clothes and having that attitude we had before, but much more forceful. We were mean and angry and we rocked. The "in your face" thing is Bill and Ernie with their affection for pro wrestling more than anything. That's the way the band's always been. These guys are huge and they're so full of energy and they push, push, push—all the time.

ERNIE BATSON: We had gone to see the Ramones when they first played in the Twin Cities. That was a real big moment. We always played fast, but we *really* picked it up. It became clear to Joe and Rick that we wanted to be a little bit faster, so they left the band. We got Randy back, and we had a powerhouse rhythm section with John Haga and Randy Weiss.

BILL BATSON: Arguably the best rhythm section in town. They could still play together. And all they care about is fucking each other up.

ERNIE BATSON: John was a very good drummer then, but now he's an *extremely* good drummer. You really have to keep your mind on the beat because he'll start to go way around it, just to see if he can fuck us up. It works sometimes. And sometimes we can all turn around and go, "Ha-ha! Not this time!"

JOHN HAGA: I'd play a beat that doesn't fit, just to throw them a left curve. It's like playing catch with somebody and all of a sudden you're throwing a rock back. I'll screw with people musically when I'm playing with them. It's a lot of fun for me.

BILL BATSON: We did a show in Minneapolis, 7th Street Entry I believe, and then we went and played Chicago. That was 1981. I'm like twenty-two, twenty-three.

This whole tour thing was crazy because we went out with nothing. We had a van full of gas and that was it. We go to Cleveland and find out that a couple of shows have fallen through. So we're sitting for five days in Cleveland sleeping on the floor of the guitar player's mom's house. We had to negotiate to feed these five people. Every day she'd come to me, "How much money do you have, Bill?" It was fun.

We played Detroit after Cleveland. Played in Bunky's, which is in a scary little neighborhood where they told us, "Unload everything from the van, park it in this ten-foot gated parking lot, and don't go out after six o'clock." The doorman was like a six-foot-eight American Indian and he patrolled the premises with two baseball bats.

The next stop from there was Washington, DC, and we're driving overnight and playing that same night at the 9:30 Club in front of three hundred people with the Slickee Boys, who we'd read about and got their single. They were pretty impressive. Then we came out and did okay, too.

We were changing over from the bowling alley, ballroom, four-sets-a-night Hypstrz to the punk rock Hypstrz. Audiences got pretty animated about us. They were starting to get pissed off at us.

ERNIE BATSON: It was pretty much brand new. If you aren't going to Oar Folk and Shinders and buying the magazines and the records and listening to stuff, you're not going to be all that enamored by it right away. If all you really know is Rush and Led Zeppelin and the Top 40, of course you are sort of put off by it. When we were younger, it was almost like a cause. You just do it like you want to do it.

In King Kustom we had our chair club, Club 35. We played park dances and school things, and we'd always steal a couple chairs as a souvenir. We had forty chairs or so stacked in our folks' basement. We would clear the basement out, put up our band equipment and PA at one end and then line chairs up along the walls so there could be a dance floor. After about 1:30 AM the place would be really full, like two or three hundred people in our folks' house. I recall some of those parties being interesting. They'd usually end at four, five, six in the morning.

Sometimes when we would tell our folks we're having a party, they would rent a hotel room. Sometimes they would stay home. I don't know if they enjoyed it, but they were very understanding, very supportive of our efforts to stay out of reform school.

When we had a weekend without a gig, we'd say, "Let's throw a party!" We would take our thirty empty cases of Hauenstein and get four more cases of Hauenstein. We'd get Flamingo, Suicide Commandos, the MORs, Flamin' Oh's, guys like that hanging out in our basement taking turns playing. It was maybe '78 or '79, because we'd gotten to the punk rock scene, when we were seeing the Suicide Commandos. The Suburbs would fill up the party easily.

HUGO KLAERS: Nobody touches the Hypstrz for me. Good singing. Everything they do, each one of their musicians is awesome, and their song choices are good. I never get tired of them.

BILL BATSON: Our first major show at First Avenue was when it was Uncle Sam's. Steve McClellan wanted us to play. He wanted to get more live music. Disco was dying. The Ramones was the first major show he booked. Steve comes back to the dressing room and says, "The tour manager for the

The Hypstrz, the Mighty Mofos, and the Batson Brothers | 61

The Hypstrz, circa 1978. Photo by Bayard Michael

Ramones says they go on at 11:30, and doors are at 8. I need you guys to start at 9. Can you do two sets?" I said, "No. If we go offstage and come back up, they'll kill us. We'll just play straight through and see how far we get." We put up a thirty-five-song set and planned for an hour and a half. We got about an hour and twenty minutes before they started throwing shit at us. We could've gone longer.

Right in the middle of the second row or so—two thousand people there, a crazy night—is Grant Hart, Greg Norton, and Bob Mould of Hüsker Dü. They're all yelling, "Get off the stage, you fuckers!" We knew who they were, but this was before we actually met them. I said, "I know you fuckers." They're laughing and saying, "Boooo! We just wanna see the Ramones." *I* wanted to see the Ramones. But I had to play. C'mon, I'm trying to make a hundred fifty bucks!

So the next night, the Hüskers are playing at the Longhorn, to nobody *again*. Me, Ernie, and Haga knock on their dressing room door and kick it open and there's Hüsker Dü, "What the hell are you guys doing?" Then they stand up and they're just as big as we are. So we decided we'd be friends instead. That's my Hüsker Dü story. That's how we met them.

JOHN HAGA: There's great stories of people getting signed for a six-week run at a club, and they're doing all this really cool fusion stuff, and the crowd doesn't get it. Case in point: we played at Uncle Sam's when they had the light-up dance floor. Steve McClellan used to bring us in to do cameos. He would say, "Hit it." It was the disco days, '78, '79, *Saturday Night Fever* is going big time. The dance floor is packed and we'd start playing—and everybody'd leave the dance floor. We'd do a twenty-minute set, and then it was back to *Saturday Night Fever*. It was almost humorous how that happened every time we played there.

JOHN KASS: Paul Stark recorded the Hypstrz's album *Live at the Longhorn*. That record is so good, man. I listen to it and I'm always astounded, like, that is the perfect garage rock record.

BILL BATSON: On Twin/Tone's *Big Hits of Mid-America Volume Three*, released in '79, we did, "6654321." Then Paul Stark recorded us at the Longhorn. A four-track recording. That's what we got all of our product from. It was two nights in a row recording four sets—thirty-six or thirty-seven songs. We repeated several songs four times to get as many live takes as possible. The first night was probably better played. Paul forgot to turn the audio mics on. So the next time we had to make sure they were on and rerecord everything, but that's okay. It was a fun time.

ERNIE BATSON: That live record was not for Twin/Tone. We just hired Paul to do the recording. We had our own Bogus Records label. Greg Shaw ran Bomp Records in California. Someone gave him a copy of the *Hypstrz Live* EP and he listened to it and contacted us.

BILL BATSON: He went, "Hey, can we sell them? I'll consign them." He took five hundred the first time. Spread them around. We sold at least a thousand to him. It's kinda fuzzy about how much we got paid for those.

ERNIE BATSON: Yeah, or even *if* we got paid. But we got some national recognition.

BILL BATSON: Bomp sold about a thousand of the records, then they said, "Hey, is there any word on tapes?" So we started working with Paul Stark on

Record covers for the *Hypstrization!* LP and the *Hypstrz Live* EP, both recorded live at Jay's Longhorn, April 14–15, 1979. COURTESY OF MARK ENGEBRETSON

putting together the rest of the tapes. We worked on the same tapes the EP came off of and put out *Hypstrization!* It is touching how many people still talk about it. There's not much we didn't put on that record.

Stark helped us print our 45. He pointed out where I should go to get the pressings done, in Memphis. We made the sleeves here and put them together ourselves. I got a die-cut place to do it and a printer. The first thousand were pink and the next twenty-five hundred were blue and green. There were a shitload of white ones, just "oops" he gave us, but we sold them.

The first fifteen hundred we put all together with glue sticks. We're writing on the inside, a lot of autographs and jokes about the times.

ERNIE BATSON: We sold the first thousand or fifteen hundred. I think we ended up with maybe a couple hundred left. I think we each had a couple boxes of 45s.

BILL BATSON: I used to give Steve McClellan a box every three years. He'd hand a record out to the Gang of Four manager or Billy Joel, Tina Turner, or whoever's coming through. "Here's a *real* band, a local band. You should listen to these guys." "Oh jeez, thanks Steve."

The first time R.E.M. played Minneapolis was in the Mainroom at First Avenue. I was working sound in the Entry, and between sound checks they were loading in. I had the first R.E.M. single, and I'm walking across the dance floor and Peter Buck looks up and says, "Hey, you're Bill Batson from the Hypstrz. I got your record!" And I say, "I got *your* record!" I became instant friends with Michael Stipe and Peter Buck. It was *really* cool. We'd talk about touring and how this one's going, how are they doing. They went a long way. Really nice guys.

ERNIE BATSON: By the time the album came out in 1980, John and Randy were gone. We had a different rhythm section. When the album came out, I quit. So you got Scott Anderson on guitar and Tommy Rey on drums, Mark Freiseis on bass.

Then you broke up the Hypstrz in '83. We did the Billy and Ernie shows for a little while with Tommy Rey and Bruce Steeples. Then we got Caleb Palmiter on bass at the start of the Mighty Mofos, in 1984.

BILL BATSON: We got him from Red House. He was in that band with Mark Freeman and Cindy Blum. We played shows with NNB. We did a show with the Overtones at St. Croix Boom Company, which is a big old bar like the Cabooze but with a low ceiling. I brought the PA and did sound for their songs, then Hypstrz played. Then we did St. Olaf with Red House and Wilma and the Wilbers. We played several places with them. Same thing with the Overtones and Danny Amis. Played lots of them.

ERNIE BATSON: The Overtones were always funny. They would carefully tune their guitars at the beginning of the show and then never touch the tuning again. It'd be all this surf music, lots of whammy bar. By the end of the night, every string would be in a different key. They were like, "To heck with it." They were fun. Great, great players.

DANNY AMIS: The Hypstrz were always a blast to play with. They were so much fun and so encouraging. They had such great attitudes.

MONTY LEE WILKES: The Hypstrz are the most rock thing you could be exposed to. Who rocks harder than the Hypstrz? Nobody rocks harder than the Hypstrz. It is incredible. And they have never let up. It's like every bit as hard and fast as it was forty years ago. John "Bongo" Haga is probably my favorite drummer. He has this innate ability very few drummers have. It's a way of hitting a cymbal where, like, time seems to stand still for just a moment. Bongo is really good at that, man. And the cymbal just slides, it's so clean. That's what I like in a drummer.

TONY PUCCI: The Hypstrz were another go-to band for me, and another reason why Man Sized Action formed. The guys decided, "Why don't we try to have a band?" Because I was the last guy to think about going to the music store, I got to be the drummer. But the Hypstrz were really influential, still are, really pillars of the music community. Absolutely, no matter who you are, they are there for you. They'll open for you; you can open for them. Just consistent, really good guys.

PAT WOODS: When Billy Batson found out that we were starting a band, he said, "Do you have a PA?" and we were like, "What the hell is a PA?" So he loaned us a microphone and a bass amp and that was our first PA. We were playing down in my basement. It was perfect. Another reason why I love those guys to this day. They were always very supportive.

Billy and Ernie Batson are really important in the work that they have done and the work that they continue to do. Their support of the scene is unparalleled. Generous and hard-working. It's really impressive.

JON CLIFFORD: The Hypstrz were the first bar band that I went to see. They were at the Longhorn. I was sixteen years old. I was terrified by them. Still am. They're one of my favorites of all time.

DAVID MOE: I think I can speak for all of us in the Silverteens that probably our biggest influence, of bands we love dearly across the board, is the Hypstrz. Speaking for myself, as a young man going to the Longhorn and hearing them play and listening to *Hypstrization!*—I wore that record out. It was fast, melodic rock and roll. And it was live. When you were a kid, you couldn't go to all the shows—this was before all-ages shows—so I lived vicariously through that album, pictured myself being at the bar, you know?

JERRY JOHNSON: The Hypstrz and the Mighty Mofos are bands that I've loved since I first heard them. I'm more in the mid-'80s, seeing the Mofos quite a bit, so I didn't get to see the Hypstrz in their original prime. I missed out. I saw the Mofos and I loved them. The Hypstrz album is just fantastic. That was a big influence on all the bands that I played in because we were like, "Yeah! Loud and fast. Let's do it. Let's take our originals, let's take cover songs and play them *that* way."

DAVID MOE: You know Hüsker Dü was definitely influenced by the Hypstrz to a certain extent. Every song is like, one after another, and Hüsker Dü loved to do that, and the Silverteens like to do that. We love that energy and it probably does go back to those boys.

JOHN KASS: I taped Mike Reiter's copy of the Hypstrz's seven-inch EP onto a cassette. I had an early version of a mono boom box made by Marantz. I had the Hypstrz cassette blaring "Action Woman," and the mailman at my parents' house came running up to me. "That song is by a band from Minnesota back in the '60s called the Litter." I'd never heard of the Litter. I said, "No, it isn't. It's this band called the Hypstrz. It's a new record." He goes, "No, no. They're covering a version."

Everybody has worked with Bill Batson since way back when. I've seen the Batsons play more than any other band. They are my heroes. Over the years I've always said my favorite bands in the Twin Cities are the Commandos and the Hypstrz. And the Hypstrz ain't running out of gas. In a lot of ways, they're better. At the Barn Party in 2015, I was watching them, thinking, "This is *it*. These guys are the best band ever from this town. Hands down."

05

CLUBHOUSE FOR MUSIC FANATICS: OAR FOLKJOKEOPUS RECORD STORE

From its inception in 1973, Oar Folkjokeopus record store was a key portal to new music discovery for adventurous fans and musicians in the Twin Cities. Located in south Minneapolis at the corner of 26th and Lyndale, Oar Folk was staffed by knowledgeable, passionate music lovers and stocked with a broad inventory, specializing in hard-to-find imports and independent labels. Along with Oar Folk, small indie record stores such as the Electric Fetus, Wax Museum, Harpo's, Hot Licks, Northern Lights, and Let It Be, among others, became the tastemakers for the growing community looking for innovative, rebellious new music. The stores became hubs and gathering places, and visiting artists went there for record signings and in-store performances. A fire in October 1985 destroyed much of Oar Folk. While owner Vern Sanden decided whether to reopen, several key personnel left and opened their own store, Garage D'Or Records, at 26th and Nicollet. Oar Folk did reopen and later became Treehouse Records, which still stands. Many of the indie record stores of the era have long since closed their doors, and many new ones continue to be valuable music resources to the community.

PETER JESPERSON: Oar Folkjokeopus was so much more than a record store! It was a clubhouse for music fanatics. It was a place where people came to listen to music and talk about their favorite stuff. The exchange of information that happens at record stores was essential to building the great community we had here.

Electric Fetus was really the first independent record store in town that catered to an alternative music audience, so to speak, the underground. That's where I was naturally drawn. My paper route distributing the *NME* led me to North Country Music, which is what Oar Folk was before Vern Sanden owned it. It was new, and I thought it was a great record store from the inception. I remember when a new album by Procol Harum came out in 1971, I wanted to find it as quickly as possible. North Country was the first store in Minneapolis that had it, so it was a feather in their cap. I started shopping there regularly.

The store moved to 26th and Lyndale in the fall of 1972. Vern Sanden bought the store and reopened it as Oar Folkjokeopus in January of '73. That April, Vern offered me a job. It was the day *Red Rose Speedway* by Paul McCartney and Wings came out. On my way to work the first day, I got to stop at a record warehouse and pick up the order, including the new Paul McCartney record. It was very exciting.

One of our claims to fame was that we carried a lot of imported records, including the British imports of Beatles albums. The American versions of the records were very different from the versions that the Beatles released in England. I thought it was important to have those available. That was a root of our clientele: people who wanted the imports, records that had been released in England but weren't released in the States. That was one of the bases for what Oar Folk did. We were buying from companies based out East, JEM Records and Records Limited, and from City Hall based in San Francisco, small distributors that carried these hard-to-find records. Eventually they started not only doing imports, but also the smaller independent-label American stuff. That was really where one of our specialties lay, so that gave us an identity.

We were always very broad-based at Oar Folk. We didn't shy away from disco, for instance. We sold lots of disco records in the late '70s and into the '80s. We had a good classical section. We sold blues music. We sold all those records the groups on the West Bank were making. So we were really quite open to stuff. But our specialty was probably the British invasion and this burgeoning American indie rock scene.

Oar Folk was a very independent-minded record store. We were shunned by the major labels for the most part. Some of that we brought on ourselves. Some of it was circumstantial, in that we didn't buy direct from the labels. In those days if you bought direct from Columbia or Warner Bros. or MCA, you got better service. The people that bought direct did bigger volume than a place like Oar Folk. Also, because we were in that great location at 26th and Lyndale, a lot of the majors wanted to put up window displays, but often they were artists we didn't like, so we would decline politely. That made them really angry. "Well, screw you. We're not going to give you any promos,

The Ramones signing records at Oar Folkjokopus, January 1978. PHOTO BY DANNY AMIS

and we're not going to be involved with you directly." We thought, "Okay, if that's the way you feel about it." We were making what we thought was an artistic statement, and we stood for something.

TERRY KATZMAN: I was shopping at Oar Folk regularly when the original staff was there, '74 to '76. I was working at the Third Stone Music locations, but then I was hired away by Peter Jesperson. Oar Folk had an opening and Peter came up to me at Third Stone and said, "We're going to take care of you." It was the obvious place for me to be. I started working there in the summer or fall of '76.

They had imports before any of the other stores. They were the store you could find a Van der Graaf Generator record, or a Taste record, or any kind of weird import, progressive rock. That's what the racks were filled with in those days, back when no one had imports. JEM was the main supplier of the import labels. We funneled all that stuff. We had English stuff in that store before anybody knew what was going on. Once the punk thing started happening, every week there's a new great record—a Talking Heads or an Adverts record, or a Saints record, or a Dead Boys record. It was a continual flow.

The clientele were musicians, record fans, just like we were, people that considered music an important part of their lives. So you really got the crème de la crème of music fans, musicians, producers and label people, people that knew label people, concert promoters. We were known as a place where people knew about music. It was the community spirit for what was going on at that time and the center point of where the action was.

ANDY SCHWARTZ: I worked at Oar Folk from '75 to '77. We had regular customers. They had particular likes and tastes that Oar Folk could supply. I remember one guy that bought every Golden Earring record—and there were quite a lot of them, if you bought the imports as well as the US releases. There were friends of Vern Sanden's who were more of the old school record collector guys buying '50s and '60s records. The store had a large stock of 45s, including rhythm and blues and early rock and roll, as well as the first wave of independent punk and new wave records, like Patti Smith, Television, Willie "Loco" Alexander. People got excited about new releases.

It was a good store to work for. Vern was a good guy, a passionate music person, a rockabilly collector. Everybody had different areas of specialization or taste. Myself, Peter Jesperson, Vern Sanden, and the record company promotion person organized the in-stores. I believe we had Graham Parker in the room, and Robert Gordon and Link Wray. Customers and employees got excited about these in-store appearances. At a certain point there were musicians rehearsing in the basement.

ED ACKERSON: I went to Oar Folk all the time, and I was very friendly from age fifteen or so with Peter Jesperson. I was a voracious record collector and he turned me on to a ton of very valuable influences. We knew all about the rehearsals downstairs, and they let us stick our heads down there a couple times. I was totally in awe.

TERRY KATZMAN: All the bands that came through town and played at the Longhorn would come to the store. They knew there was a store in Minneapolis selling their records, and it was the *only* store selling their records. That's why the Ramones and Talking Heads and Blondie and the B-52s and David Johansen all came to Oar Folk. They knew we were responsible for breaking them here. In fact, there were higher sales figures for Ramones records here than in other parts of the country. The Ramones came to the

Talking Heads pose with Oar Folkjokeopus staff, October 1977: *(back row, left to right)* Tina Weymouth, David Byrne, Chris Frantz, Peter Jesperson, Jerry Harrison, and Vern Sanden; *(front row, left to right)* Tim Holmes, representative from Lieberman Enterprises distributor, and Andy Schwartz. PHOTO BY DANNY AMIS

David Johansen at an in-store signing for his first solo album at Oar Folk, early 1978: *(left to right)* longtime customer Mike Morris, Peter Jesperson, Johansen, staffer Dan Fults, and owner Vern Sanden. PHOTOGRAPHER UNKNOWN, FROM THE COLLECTION OF PETER JESPERSON

store twice, when the second album and the third album came out. They got behind the counter and signed records. People would line up, and it was pretty casual. But everybody there realized it was pretty important, too.

The David Johansen in-store when his first solo album came out in 1978 was quite interesting. He was a nice guy. We were all huge Dolls fans, although the Dolls had been gone a couple years by that time. Nobody else in town would have the David Johansen record except for us. We snared the in-store just like *that*. "Who in Minneapolis is selling a lot of New York Dolls records?" It was a no-brainer. They knew they were going to get a lot of support and sell a lot of records when anybody came through. It was a guaranteed plus for everybody.

I talked to quite a few musicians. Talking Heads—we had a lot of good conversations with them. All the boys were drooling over Tina Weymouth. I had a long talk with Jerry Harrison. He's a really nice guy, and Chris Frantz. David Byrne was kind of eccentric, but I talked to him for a little bit. It was all very homespun then. They were coming to town with one record out, and you had no preconceptions about what it was gonna be like. They came to the store after the second album, too.

We also had a good relationship with Sire Records, because everything that they put out we promoted. I even wrote a review of the Dead Boys show, which I sent to Sire. How many people are going to write a review of the Dead Boys? I wrote Sire Records asking them to send me promos of Richard Hell. Nowadays you couldn't get them to do that if you put a gun to their head. We got attention in the store because we were the ones breaking those records and we had them first, before anybody, other than maybe Northern Lights. I have a Sire press kit from back then that has inserts about new wave and punk. It had the slogan: "New Wave. Get behind it before it gets ahead of you."

ROBB HENRY: In '75 I was playing with an R&B band called Philadelphia Story, and Andy Schwartz wrote up the band for the *Minnesota Daily*. I knew he worked at Oar Folk, and I got to know him through that. He turned me on to a lot of R&B music. Hanging around the record shop was an education. In those days, where did you hear about new music? There weren't that many stations on the radio. There was no Internet. So the record store was really where you went to hear about new music.

KEVIN COLE: Oar Folkjokeopus was the Internet of the mid- and late 1970s, basically, where you'd go to discover new music. That's where you had to go. I'd go on the day they'd get new releases or imports. You'd buy *New Musical Express*. You'd buy the *Melody Maker*. You'd buy the *New York Rocker*, all these publications that would help inform you about what was going on. What was going on in New York? What was going on in London? You had to do the work, and you had to build relationships with the people who worked at those record stores and hang out and listen. "What are they going to put on next?" They were our musical guides.

Oar Folk was for me that portal. I'd go to other record stores prior to discovering Oar Folk. I'd go to the Wax Museum on Lake Street, but I never felt like that was a scene I could associate with. I do recall buying records like Brian Eno there, just because they had weird-looking covers. Initially, I didn't know who he was. But that's where my musical exploration would go. I'd just go A through Z, and if I saw something cool looking and unusual, I'd buy it.

Oar Folk provided that mentor, so to speak, musically. And Peter was that for me. I was just kind of a shy kid who bought records there, or went to the club and heard him spin. He didn't know who I was. Later, after I got involved with Uncle Sam's, Sam's, and First Avenue, and started at Hot Licks—that I guess was a competitor to Oar Folk, but really was kind of a companion or a complementary existence, since we had a little different focus—then I got to know Peter and learn from him in person. He was a big influence on me.

PAUL STARK: Oar Folk was definitely a key store because Peter was there. Other stores in town such as the Wax Museum and Northern Lights all really helped, but in the early days, Peter holding court at Oar Folk with all the musicians coming in, showing them new stuff that just came out, that was a really big deal.

PETER JESPERSON: You think about Dick Champ or Chan Poling saying they were influenced by the music we had at Oar Folk. The Suicide Commandos, too. When Eno left Roxy Music in 1974 and put out his single "Seven Deadly Finns," we carried that record, and it was a big deal to us. I remember Dave Ahl buying that 45. I went to see the Commandos a couple nights later at the Blitz Bar and they were doing "Seven Deadly Finns" live.

A little later, we got the single of David Bowie's "Heroes," before the album was available in any other store. Bob Wilkinson, of Flamingo, was a huge Bowie fan. He came in the store to hear it and went crazy over it. I made him a cassette and Flamingo did it live the next night. Flamingo did a fabulous job. Wilkinson sang the living daylights out of that song. It was one of those immediate things.

ROBERT WILKINSON: Oar Folkjokeopus was really *the* record store at the time, from 1977 and for many, many years. Artists coming to town would do in-stores there. We did an in-store there for our first Flamingo album.

Peter Jesperson was one of the main cats who worked there. That's when our friendship developed. Jesperson was always really hip, as well as a lot of the other guys that worked there. Peter turned me on to Bowie. He was a big Bowie freak and I became a big Bowie freak. I used to go down there to get all the latest music I liked—like Mott the Hoople and David Bowie.

It was the hip place to be—great energy, great people, great vibes. We'd go down there and hang out during the day and go to the Longhorn at night. It was a really important part of my life. The Fetus was around, but Oar Folk was where we were hanging out before this whole punk, new wave thing broke through.

DICK CHAMP: Peter Jesperson and Barry Margolis at Oar Folk, and Vern Sanden, the owner—they set the tastes for the people that were going in and out of that store. And it was a pretty small group. Rusty Jones and I would be down there practically every day.

I still remember when the box that had that first New York Dolls record in it was delivered to the Oar—shortly after North Country Music became Oar Folkjokeopus. There it was—that cover! "Oh my god! Oh happy day!" The aesthetic was already in place in Minneapolis. Was there some mimicking of what was going on in New York? Yes, but there was plenty of original thinking going on in Minneapolis, when you had someone like Peter Jesperson around, with all his enthusiasm and what he found out about and shared with us. I'm sure there are a handful of others, too, but Peter was really the impresario in that world.

CURT ALMSTED: Those guys that were the clerks at Oar Folk were very passionate and they were eager to share their discoveries. You hear a song you like and you're transported away from the horribleness of reality. We wound up tailoring part of our show to those guys by doing songs that we knew they liked.

DALE T. NELSON: Peter Jesperson knew my taste in music, so when I'd come in he'd go, "Got something pretty good here." Popped on the Shoes record, I'm going, "Holy shit! These guys are great." He turned me on to *Sheet Music* by 10cc in 1974. Awesome record. Oar Folk was my gateway to the punk rock and underground scene. I'd go to Wax Museum, but the people at Oar Folk, if they liked you, they'd flip on stuff you would like. That's really cool.

TERRY KATZMAN: We all had our own records we played. Once you took the shrink-wrap off, you bought it. All my money went to records. We'd write stuff up on a sheet and Vern would deduct it from our paychecks. I think I owed him over a thousand bucks at one point. I just paid it off in a month by not drawing a paycheck.

Every Friday night it's like, "Oh my god, there's some more singles from London!" "Oh god, it's an Eddie & the Hot Rods single." A Sex Pistols single, a Damned single, a Dr. Feelgood single. For those two years, '75–'76, you're just bombarded. You don't have that kind of saturation now that you had back then. It was manual, it wasn't electronic. It was—I hate to use the word—organic. I sound like a hippie, but it was that.

STEVE ALMAAS: When I first discovered Oar Folkjokeopus, it was before the Commandos got started, the fall of '75. I distinctly remember going on my lunch break to Oar Folk and seeing the Patti Smith *Horses* album in the rack. I bought that album just by the way the cover looked. I got to know Peter Jesperson and all the guys that were working there. That was a really good crew of people that were passionate about music, and I got turned on to a lot of music from those people. Peter and I spent a lot of time listening to music.

Andy Schwartz—who ended up later being manager of my band Beat Rodeo and the editor of the *New York Rocker*—was working there, and he was an early supporter of the Commandos. He wrote for the *Minnesota Daily* and whatever the metro papers were then. He was another one that really helped the Commandos a lot in the first year. Andy was a real booster of getting the local original music scene going. A lot came out of the enthusiasm of the people who worked in that store, and we hung out there a lot.

And they got all the imports of those punk rock singles, literally as they were coming out, which most people in the States weren't even aware of. You could hear everything right away, because those guys had the wherewithal to get those records.

CHRIS OSGOOD: All those record stores—Oar Folk coming first and the Wax Museums and others to follow—had a very profound impact on our aesthetic, and all of them had erudite people behind the counters. Andy Schwartz and Peter Jesperson, then Terry Katzman and Jim Peterson a little later on, were gatekeepers and tastemakers. We would get down to Oar Folk at least once a week to see what had come in. All of us—me, Steve Almaas, Bob Wilkinson, Curtiss A, Kevin Hazlett, whoever was hanging out in those days—would go sit at the knee of Andy or Peter, and they would play us stuff in the store. "Do you like this?" Early on it was things like Big Star, and then slightly later on it was David Bowie and Roxy Music and Brian Eno. We wouldn't have known about that stuff if somebody hadn't turned us on to it. We really took it to heart, because they allowed us to listen to different things, and then we could make decisions ourselves.

As soon as the punk rock thing happened, Oar Folk was the first record store to get the Sex Pistols singles, for example. We went down and bought all the singles as they came out. Andy would call us at Utopia House and say, "The Sex Pistols single is in. Come on down and get it!" Or the Clash, or the Damned, any of those bands.

Other people like ourselves would come through the door, people we wouldn't have known otherwise because there was no scene yet. There was no club yet. We owe Andy and Peter and Terry and Jim and others a debt of gratitude because they were the ones that had access to cool. And they had an aesthetic of their own to back it up.

CHAN POLING: The little corner record store called Oar Folkjokeopus was our little clubhouse. We'd go there and get all the new records from New York and Europe. Oar Folk really was the nurturing punk rock, new wave center, definitely. We'd go to Oar Folk and hang out for hours.

MIKE MADDEN: Every Friday, Grady Linehan and I would take our paychecks from the paint shop and go spend about half of them at Oar Folk. It was a cool store. They had everything. Before I went to Oar Folk I used to subscribe to *NME*, and I would order a lot of punk rock singles through that magazine. I'd get my money order in pounds and send it off and wait for two, three weeks before this box of records, all seven-inches, would come. Then I discovered Oar Folk, and I didn't have to mail-order anymore because they had them all.

DANNY AMIS: I practically lived in Oar Folk for a few years. When I was in high school in Minnetonka, I used to cut classes once a week and drive into the city and see what they had new at Oar Folk. I got to know Peter and Andy Schwartz pretty well, as well as Dan Fults and Bill Melton.

Oar Folk was a great place to find David Bowie bootlegs. Or imports of British rock, a lot of glam rock stuff you couldn't find anywhere else. I worked at Third Stone Music in Hopkins. We couldn't get any of that stuff. That's where I met Terry Katzman. We occasionally worked together. The owner of the store thought the two of us were nuts for liking the music that we did.

When punk came along, that was it. I got fired for playing that stuff. I drove a taxi after that.

DANIEL MURPHY: I used to go to Oar Folk all the time. You could buy a used record there for $2.40, and if you didn't like it, they'd pay like $1.80 when you'd bring it back.

There was also a Wax Museum on Portland and Lake Street, and I used to go there a lot. I had a really impressive record collection as a kid. My whole life as a kid was music. It was my social life, my friends, my family—it was everything.

DAVE PIRNER: I would see Peter Jesperson and Terry Katzman at Oar Folkjokeopus. Those guys were luminaries to me. These guys were at every single event, and they seemed to know everyone. Curtiss A was playing in the Walker Art Center, and Peter Jesperson was sitting right behind me. Every time a song would come on in the pre-gig music, he knew everything about it. I was sitting there listening to him, thinking, "Wow, okay, I'm learning about this shit." That turned into going to Oar Folk and going,

"What's a cool record to get, Peter?" "What's a cool record to get, Terry?" "What's happening?" Kind of hanging out at the record store.

There was always *something someone* was excited about. There was always something like, "Oh, don't get that Cars record. Get that Iggy Pop record."

CRAIG FINN: I'd bargain with my parents: "All right, I'm gonna mow the lawn, but I don't want any money for it, I just want a ride to Oar Folk." Or I'd take the bus to Oar Folk. Terry Katzman, who I'm very fond of, would recognize me right away and be like, "I notice you got that record last time; you might like this." He is a sweetheart and obviously a huge part of this. He's one of those many unsung guys—not gonna get his name in the lights, but certainly was there for a *lot* of this stuff.

MICHAEL REITER: We'd have our moms' big '70s cars, and whoever had the car would pick up like five people and hit the record stores—Northern Lights, Hot Licks, and Oar Folk. Oar Folk was the best, in our minds. You knew you were going to see stuff there that you weren't going to see elsewhere—not yet. The Northern Lights on University Avenue was good. It was one of our stops, but we still wanted to get to Oar Folk. Maybe they were playing something you would hear and go, "Wow, what's that?" And then you buy it.

DOUG ANDERSON: I lived at Oar Folk because I was on the corner of 26th and Lyndale for years. Before the kids were going to the CC Club, we would all go in and get hamburgers. We all worked at a place called the Mud Pie for a while. Then there was Oar Folk and the Country Boy Store. That was your universe in this part of town. You go to Oar Folk in the afternoon and sit in the window and drink soda pop. It was the same guys every day. Bob Stinson would be there, Bob Mould would be there, a lot of times Grant Hart would be there. Paul Westerberg would be there a lot. Various Suburbs would drop in. Tommy Stinson and Dave Roth would come in after they got out of school. We would listen to new seven-inches all day long. We would eat crappy barbecue pork chops from next door. It was fun as hell.

The core staff at the time was Terry Katzman, Mitch Griffin, Peter Jesperson, Jim Peterson. Oar Folk was a great location for getting stuff because of guys like Jesperson and Katzman. Katzman was so smart about what his customers liked, that even when I was in hardcore bands, he would slip me the Stranglers bootleg or Devo bootleg or stuff he knew my friends didn't like. Oar Folk was there for every phase of music. I remember all the great first wave punk records and all the English records coming out. Oar Folk would have big posters in the window. It was also where we would get free tickets to everything. Oar Folk was a really important place.

MARTIN KELLER: I hung out at Oar Folk and at the Wax Museum on Lake Street a little bit. They opened a bunch of different Waxes. The smart record shoppers went to both places. I can't count the times I walked from the City Pages office down to Oar Folk and back. I lived maybe half a mile south of there. We ate at the Mud Pie a lot, next door to Oar Folk, a good vegetarian restaurant.

LORI BARBERO: I lived in south Minneapolis and worked downtown. Every time I got off the bus, I went to Oar Folk. Every day after school, after I got off work, I went there with my tips. I went there at least five days a week. I still look at my records and go, "Whoa, I paid just one dollar for this." That's where I started my whole record collecting. My first thousand records probably came from Oar Folk.

JOHN KASS: I bought so many 45s at Oar Folk, all the obvious ones at the time like the Jam and the Clash and the Ramones. I would also start buying other records that looked interesting or somebody might've recommended, like the Vertebrats from Champaign, Illinois, or Frantix from Denver. So, you'd get exposed to other stuff. I remember buying Radio Birdman, Sham 69, Velvet Underground, and the Stooges records there or at the Wax Museum on University in St. Paul.

I was standing by the front door of the Wax Museum when Iggy Pop showed up. I was the first person he saw when he walked in the store. I looked down at him because he isn't very tall and I stuck out my copy of *Raw Power*. I figured I might as well get it signed then instead of waiting in line at the counter. He looked at the copy of *Raw Power* and he looked at my face, he looked at the record again and back at me, and he said, "Where did you get this?" I go, "I got it at the store here. They brought in a French import." He goes, "This is the French one?"

He ended up going back and signing all the autographs, but I was the first one to talk to him there because I happened to be standing by the door.

MARK TREHUS: I was a frequent shopper at Oar Folkjokeopus from the time I found the first Modern Lovers album there in the mid-'70s. I admired Peter Jesperson and Andy Schwartz's passion for and knowledge of rock music. It was like postgraduate rock and roll maniac's school. The tuition was paid for with my weekly paycheck and the receipts were import and independent 45s with picture sleeves. The staff was really nice to put up with my usually drunken and stoned ass—probably because I spent all my money there.

It was there that I bought my first Sex Pistols, the Clash, Ramones, the Only Ones, Elvis Costello, the Fall records. I bought elusive records by artists from the pre-punk era that I loved, like the import twofer of Jesse Winchester's first couple of out-of-print albums, Gene Clark's "Roadmaster," Velvet Underground bootlegs. It was there that Chris Osgood handed me copy #001 of *The Commandos Commit Suicide Dance Concert* numbered LPs, which I have never broken the seal on.

Oar Folk was ground zero. There was no other store as far as I was concerned—even when I worked for Harpo's and later the Wax Museum—except for maybe the downtown Hot Licks and later Northern Lights. But even then just as an ancillary outlet for certain imports that Oar Folk, for whatever reason, didn't get.

RYAN CAMERON: My roommate Richard Elioff worked for Twin City Imports, which was owned by the owner of Northern Lights. Richard was extremely knowledgeable about music. He is an unsung hero for changing the record stores here in the late '70s and early '80s. He ordered all the imports for TCI. He would bring us all the new stuff. He was our conduit to find out about new things. Richard brought that import business to town, specifically to the Hot Licks store, and then he branched out. He convinced me that I should apply to work at Northern Lights. The store in St. Paul hired me right away. I was there from early 1980 to mid- to late 1980. Richard started to work at Hot Licks in downtown Minneapolis, and he told me I should apply there. I started at Hot Licks full-time in early '81, and by the spring, I was the manager. When that Hot Licks opened, it totally changed downtown. Prior to that there wasn't really a decent record store downtown. It later transitioned to Northern Lights, and I worked there when we moved to 7th and Hennepin in 1985. I was manager of that store until 1987, when I started my own thing with Let It Be Records.

Kevin Cole working behind the counter at Hot Licks, 1981. COURTESY OF KEVIN COLE

Kevin Cole was working at Hot Licks, and he taught me a lot. He was incredibly knowledgeable about music, and he was also DJ'ing at First Avenue. So there was that whole crossover thing. We were only a block away from First Avenue.

Hot Licks was extremely diverse. Oar Folk carried imports, but not to the extent that Hot Licks did. It was a much larger inventory of imports. Oar Folk obviously carried imports and a lot of indie and private press stuff, and they were very influential, no doubt about it.

At Northern Lights, I was involved with a Violent Femmes in-store appearance for their first record. We did a Three O'Clock in-store where they played in the basement. That was really fun. When I went to work at Hot Licks downtown, I was the one setting up the in-stores. We did two Duran Duran in-stores. We had the Psychedelic Furs twice. Those were all signings; we didn't have room for anybody to play there. We did have some local bands play in the store—Urban Guerrillas, bands like that. I remember doing an autograph session with Hüsker Dü after "Statues." We were starting to do more punk rock stuff, mostly signings.

KEVIN COLE: Johnny Thunders came to Minneapolis in 1980. We did an in-store with him at Hot Licks. He had an incredible reputation that preceded him about his drug use, and he showed up like two or three hours late and wouldn't come in the store until somebody scored him drugs; he just stood outside waiting. Three or four hours later he was okay to come in, but by that time nobody was waiting around anymore.

RYAN CAMERON: When I worked at the Musicland in Ridgedale, they said, "You like in-stores a lot right? The Musicland downtown is doing an in-store and they need help." And I said, "Yeah, I would love to. Who is it?" and they said, "It's this local guy named Prince." I didn't have a clue who that was, but it was after the second album came out.

They brought him into the employees' backroom at Musicland. He shakes my hand. He was totally shy and didn't say a word. Then we did the in-store. He might have muttered something under his breath like "hello" to the people in the room; there were probably ten people there to meet him. I could tell that he did not feel comfortable signing autographs in a local environment. They were giving away tickets to go see him, I think at the Orpheum.

By the time the in-store was done, maybe a hundred people had shown up. Mostly it was people walking by trying to figure out what was going on. People were getting tickets and literally throwing them on the floor. So the floor was just scattered with all these concert tickets that no one was going to use. But I remember going to his show that night and going, "Holy fuck! *Now* I know who this guy is!" He did a couple of kind of poppy, dancy songs, and then he said, "This next song is about a lesbian" and he just went [guitar sound]. It was like a fuzz guitar with a wah-wah pedal. That was an eye-opening experience, going from not knowing who he is, to meeting him, to that night seeing him perform. "Now I totally get it."

ERIC PIERSON: I went to Ramsey Junior High in St. Paul, and the original Cheapo Records was at the end of the baseball field. One day, right before I go to do my paper route, I hear this crazy, loud, fast music. There's some speakers outside Cheapo blasting this stuff. I'd gone in there before, but the guy behind the counter always kind of scared me. I went in, and there was the hippie guy again with no shoes and his flannel shirt open. It was Grant Hart. He was blasting the first Rezillos album. I bought it immediately, and I asked him what else was like that. The last thing I had bought there was a KISS album and *Disco Duck*. He sold me the Damned's first album, and I think I got the Suburbs' first EP there.

I started going there every day. One time, while I was thumbing through the used albums, Bob Mould and Greg Norton were there talking to Grant about getting a band together. So I think I was there when they decided to form Hüsker Dü.

Record stores were so vital. Cheapo was handy when I was in junior high, because it was right there. Then we used to take the long bus ride over to Oar Folk from St. Paul. Once Northern Lights started happening, I went there to buy records. Grady Linehan—brother of Kelly Linehan from Man Sized Action—worked there, and I asked him, like I used to do at any record store, "I like this kind of stuff. What else do you recommend?" He'd play five things for you, and you'd buy maybe two or three.

GRADY LINEHAN: I started to hang out at Northern Lights in St. Paul. Greg Norton, later Hüsker Dü's bass player, said to me, "Hey, do you need a job?" I said, "Yeah!" He goes, "Well, you can have the job if you give me a ride to work every day." I had a car that ran at the time. So I worked with Greg at Northern Lights on University Avenue in St. Paul. It was an incredible opportunity because you get exposed to all the neat new music, and things were changing fast in music at the time. Hüsker Dü practiced in the basement.

PAUL DICKINSON: There was a Northern Lights in St. Paul, which was very cool because they had shows in the basement. I saw Laurie Anderson there, I saw the Three O'Clock there, Hüsker Dü—they played in the basement of the record store.

PAT WOODS: Part of what helped was all four of us in Man Sized Action had slightly different influences. Tippy and I grew up on MC5 and things like that. The other guys had their own influences that Grady Linehan at Northern Lights was feeding them. That is where Terry Katzman comes into the picture, working at the record store, being a tastemaker for most of the scene.

TONY PUCCI: Terry and Jim Peterson and Dave Ayers and Peter Jesperson. I was going to Northern Lights in St. Paul. Grady and JC [John Clegg] and those guys would say, "You've got to hear this record" and "You need to hear the original, because that's a cover." We were ravenous, and they were feeding us. And the world just opened up for me.

It was an exciting time, there was so much going on musically. I think it's not just because of the age we were. I really believe it was different, and there were so many new directions developing and emerging at one time. We were in the right place at the right time.

DAVID MOE: I spent hundreds of dollars at Northern Lights in St. Paul, and when the downtown store opened, quite a bit there as well. Wax Museum on University was the first place I would go to. I had read about the Sex Pistols, and I saw this album. I bought it, brought it home, and was like, "Oh my god. This is the fastest, craziest stuff I've ever heard!" And now it seems so tame, of course. Because we didn't know what the music was going to sound like, even the local stuff, I would go by the album cover and the band name—if it sounded like it's gonna be new wave, punk, experimental—and say, "Hey, I'll give this a shot." You know, these tough guys on the front and it just says Tuff Darts.

JAY BERINE: We would drive over and see Larry Anderson at the Wax Museum record store in Robbinsdale. He would give us free records. When the store closed, we would go hear bands with him. Al Wodtke and I became great friends. He was the first guy I hired when I bought the Longhorn. He knew the musicians and did the bookings.

CINDY BLUM: That Wax Museum crowd was the most fun and crazy bunch of people that ever was. They were all really creative, and just a little bit off. They were always playing jokes on each other and on the customers. They had all these inside jokes, and they would do things to clear all the customers out of the store.

MARK FREEMAN: I worked at the downtown Wax Museum, and Dick Champ worked at the Lake Street store. But I worked at the Lake Street store sometimes. Those guys were a lot harder workers than I was. I don't think they appreciated having me around. There were a lot of shenanigans, but those guys knew their music. I have always been sort of a ne'er-do-well when it comes to that. I may have put Hot Licks, or whatever it was at the time, out of business. I ended up being a manager there at one point, and I refused to order anything I didn't like—which meant no Flock of Seagulls or Duran Duran or anything like that. We didn't have that because I wouldn't order it. But we had the Fleshtones' first album, probably a hundred copies. I was a terrible manager.

MARK TREHUS: I had *always* wanted to work at Oar Folk. For me, that was the ultimate job. At first Peter and then Jim wouldn't hire me. I wouldn't have if I were them either! I was admittedly a complete mess until I sobered up for good, after New Year's Eve '84–'85.

Then Jim and Terry left after the fire to start Garage D'Or on Nicollet, with help from Paul Stark, prior to Oar Folk reopening. I started working for Vern Sanden shortly thereafter when the space was rebuilt. It was an impossible act to follow. I did my best, but I couldn't. Nobody could have. The fire of '85 symbolized the end of an era, for me and a lot of other people. No single store, whether it be Garage D'Or, Northern Lights, Let It Be, or the rebuilt Oar Folk, could ever mean that much to the scene again.

Vern hired me and Bill Melton to co-manage Oar Folk after the fire. Vern took a chance on me. Once Bill left and I was anointed manager, I worked my ass off for Vern. It worked until Vern decided to get out of business around the turn of the century. When Vern told me he would consider an offer if I wanted to buy Oar Folk, I asked the landlord if he would give me a long-term lease. He told me no, that coincidentally he was preparing to sell the space, and he asked me if I would be interested in buying the property. I took out a second mortgage on my house and borrowed money from my relatives and the *sixth* bank I tried to get a loan from in order to finally pull it off. There wasn't enough money left over to buy the inventory or the business per se, so I helped administer Vern's going-out-of-business sale. In one month he made $50,000 out of his $60,000 worth of inventory. I bought some fixtures from him, he took the rest of his unsold records with him, and on April 1, 2001, I opened up Treehouse Records. I only had $15,000 worth of inventory and I was in debt and terrified of failing, but I'm still here.

Vern is an often uncredited and crucial piece of the evolution of the Minneapolis rock and roll scene. Although it was Peter's tastes that shaped Oar Folk more than any other single factor, Vern was often behind the scenes, buying cool rockabilly, blues, soul reissues, and original records for the shop. It was his vision that allowed Peter an outlet for his passion and his knowledge, which in turn played an inestimable role in fueling the scene the store fostered.

RYAN CAMERON: The one thing Minneapolis has always had—and a lot of it goes back to the beginning of Oar Folk—is really good record stores. Back then people depended on record stores more because there really wasn't much radio here. We had the college station and KFAI. I think the record stores really drove what people bought for music.

The people that worked at record stores during that time were usually tastemakers. People really trusted the taste of the particular stores they went to. The Peter era at Oar Folk to me is like the holy grail. I would go to Oar Folk and ask Peter what he liked, and that is what I would buy. People would go into Oar Folk or Hot Licks and the staff would suggest stuff, and people would buy it. I've always loved working at record stores, too. I love that interaction and being able to guide people toward something that might be outside their comfort zone. I considered myself somewhat a tastemaker because I could, to some extent, influence what people would buy. I was also learning from my coworkers about a lot of music I wouldn't have ever heard otherwise. That is how you learned about music. I never listened to the radio during the 1980s.

CHRISSIE DUNLAP: Peter Jesperson was the one who introduced a lot of us to new music. Selling records at Oar Folk, as a DJ at the Longhorn, or at after parties at his apartment at the Modesto, he loved to turn us on to new bands and records. And then, of course, he started Twin/Tone. He was absolutely pivotal in the development of the music scene in Minneapolis, in ways that go way beyond his discovery of the Replacements.

KEVIN COLE: Hand in hand with the Longhorn at that time, Oar Folkjokeopus was the place you'd go in the daytime, versus the Longhorn at night. And it was really interesting.

06

SINISTER FORCES: CURTISS A AND BOB "SLIM" DUNLAP

Curt Almsted, known to many as Curtiss A, was one of the first local musicians to put an original spin on cover songs when cover bands dominated the local scene—most notably with his band Thumbs Up, featuring Bob Dunlap. As an original artist and songwriter, Almsted went on to perform with countless other musicians in a seemingly endless array of bands and collaborations. He began playing music at age thirteen, and quickly captured attention with his incredible voice, stage presence, and creative blend of rock, R&B, blues, and soul influences. Almsted and Dunlap's successor to Thumbs Up, Spooks, was one of three bands whose records were first released on the new Twin/Tone label in 1978. A legendary local musician and visual artist, Almsted has hosted the popular John Lennon Tribute on December 8 every year since Lennon's death in 1980.

PETER JESPERSON: We first started seeing Curt Almsted's group Thumbs Up in '74, maybe '75, although he had been playing for years before that. He's been playing since he was a teenager with various bands. One long-running group he had was called Wire, and they had a seven-inch released but not widely distributed; it's something I still have in my collection.

There was a bar across from Oar Folk called the CC Tap [now CC Club]. We'd run over there from Oar Folk to grab something to bring back for lunch or dinner. One evening, I went over there to pick up a sandwich and I heard music playing. I looked in the back and there was a band onstage. I was like, "Oh, I didn't know they had live bands here."

The band was playing "Tell Her No" by the Zombies, which was a favorite of mine. I thought, "Oh cool! What a great choice of covers to do." They went into another one by a group from Chicago called the Cryan' Shames, "I Wanna Meet You." It *really* was a favorite of mine, and not as common as the Zombies song. I thought, "Oh wow, this is obscure and another great choice of covers."

I was really impressed with the group. It was Thumbs Up. The lead singer was Curt Almsted.

That was a pivotal moment for me, a real eye-opener. Even though they were doing covers, there was something really exciting and fresh about it. They put their own stamp on it. It was a mix of things—the Beatles and Rolling Stones, Small Faces, the Hollies, the Who. They were also mixing in a lot of the American rhythm and blues of the early '60s, from Wilson Pickett, James Brown, Hank Ballard, Sam Cooke. Curt had the raspy voice and he could really belt it out. We likened him to Mitch Ryder a little bit: a white guy who could sing soul music very well. But there was also that blend of soul with the British invasion, so he gave it a unique sound. That was where the lightbulb went off for me, and I thought, "Hey, there's some great music being made here in Minneapolis."

Handbill for Thumbs Up gig, with Vixen, at Kelly's Pub in St. Paul, January 17, 1977. COURTESY OF DICK CHAMP

BOB DUNLAP: I kept hearing from people who saw Thumbs Up, so I was kind of looking for them. Then they got a steady gig at the CC Tap. That's the first place I ever saw them. There was no stage then, and they were all standing along the back wall of the CC Tap. The minute I heard the band—I had such a great time that night.

I would go see them at the Tempo Bar, near where the Cabooze is. The Tempo Bar had bands with big long organ solos and guitar riffs. Thumbs Up was a breath of fresh air, because they played a lot of pop songs I'd heard and liked. They had harmonies and I was always fascinated by bands that had harmonies. They had multiple lead vocalists. That was very unusual because usually there would be a shirtless guy with a microphone swinging on a cord. Bands usually didn't have multiple guys that could carry the lead vocals like Thumbs Up did.

PETER JESPERSON: To see Curt and Bob playing these wonderful, sometimes obscure songs from the '60s was really exciting, and that developed into them writing their own stuff. We began to follow Thumbs Up all over town. Wherever they played, a bunch of us who worked at or hung around the record store became a little bit of a fan club, a posse sort of thing, and followed them around. One of the guys hauled a reel-to-reel tape recorder around to record stuff. We just liked them so much and wanted to capture those performances on tape.

That was really where my interest in the Minneapolis scene began, with Thumps Up and particularly Curt Almsted, who is, I think, one of the great singers in the history of Minneapolis rock.

CURT ALMSTED: I was born in 1951. Willie Murphy and Dave Ray and all those guys were like a decade older. They're the Dylan age, the previous half-generation, a little more Beat Generation. I'm from the TV/atomic age.

My two favorite guys when we were kids were Little Richard and Wilson Pickett as far as being "it," what you wanted to be. To me, rockin' is rockin' and soul music is where it's at and that's what I always try to point toward. That's my influence. But what comes out quite often can be something somewhat different. I want things to be unique. People who play music always want to have a new gimmick, because you can't make up new notes. Well, Buddy Guy sometimes does it, and Johnny Rotten has. There are notes sometimes that don't exist. But people try to sing them and that's fine with me; I do it all the time. I get up into some registers where you go, "What *is* that?" It's just fun. James Brown does that. That's all emotion.

Besides soul music, I enjoyed the loud English rock like the Who. Rock without much of the roll is quite attractive to young men, for whatever reason. I loved the MC5 and the blues.

In the beginning you had to be a certain way, and play songs people knew, and you had to be better than the next guys. Sometimes you'd be doing the same songs, but if you could do them better, then people would like you better. Then came the hippie days and it changed. It didn't really matter what you did, necessarily. Barriers were broken down and it's never been the same since. That started with the Beatles. People were afraid of rock and roll and by the time the Beatles came, people were ready to embrace it. Then they had to create a new scary thing and that was the Stones. Then every band that came after had to try to be better than the Beatles musically and try to be cooler than the Stones.

The first gig I performed was at the Moorhead Armory for a sock hop on Valentine's Day, the week after the Beatles arrived in America. I had just turned thirteen. It was all records, but these three friends and I got up and did half a dozen Beatles songs. That was a one-off. It was just me and a friend, a couple other guys we knew. One guy didn't even have a whole drum set. Bobby Vee's brother Bill Velline taught us the chords. I joined the Aztex in eleventh grade, October 1966. I count that as my other sort of first gig. That's where I learned to play sets. We learned to do songs we loved that were on the radio. We played five hours a night, in Chicago bars. We played New Year's Eve in the Elbow Room.

Probably the first band that mattered was Wire. Wire started February 1, 1970. I went to see the Allman Brothers and John Hammond at the Labor Temple on my birthday, January 31. The next day I got on the bus and went to Marshall, Minnesota, and met up with the guys from Wire, who happened to need a singer. I showed up at the right time. That band was relatively successful in the rural areas and even came to Minneapolis a few times and played the Depot, George's in the Park. We played out at Aldridge Arena [in Maplewood] with Gypsy and the System. Our audiences were almost all college crowds. We did it in ballrooms, and we started playing original songs but never recorded any except at the end. However, we were the first band to record an NRBQ song, called "Everybody Stomp." The flip side was "This Is It," a countrified version of Lothar and the Hand People. We had an original set, but we only got a few songs of it ever recorded professionally. There's an EP.

Wire broke up because of member changes and marriages. They went to Phoenix, and I went to Milwaukee for a year. Then we rejoined as Thumbs Up. In fall 1974, we began a year or a little longer residency at the CC Tap, across the street from Oar Folk, where Peter Jesperson, Andy Schwartz, Jim Peterson, Terry Katzman, and Mitch Griffin worked. We would do all these songs that they enjoyed, and they were amazed at what we were doing. But they were just songs that appealed to us in two different genres: '60s R&B and '60s English type songs.

JEFF WARYAN: When I was in junior high school, Steve Almaas and Jay Peck and I would go to this place called One Groveland. It was a church basement coffeehouse that did a rock music series. The first time I saw Curt play, he had a band called Wire. I thought those guys were scary good. They were like adults to me. I was thirteen years old, going down and seeing real rock bands. Back then, you really had to go see people live, and watch what they were doing, and try to learn in that way, and listen to records and sometimes slow down the records to hear what they were doing.

PAUL STARK: Curt's Beatles for Sale cover band had done gigs with Straight Up, which I was managing at the time. We'd been on the same bill at a few festivals, so I'd seen them. Bob Dunlap is a very smart, intelligent, careful player

Curt Almsted at Jay's Longhorn, circa 1977. PHOTO BY BAYARD MICHAEL

who adds color to any situation he's in. It doesn't matter who Curt plays with, it's still Curt's band. And Bob was a very good guitar player for him. He's not a front person, yet he shines brighter than anything. He's kind of like Chan. Of all the musicians we worked with at Twin/Tone, Chan Poling and Bob Dunlap were probably the two most talented.

BOB DUNLAP: I heard a rumor that the guitar player was leaving Thumbs Up, and it was crushing for me because he was one of my favorite parts of the band. I thought I'd audition, not having any chance, because he was unusually good. When you go to audition, even if you don't get it, you're better off having gone and busted through that fear wall. So I got my chance. And, through some pure luck of the draw, I got the gig. I enjoyed immensely the years playing with them.

Most bandleaders would teach you how they wanted it, and the way they wanted it was the way it had to be, or they would get discouraged with your efforts. It was fun to play with Curt because he would always be in a state of adapting things to the band. You didn't have to do it the same way every time, because he didn't do it the same way every time. It fostered a feeling that there's no one way to do the song. We could play around with it. I carried that over and tormented all the musicians that worked with me, because you're always working on a song when you do it live. Until you lay it down on a record, it's not written in stone.

Curt would come up with parts of songs he didn't alert you to, that he was going to try. He kept you on your toes. I admired that. To change something in front of a live audience is something a lot of bands don't dare do. They just do it the same way all the time. That's kind of stultifying to me. All the bands I've been in and liked weren't always the same every time. They'd change this or that and add a new thing here or there. To get a lead down and do it the same way every time, so you could do it in your sleep—that never appealed to me. I always liked to keep things moving and different.

There were some original songs in the Thumbs Up repertoire, but Spooks was Curt's original angle. He had Spooks going while he had a Beatles cover band, and Spooks became his avenue for originals. With Thumbs Up, you never knew Curt was such a good writer, because he never really pushed his own material. He came up with the key songs for his Spooks band all in a short time period. It was fun to play completely new material with Curt.

Spooks was one of the first bands to ever play the Longhorn. So Curt gets a lot of credit as far as generating the scene. There were the Suicide Commandos, who came out of left field and inspired a lot of bands locally to dare to be different. But Curt's right up there as one of the early bands to take the plunge wholeheartedly and be an original band, not a cover band.

CURT ALMSTED: I'm the harmonica player on both of Slim's solo albums. One of them I'm credited and one of them I'm not because we got into a fight. I remember one of the reasons that Slim and I had sort of broken up had to do with, I think, the way I presented originals. I wanted to reproduce them the way they were in my head and then extrapolate on that if needed. I would hear them like records in my head. I would get lyrics and I could hear it all. Some guys don't like to be told what to do. I'm sure all bands go through it. It's quite often a struggle even if you're friends.

I'm always pushing, and that's the last thing Slim does. He's not a pusher. He sneaks up on the notes. So it would lead to conflict sometimes. But I love the guy even more than the music we made. Slim was meticulous in his thing. Like drummers, there's this thing called the pocket—Tilly [Steve Thielges] and Bongo [John Haga] place their beats in different parts. It's the

Bob Dunlap and Curt Almsted at Music and Movies in Loring Park, Minneapolis, circa 1982. Photo by Michael Weiler

same with Slim and me. Usually Tilly is right in the pocket and Bongo kinda plays around a little. Bongo is the most versatile drummer I've ever worked with.

JOHN HAGA: Curtiss A and I had met when I was working at Knut Koupeé music store. He and Bob Dunlap used to come in and buy strings, then hop on their bus and head out of town and do their Beatles for Sale or Thumbs Up or whatever gig they were on. We'd talk at the counter. Curt was so shy back then. He didn't say much of anything to anyone. Imagine that. He's come out of his shell over the years. *[laughs]*

He needed a drummer; he saw me play with the Hypstrz and thought, "It'd kinda work." I started playing with Bob and Curt and Renaldo Rey, the bass player. He was a dishwasher by day and he would only use his right hand to wash dishes because he didn't want his calluses to leave his fingertips.

Bob, Curt, Renaldo, and I were in the basement of Comic City rehearsing songs that are now part of my DNA. At nineteen, twenty years old I was still finding out about Sam and Dave, and Wilson Pickett. Back then there was no rehearsal PA system. It was Curt in the middle of the room, everybody with Marshalls and big amps and an old drum kit. He's singing and he's just like this in my ear *[gestures explosion]*—that loud above what's going on in the room. I'm thinking, "Man, this guy is unbelievable."

You've got sixty seconds to take an audience and make them want to hear you. You don't start a night with "Fly Me to the Moon." You have to punch them out of the gate. That's the mentality with Curt. We'll all wander up onstage, but it's all business.

MONTY LEE WILKES: The first time I mixed Curt was sometime in '81 or '82, and we've been friends ever since. I thought his music was terrific. I think a lot of people fear his screaming, and I was like, "Fuck, this is great! Fill the meter. Yeah, go baby go!" I was a huge fan right away—"This is how you're supposed to sing!" I think I first saw him at Goofy's Upper Deck. It was Curtiss A and Johnny Rey. I mixed sound the whole night.

CURT ALMSTED: I got along with Monty Lee Wilkes better than almost anybody I ever met, and I miss him tremendously. The list of acts he helped to actualize their sound is unbelievably immense and diverse.

Courtesy is the first album I did with Twin/Tone, *Damage Is Done* is the second one, and *A Scarlet Letter* is the third. Each one has a place in my heart. *Courtesy* got four stars in *Rolling Stone*, not five. *Damage Is Done* is probably the clearest vision of just how awful things are. What I was talking about was damage, basically, to everything that can be damaged, that I felt was damaged. At the very end of the album there are three songs that are about girls and love, but they're not happy either. The same with *A Scarlet Letter*. The reason I love that one is because Al Anderson from NRBQ produced it. I trusted him to make it sound the way I wanted it to sound.

I'd come home and listen to music we recorded and kind of marvel at where all this sort of creative vibe was coming from. I would rather write about girls and being in love, nice happy things. I look back at a lot of it and usually the love songs are more angry and sad. There's a certain aspect of R&B, of dance music that I really enjoy. I've done a few songs that have a bit of that in it, but I kind of wish I'd done more. I also like the MC5-type pushing in your face, which is this proto-punk style, but I always liked soulful singing. I didn't like the way punks sang. I thought Johnny Rotten was hilarious and I thought Joe Strummer was really heartfelt but not necessarily the best vocalists on earth, the same way Dylan is. Dylan is great, but I'd much rather hear Willie Murphy doing those songs. Willie's a great singer. I think he's got a lot of different styles he can do. He's a way better musician than I am.

STEVE BRANTSEG: I was knocked out by Curt's first record, *Courtesy*. Later, when he asked me to join his band, he said, "I've got this outdoor show in four days. Can you learn sixty songs before performing it?" I think we only ended up playing forty, but, you know.... He had these weird, unexpected chord changes and rhythmic changes, too. That's the crazy unique and wonderful thing about his music.

JEFF WARYAN: I always liked watching Spooks. They were the real thing. I really wanted to do something with them some day. But they scared me, I think. I was a lot younger than they were. But I ended up playing with Curt during that period.

Playing with Curt was the university of rock and soul. I learned so much playing with him. He's such an original, real person, a real musician. I think that probably changed me in a way. My previous band, Fingerprints, was a really good band—really tight, kind of progressive rock, complicated—but it just didn't feel right for me at the time. Playing with Curt was something else entirely. Watching him do his thing was amazing every night.

Because I was so interested in being a rock guitar player, I hadn't really started writing songs too much yet. Jumping into Curt's band was perfect for me because it was big guitars, and he let me do whatever I wanted to do. It was the big guitar army. There were times when we had four guitars. It was Slim Dunlap, Frank Berry, Curt, and me. We weren't real good at editing ourselves onstage, so we all just played really loud all the time. It was massive.

KAREN HAGLOF: I remember so many times when Curtiss A would have all the guitar players he knew come up and play "Gloria." Curt would be singing and we would all be doing the guitar parts. I was the only female guitarist, which was a great position to be in at that time.

JEFF WARYAN: I played with Curtiss A in New York. Andy Schwartz moved to New York and started that whole *New York Rocker* thing. He was having a big anniversary celebration for the magazine. He and Curt are really close. He flew Curt and me out to New York, and no band. In one night, we played in three different places. We played the *New York Rocker* party, and Steve Almaas and the Bongos were our band. Then we went to Danceteria. It was a big First Avenue kind of club. That was a full Curtiss A set. The Bongos had learned all the songs, so they were our pickup band, which was brilliant. I loved it. It was really fun. After that, we went to a little club. The Raybeats were playing. We knew Danny Amis and a couple of those guys. We sat in on some songs with them. So that was a whirlwind New York thing.

DANNY AMIS: Curtiss A was quite the practical joker. I remember one time him telling me that he cleaned his guitar using Dow bathroom cleaner, and that it played much better. I almost fell for it. You never knew whether you could trust what was coming out of his mouth. *[laughs]*

JACQUE HORSCH: Curt is an interesting man. When I first dated Pete Lack, who was in bands with Steve and Kevin Foley, he used to play with Curt. When he did the John Lennon thing, they all lived at Curt's house on Garfield. Curt literally lived in the closet. Johnny Hazlett and Pete lived upstairs, and there were two other guys in the house. I think they condemned the house after these guys moved out. There was not one little piece of bare wall. It was just plastered with all Curt's stuff. It blew me away. He was an interesting guy. He scared me.

JOHN KASS: I'm so intimidated by Curtiss A because he is, in my view, the living embodiment of Minnesota rock and roll more than anybody else. To me, Curtiss A is *the* guy. I still have a tough time talking to him, just because I regard him so highly. The way he plays guitar! You can tell he's influenced a lot by Keith Richards, right? There's nobody who nails it more than that guy. When I see him I walk the other direction. I'm just too intimated to talk to him. It's so weird.

DOUG ANDERSON: Curt is one of my best friends on earth. But back then he and I weren't friends, and he was a terrifying guy. He was wild, and it was totally in his music, too. A real badass musician. He has all the swagger, he has the looks, the voice, and the ability. He was a real inspiration to people. I think his music is great, I think he is a great singer, I think he is a great songwriter. He never identified as punk, but the amount of conviction, the amount of style that Curt has—that to me is punk rock. Absolute fearlessness. He has played every kind of music with every kind of person. He is also one of those guys who is completely self-taught, that knows so much about so many things.

MARK ENGEBRETSON: The first time I heard Curtiss A was my second time at the Longhorn. Somebody told me that Thumbs Up was a really good band. It was probably Ernie Batson, and Ernie might've been with me that night. So we were at the Longhorn and it was time for Thumbs Up to play. This really cool guy was sitting at the bar. He was a rock star, you could tell. He gets off his stool and walks up to the stage. It's Bob Dunlap. He's playing with Thumbs Up and Curtiss A, and they went into a James Brown song, "Please, Please, Please." I was completely blown away. I'd never heard anybody sing like that, live at least. It was incredible. I'll never forget that moment. I'm still in awe of Curtiss A today.

DAVE PIRNER: Curtiss A's *thing* always alluded to where it was coming from. He made no bones about saying, "This is timeless music." Even though he fit in with the punk thing, he'd be the first to cite Little Richard or somebody from the past and say, "What *I'm* doing is the timeless part that connects it all together." There was always this acknowledging the rock music that led up to this kind of punk thing. He crossbred them. It was really educational in a way. There are threads that hold it all together in a timeless sort of a way.

MICHAEL REITER: Talking to Curt is like the greatest thing in the world. He could have gone to New York and been a star. The *Village Voice* loved him. It was the early to mid-'80s. They wanted to create the next Elvis Costello, and they wanted Curt to be it. I remember thinking he was going to be big, because they wanted him to be big. He just turned and walked away. You've got to respect Curt. He saw it for what it was, and he didn't want anything to do with it.

I loved seeing him live at that point. I loved that first Curtiss A album, *Courtesy*. I used to see him all the time. Years later, when I was in the Mighty Mofos, Curt would end up onstage with us a lot of times. I would be playing and, "Hey, there's Curt!" Curt being onstage is not always planned, but it is inevitable.

Curtiss A performing at the Longhorn with Chris Osgood and others, circa 1979. PHOTO BY STEVE MADORE

He was one of the first guys that would play all the time as well. He was playing every week at Duffy's, the Longhorn, wherever. Curt was always playing and then he got the regular gig at the Uptown. That was fun, too. I was there every Wednesday for years.

STEVE BRANTSEG: The first time I saw Curt I was like, "God! I wanna play with this guy! He's the coolest thing." I remember trying to introduce myself and I was so freaked out. It was so intense, man. I thought he was gonna hit me. So I was a little bit shy about it.

Jeff Waryan was in Curt's band on *Damage Is Done*. From that, Jeff and Steve Fjelstad and their friend Jay Peck, who played drums, formed Figures. It was those three guys on the first record. It was Jeff's solo record, titled *Figures*. Then he named the band Figures and started playing live. They had another guitar player who left the band. Peter Jesperson said, "Why don't you get Steve? He's not with the Phones anymore." So he gave me the record and I heard the songs and got together with them. The first show I did with Figures was with the Replacements at the U of M Field House.

Curt would start coming up and sitting in with us and then we started talking. I said to him, "Hey man, I've seen your Beatles tribute. I know all these Beatles songs." I was bold: "If you really wanna do it right, I should be doing it with you!" He was like, "Really?" So we got together and he said, "Here's my list. What do you know?" We played them all, and he goes, "It's yours, you're in. Let's do it." I've been doing every one of the Beatles shows with him since 1984.

The Lennon Tribute has evolved a lot. The first one I did was bare bones. It was him and me and Tom McKean, who was in Johnny Rey and the Reaction and was a great friend. The bass player was Caleb Palmiter. Gary Rue played some piano. It's evolved into a big thing. We have people who are aware of it worldwide. Even Yoko loves what we do and encourages it.

CINDY BLUM: I didn't play with Curt very long. We did all these old R&B standards, which I was not at all familiar with, so it was cool. It was really scary when you got onstage, Curt would yell out "Sam and Dave." And you were supposed to know what song you were supposed to play. So that was scary.

MARK FREEMAN: Cindy is playing with Curt, and she is blowing my mind because she is coming home at night after rehearsal and knows all these freakin' R&B songs all of a sudden. The night she came home and I heard her rehearsing that John Lennon song "Instant Karma," I heard that drum fill and I was like, "I married the greatest drummer in the world!"

CURT ALMSTED: The first Lennon Tribute was the next night after John Lennon died. I got a call from Chrissie Dunlap asking if I would come down and sing some Beatles songs. Slim and I had been in an argument for about a half a year. We weren't really speaking, mostly on my part because I'm the stubborn one. Chrissie says, "Slim said that we don't have to talk about anything or argue, just play songs." That sounded good to me. I got on the bus. I have this memory, when we were done at the end of the night, I just packed up my guitar, walked off the stage, and caught the bus home.

The next year we did it at Goofy's Upper Deck. Julian West wrote a review of it for the *Minnesota Daily*. The year after that, Goofy's was closed and Steve McClellan suggested we do it at First Avenue. I think we did the first few in the Entry. I remember the first time we played the big room. Jeff Willkomm must've been in Florida, so unbelievably I had to play bass. Steve Foley played drums, Slim Dunlap played guitar, and Pete Lack played keyboard. That's all we really had. We got Rusty Jones on bass because he could really approximate the Paul McCartney parts. I tried to get Tilly involved right away on the first one at the Upper Deck. At that time the band was the Supernaturals and Cindy Blum was on drums, this friend of mine Neil Chapel on bass, then Slim and me.

We did a set of R&B chestnuts I was trying to simplify into something Cindy and Neil could play with us. I would mostly handle the rhythm stuff and Slim would do this sound. I used to say he was the Edge [of U2] before the Edge was the Edge. Even though I liked certain things, my interpretations quite often bear little resemblance to the originals. Now when we do the Lennon show we try to copy everything pretty exactly. Every once in a while there's variations, but mostly it sounds like it.

CHRISSIE DUNLAP: I cannot overemphasize the impact Curt has had on the local music scene. When Bob joined Thumbs Up in 1976, they were one of the most popular bands playing around town. We used to go see them at the CC Tap. It was a big deal for Bob to get that gig, even if it did take him out on the road (and away from me at home with newborn twins). Curt excels at pop, soul, and blues, and he was able to sneak in a few original songs before that was a good thing. Curt is a great singer and a true original in every way. He is a local treasure. He's still performing around town—a fifty-year career—and of course his annual tribute to John Lennon is a popular show.

SPRAGUE HOLLANDER: I first saw Curt when I was around fifteen, and it was honestly like the clouds parted and I knew, "This is real; this is what it's about." It was profound and changed the way I heard all music from that moment forward. He was, and is, musical from his very core and has a total commitment that's effortless because he is a true singer, artist, and musician. Like any of the greats, he is what he does. It's not a job, not something that gets turned off.

Of the many people I've worked with, he pretty much stands alone in that every time he takes the stage, whether in front of five or five hundred people, anything can happen. If he's in the mood, lightning can strike, and when it does it's magic and affirming and wonderful to be a part of. You're looking at the same life force of a Jerry Lee Lewis, Elvis Presley, Muddy Waters, etc. Wherever we are playing, all that stuff is still there.

CURT ALMSTED: The only time I actually feel good is when I'm playing. Before I play, instead of being nervous, I get the opposite. I get comatose almost, because my body knows, after doing it for so long, that I'm going to expend a great deal of energy and have adrenaline. It's like Zen. As soon as I get up there I'm usually okay. Sometimes at a Lennon show I almost feel like I'm floating up there because I'm so relaxed.

In the future, you'll either be forgotten or you're remembered like Elvis, the Beatles, and now David Bowie and Prince. You're remembered as an innovator. I'm lucky I've got this sort of Curtiss A legend, myth going around town. I don't have to do anything anymore, but I still do.

I had interest from both Sire and Maverick labels. Part of me feels a little regret that maybe I should've utilized the channels that were open to me to try and be more of a success, but I sort of turned my back on stuff. Every album was a different band, and I lost interest in doing anything for a while after my kid died. I did an album with this guy that I considered the best: Big Al [Anderson, NRBQ]. I thought—and stupidly so—if I can't get a hit with him, why bother.

I've distinguished myself here, and there's a lot of talented people here. I never would've thought too much about my own self. I've had a lot of people whom I respect give me encouragement, like Willie Murphy, Maurice Jacox, and Prudence Johnson. If you think I'm that good, maybe I am slightly worthwhile, but it's a never-ending barrage of trying to top yourself. If you're successful in any way it's like an earthquake, it's exponential the pressure that is put on you. Luckily I was naïve enough in the beginning when I got a really good review in *Rolling Stone*. I swear to god, it was like water off a duck's back. I just shrugged, kind of. I knew I couldn't do anything but what I was doing anyway, so I didn't let it affect me.

If you plan for stuff it won't happen, but every once in a while cool things do happen. I've been the recipient of hundreds of those things. I've got a lot of great memories of way cool things happening. And I'm still having fun. Having friends and being in bands is a real fun thing; it's like this weird little gang you have.

All this stuff doesn't seem like it was three, four decades ago. It seems like it was yesterday.

07

WE DO WHAT WE LIKE: FLAMINGO AND FLAMIN' OH'S

Flamingo was the first band to perform at Jay's Longhorn. They went on to play there often, as well as at Duffy's and other venues. Flamingo was also one of the few early bands to perform original alternative rock music. Their previous incarnation, Prodigy, performed the ballroom and small-town bar circuit before the founding members formed Flamingo in 1977.

Flamingo featured charismatic front man, guitarist, and singer/songwriter Robert Wilkinson, guitarist Johnny Rey, bass player Jody Ray, keyboardist Joseph Behrend, and drummer Bob Meide. The band changed its name to Flamin' Oh's in 1980 and continued performing, touring, and recording through 1986. Flamin' Oh's was one of the earliest bands in the country to make music videos: "I Remember Romance" was featured on the new music-video channel MTV. Although they never signed with a major national label, Flamingo/Flamin' Oh's have long been an audience favorite and were an influential force on the local music scene.

ROBERT WILKINSON: You can blame my parents. I grew up listening to Elvis Presley, Jerry Lee Lewis, Ray Charles. My parents liked Jerry Lee Lewis a lot. I used to go to the same ballrooms in Iowa to see rock acts in the '60s where they used to go see Jerry Lee Lewis in the '50s. So I grew up with a lot of cool rock music.

I'm sure that had something to do with the path that I took later. I started taking guitar lessons when I was eight years old, but it was taking too long to learn. They were trying to make me read and learn music. I didn't want to take the time to do all that—I wanted to rock out—so I got out of it until I was twelve, when the Beatles came out. That's when I wanted to get back into music and pick up the guitar again. When the Stones came out, that was *really* it. That's when I earnestly began my journey into music. I remember sitting in my parents' basement listening to the Rolling Stones' first album, *England's Newest Hit Makers*, trying to learn the chords and the leads to the songs. Keith Richards was a big influence on me in my early days of playing. Still is.

I met Bobby Meide in high school. I must have been seventeen. He was eighteen. He was playing with this R&B band. Rather than be a real straight drummer, he had three kits assembled—very Keith Moon–like. So this R&B band was playing R&B tunes, and Meide's drumming like Keith Moon. I said, "That's my drummer right there." That was the beginning of a friendship that lasted over forty years. We played together in several different bands over the years. We were just so connected musically, and as brothers, too.

My first band was Flash Tuesday. It was a three piece that was very alternative, actually. It was me, Bobby on drums, and Cliff Holme on bass. I was writing music then, and we were doing weird stuff. A lot of three-piece bands at that time were doing Cream and Jimi Hendrix, and we were doing, like, MC5 covers. We played all these places and they hated us. But we had a great time doing it. We got to play with Wayne Kramer and the MC5. It was outdoors in Mankato. It cost five bucks to get in.

The Who and the Stones were bands that always put on really great shows. We wanted to emulate that. I don't want to loiter onstage and be that ultra-cool, ultra-hip dude who doesn't move around. Screw that. Rock and roll—you're meant to have fun and jump around. Let the music carry you where it carries you. It's not a fake energy and it's not a fake kind of "Oh, I have to do this tonight." You get up there and, boom, you're gone. You're going down that musical highway, and who knows where that's gonna lead you. But hopefully it'll be fun.

Prodigy formed in '72 or '73. It was a four piece with me, Bobby Meide on drums, Johnny Rey on guitar, and Scott Manske on bass. We wrote our own material and did cover songs of bands we liked—the Faces, the Stones, things like that. In the late '60s and early '70s, even up until 1977, there weren't a lot of bands doing original music. Prodigy was doing original music. I've always done original music, whatever band I was in, from the beginning.

JOHNNY REY: I went and saw Prodigy for years before I was in the band. I was their biggest fan. Prodigy played '50s rock and roll, like the Rolling Stones would do it. It's like you were seeing the Rolling Stones when they first started doing "Carol." They did all kinds of rockabilly stuff. I absolutely loved them.

Robert Wilkinson and Bob Meide are a little bit older than me, and they got together in 1969. They went to a festival in Milwaukee and saw MC5, the Who, the Stones, the Kinks. I had been listening to everything, I liked everything. But once I saw them, I really got into that type of music.

Robert was the only guitar player in the band for quite a while. Then they found this kid, Randy Anderson, and asked him to be in the band. He was a blazing-hot guitar player. He was my guitar hero. He was smoking hot. I was not. *[laughs]* Then he left the band. I didn't know if they'd get another guitar player. I remember Robert and me playing around on guitar one day. I showed him the intro to "Tumbling Dice" by the Stones, and he couldn't believe it. Like, "How did you figure that out?" That was my style. I'm rhythmically a Keith Richards type of guitar player. That's what they really needed. It was my biggest dream, too. He said, "Just come to rehearsal. We're going to jam on stuff." I happened to know a whole bunch of songs off the Mott the Hoople album *All the Young Dudes*. They of course knew that album left and right. So we just played the whole album. They're like, "Okay, you're not that good, but you're totally the right style." Luckily I got better quick.

I was in Prodigy for that last part of Prodigy, for maybe a year before we became Flamingo.

ROBERT WILKINSON: Prodigy used to play over at One Groveland church, in the basement, with Pepper Fog and Skogie and the Flaming Pachucos. It was a regular event. Pepper Fog wrote great original music and did some really cool covers, too. It was the Strength brothers, Bob and Dale Strength, and Gregg Inhofer played keyboards. We liked them a lot. Skogie and the Flaming Pachucos was a great band. Rick Moore was the lead singer/songwriter. He was a good cat, a really good songwriter. They were really clever, very good musicians.

Skogie and the Flaming Pachucos, Pepper Fog, and Prodigy were probably mostly known for their original music, but everybody was doing cool covers, too. We were doing David Bowie covers along with original music. We were different in that sense, too, because there weren't a lot of bands doing that around here. At that time a lot of the bands were big hair bands doing songs by Yes and Journey and things like that. When Prodigy came along, that was kind of the start of original bands.

Prodigy promo photo, 1976. PHOTO BY STEVE MADORE

JOHNNY REY: Then the Blitz Bar thing happened. We met the Suicide Commandos. We started rehearsing at Utopia House. Scott Manske, the bass player, left. There was a guy who knew Jody Ray and Mike McKern. McKern had Tracks on 5th Studios, where he recorded NNB and all those bands. He was friends with Jody Ray. Jody was a bass player who was looking for a band. This intermediary knew us and he knew them. "Well, you should try out for this band. They need a bass player."

JODY RAY: I met Robert and Bobby and Johnny in August of '76. They were looking for a bass player. A pretty instantaneous bond was created. We easily fell in with each other. We were friends and became a brotherhood. I remember playing with Bobby on drums. The two of us became one. We were so tight. It was fantastic, the feeling that gives you—let alone the sound that is coming out. It was such a great high. I was really wanting to do original music, and lo and behold, so were they. It was a perfect match.

It was a pivotal time. I never experienced such a defined music scene as back then. Punk and new wave were coming out and looked really strong. Flamingo wasn't new wave, we weren't punk. We got thrown in with them, probably from our attitudes.

JOHNNY REY: When Jody came into the band, it changed our style from Prodigy's more Rolling Stones rock and roll feeling to a little more new wave or punk. Robert was really into David Bowie and Roxy Music—on top of that, that's kind of what Flamingo was, a new wave flavor added to what we already were with Prodigy.

Everything was changing. Robert's style of writing was changing. We had a different bass player. Then we got Joseph Behrend, who had come through these other friends, to play keyboards, changing the sound of the whole band. We were like, "Now we sound different. So let's have a different name, too." Jody came up with the name Flamingo. It fit what the music was starting to sound like. Flamingo was the perfect name for our band at the time.

JODY RAY: When I showed up, there was no name for the band. Shortly after the new formation of the band, Robert and I were driving in my car, talking about needing a band name. I had one I had thought of for quite a few years. "You know what I think would be a cool name? Flamingo." Robert instantly jumped on that, and that is how we became Flamingo. We met up with the other guys and told them the new band name. Fortunately, there was no resistance.

I remember doing gigs mostly out of town in the beginning. One of the first gigs I remember playing in town was either at the Walker or at a music school on the West Bank. That was the first time people saw us in our new formation as Flamingo. That was really cool.

JOHN KASS: I remember the Flamingo guys would play over on Front Street, at the Front End, a biker bar. Can you imagine seeing Flamingo playing in a biker bar with the Suicide Commandos? But that's the way it was. That to me is just amazing, that they created this all from the ground up. It was all do-it-yourself.

JOHNNY REY: We used to play places where we would be the only band doing covers of Bowie, Roxy Music, the Kinks, the Rolling Stones, the Yardbirds. The rest of the bands were like '70s cover bands. We did three sets a night, three or four nights a week. There was very little repeating of songs. There'd be so many great songs to cover. We played bars out in like Brooklyn Center, and we obviously didn't fit in. We didn't care. That was kind of fun. Not that we got asked back.

We'd do covers, plus we were doing originals. Hardly anybody did originals back then. Robert Wilkinson, I'm telling ya, from day one, he's like a *[blur sound]*, writing songs left and right. That's what was unusual about Prodigy and Flamingo, especially in that era.

That's how it all started. It would slowly build. There'd be a bunch of people at the bar who are like, "What the hell is this?" Then there'd be ten people that are like, "Wow." Next time it would be twenty people that were like, "Wow."

SHARON SAMELS: I went to see Flamingo. Then I told my whole crew, which included Hugo Klaers, "Oh my god, we've gotta go see this band the next time they play." I found out where they're playing, which was probably the Union Bar, and brought my whole posse of, say, ten. It would start building. It was word of mouth.

JOHNNY REY: It went from us playing these bars where we didn't fit in, and then building the following until the Longhorn came along. Then it was like, "Okay, now there is a bar where we can play all this stuff." That's really the start of the whole thing. Before it was all these bands playing places where they didn't belong, but there was no place else to play. Then the audience would be building enough where now it made sense to actually have a bar.

SHARON SAMELS: That's why Flamingo was chosen as the first band to play at the Longhorn, because they had a following. They knew people would come in the door. Al Wodtke recommended Flamingo to Jay Berine.

JAY BERINE: Al introduced me to the guys from Flamingo. They played a New Year's Eve party, 1976. My roommate Marty and I lived in these apartments in Wayzata, and we commandeered the party room. Flamingo did their first paying gig. I paid them fifty bucks. It was an incredible party. People got drunk and got naked and passed out in the sauna and threw up. It was all those great things that really made for a great party back in those days! *[laughs]*

AL WODTKE: I had known Bob Meide since I was about five or six years old. Early Flamingo was like a pop version of the New York Dolls.

JOHNNY REY: It was perfect timing. Jay was going to open that bar: "Now I need some kind of band." We were just happening. We were made to order

Flamingo at Jay's Longhorn, circa 1977. PHOTO BY STEVE MADORE

for that. It made the most sense to have us be the first band that played there.

The other thing that happened was Flamingo got interviewed by Tim Carr in the *Star Tribune*, and people went: "Hey, let's go hear them." There were pockets of people all over the place that liked this new music.

LU ANN KINZER: The first band I saw at the Longhorn was Flamingo; they played for the first week there. Flamingo was one of the greatest bands of their time. They played popular rock songs and many original songs. They had an energy that kept everyone dancing all night long. Robert Wilkinson always amazed everyone by jumping so high onstage and doing the splits.

JIM FENN: My roommate Gerry Masterman and I were mid-'70s rock and roll fans. Gerry worked in a factory downtown, and he would go to the Longhorn and have a drink every night before coming home. He comes home one night at two o'clock, waking me up, shaking me in bed, telling me, "There's finally some rock and roll in town! You've got to go down to the Longhorn and check this out!"

He had been there the very first night Flamingo played there. So I went down the next night and saw them, and I was blown away. At this time most of the music of any note was what I would call similar to Lamont Cranston: blues and boogie. So I saw Flamingo one night, and I never turned back. I started going to all their gigs, started meeting all the crew people showing up.

Aside from the fact they were playing deep covers of rock and roll bands, they played fifty songs that night, twenty-five were covers and the other twenty-five were originals. That's what turned me on: that they had the chutzpah to write their own songs. They were the coolest thing I'd ever seen in Minneapolis.

The thing about them was, they weren't really punk, not like the Commandos were, not like Hüsker Dü. They weren't new wave like the Suburbs kind of were. They were just an old-fashioned, straight-up rock and roll band with a modern twist. I tell people they were kind of like a cross between the Cars and the Rolling Stones.

JIM WALSH: I was legal on February 14, 1978, and I was 19. I went to the Longhorn and saw Elvis Costello and the Attractions and Flamingo. Flamingo was really my entrée into the whole live, original punk rock music scene. They were great opening for Elvis. It was like, "This is local live music?" I was off and running. I remember going to Duffy's and seeing them that summer. A friend of mine said, "Wouldn't it be great to be in a band?" I thought, "I wanna do that." It was all exploding.

ROBERT WILKINSON: We changed to the Flamin' Oh's in about 1980, after Johnny Rey left. Johnny wanted to pursue some other music. He had been in contact with Jack Lee, who wrote "Hanging on the Telephone," out in LA. He wanted to go do his thing. That was cool. We stayed a four piece, Flamingo. We made our first album, then changed our name to the Flamin' Oh's because there was an R&B band called the Flamingos. They heard about us and said, "That's a little too close for comfort, boys." So we changed to the Flamin' Oh's. That was actually Curtiss A's doing. One night on the marquee outside the Longhorn, he was being a smartass, and he separated the "o" from Flamingo. It was "Flaming o." We took that and ran with it. We dropped the "g," put the apostrophe up there, added the "h" and apostrophe "s" because we liked the idea that it was weird and didn't mean anything. It just sounded cool. We became Flamin' Oh's and put out the record *Flamin' Oh's*, the green album.

Ad for Flamingo's EP release, December 1979. COURTESY OF CHRISSIE DUNLAP

JOHNNY REY: Sharon and I moved to LA. For one year, I played with Jack Lee of the Nerves. I got to play with the Plimsouls. I played with Flamin' Groovies. We got to play at the Whiskey a Go Go, the Troubadour, and the Roxy. We went to see South Side Johnny and the Asbury Dukes at the Roxy. Todd Rundgren sat right across from me. I'm like, "My god." His hands seemed like they're really huge. I thought, "No wonder he plays the instruments so good."

LA was a trip. It was the height of the new wave fashion out there. Everything is so cartoonish out there. You take the London, New York new wave people, and by the time it gets to California, it's like Oz. So commercial. The scene was almost like a movie out there. It was a weird scene for me.

Our son John John was born in October 1980. Two weeks later, we moved home from LA. It's funny because right before we moved back, the same guy that hooked up Jody Ray and Flamingo was friends with Mike McKern. I told him I'd be moving back, and he said, "Well, you should really start a band with Mike McKern. He's a really good drummer." Because we recorded the Flamingo EP at his studio, I knew Mike. I called him up and said, "We should do something together." First thing we did was record two songs. I released it as a single. That was in February 1981. I found two other guys, and Johnny Rey and the Reaction debuted in July at Sam's with the Crash Street Kids. All that happened so fast. Mike McKern is still the drummer in my band.

The Flamin' Oh's kept on. They were a huge part of the early '80s scene. It was the Phones and the Suburbs and the Flamin' Oh's. They were the huge things, the height of new wave.

MONTY LEE WILKES: Flamin' Oh's and the band I was doing sound for, the Bronx Zoo, played together a lot. They took the Bronx Zoo to Minneapolis for a few gigs. They had a really groovy road crew: Jim Fenn, the tour manager, and John Shanderuk, a sound guy. We went to the gig and loaded in. Everybody sound checked, and we were done. It was the middle of the afternoon. Jim said, "Do you want to come over to my place to relax and take a shower?" We get in his car and drive to this unbelievable house in Uptown. We come in, "Hey, we're home!" and out comes this, I don't know, six-foot-eleven blonde, and she has this definitive rock vibe to her. I was looking around and there's breathtaking woodwork. It was exciting. I was a hick from the sticks and now I'm at the Flamin' Oh's tour manager's house. It was pretty cool. I'm not going to lie. They took us under their wing, the Oh's did. Everybody, the band, the musicians, the crew. It was really nice. We had a lot of fun doing gigs together. The Flamin' Oh's were the first bunch of real musicians and dudes on the scene that didn't treat me like a kid. When I met Joseph Behrend, we sat down and had a nice adult conversation. He was a really wonderful person, really good dude.

ROBERT WILKINSON: Our manager at the time was John Pete, who was a beautiful person. A very devoted person to the band, put up with a lot of our nonsense. We were all bad boys with bad attitudes and not much business sense, and he was very gracious and kind and patient. At some point, we met a great A&R guy named Dougie Ackerman, who had a couple gold records on his wall and introduced bands to major labels. He was a heavy gun in the business. Good things were happening.

We didn't record with Twin/Tone. We were the outsiders. We went with some people who formed a label who weren't really known in the music business. They had some money and wanted to start their own label, and for some reason we were enamored with that idea. Some of the people on our team were pros, but the other people were not in the music business at all. After our manager and Dougie talked with them, we went with them. It started out as Fat City Records. We recorded *Oh!* at Sound 80 Studio in 1981 with David Rivkin, who later became David Z and produced hits with Fine Young Cannibals.

For the life of me, I don't know why we didn't go with Twin/Tone. I wish we would have gone with them—Peter Jesperson and Paul Stark and Charley Hallman. Dear Charley Hallman. I was friends with Peter. I knew Paul. He had done a Prodigy video for us for Channel 2. But, it's okay. Everything's cool. There were bands on Twin/Tone that were signing to major labels but never really did anything.

We were young. You think to yourself: "I'm not going with the flow. We're going to strike out on our own and do our own thing." One can never know where that's going to end up. There are so many variables involved in why and how a band makes it. You could go with the best label, you have the best team, but there might be one variable that stops it from happening. In our case, there were too many variables. *[laughs]*

We had some major label record interest. We had two instances of major labels wanting to talk to us. And each instance, the manager who was managing us at the time blew it. The one that's well known is Sire Records coming down to the Longhorn—whoever was head of Sire Records, and a major producer at the time, was doing Blondie—he came to the Longhorn, saw the show, liked the band, and wanted to come to the dressing room and talk to us. David Farrell, our manager, said, "No. We're doing our own thing." Wouldn't even let him in the door. I didn't find this out until later. I've been working hard at trying to forgive David Farrell for that. He was the guy who approached us and wanted to manage us. He made a heartfelt pitch.

When you find somebody who wants to champion you, in such a heartfelt way, you think, "Let's give the guy a chance." You want to put your faith and your trust in people. Unfortunately, he wanted to be Peter Grant, Led Zeppelin's manager. Peter Grant was evil, the biggest ego. David Farrell had an ego, too. And talk about making some bad decisions. "Dude, you just turned down Sire!" I don't know if he knew who they were or if he was just thinking they were somebody wanting to get the band.

Another time after we signed with Fat City, a guy named John Randall, J. R., who was the head of Fat City, had a meeting in New York with a big label. He came into the meeting on roller skates, as unprofessional as possible. And unbeknownst to us at the time—once again, I didn't hear about it until after the fact. We left Fat City.

We recorded a third album in Miami. It will never be released, because they brought in other musicians to play on it. Songs that should have been recorded were never recorded in Flamin' Oh's history, strong songs from our early repertoire. These are the kind of decisions they were making. And unfortunately we were going along with it.

But you let it go. Believe me, my band is not the only band to be able to tell you horror stories about inept management. There are so many stories like that out there, it's heartbreaking. So that's what happened with us. We could have signed with somebody. But our label management fucked it all up for us.

It's real important, in order to keep your sanity, to find a place within yourself where you can forgive, and let go. And understand that whatever happened at that moment, happened at that moment. And maybe there's a reason why that happened. I am totally grateful. Had I gone another route than my journey up to now, it would have been so different. I might not have had my daughters. I have a great life. So I don't really lament that part of my life, because I also had a lot of fun and learned a lot.

It gives you perspective and insight. Once again, there's a million great bands out there who could tell you the same stories. There's a lot of great bands that I love who should have gone to some sort of level of success but never did.

MARTIN KELLER: The one band I always thought would be the most successful on a major label never even made it to a major label: the Flamin' Oh's, or Flamingo. They had probably the most accessible sound, kind of an uncompromising sound with commercial edges. Robert Wilkinson is a great songwriter. They were a terrific band to see live, terrific rock and roll band. They had elements of the Stones. Occasionally some of their more pop numbers sounded like the Cars, although they were much better than the Cars, I think. That's why I thought, if they had ever gotten a break, they could have been huge. But they didn't have the right management. They didn't get the breaks. It's the luck of the draw a lot of times.

ROBERT WILKINSON: We made a video with Chuck Statler for "I Remember Romance" in 1980 when the first album came out, and then when the second album came out, we made a video for "Stop" with him. They're funny as hell. Chuck's great. He was a pioneer of rock videos. He went to school with Mark Mothersbaugh from Devo and did the early Devo stuff, and he was here in Minneapolis and worked with the Commandos and a few other bands.

The shoots were two- and three-day shoots. We would start at six, seven in the morning and shoot all day, and go to different locations. Some of "I Remember Romance" is in the Commodore in St. Paul—awesome art deco. Some of it was in a junkyard, on top of metal scrap heaps where Joseph did the solo. Some of it was at the beloved House of Breakfast on Chicago Avenue, which is no longer there. For the video for "Stop," we went to St. Paul. We're playing classical instruments like the harp. We're in tuxedos. We filmed in the Landmark Center. They had these ornately carved wooden judges' chambers.

It was real businesslike shooting, but it was awesome. Chuck was awesome to work with. His assistants were cool, too. All that stuff was really fun to do.

JODY RAY: We had a blast doing the videos with Chuck Statler. Kind of grueling, the hours we put in. Rock and roll and early mornings don't mix too well. *[laughs]* Fortunately, we didn't have to play live through the shoot. We did it at First Avenue, went to a junkyard—that's where you see Joseph playing a solo standing in front of a pile of scrap metal. It was a pretty awesome shot. There was a classroom scene where we are sitting in the front row and the girl portraying the teacher had a long wooden pointer. She smacked the desk I was sitting at, and my fingers were stretched out. She caught me. You can see in the video my hand turns into a fist really fast. "Okay, *this* is real."

ROBERT WILKINSON: That's when MTV was starting. We weren't a big name. Chuck was doing the Devo videos, "Whip It"—those were some of the first things played on MTV. There wasn't a whole lot of music videos around. I never saw ours on MTV, but my mom did. They showed them at like three AM.

Because of Chuck Statler, they were good videos. The videos were also shown on a show called *Rock World*, I think, at midnight on Friday or Saturday night. So we got a little bit of exposure.

CHUCK STATLER: I was approached by a fellow, John Randall, J. R. He had this two-story brick building with his record label, across the street from the parking lot by the Monte Carlo in downtown Minneapolis. In the last incarnation, he had a vinyl pressing plant there, Fat City. He put out two or three albums with Flamin' Oh's and at least one with the Crash Street Kids.

JIM FENN: One time Bob Meide was over at my house buying a bag of pot, and he mentioned the band was going to New York in a couple months. I said, "Oh my god, I've always wanted to go to New York City." He went, "You know what? We just lost our lighting guy, why don't you come to the gig tonight and do lights and join the band?" I went to the gig to do lights, and the manager of the band, David Farrell, came up to me and said, "What are you doing here?" I said, "Well, I'm going be the lighting guy." He says, "What makes you think Bob Meide hires the crew?" And I said, "I don't know. I'll tell you what. I'll work for free until you go to New York and then you're going to pay me."

Going to New York didn't take place for another nine months, but I was doing the lights. The band had also bought a monitor system so I was running the monitors and some lights out of briefcases. We did about two weeks of gigs in the greater New York/New Jersey area.

We did the first night's gig, and we were staying with some friends. We were upstairs talking, when Joseph walked in and goes, "Oh, you're here! Where's the truck?" And I said, "It's right downstairs." He goes, "No, it's not." We looked a couple floors down and the truck had been stolen. It was extremely disheartening. The next day I was talking to John Pete, our manager, about what to do. Somebody floated the idea, "Well, let's find some bands and let them open up for us. If we dig them we'll use their gear." And that's what we ended up doing. We stayed in New York for another two weeks.

By the time we got back, they declared, "Now you've earned the right to be a road manager." I traveled everywhere they traveled for six more years, until '85 when I left.

ROBERT WILKINSON: New York City shows were awesome. A highlight of our career was when we were touring and playing out in New York and playing Peppermint Lounge, Max's Kansas City—a place where the Velvet Underground, all these great bands had started. We were on hallowed ground, the fucking epicenter of punk rock, new wave.

We didn't fill the places. We weren't that well known. Our team had gotten a little bit of press on us, so a few people knew us. Then there were some people we knew who were living out there. We had a blast. We partied and hung out with friends, and we're in New York, in Manhattan, the East Village, and it's awesome.

You know, we're all young. We're all full of piss and vinegar and swagger and attitude. It's rock and roll. Everybody liked to party. We were all doing stuff, various things and drinking and doing blow. Then, everybody gets to a certain point and everybody's kind of crazy. But we had fun. I remember going to a party—Talking Heads were there, and the Dead Boys. If they were partying, then somehow you'd hear and get in the hotel room. One night the Faces, Rod Stewart and Ronnie Wood, were playing. Bobby Meide and I were big fans. We ended up at a party, and I was talking with Ronnie Wood for a while. They were all interested in girls, they ain't gonna sit there talking to me for more than like a couple minutes.

Sometimes the bands coming through town that we opened for were really nice; you could talk to them. Other times, they were just dicks. When we opened for Patti Smith, her band came down to the Longhorn, where we were playing the night before the show. Lenny Kaye—who's not only her guitar player but a famous music writer—and some of her band came down there and liked our band. They were very down-to-earth and very cool. We ended up partying with them afterwards.

Opening for Patti Smith at the State Theatre was really great. The place was full and we were all fans and were so excited. It probably is one of the highlights of our career.

JOHNNY REY: Flamingo opened for Patti Smith the second night. Played the State Theatre. That was the coolest. Robert Wilkinson said that might be his favorite night we ever played. Playing for Patti Smith was ridiculous. I saw her for a fleeting second backstage.

The night before, the Commandos played in front of Patti Smith. We

Promo photo of Flamingo by David Farrell, 1978. COURTESY OF JOHNNY REY

were playing at the Longhorn that night, so everybody came down there afterwards. Lenny Kaye really loved us doing a version of "Jumping Jack Flash" that we used to do. He's just flipping out about that. Somebody told me that later. He loves that early '60s rock.

ROBERT WILKINSON: Bands shouldn't be snobbish enough to think that doing their own stuff exclusively is that cool, because half the fun of seeing a band is seeing what kind of cover songs they do. I've been playing David Bowie's "Heroes" forever. I love it. I've done a lot of Bowie songs over the years, because I love him.

I'd go down to Oar Folk and Peter Jesperson would say, "Hey, you gotta hear—'Heroes.' You won't believe it." We were doing it a couple days later. Same thing with "Rebel, Rebel," and I don't know how many Bowie songs.

I love Peter. He's worked hard. I can't think of anyone who's been such an avid fan of music, so heartfelt in their love for music and exposing people to it. He loves music and it's a very simple, pure love. He loves it, he loves to talk about it, and he loves to expose people to great music.

PETER JESPERSON: To tell you the truth, besides Curt, I might've leaned a little bit toward Flamingo in the early days. It was maybe my personal taste, but I just thought Bob Wilkinson was a riveting front man and it was a great band all the way around. I mean, their drummer, Bob Meide—for years, if anybody asked me who the best drummer in town was, I'd say Bob Meide. He was a phenomenal drummer. One of the things I always remember about him was that he hit the kick drum so hard with his foot pedal that the kick drum would be inching away from him onstage. So, to try to avoid that, he wrapped a chain around the kick drum and his drum stool so that they had to stay together. That was the only way he could keep the kick drum in front of him. Flamingo was just an awesome, awesome band.

ROBERT WILKINSON: Bobby was always on, even when he was offstage. He liked to party. He liked to live what he thought was the life of a rock star. He was a cool dude.

He's also probably the reason why I'm half deaf right now. But I wouldn't have it any other way. He'd be playing these drums, and if he was overplaying the place and it was too loud, I'd turn around say, "Dude, bring it down a bit." He had this cymbal he'd ride. And there was a bell. He'd hit this and he knew it agitated the fuck out of me. *[laughs]* I'd turn around, and then he'd do it even harder. I'd be giving him the look: "Fuck. Dude." A lot of times, as brothers do, he knew how to push my buttons. *[laughs]*

When we were younger we ran around together to parties. As you get older, your journeys in life take you down different paths. We were pretty inseparable.

At his eulogy, after he died [in 2010 from complications of a neurological disorder], one of our good friends, Mike Keith, said: "The only successful marriage Bob Meide ever had was to Robert Wilkinson." *[laughs]* He got married like three times. People roared and laughed. But it was true. That's a great line.

He was an awesome drummer. He was thunderous and fierce. We had a great relationship for a lot of years.

JODY RAY: Bobby Meide and I definitely had the pocket thing going, definitely in the groove. He was crazy. He looked like Ringo and he played like Keith Moon. They were rockers and I was a rocker. It was meant to be, in my mind. He was one of a kind. I love him and his story turned out to be pretty tragic.

JOHNNY REY: Bob Meide on drums: I miss it to this day. There's nobody like him. He was like Keith Moon. There's nobody that drums like Keith Moon, and nobody drums like Bob Meide. I call him "One-Speed Meide." He's like a lightbulb: You just turn it on, and it goes. We'd practice, try to be quiet. We just couldn't. He could only play one way. He had totally his own style. He was so happy to play. Like the Stones with Charlie Watts and Keith Richards's guitar, him on drums and Robert's guitar playing was the basis for the band the whole time, no matter what the name of the band was. Robert wrote to the rhythm style that Bob played. Robert has a very distinct guitar style, and his writing goes along with it. So that guitar to Meide's drumming was so unique. Meide was absolutely fantastic.

ROBERT WILKINSON: Flamin' Oh's lasted until about '86. Then some of us got married and went off and had families, and then we came back in 1997. I've been playing ever since in one incarnation or another of Flamin' Oh's.

SHARON SAMELS: We talk about all the joy and all the good parts. In the beginning, everyone cheered each other on: "Yay. We love you guys." After we got back [from LA] in the early part of the '80s, things did start getting a little bit weird. The Suicide Commandos had broken up. Steve Almaas had moved to New York. This is the first time when egos got involved.

Actually, in the early '80s, a lot of it probably was alcohol and lots of cocaine. And ego came into play. It wasn't like that in the beginning. It wasn't all picture perfect, like it was in that '77, '78, '79 period. It got a little bit dicey after that. And I do blame the alcohol and drugs.

JOHNNY REY: At first it was just: "Oh god, finally we can just all be together, make something happen." Then the last three years of the '70s, what happened was kind of the same thing but so cool. We just never thought of it changing or ending. Of course, everything has to change. And it did. The '80s are different than the '70s.

PART 02

08

PUNK ROCK GETS A NEW HOME: JAY'S LONGHORN

On June 1, 1977, young entrepreneur and music enthusiast Jay Berine opened the doors of his newly purchased downtown bar to local indie rock and punk bands looking for a place to play and make their own. Flamingo, Curtiss A and Thumbs Up, the Suicide Commandos, and more performed there during the first weeks of its opening. Audiences grew rapidly by word of mouth. Within months, the main stage at Jay's Longhorn was also a destination for national and international punk, indie rock, no wave, and new wave bands, including Blondie, the Ramones, Talking Heads, Iggy Pop, the Dead Boys, Gang of Four, the Buzzcocks, Elvis Costello, the Only Ones, and many others. Formerly a popular jazz club, the new underground rock club became *the* place for these bands to play and for Twin Cities music fans to see live, original music in their own hometown, making the Longhorn an integral foundation of the early Minneapolis scene.

JAY BERINE: I was a kid with a pocket full of money and nothing to do but look for a good time. I spent an incredible amount of time trying to buy a bar. I had a stupid idea and I wanted to have a party for my friends. Of course you had to have music.

A broker called me one day and said, "Hey, I've got this place for you downtown. It's called the Longhorn, a jazz club. A father and son are running it. They're sick of it. Let's go talk to them." I bought the place on the spot. I paid $135,000 for the entire business. The rent was $3,000 a month; the electric bill was also $3,000 a month. So I took on quite a chunk. I think there were around fifty people on the payroll.

The original occupant had been a Sweden House Smorgasbord. The next tenant was a Nino's Steakhouse. I was told by the Blumenthals, the father and son owners I bought the place from, that Nino's manager had

Front marquee of Jay's Longhorn bar. PHOTO BY DANNY AMIS

gotten himself into some gambling problems, and apparently he got shot in the office there. So the Blumenthals bought the space, I'm sure at a bargain, and changed it to the Longhorn. They presented jazz and were fairly successful. They were very cost conscious. I have to say, they were better operators than I was. I was more interested in having fun, and I was very trusting with people.

They put in the carpeting, which was really high-quality wool, which is why it lasted so long despite all the beer and the puke! The place had cow heads, and the cow head logo was sewn into the carpet. They had plates with the cow heads on them. They had so many branded things, right down to cases of matchbooks. I wasn't about to throw all that stuff out and start over. I didn't do anything with the décor because I was so anxious to get myself a bar and I had no working capital. All the money that I could borrow, I used for the down payment. I didn't have any money for remodeling. I didn't have any money to change the name.

The reason it became Jay's Longhorn is one of my friends got a ladder and climbed up there with some paint and a brush and painted "Jay's" over where it said "Longhorn."

STEVE ALMAAS: The place was a steakhouse, and then a jazz club, and it had longhorns on the wall and weird, cheap paneling. It certainly wasn't the

Jay's Longhorn | 125

Packed crowd at the Longhorn, circa 1979. PHOTO BY STEVE MADORE

décor that brought people down. It was bigger than the 7th Street Entry, smaller than First Avenue.

JAY BERINE: The very first night, Flamingo played upstairs. That room was too small, and within the first three or four days we moved the music downstairs. We had the game company move the pinball machines and pool tables upstairs.

A couple months after that, we tore out the wall that separated the former game room. That became the music room, separated from the dining room. We put in a sliding partition. It was one of those late-night construction projects where everybody just grabbed a hammer and started beating on the wall to knock it down.

DICK CHAMP: I remember more about the downstairs bar because there were so many more shows there, not to mention that we [NNB] eventually played it. But it was upstairs to begin with, and the colors of the walls and furnishings were pink, maybe burgundy.

Eventually Peter Jesperson started spinning records, as did Andy Schwartz. And with their encyclopedic knowledge of rock and roll, blues, pop, and the contemporary sounds, you can imagine how much of a contribution it made to the atmosphere down there.

PETER JESPERSON: That crowd at the Longhorn was age eighteen to twenty-five, for the most part, maybe thirty at the outside. There certainly was a large element of people who liked to have a few cocktails; cocaine was fairly prevalent, as was pot and speed to some extent. It was a very enthusiastic crowd. A lot of college students were drawn to this new music. There was a braininess to the crowd. The people were generally accepting of different kinds of music and attitudes. It was really pretty open. I always felt good about it.

I remember a number of occasions where I'd get some skinhead with a leather jacket coming up to the DJ booth and giving me a hard time for playing Bob Dylan, or I used to play Donna Summer records because I thought she was a really good singer. "Play Devo, play Blondie." It's like, "Well, we *do* play Devo and we do play Blondie, we just don't play them all the time." I didn't feel like it was my job to play punk rock all the time. It was my job to play the best records I could think of, so we played everything from Bing Crosby to the Clash. Anything that was good was acceptable in my world. There are people who have said that that kind of approach was really important to them, like Kevin Cole. He's worked tirelessly for years and years and years to bring the best music he could to people.

KEVIN COLE: I started going to the Longhorn just as a music fan. I would go almost every night, didn't matter who played. I'd show up when the doors opened, and I'd listen to Peter Jesperson DJ. Going to hear Peter spin was great. He was doing in a club setting what I wanted to do on the radio, be a free-form DJ, full of surprises, defying expectation. You would hear him play something that you'd maybe expect, like a Sex Pistols song, but then he'd play Donna Summer, then Elvis Presley, and then the Buzzcocks, and then Eddie Cochran. It was a wonderful mix of music.

It was exciting because here was this place that was booking bands that didn't really have anywhere else to play, that weren't cover bands, that were playing original music. There were a handful of really, really good bands that you could see on a regular basis at the Longhorn: Flamingo, Fingerprints, and Curtiss A, of course. For me, it really didn't matter who was playing. There were obvious bands that I loved, like the Commandos. But I also wanted to see bands that I'd never heard of. I wanted to be immersed in that scene. Just to be in that room with that scene happening was extremely exciting. It felt very liberating and complementary to me. I felt very comfortable there. And the music was different. It was exciting music you couldn't hear anywhere else.

TERRY KATZMAN: We used to come down in '72, when it was a jazz club, to see Natural Life, which was the crème de la crème of Minneapolis jazz musicians. So I knew about the Longhorn even before the punk rock thing. I remember when I went in for the first time: "Oh, this place. Now it's a rock and roll club."

At the Longhorn I was the third-string DJ, when somebody else was sick. The DJ booth was a big, high booth to the left of the stage. People would come up and make requests, a lot. Kevin Cole DJ'd there a couple times. That set him up for First Avenue. DJ Roy Freedom did quite a few there as well. I also recorded at the soundboard with the assistance of Steve Fjelstad and other sound engineers.

ROBERT WILKINSON: The Longhorn was off of 5th Street. You went in the entryway and walked down a couple flights of stairs. There was a bar to the left and then you walked into the music room and there was a stage. There were tables and chairs, then a space in front of the stage to dance.

We'd all hang out down there even when we weren't playing. That's all we did; we didn't have regular jobs. We partied with each other and hung out with a lot of the people we met there. The Longhorn was a smaller place so it was easy to meet people. I think the capacity of the Longhorn was probably two or three hundred people. And people loved to get out and dance. The energy was amazing. There were sparks flying everywhere.

Jay Berine had a great heart. He was really personable. And he treated the bands well. He had respect for the bands. He was a big music fan himself. He wanted to bring good music in. And he did. The staff was awesome. It was definitely the clubhouse. We had pretty much the run of the place.

DICK CHAMP: It seemed to me that the scene in its very early stages was spreading by word of mouth. People would just tell their friends, "Oh god, go down to the Longhorn. That is *such* a trip. The bands are *so* great!" And in the shows that launched the club, Flamingo just rocked the place. They were a phenomenal band. You had all the rock and roll and the volume and then their bravado. It was yours for the taking.

There weren't that many people there at the beginning. When the

Longhorn opened officially and started booking our kind of bands, we were down there every night! I mean every night for weeks, because it was such a fun time. What did we have to worry about or think about? Everyone had ridiculously cheap rent. In our case we were like doubling up, tripling up, quadrupling up in apartments and houses that quickly led to the formation of bands. We had no responsibilities whatsoever, so you got to go out every night and hang out with your rock and roll friends. That's what it was about.

STEVE ALMAAS: It was the next generation after the West Bank scene people—art students, college students, a lot of other people in bands. There was a lot of drinking, a lot of dancing. There was a core group that hung out there all the time. On special nights, it would be packed to the gills.

I'm not sure playing the Longhorn for the first time was all that big a deal. But that scene revved up into something where we were playing seven nights in a row, and people would be going ape, dancing and screaming and jumping around, seven nights in a row. It took a while to build up to that, but that was something. Never before and never since then have I ever played a place seven nights in a row. It was like our living room. Everybody would be there every night. It was a very intense couple of years there, '77, '78, '79, at the Longhorn. It was pretty crazy.

JOHNNY REY: The Longhorn opening felt so exciting. It was just electric in the air. Then it shot like a rocket. The first few months it exploded.

At first there weren't all that many bands that fit the Longhorn. We didn't fit anywhere else, and we started playing the Longhorn. In really a short time, so many bands started coming out of the woodwork. It was ridiculous. So that was a very short-lived problem.

That's the cool thing about the Longhorn. We played, the Suicide Commandos played, and then the Suburbs. Every band played all these different styles. It's similar to CBGB, because Television, Blondie, Mink DeVille, the Ramones are all really different from each other and unique. They didn't fit in anywhere else, either. This was *our* CBGB. It's very parallel.

SHARON SAMELS: I remember saying to our friends: "This is it. This is *our* place." Finally, I felt comfortable. It felt like our home. Later on, it was like CBGB meets Cheers.

Jay got so busy just running the bar. He did more of the business side. Al Wodtke and Greg Gehring were helping him in selecting the bands. But at that time, Flamingo might play Monday through Saturday, three sets a night. Sunday was taco night. The next week would be Monday through Saturday, the Suburbs or somebody. You did long stints.

AL WODTKE: There really wasn't any money in the music. With all the offices downtown, you could sell upwards of a thousand meals in a day. The food was the vehicle to pay for our interests, the music side of it. Jay loved music as much as I did.

The first night was pretty good, a hundred, a hundred and fifty people. We quickly outgrew the low-riser stage. One of the bands decided to help us manufacture a new stage. It was a nice stage. It was probably forty feet wide by twenty deep.

It got to the point in three to six months where there was actually competition to play there because of the attention we were getting—*Minneapolis Star* reviews and things on several occasions. We put ads in *Sweet Potato*. Jay had marketing savvy, for sure.

There was probably more than four hundred people usually. Jay and I fought against charging a cover until we had to start regulating how many people were there, to keep the fire marshal from shutting us down. He came regularly. We fought with the city all the time. As many people as the building would hold, we would put them in there.

JACQUE HORSCH: My first experience at the Longhorn, summer or fall of 1978, I was eighteen, so I believe I was underage; I think the drinking age was nineteen. I was working downtown with my stepsister and she found the place because it was the only place she didn't get carded. So we would go there to drink.

I noticed there was great music going on. It was something I had never heard before. I figured I might as well see if I can get a job there so I could get paid to drink and listen to music. It was an interesting crew. You had some older folks behind the bar. In fact, Joanne, one of the bartenders, knew my parents from high school. It was a family atmosphere. I was always taken care of. You had Peter DJ'ing. I knew it was unique. I was drawn to it.

I loved Jay. Margaret [Duvall] left quite an impression on me. I was pretty young, and I was terrified of her half the time. One night, I walked into work and she had plastic see-through pants on! I'll never forget it.

BILL BATSON: Margaret was the door woman. Yeah, with the see-through pants. Jay's girlfriend. She was a great woman.

BRUCE ALLEN: One of the big attractions to the Longhorn was a room that was nothing but pinball machines. It was so good that Bruce Springsteen brought his whole band and crew and played pinball at the Longhorn. They did it two nights in a row. That's all they did. They watched a couple of our songs. We hung out and played pinball with them until 3:30 or 4 o'clock in the morning. It was *crazy*. It was very fun. Pinball was *really* big in those days.

MARK TREHUS: It had the feel of a cocktail lounge during the day. Upstairs had pinball machines. At night it was transformed into something unique. Tiger Night, taco night, cheap drinks. Coming downtown and walking into the Longhorn was liberating, exciting—a step into a new world that felt like it was custom-made for smarter misfits. These were artists, filmmakers, record collectors, hip journalists, musicians—rock and roll true believers, all! You had the feeling that you were in on something special. Many of us wanted to keep the scene insular for fear of outsiders wrecking it. You knew that many of these underground bands that we adored and who had played there—Blondie, Talking Heads, the B-52s, David Johansen, the Buzzcocks, the Dead Boys, the Only Ones, Gang of Four, and on and on—were too good to hold as our own for long.

LORI BARBERO: I have wings on my heels, so I just like going out by myself because I can go where I want to, when I want to. I went back and forth between First Avenue and the Longhorn. I started going to the Longhorn in 1979 or '80. I was going there for awhile before I started working there. I was a server. Peter Jesperson was DJ'ing. At the Longhorn, it was a really small crowd, and young. We were all oddballs. We liked music that the norm didn't like. It was a community. The Longhorn was our safe haven.

I saw a lot of bands at the Longhorn: the Plasmatics, the Clash, the Police. There were only a couple hundred people at those shows. Lydia Lunch and 8 Eyed Spy was touring. I loved 8 Eyed Spy; they were super good, so cool, and she was just so badass.

The Longhorn is where I learned how to do booking in a way. I was there a lot, so that's where I learned.

LORNA DOONE: There was a whole kind of art scene in Minneapolis. Real interesting people, what there was of us! Then the Longhorn kind of came out of that. And I met like forty new people, all at once. You know, mostly rock musicians, and girls too, not just guys; they weren't rock musicians, but we were all part of the scene. And then things got so exciting here in the late '70s that people were moving from New York City to come here to be at the Longhorn. It was nice that we had one venue because you knew everybody'd be there!

CHUCK STATLER: The Longhorn was kind of the gathering place. There's no question about that. It was as much about mingling with the group as it was the music. So that's why a lot of shows, it didn't even matter who the band was, you still went there. It was the watering hole.

How many times did I see the Suburbs there? Half a dozen? A dozen? Two dozen? I don't know! Flamingo and the Suburbs seemed like, on any given month, one of those bands was there, and most likely more than once in that month. The Longhorn was the venue of choice.

It was always a little bit of that battle of the bands there between those two bands. One was the clean-cut kind of poppy new wave band, and the other was the diehard rock and rollers. Different crowds, although there was a lot of crossover, too, in the crowds. People that were really the Suburbs fans, you'd see at Flamingo and vice versa, because the Longhorn was where you congregated.

CHAN POLING: At night, the only game in town, rock and roll–wise, was the Longhorn. Flamingo was playing, and they were kind of the big band in town. They would do a lot of Rolling Stones covers and some original tunes. So the idea of a young band doing *all* original material still wasn't flying. At first, the Suburbs weren't allowed to play, we weren't asked or wanted to play in any bars. We weren't a commercial concern at all at that point. At the same time, the Commandos and the Hypstrz and the Suburbs and NNB and those kinds of bands, we were all hanging out and partying together.

ERNIE BATSON: Back then the bands usually would be Flamingo three nights in a row, Curtiss A for three nights, Commandos for two or three nights, and we would do a night here and there. NNB was the first night we played there, and we headlined because we had more songs. In 1978, they had their single "Slack," but they only had maybe forty-five minutes of material. We could do four sets. We had a PA, too. I think they had lights.

HUGO KLAERS: I remember going to the Longhorn and dancing and being kicked out for being drunk and disorderly. The dance floor always seemed to be full at the Longhorn, no matter what. It didn't matter who was playing—I mean, Curtiss A, Fingerprints, Flamingo. They had tons of people. All the girls wanted to go see Flamingo, all the time.

MAX RAY: It's not like there were people that went to the shows that didn't go to see the music. There weren't incidental tourists in the crowd, so the reaction was always solid. The Wallets were well received.

BOB DUNLAP: The Longhorn had a new angle, where people wanted to hear something new and different. So, you had to impress the audiences more than you did normally. It made bands different, made bands try harder. Not just be good enough so the booking agent would book you, but good enough so people would come see you next time. You had to have a good draw. You had to keep impressing people. You couldn't rest on your laurels.

A lot of towns you'd play in, there was kind of an adversarial relationship between the band and the town. There were always a couple drunken hecklers who could destroy your act with a few well-timed barbs. Minneapolis was a different feeling, where audiences were impressed by something different. It maneuvered bands toward what audiences were expecting. It was a higher threshold that pushed bands to be better than they ever would have been, if they'd just been cover bands. So it was a new spark. And it's largely owed to the crowd.

TIM HOLMES: Everyone in the room was already a fan just because you were in the room. When the Longhorn became the venue, you'd start going because it was the Longhorn, and if a band played there you were probably going to like them because it was a place you went to hear bands that weren't Top 40 bands, and your friends were there. The Longhorn was a really comfortable venue. There was a bar you could sit in with booths. Then you could go into the music room. There were different places to go. It felt like a clubhouse.

I remember feeling like the Suicide Commandos were the house band. They were there a lot and it was always good to see them. They'd test out new songs and there'd be dancing and drinking. I would have to say my favorite would be the Commandos just because it felt like they were the most in sync with the audience and they were the house band, but they were a good house band.

DAVE AHL: When we were playing there, our fans would be there and it was a total lovefest from the stage to the audience and from the audience to the stage. They were prepared for anything that we wanted to do.

One time when my mom and dad were coming to the Longhorn to see us play, I announced to the crowd beforehand, "My mom and dad are going to be here tonight, so no smoking and no swearing." They came fairly regularly. My mom would sport her Commandos T-shirt all the time.

CHRIS OSGOOD: Audience members would often hop onstage and put me on their shoulders. So I'd be running around playing on somebody's shoulders.

Our good friend Steve Fjelstad was often the live sound guy at the Longhorn. One of my favorite moments I love to recount is the three nights that Paul Stark was recording for *The Commandos Commit Suicide Dance Concert*. Steve was the engineer at the soundboard. People would bound up onstage and play with us. We were doing a song Robert Wilkinson knew, so I asked him to come up and play guitar and sing. Dave motions for Johnny Haga to get up and play the drums. Steve gave his bass to somebody else, and the three of us met back at the soundboard, watching "ourselves" play until the song was over. That was great, because we could order a drink and the set goes way faster if other people are playing your song. Then we went back up and commandeered our instruments. That was a particularly delightful moment.

For our last show, my dream was to walk down the Longhorn bar, kicking over everybody's drinks on the way to the stage, and then hop up on the stage and play the set. I got one of the first radio setups where you didn't need to plug in. We were doing "Once Bitten, Twice Shy," the Ian Hunter song, one of the first covers we did.

The thing I didn't think about was me playing so far back from the stage, I was hearing a delay. By the time it gets to those guys onstage, they're playing way out of time with me. The distance and the speed of sound. I did get up on the bar, and I did walk down the bar kicking over drinks, so that dream came true.

KEVIN COLE: At the Longhorn, people danced. That whole area in front of the stage was packed with people. It wasn't a mosh pit kind of thing, where punk rock ended up going. It was more pogoing and thrashing about. It was a great combination of intensity that had a certain element of danger, and occasional anger, but was more just overwhelmingly fun. For me, seeing the Suicide Commandos was a ton of fun and a great release of pent-up energy.

TERRY KATZMAN: There were times when there was two hundred or more on the dance floor. Get your teeth knocked out, too. The pogoing. Stefan Hammond, the writer, had a dance called the worm. Everyone would lie down and wriggle on the floor. You took your life in your hands going down on the floor, because you could get stomped on.

DANIEL CORRIGAN: The worm was the big dance back then—you'd flop around on the floor and wriggle amongst all the broken glass and beer and whatnot. One time, this guy jumped up and smashed his head into one of those illuminated beer clocks. It was destructive. It was 1978 or '79. I was nineteen, so I was impressionable.

JODY KURILLA: If there was a band that we wanted to see, we were there. And everybody danced. We would dance until we were soaking wet. And we were kids! We were having a great time. It was something brand new. It wasn't like everything has to be one certain way. All these bands were so different. And nobody was doing it with some ulterior brand in mind. Everyone just created what they wanted to.

ROBB HENRY: I had come out of this kind of rigid club scene where bands I played with would typically do four forty-five minute sets a night. And the set list would be the same. And everything was really tight because we were playing for the dance floor. And club owners wanted the club to be packed every night.

I just wanted to let loose a little bit, and play the guitar, and play loud, experiment. I could see right away that the Longhorn was the ideal place to do it.

DANNY AMIS: I was way underage to be in the Longhorn, but they looked the other way because I didn't drink in those days. I wanted to start a band, and I wanted to do something no one else was doing. One night I was at the Longhorn and Steve Almaas was DJ'ing. He played "Hawaii Five-O." I forgot how much I loved that kind of music. That's when I got the idea to start an instrumental band. I went home and I stayed up all night figuring out how to play "Hawaii Five-O." I think the next night I wrote "Calhoun Surf," the first song I ever wrote.

I had a friend that I knew in high school, Mike Carlson, who played guitar, and I had some friends at the Longhorn. Buck Hazlett was a friend of mine and I asked him if he was interested in playing drums, but he already had something going on his own. He introduced me to Steve Foley and said, "This is the guy for you." Then we got Dave McGowan to play bass.

Naturally I wanted to play at the Longhorn. That was our very first gig ever, as the Overtones. We opened for Jonny III, who were also friends of mine. Sound check was so cool. Being up on that stage and looking out in the club and playing was so cool. Later that night, when it was full of people, we were scared to death up there.

The response was pretty good. We were just kids and we couldn't play very well. But I remember Chris Osgood coming up that first night and telling us we were the new sensation. There was enthusiasm because we were doing something no one else was doing. It fit in with the Longhorn scene just fine because the Longhorn was all about unique music.

LORI BARBERO: Danny Amis—I call him Danny Famous. The Overtones were odd because they were surf music, and it was like, "What the fuck is a surf band doing in Minneapolis?" But it was really great, because that was his roots and they were super cool.

MARTIN KELLER: Going to the Longhorn and seeing these local bands was its own reward. Music was fresh, people there were from a lot of different walks of life, and I think the universal factor in it was that the same people that would go to the Longhorn you'd also see five years later at First Avenue. They were really music fans.

I think in large part because *Sweet Potato* and the *Reader* were giving these bands a lot of ink in their pages, that drove a considerable amount of people to see bands they may have never gone to see, and bar owners to book bands they would never otherwise book. Every night you could see a great local band at the Longhorn.

Then, when the national and international acts started coming in, it was an even richer experience. You could see the Police in a room of two hundred people, and Blondie, and Talking Heads, and David Johansen, who was fresh out of the New York Dolls. Elvis Costello, the B-52s. Yeah, it was a great time to catch people whose artistic currency was going to rise pretty quickly.

JAY BERINE: Al Wodtke did the booking. I looked over his shoulder, but it was his deal. People would call me and beg to play. I would tell them to talk to Al. The phone wasn't big in those days. People would come in and talk to us.

Sue and Randy [of Schon Productions] sold us Mink DeVille, our first national act, and several more afterwards. Within the first month or two, we booked Eddie Money, Talking Heads, the B-52s—a hundred more. I loved Talking Heads. They are my all-time favorite band to this very day.

PETER JESPERSON: The first national act we had at the Longhorn was Mink DeVille, August of '77. What a singer! We were really thrilled to have something that was just dripping of New York City here in our little punk rock club. Actually, we didn't call it punk rock. It was an underground rock club.

TIM HOLMES: Once the punk thing started happening in New York, then it felt like the Longhorn was a satellite of CBGB. The Longhorn was the Minneapolis outlet for those bands. Talking Heads came to town. Elvis Costello and the Attractions played there. I was at the Iggy Pop show. The Cramps played the Longhorn. Pere Ubu played the Longhorn. B-52s played the Longhorn. Blondie. There were surprises at the Longhorn.

JAY BERINE: Elvis Costello played on Valentine's Day 1978. I paid him 750 bucks. We gave away T-shirts, "Elvis Is My Valentine." The show sold out in twenty minutes. We opened the line with a limit of four tickets per person and sold 750 tickets. I think we were rated by the fire marshal for 750 capacity. We would sell 750 tickets, but have another 100, 150 on the guest list or sneak in. [laughs]

Ticket stub from Elvis Costello concert at Jay's Longhorn, February 14, 1978. Courtesy of Johnny Rey

ROBERT WILKINSON: Jay started bringing in all these acts. International and national bands, great punk bands from New York, all came to the Longhorn. Whatever band you can name that was starting out at that time probably played there. It was amazing to see all these bands that went on to stardom and great success in their early days. Mink DeVille was the first national act, and there was Blondie, Talking Heads, the Dead Boys, the Vibrators, Rockpile, a million bands like that. The B-52s came to town on their first tour, and they had only one set worth of material, so they played two sets of the same material, which was great.

I remember opening for a lot of really cool bands. One of the best gigs we played at the Longhorn was with the Only Ones, from England. They were on their first American tour. I was a big fan and still am a big fan. So, meeting them and hanging out with them was really cool. We partied and drank and did drugs together, all that good stuff we were all doing back then.

JEFF WARYAN: Peter Jesperson was kind of the boss there. You could go there and know he was going to turn you on to something new and interesting. I remember he loved the Only Ones and started promoting them locally. I think wherever else they played, nobody showed up. But Peter got all of us to go two nights in a row. That was October 1979. A fantastic band.

SHARON SAMELS: When the bigger national acts came in, because Johnny and I were a couple, I was allowed in the green room. So I would be in the back room, and all of a sudden I felt a little smaller: "Okay. I'm maybe not so cool." Because they were from New York, they had this attitude. I didn't feel like a city chick. It was intimidating at first.

When the Police played, they came to a party afterwards at someone's apartment; Sting didn't, but Andy Summers did. They had beers with us. They were normal people, like us, hanging out, wore the same kind of clothing. Then it became a little bit more comfortable.

JOHNNY REY: Most of the bands were like that. We'd see Talking Heads a lot. They're coming from their scene that's probably like this. They're playing our scene, their home away from home. I remember being at a party with the Ramones. I had the most beat-up leather jacket you ever saw. They loved it. It made theirs look new. I remember being backstage with Mink DeVille. Because our hairstyles were so similar, we were kinda looking at each other.

All the bands we played with: first was Mink DeVille, Talking Heads, Elvis Costello, Pere Ubu, the Only Ones, the Dead Boys. That Elvis Costello show was my favorite night. We played right before him. Jim Walsh wrote about that. That's the first night he went down there. He's like: "That changed my whole life that night." Elvis Costello and the Attractions were at their peak—and at this little bar and right in your face. To be in this little bar like that, at the height of his power!

The bar would get really packed. The earlier part of the Longhorn was definitely the best. You can almost cut it in half. The second half, everything was changing and people were going other places. Management was different. It just was a different scene. That first part—'77, '78, '79—was the absolute pinnacle. Everything was smaller, too.

MARK FREEMAN: On Talking Heads' first tour, 1977, Tina Weymouth was this little nervous waif and just stared at David Byrne the entire night, watching him like the notes were coming out of his head or something. She was so scared.

MICHAEL MARKOS: One show that was the most memorable was when Talking Heads did a two-night stand at the Longhorn, October 1977. It was put together by Peter Jesperson. Once the band came on, everyone stood up and Peter made everyone sit down so people in the back could see. I was able to sneak in both nights because the Longhorn had an upstairs bar.

Talking Heads at the Longhorn, October 1977. PHOTO BY MICHAEL MARKOS

There were these back stairs in the lobby, so I was able to go down to the show. Somebody would notice I was in the lobby and say, "You can't hang out here," so I would just go into the main room.

JAY BERINE: Sadly, I saw very little of any of the shows. I was a bit of an introvert. Even though I would throw the party, I wouldn't go to the party.

I remember watching Tina Weymouth of Talking Heads play the bass, and I thought that was really cool. I probably watched more of their show than any of the others. We all partied with them after the show, and then Chris and Tina actually came back to my condo with Margaret, who was still my girlfriend. We stayed up really late.

Then, a year or two after that, Talking Heads returned to Minneapolis and played the Northrop Auditorium. I saw that show. Hartley Frank had already taken over the Longhorn by then, but I brought Chris and Tina down and we caught Grace Jones's second show. Then we partied all night with Grace Jones. She wasn't quite as strange in person as the persona she presents onstage. I met a lot of people over the years, and I really think everyone I met was just an actual person.

CHUCK STATLER: My most memorable moment connected with the Longhorn is when I met Jake Riviera [of Stiff Records]. I went down to the Longhorn, and I wasn't feeling well, so I walked out into the little vestibule there. There was the showroom and then there was a bar they called the Clown Lounge. There was nobody out there. I was seated on the bench, as they say today, "chilling." This guy came up to me. "What are you doing out here?" We struck up a conversation. Not very far into it, he said, "What's your name?" I said, "Chuck." And then he introduced himself, "I'm Jake Riviera." I told him, "I'm Chuck Statler." He went, "Chuck Statler?! Are you the one that does the Devo videos?" I claimed that, at least at that moment. He said, "Oh, I've been trying to get a hold of you!" I said, "*Really?*" He said: "Yeah, I thought you were in *Indianapolis!*" That was a common mistake back in the day, because I had no promotion, no rep, no anything.

Then he said, "How would you like to do a video with Elvis Costello?" Well, I'm not feeling well and I probably was under the influence of Nyquil or something. I said, "Yeah, okay, sure." He said, "Well, you have to be able to meet us in Vancouver in two days." I said, "Okay, all right." He said, "I'll get everything arranged. Go to the Northwest Airlines office and the tickets will be there." Miraculously I didn't feel sick anymore. I was all pumped up.

Immediately I went home and got on the phone and reached out to the crew that was helping me put these videos together. Everybody said, "I want in!" You know, we're going to go meet Elvis Costello and do a video with Elvis Costello. It was a chance meeting. If I hadn't been at the Longhorn that night—and furthermore, if I hadn't been sick—it might not have happened. I think about that, that it ended up being this ongoing relationship for a number of years. I ended up doing about twelve videos with him.

JACQUE HORSCH: I remember the Police coming in and it was my job to set up the band room, which was really just a closet. I was filling coolers with beer, and they were in there. I remember thinking I didn't really like "Roxanne" at all. So I ask, "Are you guys going to play 'Roxanne'?" They said, "Well, yeah, it's our number one hit." I'm like, "Oh god." They play it, and I was blown away. It was so crazy to hear a three piece fill the room. It was amazing.

JEFF WARYAN: I worked with Steve Fjelstad and Paul Stark on the monitors for the Police show. And right next to me is Sting, who was really bouncing up and down as he played, and when you bounced on the Longhorn stage, things moved around quite a bit! So I was holding up these tall monitor columns so they wouldn't fall over.

CHAN POLING: Can you imagine seeing the Police in this place? The stage was two feet off the ground. It was this tiny little place, a couple hundred people. We loved it. We'd go in free and see all the shows, and we were so excited to see the Police. They were pretty big in our world. We played with, saw, and hung out with everybody from Blondie to Talking Heads to B-52s. To see all those guys in the intimate setting was just amazing. We were as close as you could get to some great bands.

BEEJ CHANEY: We got to play with some of our heroes. We played with Talking Heads, we played with Iggy Pop, with Grace Jones. God, some really great experiences! We played with incredible new guys, the Stray Cats when they weren't even known. Performing and hanging out with the Talking Heads was really cool—they were at our level. We were all buddies! The camaraderie behind what all these new wave guys were trying to create was amazing. David Byrne actually taught me to use the strobe tuner. Back then they were a real luxury and they looked like some scientific piece of machinery. I was like, "God, he's really nice." We had a party; I think Dylan might have showed for that. Those were magical times.

MICHAEL OWENS: We [Fingerprints] opened for Blondie, Pere Ubu, apparently at their request—at least that's what Charley Hallman told me. *[laughs]* Debbie Harry complimented us on our show.

JEFF WARYAN: The Fingerprints guys were losing Robb Henry and thought I could join if I was interested. I had ten days to learn all their songs to open for Blondie at the Longhorn. That was the first time I played there, opening for Blondie. I'm pretty sure it was 1978.

It was a thrill. We didn't get to meet Debbie Harry, but we got to meet the rest of the band. We were all very interested in what they were doing, and having them play at the Longhorn and be so close to them. I think we got a pretty good response for our sets as well. After the show, Jimmy Destri and those guys found out that the Fingerprints guys, who had Blackberry Way studio, had some equipment they were interested in because they were mixing a side project. So they came over and worked on their project at the house until dawn. It was my entry into a more professional Minneapolis music scene.

JON CLIFFORD: Around the end of '79 and early '80, my friends and I discovered emerging Twin Cities garage rock. *The Commandos Commit Suicide, Courtesy* by Curtiss A, *In Combo* by the Suburbs, and most importantly, *Big Hits of Mid-America Volume Three*. We couldn't believe that all of these bands were right here in our back yard. We must have played *Mid-America* a thousand times.

My buddy Doug Anderson hipped me to the fact that the Hypstrz were playing at this place called the Longhorn downtown. We were about fifteen at the time. I remember lingering around trying to get up the courage to weasel my way in. Once I got past the door and inside, I was in a complete haze. All of what appeared to be the coolest people in Minneapolis were there. I was terrified someone was going to kick my underage butt out of there.

Onstage were the loudest, scariest, coolest sounding guys I had ever seen. They didn't have that polished '70s rock star look I was accustomed to seeing on album covers and in magazines. They were big and commanding and loud and fast. I knew that night that my taste in music and my life would be forever changed. My fear of being caught overcame me, so I didn't stick around for more than an hour or so.

Not much later, the Longhorn changed to Zoogie's, and that little window of history disappeared. I often wished that I were five or ten years older, so I could have experienced the whole thing, but I guess I had the good fortune of catching a glimpse of that bottle with the lightning in it. From that point, I knew that our city had something pretty fucking cool.

ERNIE BATSON: That little band the B-52s, when we played with them, had about thirty minutes of material. We were playing with the Dictators. We saw the Dead Boys. We sat in the front row and laughed at them, because they were trying to be so hard-ass and look dangerous. It was comical. My favorite moment was when the singer Stiv Bators was whipping his chains around and he caught himself in the testicles. He started to crumple up on himself. [*claps*] "Well done! Well done!" Lots of guffaws! Even Cheetah smiled at that one!

DANIEL CORRIGAN: I got to see the Dead Boys at the Longhorn with probably about thirty or forty people in the audience. And the Batson brothers—we weren't pals, but I knew who they were. It was so empty that they got a couple of folding chairs and brought them down on the dance floor and set them up like six feet back so they could have a place to sit. What an incredible show that was. The guitar player, Cheetah Chrome, came out and he had a dog chain, put it around his neck, padlocked it, and threw the key into the audience. Then at one point, Stiv Bators—this was the craziest punk rock move I think I've ever seen—he's doing this *[convulsive twitching]* getting all twitchy, totally locked up, put his arms at his side and fell forward face first, and, "Bam!" Then he flopped around on the ground for a while and then flopped over and put his head inside the kick drum. You know sometimes they put a pillow in there. He laid his head on the pillow. And you know how loud that is?! I've had to go in and fix that stuff during a song. It's incredibly loud. So he had his head in there for half a song. He was also covered with cuts—covered.

The Dead Boys at the Longhorn, May 1980. Photo by Danny Amis

JODY KURILLA: There were so many amazing shows! There was a very interesting circuit of bands, where they could come in and make money playing these small venues. The Stranglers really stuck in my mind. That one was pretty amazing. He was yelling at us the whole time. We just thought it was so funny. If we were sitting down, he'd yell at us to "Stand up, you lazy sods!" The singer was a jerk. It was fun, but that was his MO. He was known to be a jerk, his reputation preceded him, but we didn't care.

DAVE AHL: The Stranglers was a very interesting show. Don Holzschuh, from the Warheads, was heckling the Stranglers. The Stranglers were getting so pissed off, finally they said, "You are the drunkest person we have ever seen."

I saw the Iggy Pop show. That was a crazy night. That was the night where we actually got to hear Hartley Frank say the words, "Iggy has left the building."

JOHN KASS: The Iggy show had Brian James of the Damned on guitar and Ivan Kral of the Patti Smith Group. It was a really good band. They were touring on the *New Values* record, but it wasn't the people that played on *New Values*.

MIKE MADDEN: The thing I remember most about Iggy at the Longhorn was a fight broke out right in front of the stage and Iggy left the stage because he was so disgusted by it. I mean, he's a peace-loving guy. He eventually came back and all was forgiven.

BEEJ CHANEY: We warmed up for Iggy, who proceeded to be about forty-five minutes late. So all the girls were lined up at the front like it was gonna be a male stripper show. We sat on the side on our equipment because we really wanted to see him. He got the band grinding and ran into the room and onstage. He pulled his pants down to his ankles, and the front fifty girls were like, "Igggyyy!" He was such a stud. He grabbed his, uh, unit, which is already decent sized, and he started to masturbate. And he walked around on the stage saying, "This is a *prick*." Hartley Frank, the bar owner, ran up. "You can't do this. I don't have a license for this, Mr. Pop!" Iggy grabbed him by the collar and said, "This is my fuckin' stage, fat man, so get off." He drop-kicked this fat guy right in the stomach, off the stage, and then kept right on playing. Iggy pulled up his pants when he felt like it. It was like, "Oh. My. Fuck-ing. Gawd."

JACQUE HORSCH: Seeing Iggy at the Longhorn was crazy. We were underground in this dark box, and if you were claustrophobic, it was scary. It was smelly, it was hot, it was sweaty, and the energy was everywhere. Iggy Pop and some of these guys scared me. What is going to happen to this guy? He looks like he's going to implode. I wasn't into hard drugs and I didn't understand any of that. Honestly, to me, sometimes it is like watching a train wreck. It was so scary but I loved it. I was drawn to it and I kept going back. I hadn't seen anything like Iggy Pop in my life.

The capacity might have been three hundred. I think the Iggy Pop show was pretty full. I remember the Police being pretty full. I don't remember the Replacements being full. I think it was half the house. There were mosh pits. The whole slam dancing thing was starting to happen. I'm small, and I was working, so I didn't generally go up in that area. The club was so stinking small, really.

Grace Jones! I was there to set up the bar, and I come walking through the hallway between the two bars, where the entrance was. I look up, and there's this tall black being. I went running back and said, "Hartley, somebody just came in the door, and I'm not sure if it's a man or a woman, but it's tall and it's black." He just looked at me and said, "Honey, *that* is Grace Jones!" *[laughs]* She was amazing to me. It scared me because I'm five-foot-three and she must have been six feet at least. It was all very exciting.

JODY KURILLA: Grace Jones was amazing! We were right up there in front. It was a little tiny club. The fact that I could see Grace Jones there, oh my god! She must have been, like: "What am I doing in this podunk town, playing in *this* place?" She is and always will be a great artist.

WAYNE HASTI: Ben Day Dots opened for Grace Jones at Zoogie's. It was an all-gay crowd. They liked our bass player Tommy Stang. They wanted him to play and to sing. So we let him sing a song with them. That was really cool. She came out, and I was a big fan. Talking Heads were playing at the Northrop, and after the show, Tina Weymouth and the organ player [Jerry Harrison] came over. They were backstage talking to Grace Jones. That was so cool.

CHUCK STATLER: Grace Jones was so hot back then. I mean, she was *hot*, too, but her career was really happening then. To see her, you know what those experiences are like. She had one of those plexiglass bustiers. She was so severe and her music so cool. It was so of the moment, *au courant*.

The First Avenue Mainroom was a different environment. Once you get to a venue where there's a thousand people or two thousand people, it's a different experience. But you have that kind of intimacy in a room that's two or three hundred people.

JAY BERINE: The music scene was shifting. We were on the front cover of *Sweet Potato*, the *Reader*, the *Daily*, *Pioneer Press*, and *Star Tribune*. I didn't think it would ever end.

DAVE AHL: The Longhorn went at least into '82, didn't it? Hartley was a relation of Jay Berine. Jay had some legal problems and could no longer run the bar, so Hartley took it over.

TIM HOLMES: The vibe really changed when Hartley Frank came to town. Jay seemed like a really friendly person. And Margaret [Duvall], who ran the door and took the tickets, she was fabulous. She lit up a room. When Hartley came, it sort of felt—I hate to speak ill of the dead—he was colorful. I'm sure there was lots going on that I had no idea was going on.

CHRIS OSGOOD: He changed the name to Zoogie's. By that time Dave and I were in L7-3 and we were playing upstairs. Everything changed after that. By that time, the Suburbs were kind of the house band there and had their various adventures with Hartley. He was not supportive of the scene in the same way. He was supportive of the capacity of the club to remain open, a little bit more of a businessman, but a real character. Yeah, we all had our adventures with him.

DAVE AHL: He was not beloved.

HUGO KLAERS: It was so cool to be able to walk in there with my drums and eventually be able to walk in and never have to pay for anything. A lot of people got pissed when Hartley Frank took over, and that was at the beginning of our popularity. I won't call it the height, but the beginning. So we could pretty much do whatever we wanted, play there whenever we wanted.

CHAN POLING: You can imagine it was our playground. We were the local guys who got to play there and actually got paid to make music, and Hartley Frank would run a tab for us. So we could go down there and drink beer. Then at the end of the night, we wouldn't owe him anything. This tab was running the whole time. Then we'd do a gig, let's say we made $300, and he would go: "Here's your fifty bucks." Because the beer tab was $250 that month.

BEEJ CHANEY: We had a good stint at the Longhorn. It was our "learning-to-play-live" place. Everyone loved us. It was really fun. I mean in those days, I'm not going to toot my horn or encourage it, but we really did a *lot* of drugs. I was very into LSD, so it was interesting, heh heh. So we were very, very creative.

I liked the freedom of the Longhorn. Nobody gave a shit *what* we played. They just wanted to come down and see this freaky new band that played stuff like "Chemistry Set" and that fast punker stuff that was hip. And we wore weird Ragstock clothes.

MICHAEL HALLIDAY: There was kind of a political scene going on, as far as what bands played where. It was just a wild place. You'd break your beer bottles on the floor or on the walls. I remember Hartley Frank coming up outside in his Cadillac with his boyfriend. We had some kind of dispute with him, so he said, "You're not playing my bar anymore." So we started throwing shows ourselves on the weekends, like at the Podany building where we practiced, and the Longhorn would be empty. Hartley came over one time and said, "You know what, come and talk to me after the weekend." And we were back in there.

BRUCE ALLEN: The Suburbs got eighty-sixed from the Longhorn. They had a reason for each one of us. The one that sticks out to me was Hugo dancing with his shirt off at one of the early concerts there. You couldn't take your shirt off.

CHRIS OSGOOD: We played the Longhorn for a year and a half. Jay would always tell us when we were playing. When Hartley took over, he would just schedule the bands in rotation. We would find out that we were playing the Longhorn by looking at the paper. We would pick up a paper and go, "Oh, look at this. We're playing on Friday and Saturday and Sunday, in three weeks." Then we would know. That happened a couple of times, but it was notable. Hartley would just loosely pencil us in.

MARK FREEMAN: Jay worked with the musicians. It was only after Hartley took over that the band started getting billed as NNB Orchestra. The Dead Boys were playing and Harley put them in the paper as the "Dead Bags." He didn't know anything about anything. "Bag of Four" instead of Gang of Four. There was a lot of "Bag" going on.

DANNY AMIS: The Overtones played at a new band night. Hartley called it Tiger Night. He had some strange marketing ideas. Janine was running the place that night. He gave her instructions to give us a percentage of the door. He had no idea we were going to actually draw a crowd. So we got paid pretty well. Hartley was furious when he found out, so he put a cap on how much money we could make.

KURT NELSON: Simba did a record. We talked Hartley into letting us play there. We were playing weeknights pretty often. We're going, "Man, if only we could get a weekend night, we'd fill the place." Hartley would not go for it. I'm the go-between, between Simba and Hartley. Of course, I got into it with him, and I ended up being eighty-sixed for pretty much the rest of the duration of the club.

The Diamondbacks was a band I played bass in with Hugo Klaers and Beej Chaney. We're supposed to play Zoogie's, and I'm eighty-sixed. So I spray-dyed my hair silver, wore a bandanna over my face like a bandit, and still Hartley found out it was me. He got the bouncer to kick me out. Chan goes, "You can't kick him out. He's the bass player in your headlining band. And this placed is packed to see him."

JEFF CERISE: The first time the Phones played the Longhorn was probably 1979. We were setting up for sound check, and Hartley Frank comes down, he's smoking a cigarette, and he goes, "You guys mind if I audition a band out here?" And we're like, "No, go for it."

So these three guys come in and set up on the dance floor in front of the stage, and Hartley's just standing there with his arms across his chest. They plugged in and—"Blammo!" I remember Grant Hart kicking his kick drum out so far from him that he literally had to stop playing and slide it back in, and then he kept kicking it, and it would slide out and he would pull it in. So they did two pretty good thrash songs. Bob Mould was just singing over his amp and Hartley looks at him after a couple songs, flicks his cigarette, and goes, "Tuesday night." They were like, "Yeah! Sweet!" That was Hüsker Dü's first audition, and it was while we were setting up behind them.

TERRY KATZMAN: I think the last time the Hüskers played the Longhorn was in February of '81. By that time the 7th Street Entry was going. The dying plan for the Longhorn was it would stay the Longhorn downstairs, and Zoogie's was going to be the new Longhorn, sort of. That was where the punk bands were going to play. And downstairs was going to be more commercial. Zoogie's was a disaster. It would have just been better if it would have closed when the downstairs ended.

STEPHEN McCLELLAN: Hartley was so angry about the Entry opening he used to come up to the club and hand out free tickets to Zoogie's. "First Avenue is sold out, but we're open down at the Longhorn." I only knew Hartley over there. I didn't know Jay.

SCOTT MACDONALD: I didn't make it to the Longhorn until it was Zoogie's. I was underage, like sixteen, so I didn't get to see much. By the time it was Zoogie's, there was an upstairs where most of the punk stuff happened, and unbeknownst to me the downstairs had turned into a gay bar. I showed up, "Oh, it's a gay bar now." "The punk rock is still upstairs." So I went upstairs.

The band I was in, the Blaze of Glory, played new band night, which was called Tiger Night. You would play three weeks in a row so you would open [Tiger Night] the first week, then middle the second week, and the third week you would headline. Through that we got onto the permanent guest list. I would pretend I forgot my ID and talk my way in by virtue of being on the guest list. I found out later that a whole bunch of underage people went to Zoogie's and the Longhorn.

I saw L7-3 [Chris Osgood, Dave Ahl, Steve Fjelstad] at least twice there. I had talked to people at the time who knew the Commandos, so they wanted the Commandos. I wasn't very familiar with the Commandos, but I liked L7-3 a lot. I liked them too because I had just recorded with Fjelstad at Blackberry Way, so I was sort of idolizing all those guys. I borrowed cymbals from Dave Ahl to record with at Blackberry Way.

DAVE PIRNER: The Longhorn was the holy grail of gigs. It was like getting a gig at CBGB. It was the place the Suburbs and the Commandos and all those great bands I discovered through shows at Walker Art Center or at Loring Park or listening to *Big Hits of Mid-America Volume Three* [played]. I became a fast fan of the local bands. That was a bit of a revelation to find out that there were rock bands in town that were playing cool music that wasn't on the radio.

I had a band in high school called the Schitz and we played at Zoogie's, which is what the Longhorn changed its name to briefly.

DANIEL MURPHY: The only time I ever went to the Longhorn, it was Zoogie's, I was like seventeen and I was dating a girl that was like fifteen, and they let us both in. We saw Dave Pirner's band the Schitz play. They were really fucking good. They did a really good punk rock version of "Sounds of Silence." It didn't go badly for them; there was no one there. It was the first time I'd heard of Dave. I had friends go, "The band's not good, but the singer is pretty cool and he writes good songs." So I made it my mission to pry Dave away from his band.

I believe within a week or two after I went to Zoogie's, it was shut down. It was the very end.

DAVID MOE: Historically, our most interesting gig of all time was when we played the last gig in Zoogie's. We [Johnny Quest] were playing these Tuesday nights, and they were going well. We started getting folks to come, and we'd cover the Jam and the Clash, we even covered the Suburbs, maybe a Hypstrz song. But we were a likable, kind of fun band.

I was the oldest in the band and the others were just finishing up high school. That would include my cousin on bass and Eric Pierson on guitar. So there we are playing a paid gig, in downtown Minneapolis. We get there early because we're not rock stars. You gotta get there early and set up your stuff and do a little sound check. You're there the rest of the time. We don't go out and grab some drinks. We're too young.

So there we are in the basement, which is big, and they had all these pinball machines. I looked on the side and there was a big sign. I was like, "What is this?" These signs are sprawled everywhere, saying, "Tonight! Minneapolis's Biggest Gay Bar Premiere," and it had a date. I looked to Eric. "What's the date tonight?" It was that night. So there we are, four pasty white guys, very straight as far as we know, about to get a wide-open experience in the underworld, whatever you wanna say, fill in the blanks there. It was unbelievable.

We go play. We're upstairs at Zoogie's, and there is this big stairwell where people would come up. It was just men after men coming up and checking us out. Most of them went back down, but some stayed as the place filled up. By the end of the gig we literally couldn't move down the stairwell to get our gear into our cars, which are now trapped by a line of cars around the block in the alley. So we weren't gonna be able to leave.

We ended up not leaving until three or four in the morning because there were that many people crammed in that bar. You couldn't walk. Needless to say, most of us stayed upstairs the whole night. So that was our experience: We played the first night at "Minneapolis's biggest gay bar," according to the sign, and the end of an era for the old Longhorn.

ERIC PIERSON: Their thing was, fill the room and sell a lot of beer. So it was always really cheap to get in there. I can't remember if it was two bucks and then twenty-five cents for beer, or maybe it was Tiger Night—five bucks and all the beer you could drink.

Two of my high school teachers came down. I had told them, "I'm in a band and we're playing tonight." On a school night. And, let's just say that one of them scored. I didn't know what to say to him the next day.

I think it was just a dance club after that. It didn't last very long.

DICK CHAMP: I really don't know the whole story on how the Longhorn ended. Part of it is Jay Berine, who was such a nice guy, got into trouble. He got busted. He had some sort of a drug deal that went majorly bad. But that was part of that stupidity, see? People were probably getting a little too loose about some stuff. He probably was in the wrong place at the wrong time. He went to jail. So that changed a lot of what could've been or what was going on down there.

PETER JESPERSON: We were happy that the bar didn't close when Jay went to jail. Hartley was a difficult guy to deal with, but at the same time, I enjoyed his company sometimes. He was very generous to me. I think that in spite of his shortcomings and his not really being a music guy, he did a whole lot of good things for the scene and kept that bar going for a couple of years after Jay left. It lost a lot of its coolness when Jay left, but by that time the club had a little bit of a life of its own, and so it just kept going, for a little while anyway.

09

NEW WORLD: NNB

NNB was a mysterious and memorable band that had a devoted following of underground audiences. Despite releasing only two singles, their mystique lives to this day. Tastemakers Kevin Cole and Peter Jesperson and others revere NNB for being ahead of their time and consider them one of the best bands from Minneapolis. Mark Freeman formed NNB with guitarist Dick Champ, drummer Jim Tollefsrud, and bassist Rusty Jones in the fall of 1977. Over time, NNB had four different bass players: Jones, Wayne Hasti, Dave Blessing, and Chuck Hultquist. NNB released the single "Slack" on their own label, Wave 7, in May 1978. The band also contributed two songs to Twin/Tone's compilation, *Big Hits of Mid-America Volume Three*. The members of NNB moved to New York in 1980 but returned to the Twin Cities a year and a half later, reforming with photographer and keyboardist Cindy Blum as the new drummer. Blum and Freeman are husband and wife.

MARK FREEMAN: I grew up in Hopkins. I went to school with Bruce Allen, Michael Halliday, and Steve Almaas. They were all younger. Steve was playing with the band Seth. Back then, I was mostly listening to jazz, like Miles Davis, T. Monk. I heard Seth play and was blown away by how pro they sounded. I auditioned with Seth and then went back to doing jazz and conceptual stuff, and I also played with a bunch of the jazz guys in town.

Peter Stenshoel, his brother David, Jim Wilson, Steve Almaas, and I were in a band called Sky King. It did some stuff I wrote, probably stuff that Steve wrote and stuff that Peter wrote. In Sky King I played guitar and maybe flute. Then in the Infinity Art Unit I played drums and flute.

I hate to even mention who my heroes were, but they were pedestrian: Joe Walsh, Neil Young, Keith Richards obviously. Locally, when I was a kid, Robb Henry and Jeff Waryan were my heroes as far as guitar playing goes. Jeff knew how to get a tone. Charlie Bingham and Roy Alstad also used to blow me away. For me, guitar playing is all about being able to get a tone. Charlie Bingham can pick up any electric guitar on the planet, not plug it into anything, and make it scream. God's fingers live on the ends of Charlie's arms. Jeff would play with this crappy equipment, but he would get this great tone. Henner [Robb Henry] played with the worst amps on the planet and always made them sound like they were singing. If I had any major influences, it would all be really simple guitar players who like to make noise, because that is what I enjoy the most: just make noise.

My *thing* isn't really about playing an instrument as much as it's trying to figure out how other people are doing things I like. I remember spending a weekend transcribing a Rahsaan Roland Kirk [saxophone] solo because I was trying to figure out how he was coming up with the notes. I was thinking, "What do you have to do to think of stuff like that? How is that even possible to be that brilliant?" I thought if I figured out how he played it, then maybe that would give me a clue, but it didn't. I got a few good guitar riffs out of the deal, so it was good.

Skogie and the Flaming Pachucos were one of my early inspirations. I would see them pretty much every chance I got. They used to play in the basement of a church, One Groveland. It was three dollars or something, no alcohol, so anybody could go. Mark Goldstein, who played with Curt Almsted later on, was in the band. Rick Moore was a great songwriter, and they were the most professional-sounding band I had heard in a while. They blew me away.

DICK CHAMP: In that period of youth, the years seem to last forever. There's an enormous amount of time in my memory between those early beginnings and then playing with Mark Freeman, which began later, in 1977. Wayne Hasti, Rusty Jones, Jim Tollefsrud, and I all lived in the same place for long periods between '75 and '77. We even formed a band that played just one job. I don't remember what we called ourselves, but there we were—the same attitude, same inspiration, same kind of music, same kind of friendships.

The NNB thing was born out of something slightly different than what I did with Rusty and Jim and Wayne. I wanted to get involved with somebody who had songs at the ready, which Mark did. We hit it off right away. I had an AKAI GX-270 four-track reel-to-reel tape deck. I was like, "Let's do it."

NNB onstage: *(left to right)* bassist Chuck Hultquist, guitarist Dick Champ, drummer Jim Tollefsrud, and guitarist Mark Freeman, circa 1977. PHOTO BY BAYARD MICHAEL

One day I threw my recording equipment into the backseat of my car and drove over to meet with Mark.

Mark Freeman is a really top-notch guitarist. I'm kind of a hack, but Mark's the real article. So it was all flattery to me that someone of his stature would want to do something like this. Mark was very gracious, supportive even. I mean, he can outplay me to an absurd level.

MARK FREEMAN: Dick and I connected over a mutual love of the band Television. It was an amazing time in music back then; it was the end of a real long nightmare in music. We were coming out of Supertramp and stuff like that. It was awful.

The original lineup of NNB was first rehearsing in the basement of the Wax Museum on Lake Street. Practicing in the basement of the Wax Museum was one of those "we've got it made" kind of things. When you've got a place that you don't have to pay for and you can make as much noise as you want as late as you want, it's amazing. We recorded a lot of stuff down there. I don't think anybody did any drinking or getting high or anything. We *worked* down there. We didn't go there and party.

DICK CHAMP: I worked at Wax Museum from fall of '75 to probably spring of '79. By the time NNB had formed and was playing out, we rehearsed in the basement of that building. We practiced whenever we felt like it, basically every day. We had the space, the key for the store, and we knew all the security codes. When the shop would close, we'd go down and start playing, from nine 'til two AM, with all that youthful fervor of wanting to be a great band running the whole time. And it was free! So that situation helped a lot and we took full advantage of it.

Chuck Hultquist was like the fifth member of the band, and he sat there very patiently running the dials and recording a lot of our rehearsals.

JIM TOLLEFSRUD: NNB gave me an opportunity to create a style, an amalgam of different drummers that were influencing me at the time, and fit it into this context that was different than what I was familiar with, musically. I like doing really well-thought-out parts, even if they're very sparse technically. It's like Ringo—it's as much about what you don't play as it is about what you do play. It gave me the opportunity to do something unconventional with what I was able to do. NNB allowed me to do something to create a sound that was my own thing. It was angular. A few people said, "You know where it sounds like you're falling down the stairs, and then you just land." It was a good description. I'll take that. It's like things are about to fall apart, but not quite, and then everything's okay. It might have been Wayne or Mark who said that.

MARK FREEMAN: Dick and I were just like one giant guitar when we played together. It was this thing that worked. We were always shooting for making two guitars sound like three or four guitars, trying to find formulas that would give us orchestral sounds. When I was playing with Dick back in those days, I would be hearing the sound of the guitars *everywhere*. Dick and I used to work really hard on making our parts lock, so if you tried to figure out who was playing what, you wouldn't be able to. To me, that's what it's all about, finding a way to completely immerse yourself.

CINDY BLUM: When Mark and Dick would play together, there were things that would happen, you could hear things that no one was playing, that was just coming out of both of them playing together. It was really magical.

MARK FREEMAN: I used to like to bring stuff in in a fairly rough stage. At the time everybody used to complain that I was a little Hitler and I wanted everything exactly like I wanted it. Which is true, but when somebody played something that sounded good, I would try to get them to lock it in. Dick is really good at that sort of thing. Dick gets it. He understands parts. I've played with lots of guitarists who you couldn't get to play the same thing twice. I don't know if they won't do it or they can't do it. Everybody thinks that they have to be creative all the time. A song is a song; it's not like a jam session. If you want to jam, join the freakin' Grateful Dead.

Once we got the parts worked out we would just rehearse it and rehearse it and rehearse it and rehearse it. I mean we really worked hard to make sure we knew the song and that we knew where the energy points were. There is all kinds of stuff going on that you can't explain, but if it doesn't happen right, you have to change it. That is one thing that I am proud of: as a band we all were willing to really work to nail stuff down.

JIM TOLLEFSRUD: "Slack" was really thought out. Dick is playing 6/4, Rusty is playing 5/4, Mark and I are playing 4/4. So it had three different time signatures. It creates a rhythmic bed, the guitar and bass are shifting against each other, and Mark and I are playing 4/4, which makes it more interesting. I think it adds this sort of pull, kind of an undercurrent. It adds a level of intrigue.

RUSTY JONES: The night that "Slack" came together was a real memorable moment. It was like, "Shit, boys, I think we've got a real good song here!" Even Mark goes, "Yeah, Rusty, when you started doing that 5/4 against Dick's guitar, that's when it really just..." It was against what Jim Tollefsrud was doing. Then we could pull it all together in the chorus, as it were.

When I was in Arizona I got a part-time job at a record store. Dennis Maxwell is one of the most brilliant minds I ever met, and he was the guy that brought me in. He was listening to way-out-there shit. He liked all this electronic music.

So we had the NNB thing going and we had the background of more progressive music and bands I learned about in Arizona: The Residents, Faust, and Henry Cow. So when Mark was doing "Slack," it was like, "Yeah, sure man, I can figure out how to do something weird." I wrote the bass line for both songs, "Slack" and "New World" on the B-side.

DICK CHAMP: "Slack" was released on our own label, Wave 7. We just did it ourselves, the recordings, the artwork, the folds, the picture sleeve.

We were operating very secretively; we just snuck into Tracks on 5th in St. Paul armed with a very, very good demo. When we played it for the engineers during the one meeting we had with them, before we actually started recording, we said, "Here's what we want to record." They were like, "Jeez, this thing is ready." Well, it was because we had worked so hard on it already. We had the song all worked out, had all kinds of notes and diagrams on paper about the different time signatures that are running at the same time and resolve themselves.

MARK FREEMAN: When we started it was Chris Hinding and Mike McKern at the soundboard, and it ended up being mostly Mike McKern toward the end. He just seemed to have a better feel for what we were trying to do. It was a nice studio, the room was nice. I don't think they had a huge amount of outboard gear or anything, but it was plenty for what we needed to do. We didn't want to go nuts on crazy effects or anything like that.

MICHAEL McKERN: NNB had heard some stuff that I had done, and somehow, I believe it was Mark, we started talking, and he said they were thinking about doing a record. It was their first record. I think they had done some demo tapes.

So we agreed to work together, and they came over to Tracks on 5th. Both songs were done pretty much in one night. The thing that sticks out to me the most about that whole thing was on "Slack," that little beep noise that sounds like a radar blip? That was a guitar thing. It was funny because they were looking for something to have that kind of sound, and that was developed in the studio. It was the band and me and Chris Hinding, who was a partner of mine at the studio at that time. We were goofing around in the living room. He had this little amp and he had it really cranked up and I went into the control room and I put it through a spring reverb, but it made it have this really sonar sound. I always thought that had a lot to do with the sound of that record. Stupid little things sometimes make the record, right?

Most of the recording was done live, and we overdubbed some guitar stuff. Maybe we redid the vocals. It was a spontaneous, basic live recording kind of record, which is the way that I like to work. That is not something that's done much anymore. I believe you get a lot more feeling from a band if they are actually playing in the studio, instead of building tracks one by one—you lose the soul of it that way.

And NNB were all really nice guys. That is the important thing: when you look back on it, you make a good record, you capture it, and everybody was good people. That is the jewel there. The whole thing, sonically, was a lot of fun and we liked the record. I had no idea it would have the shelf life that it has had.

To tell you the truth, when we were recording, I liked the song "New World" better than "Slack" at first. I thought "New World" was catchier or something. I thought "Slack" was a little dark. It sounded more Nick Cave-ish. "New World" had this up feel to it and I'm more of a pop guy.

MARK FREEMAN: The B-side of "Slack" is "New World," which, even at the time, I thought was a horrible piece of crap. The reason we put it on there was because someone told us to put a bad song on the B-side, so no one would listen to it. We wanted people to listen to the A-side.

RUSTY JONES: We did everything ourselves. I believe I was the guy who told the band that night, "Well, what are we going to do? Wait for Twin/Tone to do it? Why don't we just put our minds to it and do it?" Everyone was like, "Yeah, why don't we?" Both Dick and I worked in the record store, so it was a piece of cake. We just put it up for sale. We already had the distribution.

I quit before the record came out because I just felt like there really was no place for me in that thing. Everything was so angular. I'm way more at home with the Front Porch Swingin' Liquor Pigs. I was listening to country music at that time, too.

DICK CHAMP: Once we had the recording in the bag—we had it pressed ourselves—Cindy Blum took a beautiful photograph for the front cover. Cindy became our drummer in the second incarnation of the band. And we packaged the record up and brought it around to the record stores ourselves.

We only pressed a thousand of the "Slack" single. It has a fold-up sleeve that you put into a plastic bag, and we probably ran a couple thousand of those sleeves. It worked spectacularly well to launch the band: tremendously good record, by a band that had yet to take the stage. Just a year later, the summer of '79, we went out and played in places like Milwaukee, Boston, and New York.

MARK FREEMAN: We released the "Slack" single before we had played anywhere. We picked the name NNB because we didn't want anyone to know what the hell was going on when we started playing. People were always guessing what the name was about. I was like, "Why does it have to stand for something?"

NNB on the cover of *Musicians' Insider* in April 1979 after being named Connie Award winner for Best Local 45 for "Slack." COURTESY OF DICK CHAMP

This was a band of guys who were huge Beatles fans, Stones fans, and we were also rock and roll fans and theorists. We would talk about how the Beatles was a shitty band name, the Rolling Stones was a shitty band name. The band makes the name, right? So we were trying to go for something that would be nearly impossible to make, so that it would be ours.

When we put the single out, we weren't on the record cover, so nobody knew who we were. When we played the first time live, everybody was like, "Hey! Those are the guys from the Wax Museum. Those losers!" [*laughs*] Tim Holmes was our most avid guesser.

TIM HOLMES: I don't remember NNB doing very many shows. They had sort of taken the threads of the post-punk, new wave thing. They were virtuosic; the playing meant something. With NNB there's a lot of technical stuff. And atmospheric, really going deep in whatever the mood was they were creating. Mark was serious onstage.

RYAN CAMERON: Mark Freeman used to come into Hot Licks quite a bit, and we sold a shitload of the "Slack" single there. I think it was one of the best singles to come out of this area. It's up there, it's so great.

PETER JESPERSON: I saw NNB as many times as I could. They were absolutely astonishing onstage. I thought they shared elements with two other bands that I loved: Television and Pere Ubu. And I thought they did it very well. It wasn't copycat stuff. The shows were very dark and intense. Mark Freeman had a real vision.

JIM TOLLEFSRUD: We opened for Pere Ubu in Milwaukee or Madison. We loved Pere Ubu. We were kind of influenced by Pere Ubu. We'd do "Final Solution" in our live show.

ERNIE BATSON: To me, NNB was a better version of Television. I never was a big Television fan. Too much noodling. NNB were very controlled. That's perhaps always been a problem with Mark Freeman and any of his efforts: very in control and seeking to have more and more control. When I heard that "Slack" 45, it was like Minneapolis's version of Pere Ubu to my mind, without the synths, though.

BILL BATSON: NNB played short songs, very concise. NNB was a different band than Red House later on, but that was still Mark Freeman and Cindy Blum on drums. She is really good. A natural. Solid, kept it simple. The way that Mark would write a song, he'd make everything fit just right for her and him. He was a great songwriter. I think one of the best in this town, ever.

MARK FREEMAN: Our first show was probably at the Longhorn, whenever the "Slack" single first came out, 1978. The acoustics were great at the Longhorn. The soundperson was Terry Katzman or Billy Batson. Billy is a great soundman.

Billy did sound for us when we were on the road. I remember playing the Cubby Bear in Chicago right after a Cubs game. There were a bunch of Cubs fans, who absolutely hated our guts, sitting in the bar on the other side and three people in the audience, including Jeff Pezzati [of Naked Raygun] and his girlfriend, who danced the entire time. The guy who booked the place kept saying, "You guys don't have to keep playing if you don't want to. I'll still pay you." And Billy sat behind the soundboard the entire night with a microphone in his hand going, "Get off! You suck!" Yelling shit through the PA at us.

WAYNE HASTI: I was waiting in a long line at the Häagen-Dazs store in the IDS Center, and I saw a guy in line that had a Ramones shirt on. I went up to him and talked to him about music. That's how Mark and I met. I think that's where we first started looking at his songs. They must have asked me when Rusty left the band.

When I saw NNB perform for the first time, I was amazed because they would play four songs, no one would be on the dance floor, and then they would go into their fifth song and the whole place would dance all at the same time. That happened the next night, too. They knew what they were doing.

DAVE PIRNER: NNB were probably one of my more favorite bands. I think the way that the rhythm section operated was really, really interesting. Deconstructing and reconstructing, all at the same time. It seemed like very, very smart people messing around with a format that is rock and roll—for lack of a better expression—but really trying to push the boundaries of it, and present it like an inside-out skeleton.

I specifically remember seeing them at Walker Art Center and the singer coming out and saying "hello" very quietly to somebody in the front row. It was something that really stuck: he saw somebody in the audience and was like, "Oh hey, how are you doing?" That was interesting to me. The more I realized that the line between the people that are onstage and the people in the audience was not a huge barrier, the more I wanted to be on the stage.

JOHN KASS: I was in the high school class of 1980, and some older guys from the class of '78 got into KISS really heavily, and so we followed them. The class of '78 also turned us on to Alice Cooper, the New York Dolls, the Stooges, and the Ramones.

One of the guys really liked the NNB record and the fact that if you listen to the lead guitar part, it sounds like somebody is taking like a glass bottle on the guitar strings and going *[eeeeeaaaaaaaaawwwwWWWWWW!!!]*. That was blowing our minds. We'd never heard anything like it. We'd listen and just laugh, "I can't believe this guy did this on a record."

That record, "Slack," had a huge impact on us because it wasn't, "One, two, three, four!" Ramones. It was something beyond that.

MARK FREEMAN: "Listen" and "Uruguay 1983" are on Twin/Tone's *Big Hits of Mid-America*. "Uruguay" was strictly a Dadaist lyrical experiment. I was trying to make the lyrics as meaningless as I could possibly make them.

Dick has a recording of "Listen" that is a billion times better than the one we released. We originally recorded it on Dick's four-track in the

NNB at Blackberry Way studio during the recording for *Big Hits of Mid-America Volume Three*, October 1978: *(left to right)* Jim Tollefsrud, Mark Freeman, Dick Champ, and Wayne Hasti. PHOTO BY JOHN TOLLEFSRUD.

basement at the Wax Museum. My memory is that it is amazing. And my memory of it also includes Dick standing in the middle of the room in wingtips and knee-high dress socks and a pair of Bermuda shorts with a hose in his mouth going "whoooOOooo!" That point in our band was as creative and engaging and perfect a situation as I've been in in my life.

We recorded "Well, Oh Well" at Blackberry Way. It was a flexi disc for Chris Nelson's *NO Magazine*. Dick Champ was in Chris Nelson's band the Scene Is Now, which got pretty big in New York. Dave Blessing played bass on "Well, Oh Well."

David Foley is also on "Well, Oh Well." I said, "I want Davey on this one." Everyone was like, "*Whaaat*?! Wait. *Whaaat*? He's not in the band!" I really just wanted what he does. He makes the cool guitar stuff on it. He made some sounds on there that were just so cool and perfect, exactly with the lyrics and stuff, the train sounds.

DAVE FOLEY: Mark Freeman, Cindy Blum, and I lived in a building behind Comic City on 31st and Hennepin. Mark would sit in his room and taperecord riffs off of guitar players and play them over to learn how to play guitar because he wanted to teach guitar. He's good at all that kind of stuff; he's a genius. I said I wanted to put a band together, so we put this band together. Cindy played drums, Mark played guitar, and I played noisy guitar. Mark Luers from Tatters named the band Modern Corduroy. That was a great name. Steve McClellan gave us a gig in the Entry.

MARK FREEMAN: I recorded the flip side of the flexi disc at the *New York Rocker* office, using Chris Stamey's four-track reel-to-reel machine, which was actually a three-track reel-to-reel machine at the time because one of the channels was blown. There seemed to be a general agreement that that was even cooler, that we had almost nothing to work with. It was fun, actually. The police were called at one point and shut us down.

NNB played CBGB right after "Slack" came out. That was the weirdest, most confusing tour because we didn't know we were getting airplay. We were playing places where crowds were showing up, and we were like, "Why are people coming to see us?"

The first time we played CBGB, we were terrified. Like when you hear those hazing stories before you go to high school and you think you're going to get beat up and stuck in a locker. We had heard, "If you play New York, if anybody claps, you're lucky." So after the first song, people clapped, and I said, "Wow, thank you! I heard audiences in New York didn't clap." Some guy in the audience yelled, "We heard bands from Minneapolis couldn't play." It may have been Andy Schwartz who did that.

We used to play with Information and Mofungo every once in a while. I think we played with them at CBGB. At one point, between three bands, we split seventeen dollars. When I asked Hilly Kristal about it, he said, "Well, everyone was on the guest list." I remember asking somebody, it may have been Richard Lloyd of Television, "What's the deal with that?" He said, "He will pay you after a while, but when you first start, he doesn't. He has to get to know you and like you."

Then we played Boston. We got to the Rat, and I said, "So, who is headlining?" and the guy said, "You're fucking kidding, right?" I said "No." He said, "*You* are." I said, "Why?" He said, "Are you joking? Your song is on the radio like every five minutes! You can't get away from it."

JIM TOLLEFSRUD: We were a big hit on a show in Boston hosted by Oedipus. He really loved "Slack," so he played it quite a bit. We found the show as we came into town, and we were literally pulling up in front of the place and—boom!—there's our song, it came on the radio. We're in Boston and we're hearing our song—it's really cool! It sounded great.

DICK CHAMP: We just about died. Every band probably has a story like that, but this was particularly sweet. So the record did get around. They really liked it up in Boston. Oedipus had an underground radio show there, very well known. God bless him. He printed up a Top 10 list or something like it, with all the underground rock that was around at the time. He liked the "Slack" single. Probably had it in his Top 20. For a bunch of Midwestern hillbilly boys, that was pretty cool.

MARK FREEMAN: When we went to Maxwell's in Hoboken the first time, we were on the jukebox there. So, when we played, everybody had already been listening to us, and they knew who we were.

One of the most valuable things I have in life is my anonymity. So for me, it was really cool and really creepy. It was working for us; people liked us. But I kind of like to be able to disappear when I feel like disappearing.

DICK CHAMP: Being on the road, it was just the lowest-budget affair you can imagine. You would wind up staying with one of the local scenesters, in some cases it could even be the apartment of the person who booked you in the club. We didn't stay in hotels, that's for sure. It was always a real hassle. I mean, you had all the security concerns about a van, a car, or a trailer that could easily be broken into—the Suicide Commandos lost everything—so we had our guard up against that stuff. We had the added misfortune of being on the road during the so-called energy crisis, when the gas pumps at stations were turned off at night. At least once we slept in our car and U-Haul trailer in the parking lot of a closed gas station.

MARK FREEMAN: It was fun. What better time can you have than driving around the country in a van with no heat with a bunch of smelly, sweaty guys who haven't showered for—I mean, that's *living*, you know.

DICK CHAMP: In all honesty, I don't think the original version of the band was really ready for primetime. We had the "Slack" record, then the tracks on *Big Hits of Mid-America*, and then our flexi disc in *NO Magazine*. But

I don't really think we had enough good material until that '79 tour was completed and we came back home. By then we had really gelled and were quite comfortable playing the Marathon '80 festival, for example, that took place later that year. I mean, there was sincere label interest by then, so it's fair to say we had our sound together. There were some record people that came through to see the M-80 festival. Capitol Records was interested; I think A&M might have been as well. We were very flattered, probably made ourselves available to discuss it.

MARK FREEMAN: I know "Slack" was getting played in clubs in Europe. We never went over there and we didn't have any spies over there to let us know what was going on. But we were getting letters from people saying they heard it at such and such a club. It was happening a lot, and then we got a publishing offer from Chappell Music in Belgium [a division of Warner Music Group]. At that point we were like, "Why is all this stuff coming from Europe?" We didn't find out until later that someone had licensed it to a lot of labels over there.

DICK CHAMP: Unfortunately, right around this time, we had all grown tired of it. Anyone who's ever been in a band has had that moment when you're trying to call somebody else in your outfit to say you want out, and all the phone lines are busy because everybody else is trying to do the same thing. We all kind of had had enough. I don't know what was going on then, but we were tired of it, you know?

I went down to Florida—my parents were living there—and I didn't know what on earth I was gonna do. I was totally without a way because the band had collapsed, I wasn't working at the record store, and the Longhorn had come to an end. I went down to Florida for about a month, an attempt to regroup.

I came back around February 1980, and Mark and I, Cindy, and Chuck [Hultquist] reconstituted NNB in late winter or early spring, if memory serves. NNB really came together when it reunited with Cindy on drums, although that created all kinds of problems for me personally because Jim Tollefsrud is absolutely one of my best friends. I've known him for over forty years, but he was out of the band and Cindy was in. But Mark had all kinds of new songs. And 7th Street Entry had opened and I just wanted to get on that stage—I love that room. And there was that verve all over again, all that desire to get in there and play at that club as soon as we possibly could, you know? A lot of people couldn't understand why we ever broke up to begin with. So when we did our first shows, people went crazy. No shit. We had lines around the block. I mean, it was really a big deal, a madhouse. It's fair to say that 7th Street Entry took off on the strength of our gigs, us and the Wallets. It was really hysterical. There were huge crowds. That place was packed.

Handbill for NNB concert, with 8 Eyed Spy, at 7th Street Entry, July 14–15, 1980. COURTESY OF DANIEL GROBANI

MARK ENGEBRETSON: It must've been summer or fall of 1980, and NNB had been to New York and back, and it was really early at the Entry. NNB asked if we, the MORs, would open for them. That was the most crowded I'd ever seen the Entry. It was sold out, clearly. They did two sets and we did one set, and at the end of the night Freeman settles up with us: "You guys played one-third of the night, so here's one-third of the money." Nobody was there to see the MORs, except maybe our friends, who were probably on the guest list. And he still paid us the money, which was really cool.

DANNY FLIES: NNB never played much. They were reserved. They selectively played when and where they wanted to play. But if it weren't for NNB—they basically kicked the door open for the 7th Street Entry.

CINDY BLUM: I was doing freelance photography for *Musicians' Insider* and for *Sweet Potato*, the precursor to *City Pages*. I was hanging out with the Suicide Commandos and that crowd. And then I started going out with Mark. Sometime after NNB had broken up, Mark was forming another band with a friend and asked if I wanted to be in it. I said, "Well, sure!" I started playing keyboards. We bought a funny little keyboard with some Astro Sound—it was really hysterical.

MARK FREEMAN: It was crappy and cheesy and awesome. That band was me, Cindy, and Mark Powell, who is a really good guitar player. He is the son of George Powell, who owned Hot Licks.

CINDY BLUM: We were getting things together. We were looking for a drummer and couldn't find one. Mark brought in this little rinky-dink drum kit. He was goofing around teaching me how to play drums.

We had a rehearsal studio downtown on 1st Avenue. There was a fire in the studio and all our equipment was burned up. Mark said, "What do you want to replace: the keyboard or the drums?" So, that was my choice there.

MARK FREEMAN: The fire was a pretty amazing thing. We were at Cindy's parents' house, and the news was on and we were watching the fire on TV. I said, "Wow, that is one hell of a fire." There were flames shooting out the windows. All of a sudden Cindy went, "Wait! That's our studio." So we went racing downtown. They wouldn't let us in.

Finally, not to get anyone in trouble, but one of the firemen told us how to get into the building safely. We went in to see if any of our stuff had survived. Because it was winter, my amp was frozen in like four inches of ice—it was basically a cube of ice. I brought it back to our apartment and threw it in the shower under hot water and then let it dry, and it worked perfectly. My guitar was a Travis Bean. It had an aluminum neck. I had to cover up the fire damage by painting it flat black.

CINDY BLUM: We bought some Pearl drums from some guys at a halfway house up on Ridgewood. They served me well, actually.

MARK FREEMAN: The drums were not great. The cymbals were great. But the deal was, she said she would play drums, and we had a gig coming up in a week. I said, "Well, you're going to have to get to work." And over the course of a week, she learned all of our songs, having never played drums before! She was ready to rip my face off. She was angry and in tears a lot of the time when I would say, "Hey, you committed to this, you've got to do it."

Well, we got up onstage, and she played all the songs. Later we found out her mother was a drummer and her grandmother was a drummer.

CINDY BLUM: Mark was good at creating bands where he would say, "You don't have to really learn to play, you just need to learn how to play *these* songs." He did that with other people, too. You just learn and it's fun.

It's great playing drums because you get to watch, too. It's such a great seat back there. All the other people are in front of you. The audience is in front of you.

MARK FREEMAN: Cindy was thrown into the fire probably more quickly than most musicians ever have to be. So for her, being onstage in reasonably major situations is the norm. She can't look back on her early days and say, "Well, when we first started, we were like..." It was straight from the Longhorn to 7th Street to the First Avenue Mainroom to Irving Plaza. She didn't get any break in time.

Cindy, Steve Almaas, and I played together in a band, in New York. I was a big Suicide Commandos fan, and so I always wanted to try the three-piece thing, which absolutely does not work for me. I don't know how anybody can take a guitar solo over bass and drums. But anyway, we wanted to try it, and Almaas, as far as I'm concerned, is one of the best bass players I know. So I figured, if it was going to work with anybody, it would work with Almaas. Besides having a great bass player, I think you also need a drummer who knows how to completely go crazy, and I hate that kind of drummer. I just don't like busy drums. But we tried it.

CINDY BLUM: I don't think being on the scene as a woman drummer was much of an issue except maybe with other drummers. Guy drummers were always the most annoying part of it, really. They would always be telling me I was "pretty good for a girl" and "you should let me help you tune your drum." I was so sick to death of it. It's like, "Can't we all just be people, like humans?" We are all just doing our little jobs, you know, whatever.

I definitely had a thing, I always wanted my snare drum to sound somewhere between a gunshot and punching someone. That's what I was going for, somewhere in there. I always used giant sticks at first, like LP 5Bs. They were like baseball bats.

MARK FREEMAN: Jim Tollefsrud is the guy that taught her about doing the rim shots to get a cracky sounded snare. I think back in those days we were all completely in awe of Scott Krauss [of Pere Ubu]. After John Bonham, Scott Krauss was a god.

CINDY BLUM: Jim was a hard act to follow, because he is so fabulous. I of course would get compared to Moe Tucker, of the Velvet Underground, which is fine. She's cool.

MARK FREEMAN: Cindy is better, though.

KEVIN BOWE: Cindy Blum was great on drums. She was fun to watch because she looked like she was in her own little world, but she laid it down.

LORI BARBERO: Cindy's one of my heroes, for sure. I saw Cindy Blum drumming with NNB at the Longhorn. I remember seeing her as being one of the first female musicians, female drummers ever. It was one of the coolest things. Seeing her drum really encouraged me to become a drummer. I was nineteen or twenty when I saw her. I saw NNB often. I loved them.

ANDY SCHWARTZ: NNB was really different because they were more inspired by a band like Television than they were by the Ramones. NNB was kind of experimental. They were on to something and they had a female drummer and there weren't a whole lot of female musicians involved in that scene. We had one female band, Spitfire.

NNB were ahead of their time, in a way. And they were sort of out of time because they weren't really playing pop songs. It was two-guitar texture things. It was different. It wasn't punk rock the way that people think of punk rock. I don't even know what NNB stood for. That is an example of a band trying to establish a certain unknowability, a certain air of mystery, if you will.

JODY KURILLA: NNB were *way* ahead of their time. And they were *amazing*! Those singles, to this day, have not aged; it doesn't feel dated. They were really good. NNB were the Television of Minneapolis.

TERRY KATZMAN: NNB is the more serious side of our punk rock. Clearly they were our Television. Everybody was very into [Television's album] *Marquee Moon* at that time. NNB did their own thing, but were definitely very influenced by the New York scene, more straight-laced "We play our songs and don't talk so much." You had a sampling of different things you didn't get from other bands. That was neat for that time.

DOUG ANDERSON: I was lucky enough to get in one night to see NNB. I know the comparison is always there with Television. To me they were not copying Television, but Mark Freeman, not only is he a great songwriter and a great guitar player and a really good performer, but he was like an antenna. Freeman was one of those guys who the most advanced shit would come through. Freeman was probably the first diehard Pere Ubu fan in town.

Freeman had been around interesting experimental music for so long that it hit him like a lightning bolt. He has this ability to divine what is truly cool and truly interesting. Dick is that way, too, and they're both in the band. Dave Foley is that way, too; he's just got this *thing*. I guess that was the thing with those guys and girls: they all had this openness to the most interesting stuff that would just go through them. And other people learned to be *cool* from those people. It was a way of living, a way of talking, a way of thinking.

MARTIN KELLER: NNB were self-consciously cool and they didn't care what anybody thought of them. Freeman has always been an enigma to me and, to a certain extent, Dick Champ, too. Dick I would call an intellectual. He studied philosophy in college and he's very bright. Everybody thought this was a band that could go places, because they had the sound of the new wave rock scene before people realized what the sound was. They didn't play hardly at all, but they left a pretty deep footprint.

MARK ENGEBRETSON: NNB is a band I think in danger of not being remembered as prominently as it should be. They were a tremendous band—really, really good. They never played that much, so that's why people sometimes forget about them.

TERRY KATZMAN: I think they were perfectionists almost to the point of hurting themselves. NNB had just two singles. They should've had an album and it just didn't happen. When they were getting *Big Hits* together it was like pulling teeth to get NNB to figure out which two songs they were gonna put on there. When I get done working on something I want it out like tomorrow. But they were a professional band. They were very focused about what they did, so that put them outside the normal nucleus, though they were very much a part of it anyways because "Slack" is as classic as any record that's come out of this town.

MARK FREEMAN: We were never trying to be the next local heroes. We had our own thing that we were doing. It was all about creating. When I say we rehearsed the hell out of the songs, it was for us. We just enjoyed playing them until we had them nailed. We didn't release more of our music because we were doing other stuff. We recorded a lot; we just didn't feel like releasing it. Also, there is economics involved. It wasn't free to put that single out, and we basically had to scrape that cash together. We never got any serious offers from any labels that we wanted to be on. It is expensive making a record.

KEVIN COLE: Criminally overlooked, NNB are the best-kept secret of the late '70s Minneapolis scene. While the Suicide Commandos brought the punk pop fun, NNB owned the metaphysical void, riding an undercurrent of tension with an occasional cathartic release through a soaring guitar riff, shimmering chord, or hook. But they didn't waste much time in resolution, as the joy was the musical interplay in the darkness. They utilized dissonance, dirge, and feedback, while at the same time being so taut, restrained, and clean. They were never sloppy—every piece in place—but never mechanical; there was always an edge, a jagged and real emotional quality to the performances and songs. Like Television, the guitar interplay between Mark Freeman and Dick Champ was majestic. Transcendent. They were fantastic live, and their limited recorded output of five songs is equally brilliant.

Post NNB, Mark Freeman formed Red House and released only one single, in 1983, "25 Reasons"/ "Teenbeat," which is also brilliant. After that, he seemed to disappear. I guess he bought a little boat and just sailed away. [A reference to a lyric in "25 Reasons."]

10

PARTY UNDERGROUND: THE PODANY AND THE MODESTO

After shows at the Longhorn and other venues, bands, artists, and music fans regularly convened at after parties at locations around the Twin Cities: in warehouses, basements, apartments, and other spaces. People like Jody Kurilla, the Batson brothers, Jim Fenn, and more were frequent hosts of such gatherings. Peter Jesperson hosted after-hours record listening parties at his apartment in the Modesto apartment building, located behind Oar Folkjokeopus at 26th and Garfield. The Podany Office Furniture Warehouse building on East Lake Street in Minneapolis served as studio, rehearsal, and living space for numerous artists and musicians. The Suburbs formed at the Podany and had their first practices there. They rented the two-thousand-square-foot basement space, including a former rathskeller, which became a notorious spot for their popular underground performances and parties.

DICK CHAMP: Podany's! My goodness! It was really something amazing, especially to drive by that intersection now and to see a Denny's. Well folks, there weren't no Denny's booths in that place back then.

The Weaver brothers—Jay on lead vocals, Tom on guitar—had a really good band called Seconds with Tim Mauseth, Rusty Jones, and George Clifford. I'm pretty sure the third-floor sort of office space that I began at was one I shared with those guys. This would've been in the late spring of 1977, shortly before the Longhorn took off. The rent was peanuts, probably like seventy-five bucks a month for electricity and a room. I would go over there, plug in my Pignose portable amp, a cassette deck, and just play any old garbage. That was one of the first places I had where you weren't attaching yourself to the basement of somebody's house or, like we did later, to the basement of a record store.

At Podany's you could rent a space and rock out any hours of the day. Right around the same time, Bruce Allen and Michael Halliday had their space on the second floor, I think, and they were calling themselves the Tsetse Flies. We were all walking back and forth between the floors there, checking everybody out. It wasn't long before we finagled renting the legendary basement of that building. This was like the biggest coup d'état of all time in that scene.

BRUCE ALLEN: Podany's! The Suburbs formed in '77, and that's where we formed. There was a bar off to the side, and Hugo Klaers, Michael Halliday, and I started rehearsing in that office area. We were the Tsetse Flies. Michael was living there, too.

We worked our way down to the basement. *[laughs]* Podany offered us the basement. It was perfect timing because we were so crammed in, and Chan Poling and Beej Chaney had just come to town. So Chan, Beej, and Michael all lived in the basement and we got this great deal. We broke down this door and there was this bar: the Rathskeller. We did gigs there all the time.

Once we got eighty-sixed from the Longhorn, we had parties at Podany's. Everybody went to our parties. It felt so cool. We'd have these huge kegger parties. Us and the Commandos and other bands would play. That's how we paid our rent. There was a big room, and I remember playing in that room and the Commandos playing in the Rathskeller, and we switched members.

CHRIS OSGOOD: It was like a rent party down there, with kegs of beer and people flailing away in the semi-darkness.

We would rehearse upstairs in Podany's little offices. The windows would rattle as soon as we started to play.

DICK CHAMP: I may have already gotten off the original lease by the time the Podany's party scene came into being. But I was an original leaseholder with those guys. We simply divided the space in half and threw up a big curtain, or sheets draped over a clothesline, to make two large work areas. The space was kind of dumpy, like the previous tenant had left behind a lot of stuff you had to walk over or around. I didn't really go for that whole curtain situation, because I found it a little difficult to rehearse a band when somebody else was just hanging out on the other side. I was pretty uptight about the whole thing. But we had that space, and in that "Well, the bar's closed, now what?" spirit of the times, the Podany's space became one of the prime targets for after-hours merriment. It was pretty crazy. I can't believe we didn't get busted.

The cop shop was near there then. No one was too worried about stuff like that. Goes to the outrageous rebelliousness of the times, you know. Like, "Screw 'em!" Nowadays a place like that would be found out and just scratched off. It boggles the mind what we got away with. There was all kinds of drinking, and who knows how old the people were that were going in and out of there for those parties. We didn't have somebody checking IDs, that's for sure. Granted, it was mostly the clique—the bands, their girl-friends, and the hangers-on—but even so. It's unimaginable that that sort of place could survive today. A lot of people would have paid the price big time—yours truly included—had we actually gotten busted. I feel so lucky.

A big part of its charms was that it had restaurant booths that the previous tenant left intact along the perimeter walls of the space. You could probably seat three people on each side, like in a normal restaurant. So, when you were down there partying, it felt like you were at a club, but you definitely weren't at a club. You were in a madhouse!

JEFF BUSWELL: Podany's was the first place I saw the Suburbs. Before they got to the bar scene, they used to throw parties pretty much every weekend. All the bands that were part of that time seemed to pop in there and play once in a while. I wandered in there one time: "My god! These guys are really having a good time down here. I need to be a part of this." So I pushed my way in.

TERRY KATZMAN: Podany's Office Supply was four blocks from my house. I used to walk over there every night, when I should have been doing homework. The Podany was a fantastic space. There was a foot-high stage where the Suburbs rehearsed, so you could just sit in a booth and bring some beer in and watch them rehearse. That was a good place to see the Suburbs because that's where they stretched out and did some different things that you would never see in a club. That was when they were really formulating their sound, and it came a lot from earlier jazz improvisations.

ERNIE BATSON: We wrangled an invite to a Podany party. We got there at four in the afternoon. We played at like three in the morning. The Suburbs played after us. That was our entry into the scene, our first exposure to the Longhorn crowd. After that, people liked us. Before that it was like, "I don't know about you guys."

LU ANN KINZER: I remember being at Podany's and other parties where several bands would be playing all night, until the wee hours of the morning. Everyone knew each other and they were all friends. There were a lot of parties in a lot of warehouses and practice spaces. There would always be two or three different bands playing all night. There were a lot of other bands: the Wallets, the Warheads, Things That Fall Down, the Hypstrz, and the list goes on.

DICK CHAMP: With today's nightclubs, the second you walk in, even while they're setting up the bar, it's a constant barrage of sound. That to me doesn't much lend itself to even the most basic socializing. I'm not saying that because I'm sixty years old, because I didn't like it then either. That was my own personal aesthetic. But I really loved meeting all these new people from all these different places around town. It was irresistible. One of the avenues for finding out about them and what they were interested in and so on could be in the downtime between sets of live music.

Once the DJs were in place, many of us took to the Longhorn's afterparty scene. It really was a huge part of the experience. As soon as the bar was closing, everybody would be milling about on the sidewalk along 5th Street and there would be all this whispering going on, people trying to find out where everybody was going to go next. "Oh, we're gonna go over to Cedar Lake. See you there," or so-and-so's house. And a good handful of us would continue on, which was a lot of fun, to put it lightly.

The after parties went into the wee hours, just dangerously late in retrospect. I can remember a lot of evenings that would wrap up when the sun was coming up. We'd still be hanging out with the survivors, the five or six people from the original fifty, let's say, who left the bar in search of more kicks.

HUGO KLAERS: People used to leave the Longhorn and stand out on the street until someone would relinquish and say, "Okay, here's the address, here's the house we're gonna go trash." Parties at Jody Kurilla's house were legendary.

It was kind of a selfish era, really. Everything was fair game. You could just do what you want. A lot of times I didn't even know what I was taking, and I'd take it. I realized right away, being in the Suburbs and hanging around Beej, that hallucinogenics were not for me, and not for drummers. Beej used to take like three hits of acid before we played at the Longhorn.

JODY KURILLA: People remember my address. Friends made a song about it. Everybody would just sing the address. It had a little rhyme to it.

LORNA DOONE: Sometimes your friends would go to the Longhorn at eleven, twelve at night and ask where the party was. My friend Jody had most of the after parties. She had a big pajama party one time. It was so cool. We really had a good time.

DAVE AHL: I went to Jody's parties all the time. She was so much fun and there was always a great crowd of regulars there. Jody and Ellen Morgan and Anne Peil were collectively known as the Mod Girls. They would wear all '60s mod fashion.

Invitation to a party at Jody Kurilla's house, June 1979. COURTESY OF DICK CHAMP

CHRIS OSGOOD: When the Longhorn was over at one o'clock in the morning, it was never a consideration that we were going to go home. Always by the last set of the evening, there was an address that would circulate. We would go, lots of times, to Jody Kurilla's house. The Mod Girl parties would be themed sometimes.

DANNY AMIS: Of course, Jody Kurilla always had parties at her house. I remember standing in her kitchen and drinking beers with Talking Heads one night and Devo another night. We talked about music a lot. And New York. I was fascinated with New York.

JODY KURILLA: The first thing I remember is being eight years old and inviting so many people to my birthday party that my mom had to borrow tables from the neighbors. Then she had to run to the store to get extra cake.

So it's always been something that I've just done. I always had parties at my house when I was a kid, because my dad was a bouncer, so he wasn't home at night. We would all clean up the house by the time he got home, at about two in the morning.

Somehow I got Talking Heads to come out there. I have a photo of Jon Bream, the reporter for the *Star Tribune*, interviewing David Byrne in my parents' kitchen. *[laughs]* It's like, how did I get these people to drive all the way out to West Bloomington? I'll never know.

When I moved out on my own, it made sense that I would continue having parties. My house was easy because it was five minutes from downtown. I had a double bungalow, and my friends lived upstairs. So we would have these big parties. My neighbors were very tolerant. Some of them thought it was pretty hilarious.

We would have these funny little themes. We would have Tom and Jerry parties. We would have pajama parties. We'd make homemade postcards and hand them out to everybody. There was maybe a hundred people or so that would wander through during the night. It wasn't just getting together and getting very drunk—we did that, too—but there was always some reason for it. You had to think a little bit about the theme, why we were going out.

When I would have parties after the venues, those were sort of impromptu. If somebody was in town playing, we probably had a party. I DJ'd, and for some reason I was able to get all these bands to come to my house. Gang of Four at my house was a favorite night.

Other people had parties, too. There was the shop Lorna Doone had with Michael O'Neill, called Rock-It Cards. They would have theme parties. So it was art and parties, and everybody had to be involved.

LORNA DOONE: Rock-It Cards was a small space. We had one party called "Clash or Match," where we invited people to come and either clash or match with the hot-pink walls. All these people were there, and that was a rousing success. But we got thrown out about a year later because when we'd have these parties, well, for one thing, the hallway smelled like beer all the time! But our friends and customers would also go through the building and ride the elevators and poke around, and the building really didn't like that, you know. And so we got kicked out.

KAREN HAGLOF: Comic City was definitely a place to go to after the clubs closed. There was always some place to go. I could go out every night, then go to work at the music store at ten or eleven in the morning. I did guitar repair and counter sales at Knut Koupeé. I used to run into musicians all the time as well. Knut Koupeé was here and Comic City was here, kitty-corner in Uptown. It was a hip guitar hangout for inner-city musicians. It was pretty excellent.

Prince used to come in and get his guitars done. This was when he was nineteen, before he was known, and the rumblings were that he had this big Warner Bros. contract and was going to put a band together. He got some of his musicians through connections at the store. Other luminaries would come in. The guy from Cheap Trick would come in. Bonnie Raitt would come in every so often. All the local guys would always wander in, Curt or the Commandos. Everybody would be checking out all the little gadgets, trading guitars for organs, all that. It was a real hangout place, very loose vibe. It was a great job.

DOUG ANDERSON: I remember Jody's and going to parties there with my girlfriend, Deb. You would see these really amazingly beautiful women and men. That world was real nocturnal and separate. What they brought was that sense of self-dictated style. They would see things but turn everything into their own. I would see those girls and think they were so powerful and so great and so beautiful and so wild. Those were the girls that were just untouchable, smart, and completely unwilling to take shit from anybody, right? That was also a great thing about that scene then: those women seemed more empowered in many ways because they were not afraid to say anything. A man could say anything to them and they would just answer them back.

CINDY BLUM: David Foley introduced us to Jody. David Foley introduces everyone. David Foley is the glue that binds us all. He was just omnipresent at the time.

MARK FREEMAN: David Foley is the glue that binds humanity. First time I saw Davey was at that Riverside bank on the West Bank. He was wearing a trench coat and red horn-rims and he had this big afro. I thought, "Who is this fucker?"

Dave Foley, with Bruce Allen, at a house party, circa 1978. PHOTO BY BAYARD MICHAEL

DAVE FOLEY: I would have a party down the street from First Avenue, and Steve McClellan would go, "I'll get you a keg." So I would get a keg of beer from him and they would wheel it down to my place after bar close and I would pay him for it. They would drag it up my icy steps at the Glenwood.

There was this girl named Eloise Bryant, a real go get 'em kind of girl. We had this band once. Eloise wanted to be in a band badly. So we had this loft and we were just friends hanging out.

The Church had a rerelease of their *Starfish* album, and they did the party at Runyon's on Washington and 1st Avenue. Eloise staged it, all these candles on all the tables. She was friends with Paul Runyon, so he let her do the party there.

DOUG ANDERSON: Eloise Bryant used to have these great loft parties. Foley was down there all the time. Jon Oulman had a loft that was cool. He had a lot of great after parties, too, after First Avenue. You could walk right over to Jon's place.

ROBB HENRY: At that time, in the whole north part of downtown, there were a lot of loft spaces, and we were going to a lot of after-hours parties at those places. Back then it was like the wild west. People had loft parties and storefront parties.

CHRIS OSGOOD: After parties were a big part of the socializing and relationships. Later on, Hartley Frank got wise to them, and sometimes they were big enough that they would threaten attendance at the Longhorn, and he would call the cops on them. He called the cops on my wedding reception, thinking it was one of those parties. Hartley didn't engender any friends amongst the musicians for doing that. It was uncool for him to do that, since we were sort of his indentured servants.

PETER JESPERSON: A lot of times after the Longhorn closed, people would stand around on the sidewalk and say, "Where is the party?" I never had that kind of place, but there would often be a few people—like five or six, or ten on a crowded night—and we would all head back to my place and hang out until the sun came up the next morning. We would just listen to records, drink, and do whatever other nasty shit we were into at the time, and it was a lot of fun. A fertile period for that scene. Mine wasn't a very big apartment. If people came to my place, it was to listen to music. I know that I offended a number of people by saying, "Be quiet. You need to listen to this song." That was what we were there for. I was there listening to music, and if other people wanted to come listen to it, that was good. But there were many times when I'm like, "No talking!" and people would be like, "Fuck you. I'm leaving."

A bunch of us lived in the Modesto apartment building, behind Oar Folk. That was the den of iniquity back in the day. That was a wild place. People didn't lock their doors, and we would be running between floors going to somebody's fridge to get beer when they were out. It was pretty intense. Tim Carr lived right across the hall from me. Curt Almsted lived downstairs, on the first floor. Terry Katzman was in the basement in an apartment on the front of the building. Steve Klemz, who was a part-timer at the store and my best friend, lived at the Modesto.

I remember specifically Paul Westerberg and I being in Terry's apartment when Terry played us the tape of the Minneapolis police from the Harmony Building show that got busted. We had just recorded "Kids Don't Follow" and the other songs for *Stink*, so that would have been March of '82. I don't remember whose idea it was, but it was one of the three of us who said, "Let's take that tape of the cops and cut it into the beginning of 'Kids Don't Follow.'" Terry did a little test cut and paste there in his apartment and then hit "play." We just fell off the chairs laughing, it was so cool. That was one big moment, I guess, in Minneapolis music history.

Later my apartment became the Replacements office. A good portion of the day when I wasn't at Oar Folk, I would be back at the Modesto working on the Replacements business, especially when the touring began. The guys would come and hang around, and they wanted to hear what kind of business was going on. I was always fine with having them there, especially Westerberg. He would sit in front of the turntable and play 45s all day. I would be on the phone and he would dig through my collection because I have a lot of singles. He is also one of those guys who, when he found one he liked, would play it over and over and over again. I would practically have to physically stop him. "Paul, do *not* play that Mission of Burma record again!"

DOUG ANDERSON: Arpad Kolath lived in the Modesto building. It says Modesto on the building, and it was very modest. Arpad had a bar in his apartment called the Blam Bar, and the only beer up there was Blatz. On any given day there would be Arpad, Bob Mould, Jesperson. Bob Stinson was there all the time, Westerberg was up there a lot, Chan and Beej would go up there. You'd sit around and listen to records. Things from Oar Folk that were brand new would ultimately end up at Arpad's. That was a very important place, particularly for hardcore. Arpad straddled both sides.

LORI BARBERO: I lived at 23rd and Garfield. I don't know how many years I lived there. A lot of bands stayed there. I remember the Minutemen staying there, and we had a party after their show with Hüsker Dü. That was fun. Drank from a beer bong. I remember the Gun Club staying at my house. There were a lot, but those two really stick out. R.E.M. came to my house. Sometimes it was just bands at my house, and sometimes there were parties.

DOUG ANDERSON: You'd go to Lori's house for parties. Anybody who was involved and any band that was in town was at those parties.

JOHN KASS: By the hardcore days, I would go to some parties at Lori Barbero's. And we would get the Minneapolis punkers to come over to the East Side keg parties in St. Paul, too, like the guys in the Replacements. Hüsker

Dü would always come to our parties, especially Grant. Bob Stinson used to come over, Paul Westerberg used to come over. I remember going to parties over in South St. Paul. That's where Grant is from.

TONY PUCCI: There was that Cold Party, over by the U on the West Bank. A half-baked idea. We almost died.

We [Man Sized Action] and the Hypstrz and a few other bands were on the bill. We're there for sound check in the afternoon, and it's a blizzard and it's way below zero. Tommy Rey was gonna start hitting his drums. I was looking at him. He says, "What are you looking at?" I said, "I want to see if they break, because I was afraid to hit mine." We were doing sound check in gloves and winter coats.

The cops busted it. And then nobody's car would start.

PAT WOODS: It was a January night, probably fifteen below, and in this empty warehouse that had no heat. Somebody had the bright idea of booking five or six bands in there. It was so flipping cold, guitar players were playing with gloves on. At some point, somebody came in with sacks and sacks of White Castles. It is often referred to as the White Castle Party. Only three bands played, and then it got busted.

DAVE PIRNER: The party where they made the recording for the Replacements' *Stink* record was the *second* best warehouse party ever—making the Cold Party the best. I don't know what made it so magical, but I think it was everybody was sort of amazed that all these people were there. You could see everybody's breath, and there was something very amusing about everybody weathering the storm and not giving a shit—it was seriously fucking cold! I remember Man Sized Action trying to keep their hands warm, and everybody had full winter gear on. Everyone was looking at each other and going, "I can't believe we're here. This is hilarious." That's what gave it so much of its charm.

At some point they brought in a shitload of White Castle hamburgers. I don't know how they pulled that off, but it kind of made the whole thing that much crazier. It felt completely natural to be involved in this sort of collective absurdity. Everybody was laughing and having a great time and blasted.

As far as the cops coming and breaking up the party, that was very common. That is just how a lot of these parties would end. You carried on until the cops threw you out. And you kept moving the party from one warehouse spot to another. I'm sure it was a very common thing in the city. Kids are trying to have parties, and then the cops find the spot, and then you try to establish a new spot. And you keep trying to find some place where the noise is not going to bring the cops, and the crowd is not going to spill into the streets and attract attention. It's kind of funny because you are trying to have a secret party with a super-loud punk rock band.

It does seem like one big, long night that lasted forever. It's that thing where you are only going to be in that situation and that place one time in your life. That's the point where you've gotten to know everybody. You know you can go to a house party and it's all friends. It takes a while for that to develop. But the beauty of it is that you can feel so comfortable walking into a house full of people—and it's not always going to be that way. Sometimes you're gonna be the stranger at the party, or the person nobody likes or something. Sometimes there was music, sometimes there wasn't. I don't remember too much trouble at all. I remember some kind of weird druggy-type things that would happen now and again. It seemed that the most violent people at all those events were the cops when they came to break the party up. *[laughs]*

The cops didn't beat people up really, but they had to be tough, because there was a lot of opposition. Mostly a lot of people that just didn't give a fuck. We weren't really doing anything wrong. Nobody was running. They were just going, "Oh, here comes the fuckin' cops again. Let's dissipate and wait for a half an hour until they leave." We weren't operating anything other than music really. It's all connected to the music and that's why it was such a comfortable environment for me. That's why it was easy to say, "Hey, here's a musician from out of town! All right, let's celebrate. Make him feel at home."

11

LADIES AND GENTLEMEN, THE SUBURBS!

The Suburbs formed in 1977 out of childhood friendships and introductions by the Suicide Commandos. The five original Suburbs were Chan Poling (keys, vocals), Beej Chaney (guitar, vocals), Bruce C. Allen (guitar, vocals), Michael Halliday (bass), and Hugo Klaers (drums). Their amalgam of punk, funk, no wave, new wave, jazz, and soul sounds combined with their brilliantly funny lyrics, unique fashion sense, and great musicianship to take the scene by storm—rapidly building audiences drawn to this new sound. Renowned for their outrageous and exuberant live performances, the Suburbs were one of the first three bands simultaneously released on Twin/Tone records in 1978. They would go on to be the first Twin/Tone band to sign with a major label. The Suburbs continue to perform and record, in a slightly different incarnation, forty years after their founding.

PETER JESPERSON: There was this band that played a couple times at the Longhorn. I remember thinking this is some goofy art rock along the lines of Devo, a little bit Talking Heads. They had some funky dancy beats. They just charmed me. They played with such enthusiasm and determination. They were called the Suburbs.

STEVE ALMAAS: Bruce Allen, the Suburbs' lead guitar player, and I went to first grade together. He was really my oldest friend. We got guitars around the same time and played in bands in junior high together. Around ninth grade, we drifted into different bands. Later, Bruce and I lived together when we moved to downtown Minneapolis. I had quit college and was playing with the Commandos. He was working as a commercial artist.

Mike Halliday, the Suburbs' bass player, went to junior high and high school with me, too—another old friend. Beej Chaney and Chan Poling were Minnetonka guys that knew Chris Osgood and Dave Ahl. Beej and Chan had been out in California and came back to Minneapolis. They wanted to join the Commandos, but we were quite happy as a three piece. So we said, "Hey, we know these guys that play: Bruce Allen and Mike Halliday." Bruce and Mike knew Hugo. So it was directly from us knowing these guys that they all got together as the Suburbs.

MICHAEL HALLIDAY: All of us kids were neighbors. It was through that Hopkins–Minnetonka connection, a lot of musicians came out of there: Jeff Waryan, Jay Peck, Robb Henry. We used to hang out in the music part of the high school and jam. I played harmonica back then. I played piano a little bit. We were all the same age and just hung out together.

HUGO KLAERS: Michael and I worked in a restaurant, and we just started talking about music. He said he played bass. I said I played drums. What it amounted to is, he had a bass and I had a drum set. So he goes, "I do know a guy that really knows how to play guitar, though." That was Bruce.

MICHAEL HALLIDAY: Tsetse Flies was me and Bruce and Hugo and Johnny Knaeble. The Tsetse Flies were joined by Chan and Beej and became the Suburbs.

CHAN POLING: I went to high school in Minneapolis. The rest of the guys were from the suburbs. I was pals with Beej since I was thirteen or fourteen years old. So we were in the same scene and hung out.

I had a friend who sang with the Litter, and there was a hard-rock band called Cain. So we were playing a lot of Long John Baldry and Stones influenced stuff. I started breaking away a little bit—really was into jazz, and I still am. My last year in high school, I did a concert at Walker Art Center, where we did very avant-garde new classical music. That's the direction I thought I was going to go in, or some new jazz thing.

Right around 1975, I went out to Los Angeles to go to school at Cal Arts. The classical world was spinning off into minimalism and into more atonal kind of music. I was interested in *that*. At that time Terry Riley and Philip Glass and those kinds of guys were brand new.

Then I heard David Bowie and the Sex Pistols and all those guys, and I went off in that direction. I left LA and returned to Minneapolis. I told my good friend Chris Osgood, "Here's some songs I want to do that I've been writing lately." They were songs that ended up on that little red record, the

Suburbs' first EP: "Stereo" and "Go" and "Your Phone" and all those short little punky tunes. Chris said, "Oh, you know who would be great for you to meet is Bruce Allen and Michael Halliday. They're on the same direction. I think you'll really get along with them."

I brought Beej into the fold, too. Beej and I had a band in LA called the Technocats for about twenty minutes. Beej and I came back and hooked up with Bruce and Michael, and we hit it off right away. We started writing original songs together. That was in '76 or '77.

BEEJ CHANEY: In the beginning I was a very angry, scared young man in high school. I just wanted out, somehow. I was a pretty shitty guitar player. But every guy wants to be a rock star when he's seventeen, get all the girls. [laughs] I wanted to do something *I* wanted to do. The anger isn't there as much, but the *hunger* in the beginning was what was fueling us.

Chan was at Cal Arts and he called me one day and said, "You've got to get out here. We've got to start writing some songs." He said, "I'm renting this place for like a hundred bucks! It's out in the middle of this valley." Chan and I lived there for about a year, and we wrote "Girlfriend" and one of the biggies, "Spring Came." That classic wouldn't be written without the Suburbs, but the concept definitely came from Chan and me living in this valley. We pretended, "Wouldn't it be funny if this valley was like a boy's camp?" That's where that little rap came from, "Where boys run free!"

I was about ninety pounds and I had a little motorcycle that I'd ride around on. I finally just went, "You know what? I'm going to die." I was starving. A can of Colt 45 and a bag of peanuts was my life. So we moved back to Minneapolis and started fishing around to start a band. We met the Tsetse Flies—two out of three of the Tsetse Flies, because Hugo was out of town. We met Bruce and Michael at the Longhorn. Then Hugo came into town. We started to rehearse and the Tsetse Flies joined the Suburbs—Chan and me—as songwriters, like Bernie Taupin and Elton John made a band. "We like your songs, too." So, "Let's punk it up and let's rock." That's how we started.

HUGO KLAERS: Chris Osgood introduced Michael and Bruce to Chan and Beej. Then they started jamming in Podany's and auditioned a bunch of drummers. Apparently the whole time Bruce and Michael are going, "We got somebody in California," and they said, "Call him up."

I wasn't doing anything, kind of bored in San Diego. Bruce called and said, "We met these two guys. You gotta come back." He actually sent me a bus ticket because I didn't want to hitchhike back.

I came back and we had our first practice the day after Thanksgiving. We played "Chemistry Set" and "Bongo Rock." It just all came together.

MICHAEL HALLIDAY: We were all knuckleheads. It was great, great chemistry. All five of us really entertained each other and really got the same thing. Always, in the early band days, it was a lot of inside humor and blah, blah, blah. But yeah, they fit in just right.

CHAN POLING: When you're in that stage of your life, energy is the thing, right? The old rock bands that were playing at that time were a little more staged and a little more staid. So our goal was to have energy. We liked to be intense, and one thing we liked was to be a little bit different. We liked to get the people moving. So yeah, we always tried to come out electric and keep the energy as high pitched as possible. It was super wild. Sometimes it was fueled by substances, but the reality is, you actually have to play and you have to sing and remember your lyrics, so there's not as much of that drug use as you may imagine.

HUGO KLAERS: Andy Schwartz came up with the name for the band. It was either gonna be Chemistry Set or the Suburbs. I almost liked Chemistry Set better. Bruce came up with the logo. He sat down at the bar sketching on a napkin shortly after he came out of the bathroom, where the guy was on the door. That's basically what he lifted it from. It was a brilliant logo.

BONNI McCONNELL: The most iconic thing Bruce brought to the band was the logo. This logo is five guys. They decided everything's going to be split five ways, equally.

I think Bruce kept the spirit of the band up. When you're on the road for hours and hours, you've got to be somewhat humorous about stuff.

BRUCE ALLEN: It was really fun doing the art direction for the Suburbs. For *Love Is the Law*, the collage on the back was supposed to be the cover. PolyGram said it was way too controversial because of the devil and Lincoln and dice—I'm serious! The back was supposed to be just this bear basking in a reef.

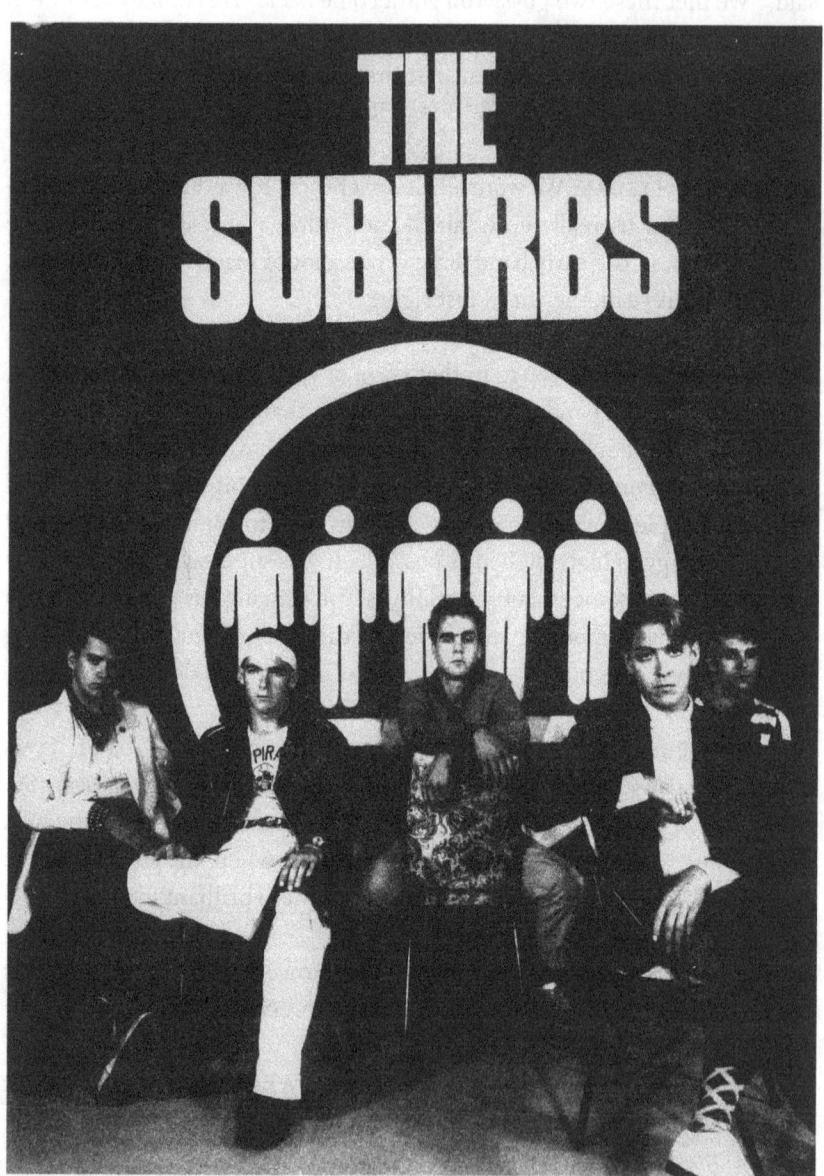

Poster of the Suburbs: *(left to right)* Chan Poling, Beej Chaney, Hugo Klaers, Bruce Allen, and Michael Halliday. COURTESY OF MIKE MADDEN

BONNI McCONNELL: Bruce was an incredible artist. *Love Is the Law* was his favorite album cover. He said the record companies didn't always approve of his artwork.

It was Chan's idea to make the record in 1992 called *Ladies and Gentlemen, the Suburbs Have Left the Building*. Bruce said, "Well, let's just make it on fire, so we had to leave."

HUGO KLAERS: Bruce was pure genius because, if we even had an idea and said, "You know...," Bruce would just run with it. The next day he'd come to practice and go, "Is this what you're talking about?" You'd be like, "Fuck, how'd you do that?" He made all the posters for every show we played. Michael and I worked for Pro-Color. We'd walk around downtown stapling up posters and delivering film to ad agencies.

BRUCE ALLEN: We had cool gigs at the Minneapolis Institute of Art. We did an opening for a Frank Stella exhibit. That show was really cool because we played right in front of Stella's art. We played Walker Art Center as well. Loring Park Music & Movies was a real exciting gig. We did Halloween gigs when we were starting out at MCAD [Minneapolis College of Art and Design].

JEFF BUSWELL: The Suburbs played Loring Park twice. The second one we trashed the park. We had like seven thousand people. The park board at the Walker was not prepared for something like that. I guess we were the first band in the park. It had to have been '81, '82 because it was all exploding for the Suburbs at that time. We were getting shows like crazy. I don't think they were getting paid a lot of money, at least not until they started headlining at the Cabooze.

CHAN POLING: The Suburbs were new on the scene and some people loved us, and some people thought we were the worst thing they'd ever seen. It was exemplified in this article that came out in the U of M paper, the *Daily*, and it had a big picture of Beej with his goggles on. It was a dual review, took up the full front page of the entertainment section. The title of the article was: "The Suburbs: A Blight or a Blast?" Down the left column was the "blight" side of the review, and the guy went on in a very reviewerly way and said how bad we were and why we stunk. Then on the right side the "blast" review said how great we were. *[laughs]*

What we were doing was brand new. If you listen to the Suburbs' music and the Commandos' music, compared to Foreigner or REO Speedwagon or something—I had a brother-in-law who loved REO Speedwagon, thought that was the coolest thing. And our music was just noise to him, just crazy nuttiness.

HUGO KLAERS: Categorizing our music, that's almost the hardest question for me to answer.

MICHAEL HALLIDAY: It was blatant: we tried not to sound like anybody else. There were a lot of bands coming out. Everybody had that sound they wanted to sound like. And we go, "Whatever we write is whatever we write. And it sounds the way we want it to sound." Some of the New York rags used to call us "Midwestern cow punks" and goofy stuff like that.

BONNI McCONNELL: The Suburbs didn't appeal to the average person on the street. They were on the fringe. Especially their early stuff. When working with a record company, how do you sell something like the Suburbs? They were so undefinable.

TERRY KATZMAN: The early Suburbs had a much more zany, irreverent sound than everyone's familiar with now. The Commandos were more the meat and potatoes punk band. And the Suburbs were the art punk band. They were the artists. A lot of it fed off Chan's talent; at that time [he was], I think, the most skilled musician in the band. But it was very new wave, too. They were a different experience than the Commandos. The Commandos were a little more focused, whereas the Suburbs would go every which way.

PETER JESPERSON: The Suburbs weren't really a punk rock band, but they had certain punky elements. And they had one of the classic punk elements, which was they got together as a group of people and not necessarily a group of musicians. I think Michael Halliday was a beginner on the bass. He was determined to get better, and he did. He had a great stage presence. Bruce Allen was one of the absolute best guitar players in the scene at the time and also one of the most stylish dressers—Bruce Allen was so fucking cool looking. He was very much a rock star. Chan is clearly a genius musician. Hugo's a great drummer. Beej is a great rhythm guitar player and an incredible performer.

I think musicianship is important, but sometimes some of the worst music made is by people who are great musicians, because they're so caught up in the playing of the instrument that they forget about the other aspects, like the writing of the song or the energy of the performance. In terms of what I look for, it's not always looking for a great musician, it's looking for somebody who can play with an exciting angle on music. The Suburbs did that.

When they first started, there were a lot of people that didn't care for what they did.

JEFF BUSWELL: At first a lot of people hated the Suburbs. A lot of people didn't like thrashing, loud music. Bars always wanted a band to do multiple sets. The Suburbs did it once or twice and quickly realized they hated it because they worked so hard, and sweated so hard, they needed to put on new suits to play a second set. They decided, "We're going to be a concert act. We're going to play ninety minutes, or seventy-five. We don't like being an opening act." It all changed beginning around '81. We slowly took over the music scene for a few years. And we were able to do what we wanted to do. Not a lot of bands can do that.

PETER JESPERSON: When Twin/Tone picked the Suburbs as one of the first bands to release, Jay Berine said to me, "Peter, they sound like they stepped right off the playground and onto the stage." I laughed and said, "What a great thing to say! Do you mind if I quote you in the press release? That's a brilliant summary of what they do." They were just like these little kids who were full of enthusiasm and excitement.

JAY BERINE: I hated the Suburbs the first time I saw them. I don't remember why, but I am also the guy who passed on Devo, so.... The Suburbs started a guerilla marketing campaign. They or their fans would call the club a dozen times a day asking when were the Suburbs going to play again. I gave in, and you know the rest.

LESLIE CARLSON PERKINS: Everything was happening. The Suburbs were taking off. At one point, my brother, Dann [Carlson], was getting them gigs. They were basically nobodies. Then the Longhorn made them into this house band, and they took off. Their music was fun and fast and the songs seemed like they were only sixty seconds long. It was just new to me. When I moved into the city and the Suburbs started practicing at the house I was living at, that's when I found a new appreciation of their music, hearing their new stuff coming out of my basement.

LORNA DOONE: I met the Suburbs early on in their career, when they were downstairs at Podany's. They had their idea down of the band they were going to be even before they wrote songs. They had that artistic bent. They played a lot. I mostly remember nights they played, because we'd dance and dance and dance.

CHUCK STATLER: A good friend of mine introduced me to the Suburbs. He said, "I'm going to go see this band the Suburbs. They're rehearsing. Do you want to come with me?" We went down to Lake Street, and there was Podany's. So the first time I saw them was not in a club or a venue; they were rehearsing. They were great because they were refreshing. It was different. It was poppy, but it was also new enough that it had an edge to it. And the guys were cool. They were in the groove at that moment.

I think Randy Levy was doing their management back in the day. I think he helped them get their record deal. I know he tried to hook us up to do a video, but it never came to pass for one reason or another.

I saw them a number of times, and they were a good live band. Beej was really in his prime then. He was really a showman. I mean, he's a performer!

HUGO KLAERS: We took a lot of pride in our shows. We didn't want to go onstage wearing the same stuff that we wore walking around. Bruce was the pioneer of dressing in a sport coat. That's what he did for his job.

MICHAEL HALLIDAY: Bruce always had the thing with the white button-down shirt; he always wore a vest, even in high school. He just carried it on with the band. He always wanted to be the dapper one.

BRUCE ALLEN: It was a very decadent existence. It was really wild because I was working for an ad agency at the same time, so I was living a double life. I'd wear a suit by day and rock out at night, but keep the suit on. That's how that started, us dressing up.

BONNI McCONNELL: Initially when they played concerts, they would perspire so much. They'd buy used suits like at Ragstock, then they'd probably throw them away after the concert because they were just toast.

Bruce was really stylish. He liked to mix up designs and colors; he didn't like anything matching.

JEFF BUSWELL: In the Longhorn days, they'd all dress any way they wanted to. Michael and Bruce dressed nicer than the other ones. Chan was more likely to wear plastic see-through pants. Then he outgrew that and wanted to be more of the sharp-dressed man. I think they all adopted that as they were turning more into the dance rock band. Except for Beej. Beej always wanted to remain quirky—duct tape around his ankles, or baby powder and glitter in his hair. He always would be left of center. That was part of the appeal of the band, I think. Beej was the show, for a long time. Beej impressed me because he was hardcore and different, like Iggy Pop was. A lot of people compared him to Iggy Pop because he profusely sweated onstage, which added to the mess he would make. You've never seen anything so bad as a guy's guitar crammed with sweat, glitter, and baby powder. There was nobody else doing what he was doing at the time. Beej was the messed up shtick part of the slick band that we had.

You didn't know what Beej was going to do, whether it would be jump into the audience or climb up some PA. Kick somebody's drink off the table, or, as he did at the Longhorn or the Cabooze, reach behind the bar, take a quart of booze, and start dumping it in people's mouths, walking down the bar, while he was singing.

It was probably at the Cabooze when he really started diving into the audience. People liked holding him up and pushing him across the crowd. Nobody ever dropped him, so he felt pretty comfortable out there for a long time. And he was always a climber. Scared us quite a bit, some of the leaps he took off speaker cabinets and stuff. He was lucky not getting hurt for the amount of things that he did over those years. Especially in the state of mind that he was in, probably.

DEBORAH HOUGH HEWITT: The first time I met the Suburbs, I met Chan and Hugo at this party. This guy I was with went to school with them. I had never heard of them. They looked like little preppy Wayzata boys. They were like a comedy team and just ping-ponged off each other. I ended up seeing them play, and I remember being blown away by Beej, because Beej was just so nuts. Beej was a little bit more on the daring side. He did a lot of things where he really could've gotten hurt—crawling around on the lights up on the stage, jumping off the stage into the crowd. Sometimes you wondered if it wasn't an act, because he would get so crazy nuts. He'd dress up in the goofiest little outfits.

Beej Chaney, "goggles on," at Jay's Longhorn, circa 1978. Photo by Bayard Michael

They had big crowds from the beginning. There would be two hundred people regularly attending their shows. When they first started at the Longhorn, I remember them looking a little bit Devo-ish. They wore hazmat suits, and the outrageous, ugly makeup was as weird as possible. I remember Beej singing and belting into the microphone and spitting all over.

CHAN POLING: Coming from LA, the style was more flamboyant there than in Minnesota. One night, I had on my plastic pants, which were taped up with artfully placed electrical tape and had paint spattered on them, and big high-heeled boots and spiked-up hair and a plastic coat made out of bags. I think I stuck out a little bit. *[laughs]* But I ended up toning it down a little. The Suburbs ended up wearing suits and that kind of thing in the '80s.

Beej always dressed crazy. There were a few people like that, but it's the Midwest. You'd look out in the crowd and there'd be just blue jeans and sweatshirts, the Converse tennies and peg-leg pants and leather jacket crowd.

At that point, there was a weird mix of disgust at the consumer culture and the "me" generation and the yuppies, of that "screw the man" kind of thing, and also chasing after it, too. You see that with some of the bands in England and the New Romantics and Depeche Mode and those kinds of guys. It was this new luxe, the hairdos and the clothes. The clothes were getting nicer. We were dressing a little nicer, too. So it was kind of alternative, but there was a decadence to it, too. I mean, rock bands have done the suit thing, obviously—the Beatles did it. We weren't the first ones. But I always liked the idea of subversion while being dressed up in the conservative costume, rather than being the obvious rocker, you know? I thought it was cool; we'd come out in our suits, and at the end of the night, everyone is trashed and sweaty. To me it seemed more interesting that way.

TIM HOLMES: David Bowie was straight-up costume. He'd wear feathers and weird space gear, breakaway pants, and stuff that wasn't like anything you'd ever seen before. Bryan Ferry is on the other side of the glam coin. That glam rock where Brian Eno wore the peacock feathers and they all wore like weird space gear, and then Bryan Ferry wore the tuxedo and it was traditional, classic, Humphrey Bogart kind of Hollywood glamour. That's where you get the Suburbs' look. It was about looking really good, not about freaking people out. The first time I saw the Suburbs they were like that, except for Beej. I picture them all in evening wear except for Beej. I picture him with his shirt off. He was the Iggy Pop of the Suburbs.

I remember liking the Suburbs right off the bat. The songs on that first EP they put out—"Chemistry Set," "Prehistoric Jaws." I don't remember the Suburbs playing a cover song, ever. That was usually how bands would draw you in. You'd go to a show and you'd know enough of the songs that they could slip in a few originals. The Suburbs didn't. Each individual song had its own character. All the songs had a Suburbs sound. They really did have a sound as a band that you could pick out of a lineup, and they had a look. It seemed like there was a weird mishmash because you had the Stooges, you had Iggy and rock music at the same time, and then there were all these things you could sing along with even though they weren't melodic hooks.

Whole rooms of people would just be screaming a certain way. It was like you knew these songs already, even though you'd never heard them before. It was that weird thing when everyone in the room is kind of on the same wavelength; the Suburbs could do that. They weren't trying to win you over. The Suburbs seemed like they had their stage act together, like they were a show band.

HUGO KLAERS: We played with the Lounge Lizards from New York, and they had sharkskin suits. When we saw them, we were like, "Suits are pretty cool." They had horns. They were kind of influential on us. That's when we started asking Max Ray to play with us. Chan invited him to play with us in New York a couple times.

CHAN POLING: I was really into some new wave bands in New York, like James Chance and the Contortions. I've always loved jazz, and all the great jazz big bands had horns. Bill Haley was real horn-driven rock and roll, too, and David Bowie played with a sax, and I liked mixing those textures together. We added Max and those guys, and they've been with us ever since.

MAX RAY: We [the Wallets] played a lot of shows with the Suburbs. We were compatriot bands and shared a lot of bills. They called me to play some horn parts on *Credit in Heaven*, which Paul Stark recorded for Twin/Tone at Blackberry Way. It was in a house with a cord running out to a Winnebago. I sat in the passenger seat of the Winnebago and played horn tracks in four, five, or six songs on that record.

PAUL STARK: You start with the rhythm section. Hugo was always more *feel* than steady beat, and Michael is a typical bass player, one who really depends on the drummer. And so the conflict in the band was always who's going to catch up with whom, which many people don't really perceive. But it gives the band such a nice, colorful character trait. Of course, Chan and Bruce had to follow that. So that even added more to it.

Chan is an orchestrator. He thinks in terms of the big picture. He's doing kind of a color backdrop with his keyboards. Bruce was just a maniac. He was always trying to invent new things to do and new ways to do it. And Beej, I have no idea what he came from. I don't know if he picked up a guitar one month before the band started or what. He was more of a character. I think the intention was that he was going to be the front man.

CHAN POLING: Twin/Tone signed Fingerprints, Curtiss A, and the Suburbs. The Suburbs' EP came out in 1978, the same year as Talking Heads' *More Songs About Building and Food* and the Commandos' and Pere Ubu's records.

We were a little younger than Talking Heads and Television and the Ramones and the Commandos, so we were this little second wave. Pop culture changes constantly. At that point there were these little waves. There was really a break from arena rock and corporate rock, a complete watershed, with the Ramones, Television, Talking Heads. These are just examples, there were others. To me, that was a real cultural shift.

MICHAEL HALLIDAY: We tried to evolve musically, too. When Talking Heads and some of these other bands came out with more of a dance groove thing, that was right up my alley, being a bass player. I loved it.

Everyone came in with their certain part and we'd just try to configure it. Chan was always the arranger, him and Bruce. We'd come in with, "Hey, I've got this part, what can we do with it?" That's basically how most of the songs in the beginning were done.

Chan and Beej brought a few of the songs back from Los Angeles when they were out doing LSD in the desert. They wrote "Bongo Rock" and "Shooting Pistols" out there. There were nine songs on the EP. All crammed onto a seven-inch.

HUGO KLAERS: We'd all contribute bits of lyrics here and there. I wrote the lyrics to "Baby Heartbeat." Michael wrote the bass line. Michael was the funk and soul in the Suburbs. We jammed, took a break, and then we went back and I had words for it. After I heard myself singing on *In Combo*, I opted to just stick to drumming.

In the early days, every idea was a song, or could be a song. It was always thought through to the end. We took a lot of pride in playing. We just always wanted to never let the energy drop, even when we were playing two sets. We'd have to take a break and come back.

MICHAEL HALLIDAY: We also did slow songs like "Girlfriend" and some ballads. Chan was the balladeer. Beej too. I think for the dancier stuff, I probably had more of an influence, like on "Waiting" and "Music for Boys." But in our first couple years, it was three-chord "wham-bam thank you ma'am!" It was an assault, for the most part.

I never had much to do with the lyrics, other than a funny line or something said on the bus. We'd be out of our minds having fun at the end of the night, then we'd jot down these things and, "What did you do with that piece of paper with that lyric last night?"

HUGO KLAERS: Like "Dish It Up": "We're a bunch of characters, sunglasses and the works" was written at a truck stop. I was standing at the counter and those guys were eating and laughing and being loud. One of the waitresses behind the counter was like, "Look at those characters, sunglasses and the works." I wrote it down and gave it to Chan.

I think sometimes we suffered for having two singers who crafted a song, and it didn't matter that it wasn't commercial. What was important was what the song was and what it was about. And a lot of times I think we suffered for our sense of humor. There was a lot of inside humor. We weren't competitive with other bands, but we did make fun of what other bands were doing.

CHAN POLING: Suicide Commandos were a great influence on us. Chris Osgood has always been one of my good friends, way before we even started playing music. So I definitely tip my hat to Chris Osgood and Dave Ahl and Steve Almaas. Steve and Bruce were childhood friends. Isn't that funny? We're all connected. And I always loved Flamingo. They had a great pop rock sense to them. They were one of my favorite bands. And the kind of art rock of NNB and those kind of bands are excellent. And the Hypstrz's energy. They would play some of the early parties with us, and we were just blown away by them. We really admired the Hypstrz.

BILL BATSON: I enjoyed the Suburbs when they first started. It was a spectacle. We did several shows with them.

JOHNNY REY: The night the Suburbs first played the Longhorn, they opened for us, Flamingo. We really liked them. They were really different. Right away, they were absolutely unique.

MIKE MADDEN: It was Flamingo that got me into the Longhorn, and the Suburbs was one of the first bands I saw there. It was something I'd never seen before, growing up with AM/FM rock and roll out in the suburbs. Beej would sing through clenched teeth and the veins on his neck would be popping. Really great shows, really entertaining.

MONTY LEE WILKES: I was eighteen or nineteen when I first saw the Suburbs. It was at a roller rink. I had never seen anything like that in my life. Bruce looked like he was in a continual orgasm. Beej was dripping sweat as though there was a fucking garden hose off the end of him. And Chan was

The Suburbs performing at the Longhorn, circa 1980. PHOTO BY STEVE MADORE

foreboding, ultra-handsome, sinister, yet intriguing. And then the rhythm section was like, "Holy fuck, I want to do *that*! I want to be in a rhythm section like *that*." Jesus, it was good, so fucking tight. I'd never heard a rhythm section like that. I decided I wanted to play bass, and I bought a bass just like Michael's. Michael Halliday was a rock-solid bass player. I liked everything about him. I thought he was amazingly cool. I liked his look, I liked his sound. I bought the same model bass because I wanted to look like him.

One of the things I liked so much about mixing with the Suburbs is that it was clean. There was a lot of room. They were very much one of my favorite bands to work for. I toured in their bus with them. I worked for them as long as I could before I had to go on to something else.

CHAN POLING: I loved Monty Lee Wilkes. Monty had something special about him. We really liked working with him. Towards the end of our run in the '80s, he had a giant, big, pro sound. He was just a joy to work with.

DANN CARLSON: I was the first person to ever play the Suburbs on the air. My show was Dr. Dann Placebo on KFAI. I had the three to six PM slot on Mondays. Garrison Keillor asked me, "How about midnight to six AM, Saturday morning?" That was a real good time slot.

I started bringing in Dead Boys and Devo and all sorts of fun stuff. And, of course, the Commandos, the Hypstrz, the Suburbs, Simba, and a few other people. I would record them at the Longhorn and play the best cuts on the air. I would say it helped the Suburbs, because people didn't really know about them at the time. More and more people started coming to the Longhorn, and then they told friends. It was mostly word of mouth. It was a big deal.

HUGO KLAERS: We used to do these weird gigs. We'd play as the Diamondbacks, Crabs of Culture, the Roamin' Catholics, Gargoyles, the Gay Pirates. We'd get dressed up for Halloween and change the name of our band for that. We could go in the Longhorn on a Sunday night and have me singing and playing guitar, Dave Ahl playing audio generator or tone generator, my sister Liz dressed like a nun singing backup, and we'd just play songs that we made up on the spot. There'd be a hundred fifty people down there on a Sunday night and they'd be happy as could be. We wouldn't practice or anything.

We weren't really competing with bands from Minneapolis because we wanted to play in New York and LA. We took off really early in a Volkswagen van and did driveaways. Remember driveaways? People used to bring their cars to a place and say, "I need this car in Los Angeles in such and such amount of time."

JEFF BUSWELL: Around 1980, Casey Macpherson offered me a job with the Suburbs. He was managing them, and they had just started doing tours. They had done one major tour before I started. I was a good driver, and that's probably what they hired me for, to be a great driver and an organizational person for them.

It was the East Coast for around five weeks, quite an adventure. The band was all excited because it was their second real tour. They'd all quit their regular jobs. For the first time, they were going to rely on the band to provide for them. We were all twenty, twenty-two, twenty-four years old. We had the world by the tail.

We left in our fifth-wheel trailer and pickup truck. We didn't get as far as Bloomington, Illinois, because the transmission blew up. We had three gigs to get to, so Max Ray and I rented a big U-Haul truck, and we put everybody in the back. We put all the cushions, pillows, and blankets in the back of the truck with all our gear. Two or three of us would fit in the front seat. It was insanely illegal. But we did it, with the door open, driving down the road.

The truck broke down on the way into New York. We were supposed to go to Albany. I called the guy to tell him that we were broken down and needed help. He hung up on us. So we decided, "We're not going there." We limped our way into New Jersey, across from Manhattan. People were getting ripped off in Manhattan, like the Commandos and the Flamin' Oh's, so we kept our gear in New Jersey, brought it over for the show, and brought it back. We went to Boston and the 9:30 Club in DC.

HUGO KLAERS: Bruce would have conversations with anybody. These guys would come back after the show and Bruce would be talking to them. We'd be like, "Is that your cousin or something?" He'd say, "No, I just met them."

But it also meant you'd walk into your hotel room and Bruce would be in there freebasing with guys he just met. He's like, "You gotta try this!" I'm like, "No, I don't. Do you know who those people are? What are you doing?" I didn't even know what freebasing was.

One time we played at the Ritz in New York, and some guys from Colorado had a room at the Waldorf Astoria. We went up on the roof at like two in the morning and we're lighting fireworks off and there's a penthouse suite that has a sliding glass door onto the roof. We went in and there were two cases of beer in the refrigerator and there was a grand piano. We sat there until six in the morning.

MICHAEL HALLIDAY: We're doing grand piano lines of cocaine and didn't get charged a dime. We left and the place was a disaster.

And then, Chicago. I think we were with PolyGram then and things were just starting to take off. We were not getting a lot of support from the label. The one thing about the music business that used to rub me is they'd stick us with a heavy metal band. I'm telling you, you're at Navy Pier and you've got Chicago's finest in their little checkerboard hats and it's black asphalt and you see thousands of people—not for us, but for the band that's coming up later. And I was really egging them on. These guys were foaming at the mouth. You could see the blood in their faces. They weren't even finishing their beers. They were just whipping them at us, picking up pieces of asphalt.

HUGO KLAERS: Chan said, "Come on, give us a chance." And the deluge really began. We made it through three songs.

It was Chicago Fest, so they had hundreds of bands. After we're done and we were walking off the stage, stuff was going all the way over, hitting the trailers behind us. There was a band—Krocus, I think, some heavy metal band from Sweden or something—and they were just looking at us like, "You guys are fucking crazy."

BEEJ CHANEY: One time when we played Chicago, three people showed up for the show. In the old days, we didn't give a fuck about anything. We didn't have any responsibility except playing. Our deal there was, I think, the door and four cases of beer. The place was honestly insane. But it broke us into Chicago a little bit. These people were floored. I swear, it was like, "We are gonna fuckin' play for these three people." Their mouths were open the whole time, the energy we were putting out there.

CHAN POLING: The Suburbs played a few shows with Iggy Pop. We opened up for Iggy in Madison and Detroit and Minneapolis. We shared a few drinks and stuff. Mainly just backstage party stuff.

BEEJ CHANEY: That guy is the greatest front man in the world, hands down. He makes Mick Jagger look like a shoe salesman. He's so spontaneous. Yeah, I'll say it. I'm like that. If I feel like doing something, I'm doing it!

CHAN POLING: We had a lot of those connections. I remember U2 hanging at my apartment in south Minneapolis. Time chatting with Bruce Springsteen and Prince, and even passing "hellos" with Dylan at parties. We rubbed elbows with all sorts of people back then. I wouldn't say we were best friends, but I had a lot of really neat experiences.

JEFF BUSWELL: Kurt Nelson always liked to play with the guys. He was always at our gigs. Beej would set his guitar down, Kurt would pick up the guitar and do Beej parts or his own. He was very much a regular, for a long time. Kurt had good bands, like his reggae band, Simba. The Pistons were a great band.

KURT NELSON: Simba was right after the Pistons. I got kicked out of the Pistons, and I just went: "Well, everybody's playing punk rock, so I'm going to play reggae." I'd already done punk rock. I had my foot in punk rock with the Suburbs. We used to get together and have off bands with various members. I played a bunch of those. So that was my punky-rocky fix.

MICHAEL HALLIDAY: We were getting really popular. I mean, lines down the block. Every time we'd play on the weekends, we'd do two nights. One time when we were playing the Longhorn, Bruce Springsteen was in town playing the Met Center.

HUGO KLAERS: Springsteen came over to the Longhorn and was playing video games. He talked to me, Michael, Chan, and Bruce. He said, "I'll come back Saturday night and play." So it was all over town that Bruce Springsteen was gonna play with us on Saturday night.

The place was packed. We were going to do our encore, and Springsteen came up and said, "It's too crazy here. I'm gonna get out of here." So we brought Kurt Nelson out, and we go, "We've got a special guest." People were just going crazy! They thought it was Bruce.

KURT NELSON: Everybody heard the buzz throughout the Longhorn: "Springsteen's here." It was packed as usual for the Suburbs. I hop onstage, and the next thing we do is we're all in a cluster crumbled on the floor, writhing around together. All that the people in the audience saw was a guy dart onstage, put on a guitar, and then disappear below eye level. The whole place crushed to the front of the stage. I'm down there on the ground, and Bruce Allen has the mic at my mouth. I'm doing a Springsteen imitation. Everybody thought I was fucking Springsteen.

HUGO KLAERS: We went to Springsteen's show on Sunday night at the Met Center, and afterward everybody's in this locker room. It was like sixty people just hanging around for like a half an hour. Then this guy comes in and says, "Everybody's gotta go." So we're waiting to walk out, and the guy goes, "Is there anybody from the Suburbs here?" We all sheepishly raise our hands, and he's like, "Come with me." There was a bunch of beer sitting out. Springsteen came out when he'd showered and sat with us for three hours. He told us, never sign with a major label. After we signed with PolyGram, Michael and I were like, "We shoulda listened to the Boss."

CHAN POLING: Back in 1979 or '80, I'd basically broken the Suburbs up and moved to Chicago. They said, "How can we get you back? We've gotta keep making records." I said, "Well, I want to do something different. I want to have piano and I want to have percussion. I want to have strings and I want to use different textures, and I want to use disco music or jazz or whatever. It's going to be funky or punky. I don't want to be stuck." Everyone said: "Yeah. Let's do it. That sounds great." So I moved back. I think the band really opened up a lot in *Credit in Heaven*, which was released in '81. That's one of my favorite records.

Then we made an EP called *Dream Hog*, which got the interest of Mercury. Mercury signed us. At that time the labels put a ton of money into your band. We made a great record for them: *Love Is the Law*. We made videos and toured all over, and we got to go to New York and do shows. Then that record didn't perform well enough for them. So we tried again. We got signed to A&M Records and made, I think, a pretty okay record called *Suburbs*, in '86. "Life Is Like" came from that record, which still is a favorite of a lot of people's, and of mine, too. It was like number one in the Twin Cities, but it didn't catch on. And the frustration of watching R.E.M. go and Replacements go and sell more records than us—we were going, "Why can't we catch on in a bigger way?" We were angry and frustrated, and not having fun. I'd be on the road for two months sometimes. I was twenty-six or something, I had a kid, and so we just called off the band. It was getting to be a drag. But we were back at it pretty soon in the early '90s, playing together again.

HUGO KLAERS: When Beej moved to LA in 1990, everything changed. It kind of put a dent in his creative juices, because the rest of us started developing. We would give Beej songs and go, "All you gotta do is write lyrics for them. Here's the chorus, and you write the verses." He was kind of stymied because he didn't have anyone to work with. Chan was his working partner. They were like Simon and Garfunkel or Hall and Oates. Chan would help arrange Beej's ideas. Toward the end, Beej stopped traveling with us.

MICHAEL HALLIDAY: Beej would just fly in a week ahead of time, rehearse a few times, and that was it. Mainly it was Chan and Bruce and Hugo and myself doing all the rehearsing. Then there were certain times when somebody was drinking too much, or doing too much of this or that. But we made it through.

JEFF BUSWELL: The Suburbs were playing ten, twelve times a month and not making any money. So they decided to call it quits. Almost immediately after they broke up, they talked about getting back together. In 1989, we did a New Year's show. We sold out the Holiday Inn on the West Bank.

MICHAEL HALLIDAY: After the Suburbs, we did the Chan Poling Band thing for a while at Harriet Island and a few other things. I really liked it because it offered me more room to grow as a bass player.

JEFF BUSWELL: Paul Stark called the shots for the reunion in the '90s. I stepped in as production manager again, and again in the early 2000s. When Bruce passed away in 2009, it made us all want to try it one more time. We've been together since then.

BEEJ CHANEY: Some of our classic songs—I swear I could barely play them, they bring me to tears every time. I didn't hang with Bruce socially because I was in California. But when I realized what it did to the music when he wasn't there anymore, it really shook me up.

BONNI McCONNELL: Bruce had a personality that was a rock musician. Even if a guy was three times bigger than him, he'd growl at him and intimidate him. He would just have so much passion that it'd freak everybody out. Bruce got along with everybody. He had friends that were musicians, artists, theater guys. He was a very popular guy in high school. Bruce felt that he had the best friends in the world and he was so blessed to have them. I think that's his legacy.

Sometimes I hear something he did, like "Rattle My Bones," he's playing guitar, and his spirit lives on in that song.

JEFF BUSWELL: I miss Bruce every day of my life. He was one strange character, but he was so funny. He was probably one of the funnier personalities in the band. Bruce was always the last person awake in the bus at night. He would be in the front seat, trying to talk while I was ignoring him most of the time. He would talk until he passed out.

TERRY KATZMAN: The Suburbs always, always made you smile. You never knew what they were going to do. It was always unpredictable. They lost

206 | *"Wham! It's a Scene": 1977–1979*

Bruce Allen of the Suburbs, at the Mudd Club in New York City, 1981.
PHOTO BY MICHAEL MARKOS

something that they can't recover without Bruce. Bruce had something special that can't be duplicated. Bruce was a good guitar player. He was, "This is my own thing that I'm going to do," and have everything revolve around it. They're still playing and they're still really good, but it's a different band.

That's one reason why I issued the *High Fidelity Boys Live 1979* CD on my Garage D'Or label in 2006. Those were songs most people didn't know about, that preceded the first record. I merged three different sets within the same time period from the Longhorn into one composite set.

STEVE BRANTSEG: Bruce Allen was the *coolest* guy. He was the first one on the scene that was really welcoming to me. After the first gig we [the Phones] did with them, he was like, "Hey, can I carry your amp? Can I carry your guitars to your car?" I'm like, "What?! You're in the Suburbs, man, and we just opened for you." In my mind they're stars and I'm just feeling eighteen years old. He and I hit it off right away.

DANIEL MURPHY: The Suburbs were so big and they were so popular. I saw them play a lot, but it was a slightly different generation. They used to pack First Avenue, and they had way more fans than the Replacements back then. The Replacements would play the Mainroom and get four hundred to six hundred people on a good night. The Suburbs would sell it out every time. It didn't really translate out of the city, but during the '80s they were the biggest thing in Minneapolis by far.

ADAM LEVY: I heard the Replacements before I heard the Suburbs, but I think the Suburbs had more of an impact on me. I was also really into Prince and that stuff, and I felt like there was this kind of color dividing line. But for some reason, the Suburbs seemed kind of soulful, as well as angular and rock music and Iggy Pop, but also this soul stuff that was happening. They were just like a consummate rock show.

JACQUE HORSCH: You had your Suburbs camp and you had your Replacements camp. It was kind of weird. They both seemed to be coming up strongly at that time. I was more of a Suburbs fan. They were an incredibly talented mix, and their writing is so beautiful and crazy at the same time. I just loved their mix; it was very catchy.

I felt they never got the right representation, and they should have been way bigger. They really should have made it. That is what I always felt. The Suburbs had a unique sound. It was danceable and super fun. They were different than the rest of the crew coming up. I couldn't describe them as punk, really. You had Beej up there, who is unique. Chan's melodies were just amazing, and Bruce's guitar playing...

MICHAEL REITER: Everyone glamorizes the Replacements and Hüsker Dü, and I do, too. I like them more than the Suburbs essentially, but everybody was going to *see* the Suburbs. The Suburbs were everywhere. They played every college show, every bar, every outdoors thing that anybody asked. They were always top notch. They always delivered. They still do.

That first record, *In Combo*, was amazing. The Suburbs were the first band out of that scene to make what seemed like a really professional record that belonged out in the world. They were the first non-mainstream band in Minneapolis that was professional. They were creating something that didn't sound like anybody. Yet, people could dance and they were a great party. They had a sweet spot.

The Suburbs were the band that should have been *huge* out of this whole thing. They really, really should have been. They got as fucked as anybody by labels and management. Everybody I knew that dealt with a label has nightmare stories about what those people do. The Suburbs were the first, biggest thing around here to get put into that machinery, where someone would go, "Wow, we are getting fucked every time."

JODY KURILLA: The Suicide Commandos weren't around that long—they committed suicide, as they said, pretty quickly. The Commandos will forever have a piece of my heart. I adored them. The Suburbs, they hauled. They were around for a while. They had a musicality to them, beyond just little punk rockers. They evolved and grew. They were very, very talented.

DAVE PIRNER: The Suburbs were very stylized. Not new wave, but more experimental in a way that involved pianos and really interesting song structures. I think the whole Roxy Music thing came a little bit later. But in the beginning, it was like, "Who the fuck *are* these guys?" They seemed to be from a different planet. Or perhaps from the suburbs, I don't know. *[laughs]*

DOUG ANDERSON: The Suburbs' first record was fucking great. I thought the Suburbs were all really good. Chan is a good composer. Bruce Allen was actually my favorite guitar player in Minneapolis. He had a real unique way of playing—you always knew it was him.

TONY PUCCI: The Suburbs were a great band. I had a lot of respect and I loved Hugo as a drummer because he was just so damn rock steady. I like the signature beat of Hugo a lot.

LU ANN KINZER: The Suburbs did some really good shows at the Cabooze and First Avenue. Sometimes a bunch of us would take a road trip to Stillwater and see them at St. Croix Boom Company. Their horn section, that's when they really upped the ante. That double album, *Credit in Heaven*—I was blown away.

CHUCK STATLER: The Suburbs have created music that stood the test of time. It sounds current; it doesn't sound dated. They could have and should have gone farther.

JEFF BUSWELL: It seemed like the Suburbs never quite had all their oars in the water at the same time. They would have a management company and a booking agent, but wouldn't have a record company. Or have a record company and a booking agency, with no management company. Or a record company and a management company without a booking agent. We always had a hard time getting along with our agents, because we didn't like the kind of shows they put us on. I think they always thought we were a punk rock band.

Then the Suburbs were categorized by other genres. I'm not sure if it was the band's idea or Steven Greenberg's idea to create more of a dance band out of them, when they started doing these dance mixes. Like "Music for Boys" and "Waiting," they'd do eight-minute dance versions to hit the dance floor.

We lost our PolyGram [Mercury] record deal to the likes of Bon Jovi, Cinderella, and Ratt, who were coming out on PolyGram in '84. When we first got signed, it looked like it was going to be good. They made the video for "Love Is the Law." Then all of a sudden Bon Jovi came on the scene, and PolyGram didn't care about us anymore. It never really got to where they wanted it to be. It was a tough time for the Suburbs.

The same thing happened with the A&M record [*Suburbs*]. We lost out to Janet Jackson and the Human League. All the records were done here in town [at Flyte Tyme Studios]. A&M's pouring all this money into the music here in Minneapolis, and we were the odd man out. The *Rolling Stone* review didn't come out until six months after the record was released. We went on tour to support the record, but the A&R people weren't there to support us.

We made our mistakes and we got taken advantage of just like everybody did in the era of major labels. Prince went through this, and anyone with any brains at that time was expressing the idea of controlling and investing in your own royalties and publishing. The worst-case scenario is the R&B guys who signed away all the rights to their songs for a little bit of cash and were just exploited. So there are varying degrees of that that we had to negotiate. At the same time, we got to make records for a larger audience.

STEVE BRANTSEG: The first time I saw the Suburbs live I was just blown away. I'd heard them on record before that, but seeing them live was so outrageously cool. I loved Chan's keyboard, and I loved Beej's weird faces and gestures, and Bruce's tasty guitar licks, and the funky rhythm section of Hugo and Michael.

When they broke up, Chan, Hugo, and Michael started the Chan Poling Band. They asked me to be the guitar player. It was kind of like the Suburbs without Bruce and Beej. We had a couple of horn players, too. That was the first time I really played with them.

Cut to some years later, I heard Bruce was sick. When he passed, it left a large Bruce-shaped hole in the music community. A couple weeks after Bruce's funeral, Chan called and said, "Hey, we're going to put together this tribute and all these friends of Bruce are gonna do songs. We'd love you to play the part of Bruce." Of course I said, "I'm totally honored." We had no intention of staying together as a band, until afterwards, it was like, "Wow, this is really fun. People love it."

CHAN POLING: We had so much fun, and Brantseg was a great collaborator. He was kind of reincarnating those Bruce licks and everything, plus bringing his own great skills. Michael Halliday had stopped playing for a while. He suffers from arthritis, and he couldn't play and kind of gave us his blessing. Beej was with us for a while, and we just kept on going. We had a huge catalog of music people loved, plus I started writing more new ones. We started enjoying ourselves again, and why not keep playing? After a few years, *Si Sauvage* came out. That album evolved out of the reunion for the Bruce tribute. Bruce gave us a reason to put it all together. It's a beautiful thing, you know?

12

LOCAL WAX: TWIN/TONE RECORDS

With the emergence of more bands on the Twin Cities scene, three men got together and decided to form a label to record and release these local acts. DJ and Oar Folkjokeopus manager Peter Jesperson, recording engineer Paul Stark, and music enthusiast and funder Charley Hallman founded the Twin/Tone record label in 1977. In the spring of 1978, Twin/Tone released its first three EP records: *1980–1990* from Curt Almsted's band Spooks, and the Suburbs' and Fingerprints' eponymous debut recordings. A year later, Twin/Tone released *The Commandos Commit Suicide Dance Concert*, recorded live at Jay's Longhorn, and shortly thereafter released the compilation double album *Big Hits of Mid-America Volume Three*. The year 1980 saw the release of the Suburbs' full-length debut, *In Combo*. A year later, Jesperson brought the up-and-coming Replacements into the fold. By 1984, Twin/Tone had released forty-one records, and they would soon add such emerging acts as Soul Asylum, the Wallets, Babes in Toyland, Trip Shakespeare, the Jayhawks, and more.

PETER JESPERSON: When we were coming up on the time Twin/Tone started, I thought that there needed to be records made of Curt Almsted, because he was such an important figure on the local scene. We've often said that Twin/Tone was practically forced into existence just by the number of great groups in that burgeoning scene—Curt, Suicide Commandos, Flamingo, etc.

It was a really exciting time because you could feel something starting to develop, and we were right there on the ground floor. Paul Stark, who was a recording engineer, had a studio over in Dinkytown called p. david studios, where he had recorded the first couple of Suicide Commandos 45s, among other local groups. Paul also did live sound for several bands and helped groups get their stage act together. He was involved with setting up lighting systems and PAs, so he was one ingredient.

Charley Hallman was a sportswriter for the *St. Paul Pioneer Press*, but he moonlighted writing record reviews and was a big music fan. He took a challenge from his editor who said, "Hey, you're always writing about these national or international groups. Why don't you write about the local bands?" Charley said, "Well, I don't really know much about the local bands." His editor said, "I'll challenge you then. Why don't you go find a great local group to write about?"

So Charley started trolling the clubs and ran into the Suicide Commandos and fell in love with their music, and consequently met Paul Stark. Paul and Charley had it in their heads—this is right as independent labels were really starting to happen—that maybe they could start an independent label.

After Charley and I met, he became a regular at Oar Folk. Charley was one of the dearest people, a little wacky but in a good way, and a super big music fan. He was the biggest Beach Boys fan I ever knew.

CHRIS OSGOOD: Paul Stark noticed there were about a thousand people that went out to support bands at the Longhorn regularly—us, Curtiss A, Flamingo/Flamin' Oh's. And he thought: If these thousand people bought the records of those bands, it could be viable to start a record company. Twin/Tone could have enough of a fan base to, if not grow, at least survive. That was honestly his thinking. And it worked. And the impact, with the Suburbs and the Pistons and Curtiss A and all the bands that were immediately to follow, was a big shot in the arm.

Charley Hallman and Paul Stark—whom I knew from us recording at his studio—were looking for a third person to join them. They wanted a triumvirate to start what would become Twin/Tone Records.

Charley loved the Commandos, and we loved him, too. He wanted the Commandos to be the first band signed to Twin/Tone. The Commandos were going to be the first release. I was thrilled, but at the very same moment, in October of '77, we got an offer from Cliff Bernstein and Blank Records via Phonogram and Mercury. We took that instead. But I went to work for Twin/Tone a few years later. Our next record was a Twin/Tone record, as a matter of fact: *The Commandos Commit Suicide Dance Concert*.

PETER JESPERSON: Chris gracefully bowed out. He thought I might be well suited to be involved as far as starting a record label was concerned. So Chris called me up and said, "Hey, I'm talking to these two guys who are

Paul Stark recording *The Suicide Commandos Make a Record* at Sound 80, November 1977.
Photo by Danny Amis

interested in maybe starting a local label. Would you like to get together and have lunch with them?" I said, "Sure." And we all met at William's Pub, in the Uptown area. They invited me to join and I accepted. That's where the seeds of Twin/Tone were sown.

Flamingo, Suicide Commandos, and Curt were the three most popular groups at the Longhorn at that time. I said, "Curt has got to be the first artist that gets signed to the new label. We've got to sign Thumbs Up." I love the Commandos and I love Flamingo, but Curt was always my—I don't want to say favorite because I loved them all—but Curt was someone who really spoke to me. When I heard Curt, I thought, "This guy is as good as anybody going right now." He has such a vast repertoire and by that time had just started to write songs and play more original material in the sets. So Curt was a given.

Also around that time, some high school buddies of mine, Mike Owens and Kevin Glynn, had the band Fingerprints, and they had a recording studio and a bunch of recording gear set up in Mike's parents' basement in Minnetonka. They called it Blackberry Way. They ended up moving their gear into Paul Stark's studio, p. david studios in Dinkytown. I don't know if I introduced them to Paul, but it quickly coalesced into them saying, "Hey, we want to move our recording gear into the city. How about we combine our stuff with your stuff?" Paul said, "Okay, sounds good." So, if these guys are going to be involved in the studio, Fingerprints is a little bit of a given to be on the label as well. But of course they were unquestionably one of the best bands on the scene.

CURT ALMSTED: A couple of the Fingerprints guys, Mike Owens and Steve Fjelstad, lived at Blackberry Way, where the recording was done. They did some of the engineering on the Spooks recording.

MICHAEL OWENS: We were starting the studio, and Fingerprints was starting. We went there to try out for Twin/Tone, and I think we were kind of a done deal. Paul had p. david studios in his house, and he had equipment that wasn't anywhere near as good as what we had. He wanted to concentrate on Twin/Tone, and we needed a place to work out of. And so we moved all of our stuff down there.

PETER JESPERSON: On January 31 of '78 we auditioned and recorded five groups over a two- to three-day period at Paul Stark's studio. There was Thumbs Up with Curt—by the time we were ready to put the record out, he had changed the name of the band to Spooks—the Suburbs, and Fingerprints, but we also recorded Riff Raff and Ice Stars. We tried to decide what came across best on tape.

Robert Ivers and Ice Stars did some recording. Riff Raff had Kevin Hazlett, who had two brothers that were later very prominent in the music scene: bassist John Hazlett and drummer Buck Hazlett, one of the all-time best drummers in Minneapolis.

The Suburbs were the new young upstarts when Twin/Tone first met in October of '77, a little less rock and roll and a little more modern than Curt Almsted or Fingerprints. I was struck by them, and I said, "We've got to bring the Suburbs into this audition." I remember everybody looking at me, "Really? The Suburbs?" They just had a charm and a quality that I thought, "This is really something to seriously consider." Maybe I saw them more than Paul Stark or Charley Hallman had, because I was at the Longhorn more.

People were ticked off that we were looking at the Suburbs, because there were other musicians that had been around the block a few more times and "paid their dues." They were like, "Why are you inviting these guys?"

PAUL STARK: They were quirky, fun songs. Chan Poling went to the same high school I did. I had recorded him in a jazz fusion band a few years earlier. Peter arranged for me to see the band. I recognized Chan right away, and that sparked my imagination. Chan's a very talented musician. And the band was really a bunch of misfits that complemented him.

PETER JESPERSON: All this had been planned before we'd even come up with a name for the label. I was thinking that it would be cool to have something that had a local feel to it but would still be a name we could live with for many years to come.

We used to have our meetings on Tuesdays at the CC Tap, before we had an office. We said, "Hey, we've gotta decide on the label by next Tuesday because we're gonna press the records, and we need to come up with a logo." So the night before the meeting, I literally had a dream of a label called Twin/Tone, and I woke up enough to jot it down so I wouldn't forget.

The next morning I didn't really remember the dream but luckily there was this matchbook on my nightstand with my scribbling on it. "What's this? Twin/Tone? Oh yeah, that was the name I thought of for a label. I like that." It had the word "Twin" with the slanted line after it. I brought that to the meeting and everyone liked it.

Bruce Allen's sister Cynthia—who married Dave Ahl—designed the first Twin/Tone logo. Bruce did a lot of our graphics, and he revised the Twin/Tone logo a few times over the years. He did so many of our early album covers; he was our in-house designer. He did the Replacements' *Sorry Ma, Forgot to Take Out the Trash*, and he built the template for the stamps we used for *Stink*. Then Grant Hart did *Hootenanny*, then Bruce did *Let It Be*. So Bruce did three of the four Twin/Tone Replacements album covers.

It was a great period. Great community and everyone could feel something was beginning. It was a very heady time, when we really felt empowered and we'd heard about all these scenes developing different places. We thought, "Wow, it's happening in Minneapolis and St. Paul as well."

The Suburbs, Fingerprints, and Spooks were the first releases. We did three seven-inch EPs. It was a trend to do things on colored vinyl, so we did them on red vinyl.

The first three Twin/Tone EP releases: *The Suburbs* (TTR 7801), *1980–1990* by Spooks (TTR 7802), and *Fingerprints* (TTR 7803). ALL IMAGES COURTESY OF DICK CHAMP

HUGO KLAERS: When Twin/Tone formed and the red records came out, I mean, we were blown away that we even got asked. I know the Flamin' Oh's turned them down and I don't know if that's why we got asked, but somehow we wound up with Paul Stark. He got his hooks in us. Paul, sweetheart that he is, he's kind of like Mr. Spock. Everything's just logical to him.

We had a ton of songs that were all like a minute and a half long. We said to Paul, "How many songs can we put on it?" He said, "You can put on as many as you want." So I don't know how many we recorded—but we put nine on there.

When it came out, we listened to the records and were like, "How come the Spooks record and the Fingerprints record sounds so much nicer than ours?" Paul goes, "Well, that's because you put so many songs on it. The grooves are so close together." We were like, "Well, you said you could put on as many songs as we wanted!"

PETER JESPERSON: We were novices learning, flying by the seat of our pants, but I think everybody understood that. One of the greatest examples documented was Bruce Allen had designed those EP sleeves and mistakenly made them a fraction of an inch too big for the automated folder and gluer machine at the pressing plant.

So we had them send us the sleeves and we folded and glued the first few thousand by hand. We did a lot of that at the Longhorn, and a lot of the bands would do it with us. We would say, "The room opens up at 9:00 PM, Paul Stark and I are going to be down at the club at 7:00 PM. Anybody that can give us a hand, please come ahead of time." We had bunches of people sitting around tables folding and gluing those EPs. It felt so good.

JOHN KASS: When the first three little red seven-inch EPs came out, I bought all three and I thought they were amazing. We were trying to get everything we could that was local and new wave, so the Flamingo record, the first three Twin/Tones, Hüsker Dü, and the Dads 45.

ROBB HENRY: Back in the early '70s, high school friends and I used to have a lot of jam sessions out in the Minnetonka–Hopkins area, where I grew up. I jammed with Steve Fjelstad quite a bit. Around 1974, I met Mark Throne. We had jam sessions. Kevin Glynn was on the drums. I was playing clubs with these semi-professional bands. It was fun to go to the garage jam session and turn up the volume to eleven.

When the Rolling Stones album *It's Only Rock and Roll* came out, they had a song called "Fingerprint File." I remember thinking, "That would be a good name for a band: Fingerprints." Mark, Steve, Kevin, and I started to play a lot in Mark's garage and got a few little gigs.

In the spring of 1977, I was sharing a duplex with drummer Jim Hines, from Sweet Thing, the band that I was in with Carol Peltier. We had a little attic studio up above our duplex. Mark had songs he wrote, and we would record them. I would play the guitar and bass parts, Jim would play the drums, and Mark would put the vocal on top. They were nice recordings. That was probably the first actual Fingerprints stuff. We tried to redo them in the studio later, [but] that didn't work out. Sometimes the demos that you make are better. *[laughs]* Plus, it was different musicians.

A couple of years later, Mike Owens started playing with Mark and Kevin and Steve, and he called me up one day and asked if he could use the name Fingerprints. This was probably September or October of '77. I said, "Yeah." He said they were playing at the Longhorn downtown. I went down to see him, and I thought: "Well, it sounds pretty good, but I think they need a lead guitar player." So I said, "I think you guys need a lead guitar player. I'm available." So, boom. I was in the band.

It was fun to play in a group like that because I had never been able to do it out of the garage. And there was actually a place to do it then, because the Longhorn would hire rock and roll bands. I could let go a little bit more and it was nice to do that. You know, going from something where it's really disciplined, going into something where it's pretty undisciplined was refreshing.

MICHAEL OWENS: Fingerprints is kind of the forgotten band, it seems like, because we didn't get an album out. But three of us owned Blackberry Way, and we had as much to do with anything that happened here as anybody did. But what happened was we had this eight-track Scully one-inch tape machine, and it didn't have a tape counter, so it was hard to find where the songs were. I don't remember if it was Steve Fjelstad or myself who had the idea of these Scotch stick-em dots—you put them between the songs, and then when it rewound, it would go click-click-click, so you could tell where the beginnings of the songs were. I got the brilliant idea of marking the third verse of the lead solo. And the dots ate through the tape.

So the Fingerprints album never got done. We probably had alternate versions of songs, but at the time, you think the ones you're picking are the best version. And that was towards the end of the band. Otherwise, we would have recorded everything over again.

TERRY KATZMAN: Fingerprints would be another example of a band that should've had their full-length release that didn't. That's another thing that I've thought about resurrecting, but the source tapes we have are really, really poor. It's great stuff.

I did an interview with Curtiss A and Jesperson shortly after the first record came out, when I was writing for the *Insider*. Curt was another section of the pie like NNB, like Flamingo, like Suicide Commandos. They all had an appeal basically to everyone, but they had their own niche of fans. And everybody played together back then. NNB played with the Commandos two or three times. There's some pretty solid tapes that we made of NNB. Everyone would love to hear it. They had enough for one album.

DICK CHAMP: It was kind of funny because we decided not to go to Twin/Tone for our record "Slack," mostly because we wanted more control, to do things our way. I suppose we were a little bit uppity in that respect. For that I apologize, especially to Peter.

It was in June '78 and Peter and Charley and Paul, the Twin/Tone folks, were just about to release the Spooks, Fingerprints, and Suburbs records. They were like five minutes behind us. So we thought the timing was hilarious. There was no malice involved, but I could tell they were a little bit worked up about that, that we were kind of stealing some of their fire. But we just thought it was funny. And "Slack" is a good record. It's really well made, great rock lyrics, great guitar stuff. The fact that we just laid it on the public was a hype. We rode that pretty good. We thought it would be an effective sort of publicity stunt so we would be sure to get some attention, which it absolutely did.

JOHN KASS: I couldn't find the NNB 45 anywhere. My friend had it and I loved it. So I got Twin/Tone's phone number and I called one night and I ended up getting Paul Stark on the phone. This is when I'm like seventeen. Paul's like, "Oh yeah, just send me three bucks, and I'll send you a copy." So that was my introduction to Twin/Tone directly.

Wave 7 is Mark Freeman's label. Twin/Tone was distributing it. Twin/Tone distributed a couple of other things like the Hypstrz EP and the "Slack" record. Both of those bands were on *Big Hits of Mid-America*, but they weren't on the label.

PETER JESPERSON: At that time Twin/Tone was the only game in town really. I believe we did have a big impact, and it gave a lot of people not only a reason to tour but something to tour with. You needed to have records out to get people into the clubs in the various cities you were going to. At that time people didn't carry merchandise on the road and sell their records like they do now. We tried to get the records in the stores in those cities. I'm sure a lot of those bands were able to expand their reach outside of the local market.

Twin/Tone was so exciting and we were early in that era of the indie labels and we really didn't know how to go about it. Because none of us had spent a lot of time outside of Minneapolis, there was a naïveté to some degree, which I think is good in some ways and not good in other ways. Some of those records maybe haven't held up as well as they could've if we'd had a little broader knowledge, but I'm immensely proud of what we did with Twin/Tone. I think that we generally speaking made pretty good decisions and we made some really good records. It's amazing to me now how I run into people who work for major labels or big-shot law firms, or *Rolling Stone* or *MOJO* or whatever, and they say they grew up on Twin/Tone records. I think some of those records really influenced people in a positive way. Certainly there's a lot of local Minnesota pride, and it's pretty far reaching.

CURT ALMSTED: The Suburbs and Spooks, Paul Stark, Charley Hallman, and Peter Jesperson each brought something to the party. They each had assets that would complement each other. Peter had a lot of musical taste and promotion ideas. Paul had the equipment and the tenacity to sit through all the BS of recording people, and Charley brought some financing and a lot of enthusiasm. There was a sense of camaraderie.

Twin/Tone showed people that you could start something small and have success, get noticed and get notoriety. They gave us not only the Replacements, but Soul Asylum, the Jayhawks, and others.

BOB DUNLAP: You always knew you were doing good if Peter showed interest in you. It was a time when it was very difficult for most bands to afford to make a recording, much less putting it on any kind of label that would garner publicity. So Twin/Tone was a very key thing for bands to get anywhere. You had to get some press interested in you. There were other labels back then that sure played a key part in it, but Twin/Tone was a tastemaker label, where if Twin/Tone would take you, it was a good thing for your band. Peter was instrumental in guiding, a real key figure in the local scene—not that the other two guys involved in the label weren't in their own way. Peter was always helping songwriters find their style and harness it, just by showing interest in it, because that's what you're writing songs for, to spark interest. If Peter was interested in it, you knew other people would be interested in it. He played a key role in that way.

All songwriters need a window to create their vision in. There is always someone like Peter who plays a role in guiding what that vision is, because you can't do it self-contained. You need somebody to bounce it off of, to say, "Is this any good?" There is no one capable of writing only great songs. Even the best songwriters write horrible clunkers. You've got to have somebody close enough to you to tell you a song is *not* a good song, without you getting angry and yelling at them to get out of the room. All artists need a wall to bounce off of.

The worst thing you can do as a songwriter is write a bad song. It could kill your career if you're not careful. All the great songwriters I've ever been around have those real stinkers in the back closet somewhere, what they thought was the best thing they'd ever written, and everyone around them said, "No, it isn't." So, Peter was good at discriminating among what was good about your newest pile of songs and what was not.

CHRIS OSGOOD: After doing *Make a Record* with Blank, our next record was a Twin/Tone record, *The Commandos Commit Suicide Dance Concert*. Then we recorded *Big Hits of Mid-America Volume Three* in December 1978. It was released in '79.

The band had broken up Thanksgiving weekend. *Commandos Commit Suicide* was recorded Thanksgiving weekend of '78, and then posthumously we recorded three songs for *Big Hits of Mid-America*, including Dave Ahl's "Weekend Warrior," Steve Almaas's "You're Not the First One," then my song, "Complicated Fun." Those turned out to be some of our most popular songs, which we didn't get a chance to record until after we'd broken up. I don't know how many other bands can say that.

STEVE ALMAAS: Twin/Tone is really sort of post-Commandos. With regard to *Big Hits*, I'm sort of tickled now by how many different groups I play with on that thing. I play with the Commandos, then Karen Haglof's band with Jan King, the Wad. I played one of Curt Almsted's things on there. That extracurricular stuff on *Big Hits* was a lot of fun.

WAYNE HASTI: It was an honor to be on *Big Hits*. All the other bands were really cool. That was a really good thing. So we recorded and were really happy with how quickly we were accepted. We hit the nerve. We were really proud of our music. We knew it was good.

I was familiar with the two Soma records. It was really strange Twin/Tone used the name.

CHRIS OSGOOD: We called it *Big Hits* because we were fans of Soma's *Big Hits of Mid-America Volume One* and *Volume Two* [local compilations from the '60s]. I'm the guy that got to write the liner notes for *Big Hits of Mid-America Volume Three*.

There's a fun spread on that double album, because we all went to the photo booth at Woolworth downtown to get our pictures taken. And if you hold *Big Hits* out, you can see all of us around the counter in that sort of posterized picture.

JOHN KASS: That compilation, *Big Hits Volume Three*, was so influential for me and my friends. There were kids in garages everywhere trying to learn how to play half the songs on that record.

Poster for Twin/Tone's *Big Hits of Mid-America Volume Three*. COURTESY OF DICK CHAMP

KURT NELSON: On *Big Hits*, the Pistons did "She Got Sex" and "Misery," a country song. Guitarist Frank Berry had a reputation from playing with Curtiss A's Spooks, so we got a go-ahead to record something on their *Big Hits* thing.

Frank was trying to be country ahead of all the country, which was actually just keeping up with the Rolling Stones, because that was when they did "Faraway Eyes," that stuff. Frank taught me the Keith Richards five string open tuning trick, which Keith Richards does on half the stuff. That's why Keith Richards sounds like Keith Richards. "Brown Sugar," "Can't You Hear Me Knocking"—that's all five strings and tuned to an open chord. I played nothing but for ten years with You and Whose Army. No Stones covers, though. I wrote a shitload of songs using that.

Frank quit, they got me in, and we finished the rest of the album. The Pistons' *Flight 581* and the Suburbs' second record, *Credit in Heaven*, and the Replacements' debut album, *Sorry Ma, Forgot to Take Out the Trash*, were all put out at the same time, and Twin/Tone put their weight behind the Suburbs and the Replacements. After that, they were getting new bands. They never came back to the Pistons to say, "Hey, you guys should record some of these new ones." I was writing like crazy with the new Pistons. We were still playing good shows and writing great songs.

GRADY LINEHAN: I was working at Twin/Tone at the time of *Sorry Ma* and *Stink*. I did all sorts of stuff for Twin/Tone. I did a lot of their national distribution. Peter Jesperson and Blake Gumprecht did a lot of the radio and press, I was more of a retail and distribution guy. I was the guy the band yelled at when they would get to a town, "Can't find a fucking record anywhere. Jesus, what's wrong with you?" I was always like, "They've got to be there somewhere. I even sent them some copies for *free*." So they'd go to the used bin, and they were all in the used bin. And Paul [Westerberg] used to go just nuts. Just *nuts*!

We had a game plan at that time. It was really hard to get a distributor to take your records. There were a lot of reasons for that, but the trick for a new band was basically, "Here, I'm going to send you this box of records. I want you to get them out into stores for me. They're no cost. Get them into three or four of your best stores in town, *please*." In Boston, you'd go to some stores and there'd be stuff. Philadelphia, there'd be stuff. DC, we would find records. But New York was a waste of time. There wasn't a record to be found. And it was sad because Robert Christgau, the writer for the *Village Voice*, was high on Hüsker Dü and he was increasingly high on the Replacements. So he was building some action for them, but you couldn't get their music anywhere. I'm sure it was frustrating for the Replacements, because they were starting to play a lot, and to get the records out was almost impossible.

I recall Peter and me sitting in Paul Stark's garage with the white jackets for *Stink*, and we were literally hand stamping the covers. And so you're sitting there with an inkpad, a case of beer, one after another, cases. We had to do like a thousand, because we had to send them to the pressing plant to run the vinyl. Tower Records in New York said they wouldn't take it without a bar code. Peter and I said, "No problem." So we made punk rock–style faux barcodes—got forks out, dipped them in the ink, put them on the back bottom right corner, put them in the dang box, and sent them off. I don't know how many hundreds Peter and I did with the fork. It's absolutely true.

CHRIS OSGOOD: The Replacements started to take off, so [since Peter was away a lot] in November '84, I came back to Twin/Tone to be A&R guy. I had to work for free for a month, until January 1. Paul found it in his heart to give me a small paycheck after that.

The Replacements already had *Sorry Ma*. I remember stamping *Stink* right after I got there—or maybe it was before. The Suburbs were the big band when I came back in '84. The Replacements became the big band after that. *Let It Be* was the forty-first release on Twin/Tone. And it was in 1984.

GRADY LINEHAN: By god, it was fun. It was really a different time. Safety Last was on the label, Loud Fast Rules was at about the same time I was there, before they became Soul Asylum. The Phones put out an album, and Jeff Waryan's *Figures*. We all loved it. It was tough to sell, but it was a great record.

STEVE BRANTSEG: Peter Jesperson, especially, was really hot on the Phones. The Phones were a fun, energetic rock and raw live band. I don't think it translated into the recordings, at least with the Twin/Tone records that the Phones did. The recordings aren't as rocking as we were live. The records sound really polished, very atmospheric, and overproduced. But Twin/Tone wanted to put it out, so they put it out.

Twin/Tone did help immensely. They encouraged bands to sound like themselves and not try to sound like they were from anywhere else. They encouraged the originality of the bands. I think they were a *huge* influence, still to this day.

There were quite a few independent labels that tried coming up and didn't make the impression or have the influence that Twin/Tone did. You'd hear about other independent labels that tried to market bands to do whatever was cool at the time. Twin/Tone seems to carry a lasting reverberation in Minneapolis history. They had so many amazing bands: the Suburbs, Curtiss A, the Replacements, the Phones, Soul Asylum.

CHRIS OSGOOD: I was the in-house producer for Twin/Tone for a while. I did Soul Asylum's *While You Were Out*. Chopper remixed one of those songs we were going to release as a single, "Closer to the Stars." And we went on before and after that, in the very room, Studio A, in Nicollet Studios that Dave and I recorded in, in 1971 as Sue Veneer and the Mementos, when it was called Cookhouse—a hundred Twin/Tone records we recorded there. That's where the Hüsker's *Warehouse: Songs and Stories* and the Replacements' *Tim* happened. I'm on *Tim*, foot stomping. Felgie [Steve Fjelstad] was the engineer for almost every record I produced there, except for Têtes Noires' *American Dream*—Jerry Steckling was the engineer on that record. It's called Creation Audio now.

ROD GORDON: The Wallets recorded the *Take It* record in New Orleans, and it came out on Twin/Tone [in 1986]. It seemed like they didn't really want us at first. But then after we started recording in New Orleans with Allen Toussaint, we ended up bringing all the tapes back here and mixing it at Twin/Tone. So they decided we were okay, I guess. *[laughs]* They were good guys.

DANIEL MURPHY: Dave Ayers was a really good friend of mine, and he later became our [Soul Asylum's] manager. We opened for the Replacements in Merlyn's, a club in Madison. After the show Peter Jesperson comes into our dressing room with two pitchers of beer and says, "How would you guys like to record for Twin/Tone?" We're like, "Holy fuck." So it was really one of our most exciting days in music, because at that point Twin/Tone was the only game in town. You're not gonna sign to A&M Records from Minneapolis. There was just no interest. So that was really cool.

DAVE PIRNER: That was the biggest day of my life! I don't recall being more excited about anything than when Peter Jesperson decided he wanted to sign us to Twin/Tone. I thought, "I have gone as far as anyone can go, and I've gone farther than I expected." I was beside myself with excitement. I was going to make a record! I couldn't believe it. It was my dream. That was a big deal. I remember sitting with Karl [Mueller] going, "Holy shit man, we got a fucking record deal! And Twin/Tone is where it's at." I met Paul Stark and the gang and things went from there.

DANIEL MURPHY: Our first record was kind of a disaster. *Say What You Will.* We didn't have our shit together. There was a ton of stuff we recorded, maybe twenty songs, and we put eight or nine on an EP. We hired Bob Mould to produce it. He said, "Why don't you put all your amps in a circle in the studio." I didn't like the studio; they didn't like us. It was Blackberry Way. Steve Fjelstad and Dave Pirner did not hit it off at all. We had two or three days to do the whole fucking thing. We just didn't know what we were doing. We were freaked out by the studio. I think Twin/Tone lost faith in us. I mean, our first EP just wasn't any good. We wanted to capture what we did live. It didn't sound like us, it didn't have any charm.

Making a record is really methodical, and it's not about your impulse. Your impulse is to be a bratty kid and yell and scream. It's more about the sentiment you were thinking of when you wrote the song. You need to capture the pace of that and the feelings you had. And you can't really do that if you're going to record twenty songs in three days. Everything gets two takes.

Chris Osgood wanted to have stationery printed up that said: "Twin/Tone, where artistic dreams get dashed on the shores of fiscal reality." That was like his motto for the label. He's such a funny guy.

DALE T. NELSON: I worked at Twin/Tone from '87 to '91. There was Paul Stark and Dave Ayers and Jill Fonaas and Abbie Kane. They started hiring more because the catalog was getting big and the Replacements' *Let It Be* record became the best selling record on the label. We're going, "What the fuck, man? We've only got four people in the office."

JOHN KASS: In the 1980s, there was no other independent label as successful as Twin/Tone in terms of getting records out there and then also getting the bands onto major labels. Twenty-five bands graduated to major labels. That's *insane* from a town like Minneapolis. They had records by Robyn Hitchcock and Pere Ubu. You think of all the stuff that was on the label, it's pretty bizarre that they had such a long shadow in terms of influence.

As Twin/Tone was becoming more and more successful, more and more people wanted to carry their records. Chris Osgood was in charge of the distribution; I think he got it up to thirty-five different distributors handling Twin/Tone product. Chris was the guy who ballooned the number of customers Twin/Tone had during that era when everyone wanted the Replacements records, and the Suburbs records were getting played on Top 40 radio stations. Even the Wallets had a Top 40 hit.

Usually the radio and press was handled by Peter and a guy named Blake Gumprecht. Jill Fonaas and Blake Gumprecht had a huge impact on Twin/Tone becoming more hip to the *Village Voice* and college radio stations. There was also David Ayers, a writer from the *Minnesota Daily*, who ended up working at Twin/Tone. And then Chris was there to up the distribution quotient. Peter was always good with the press. Paul was always good with taking care of the business and technical stuff. Paul was a technical wiz. So it was like the perfect storm of all those people being together.

Paul's a genius. I love Peter, but Paul, he's like the mad scientist. I learned so much about how to get around the rules from Paul because he was the master at it—in a good way. I don't mean it in a bad way. It's just that he's a crafty son of a bitch; my hero for sure. I learned how the record contracts work. It's like a chess game, and that's the first maneuvers of a label. Also how Paul would get the process of coordinating getting the recording and manufacturing done and when to do the promotion for press, when to do the booking, and how they all related to each other. If you're gonna do this business you need to have all the pieces of the puzzle. You need to have a booking agent, a label, a publicist, and a manager. If you're missing one of the pieces, there's no way it can work. That's what I learned from Twin/Tone.

DANIEL MURPHY: Twin/Tone was a weird place to work. Paul Stark, I never got him. I don't think he got us either, but I think he was bright. Everybody at Twin/Tone was in the past, but Paul's like, "Music's gonna be on a plastic storage disc." And we're like, "No fucking way, dude, you're crazy. Vinyl will be around forever." So he was *that* person at Twin/Tone.

The rest of Twin/Tone loved rock and roll, and Paul didn't love it at all. The first time we recorded for Twin/Tone we went out to their mobile truck, parked out in Roseville somewhere, and Paul was in there and Peter was there, and we set up—"Play some of your songs." And that didn't go well at all. Paul thought Peter was crazy for signing us. We weren't very good. We had a spark and we had a lot of complex ideas for songs that had tons and tons of parts, but it wasn't focused. It took us a while to write simpler songs that were more fun to play rather than a song that had eleven parts when you could've gotten by with three.

TERRY KATZMAN: Reflex Records was, really, a reaction to Twin/Tone Records passing on Hüsker Dü. That's a simplified version of it, but it was clear that they weren't Twin/Tone material back then. They did submit the early demo to Twin/Tone. I think there was a comment, from Charley Hallman or Peter: "Sounds too much like Public Image Limited." Which it did, actually; take that as a compliment.

Hüsker Dü and I formed Reflex together. They didn't want to wait around for somebody to put a record out, so they just said: "We're going to do it ourselves, and promote it ourselves, and have something to take on tour with us." And that's how Reflex started.

It gradually turned into something else, where we started looking for other bands to record. It developed into this little co-op. Bob had his bands, like Articles of Faith, and I had my bands, like Rifle Sport. We did the first Man Sized Action record.

The first release I worked on was the "Statues" single. Then *Everything Falls Apart* was the first full-length on the label. Rifle Sport's *Voice of Reason* and Man Sized Action's *Claustrophobia* became the next two full-length LPs. Shortly after that, we started working with Ground Zero and Articles of Faith from Chicago. That's when Dutch East India started to set up a distribution deal for the Reflex stuff, which lasted three, maybe four years.

We did a second session with Rifle Sport, and it's too bad that never came out, because it was way better than the first album. It was basically the label was not as interested in doing a second Rifle Sport as I thought they would be. But that was fine and I knew it wasn't gonna happen and they knew it wasn't gonna happen, so we made a really good demo, which still exists.

Dutch East India did distribution for our last four projects: Articles of Faith's *Give Thanks*, Man Sized Action's *Five Story Garage*, the second Ground Zero record, *Pink*, and then the Minutemen EP *Tour-Spiel*, which was sort of a payback to them because they put the Hüsker's "In a Free Land" on their New Alliance label.

By that time it was almost over. I knew Hüsker Dü was getting so busy with playing and touring, which sort of started the rise of Reflex and also the end of it, eventually. They couldn't give it attention, and I didn't have the time to do it. I had the record store, and it just wasn't working. But we did twelve records altogether. That's pretty good for back then.

TOM HAZELMYER: I did a bunch of work with Reflex in the couple of years leading up to the Otto's Chemical Lounge seven-inch [released by Reflex in 1983]. It was about as DIY a label as it could possibly be, and Bob and Grant weren't shy about doling out some of the work to us hangers-on. It was my first experience in dealing with a label.

I got to watch Hüsker Dü go from local heroes to a national act from the inside. A lot of valuable knowledge was gained there that came into play years later when I was doing Amphetamine Reptile Records. One of the big lessons was that you *could* do it from here without hightailing it to LA or NYC.

JOHN KASS: Around 1984 and 1985, the scene in the Twin Cities switched over from individual bands to bands being identified with a label. So the Entry started doing Treehouse Records night, Amphetamine Reptile Records night, Crackpot Records night, Big Money Records night, or Susstones Records night. These labels all formed around the same time, '84, '85. And each of those labels had a sonic identity that's different from the others. That was the beautiful thing about it.

Think about this: the first Susstones 45 and the first AmRep 45 were recorded the same month in the same tiny basement studio in St. Louis Park. Nobody in that whole world knew about each other at all. But that's exactly what happened. Look at Tom Hazelmyer now; look at how many records the guy's put out—hundreds! Look how many records Ed Ackerson and I have put out on Susstones—hundreds, right? They all started in spring of 1984 in Neil Thorgrimson's studio in St. Louis Park.

CHRIS OSGOOD: Suddenly everybody had some vinyl that they could tout as their own. And it became almost a self-fulfilling prophecy, because now there was a club to play in, the Longhorn, and there was a record label putting out records of the bands. We had Blackberry Way recording studios. And from there, other clubs followed: Duffy's, First Ave., and all the rest of it. And certainly other labels and recording studios. It all established the Twin Cities as a base of operations, as a scene.

13

THE WALLETS TAKE IT—TO MINNEAPOLIS: THE ART ROCK SCENE

During the late '70s and early '80s, several indie bands began melding the new wave or no wave style with jazz, funk, theater, and performance art in their music and live shows. Leading the way on the local front were the Wallets, a five piece consisting of lead singer and accordionist Steven Kramer, keyboardist Rod Gordon, bassist Jim Clifford, saxophonist Max Ray, and drummer Erik Anderson as core members. Kramer formed the Wallets in 1980 in his native Minneapolis after spending a few years in New York's no wave scene. He brought those experiences and his own unique personality to inform the Wallets' absurdist humor, outrageous costumes, and over-the-top theatrical performances. The Wallets and the bands that followed in that vein—such as Things That Fall Down, Têtes Noires, 2i, Fine Art, Urban Guerillas, and Warheads—defied categorization but built loyal followings. They could be enchanting, confrontational, confusing, and inspiring all at once.

LU ANN KINZER: The Wallets were very creative and artsy. They performed in costumes and surprised their audience a lot. You never knew what Steve Kramer would do next.

ROD GORDON: Before the Wallets I had a band with my brothers, the New Psychonauts, for four or five years. That was the late '70s, early '80s. We called ourselves the New Psychonauts as a joke. There was no old Psychonauts. There were four of us Gordons, and then a couple other guys. Both the New Psychonauts and the Wallets were two-keyboard-player bands. Dueling keyboards, I love it! I like it better than a bunch of guitars, frankly.

Our mom was a piano teacher, so she taught us. In our preteens she sent us to MacPhail to study. It was fun around the house; we used to play and make up tunes. We used to bang on pots, and a couple of us played keyboards. We thought we should try to be a real band and rehearse more seriously. We had to collect money to get a set of drums. We had nothing at first, but we put together a bunch of junk and rehearsed. It was definitely a basement/garage band. Then we started playing out in public.

I came out of the '60s, and I really saw everybody. I saw Jimi Hendrix. I saw the Doors. I saw Janis Joplin. I think that had a big influence on me. I worked at the Guthrie Theater as an usher for years, and a lot of people came and played at the Guthrie before they were very well known. Frank Zappa, the Who played at the Guthrie Theater. Sue McLean was booking these people in the Guthrie, and they were on the verge of being huge. But they really weren't that huge yet, so they could actually play the Guthrie. It was pretty amazing to see that stuff.

The Bonzo Dog Doo-Dah Band from England played at the Guthrie. They had all these props and funny, goofy things. That's what inspired me, when I started working with the Psychonauts. It was like, "Why can't we be goofy like that, and have a great time?" I never wanted to take myself too seriously and pretend I'm a great musician. It's more like, have fun, have a sense of humor, play goofy songs. A lot of the Psychonauts stuff was all humor. We tried to have the music be interesting and sort of challenging, but at the same time, it was all kind of tongue in cheek. With the Wallets, our humor was mostly planned. Or we'd come up with some spontaneous choreography that was kind of goofy, and it would just stick.

Steve Kramer and I grew up in the same neighborhood. We'd goof off in high school and jam. I was always impressed with his creativity. He used to come over and play the piano at our house. I always admired his originality on the piano. Sometimes I thought, "I don't have a chance to be that creative." But we always had fun. When he wanted to start a band, I said, "Sure."

The Psychonauts played at the M-80 festival in the fall of 1979. Steve was there with James Chance. Steve had moved back to Minneapolis from New York after having an accident, falling off a building. He had this idea that he wanted to start his own band. He said, "It's really easy. We can make a lot of money, you know. The songs will be really easy." It turned out, they weren't that easy. But I started playing with him. He came and played keyboards with the Psychonauts a few times, too.

ELLIOT GORDON: Bands like the Wallets, the Hypstrz, and the New Psychonauts influenced everything I did after I heard them. When I was thirteen

Rod Gordon and Steve Kramer of the Wallets, playing dueling pianos at the Peppermint Lounge in New York City, spring 1982. PHOTO BY MICHAEL MARKOS

I got a Psychonauts tape from my dad, or maybe took it. It had all the professional recordings they made, plus a bunch of live cuts. I played that tape so often that it broke in under a year. It was the only copy in my family's possession. Some of those songs are now lost in time because of my obsession.

DANIEL CORRIGAN: I'd seen the New Psychonauts a couple times at the Longhorn. They were kind of an art band but still a rock band. One of my favorite songs was "Mannequins Drink 3.2." It has a beautiful story about a guy waiting for a bus and he falls in love with a mannequin in a Dayton's store window on the Nicollet Mall. That really spoke to me because I was working at Dayton's downtown at the time. If I remember correctly, they break the mannequin out of the storefront. They're wondering what they're going to do, and it's Sunday, and they could only get 3.2 beer. But it's okay, because "mannequins drink 3.2."

And there was another song, "Walk on Water"—at least that was the chorus, maybe it was the name. The drummer sang it. This is before I was a photographer, so I didn't get pictures of it, but it's indelibly printed on my mind. He was singing the chorus "walk on water," just screaming and screaming it, and he started bleeding from the nose copiously but kept on performing while he was bleeding.

ROD GORDON: We'd play the Longhorn pretty regularly. Then we did other places, mostly Duffy's, Goofy's once or twice. The Wallets played warehouse things downtown, private or house parties. They were fun. It was wild parties.

It was a lot of fun playing the Longhorn. It was a different scene from what came later, like at the 7th Street Entry. I liked the crowd; the ambience was fun. Energetic, young! We were pretty wild. We were crazy kids. I think we got a chance to warm up for the Suburbs. We all just called everyone we knew and asked them to come, so we'd have a big crowd and make a good first impression. The guy that was booking there, Hartley Frank, saw the big crowd, so he started hiring us regularly.

Our audiences danced. I think that they felt they were in on something special that other people didn't know about, or maybe that was part of our mystique, that we weren't real poppy.

MAX RAY: The Wallets started in 1980. It was Steve's band, and I joined because of the music and stayed in it because of the music. There was never any question in my mind that it was really interesting music, really fun to be associated with.

We opened for Talking Heads at Northrop Auditorium in October 1980. That was extremely exciting. As the opening act, we got booed: "We want Talking Heads!" And then when Talking Heads came on David Byrne bawled out the audience: "You shouldn't boo those guys. They're great. They're friends of mine." I'll never forget that.

ROD GORDON: The Wallets had five players most of the time. Sometimes people sat in with us. We would often have a big, big band kind of thing. A lot of my parts were like a repetitive groove that I would just play for five minutes or something. Actually that's quite difficult, believe it or not.

When we first started working with the Wallets, I was sometimes coming up with ideas. But I realized Steve just wanted to do it his way. I was fine with that. It was different for me, but I enjoyed it. I mean, the music was great, so I loved doing it and I was very happy with all that. But it was mostly Steve who came up with performance ideas and themes. We came up with certain moves we'd do. Max and I were over on one side of the stage, while

Steve would be off doing something like jumping onto the audience. We'd just have to stand there and play until he came back up onstage and decided to do something else. So we'd do things like spin around or do it in sync just to keep it interesting. A little choreography, yeah.

I had an old portable organ initially. It might have been a Yamaha. There were not a lot of keyboards for a few years. You could get like a Fender Rhodes electric piano. They were always breaking down, and you had to replace these little metal tines before every gig, practically. They were tuned by moving these little springs up and down. And then you throw it into the car and drive a couple thousand miles, it's always out of tune and you have to retune it. But now they have all these great little computerized portable keyboards.

I was using an Ensoniq keyboard for years and years, because it had sort of a reasonable piano sound. Basically, all I really want to do is play the piano. But that was so big and heavy, and I finally just decided to replace it with a littler and lighter keyboard made by Yamaha. It really sounds like a piano.

We didn't have any guitars. And that was part of our plan. I think people liked the uniqueness. Sometimes you can get sort of tired of guitar. *[laughs]* You just hear it all the time. Steve didn't want to have a guitar. When Jon [Gordon] played guitar, I think it was mostly because he had that percussive, really staccato sound. Almost like there weren't even any notes. So that fit in pretty well.

MICHAEL HALLIDAY: I was the original Wallets bass player for the first couple months, until Steve Kramer actually got a band. But he really wanted me. He said, "I just like the way you play, blah, blah." I said, "I'm not good enough, blah, blah, blah." He was a pretty funky and cool guy; I always liked him. He was one of my favorites. A genius, in my mind.

CHARLIE LAWSON: I believe I was in the Wallets after Halliday. These guys went to New York, and I had been living in Manhattan. I kept telling them I'm not a bass player, I'm a blues guitarist. And they kept saying, "Yeah, yeah, we know. Now here's how the song goes." When they went to New York they picked up Jim Clifford, a great bass player. He was in Marbles at the time with Erik Li.

MARK FREEMAN: Cindy and I were in the Wallets early on. Two gigs maybe? Steve Kramer tried paying us in liquor and drugs and so we quit. They rehearsed in our loft, downtown. I think that was the main reason we were in the band, because they needed a place to rehearse. We had this awesome place where you could pull your car or a Greyhound bus or whatever right in the door.

CINDY BLUM: It was kind of crazy at that time. There were like a million people in that band. When we couldn't get together to rehearse, Steve would call people up and say, "Okay, here's your part," and he would tell you over the phone.

DAVE FOLEY: I was the first guitar player in the Wallets. When Steve Kramer got back from New York, he decided he wanted to put this band together. So I got Bill Martin, who became the saxophone player in Things That Fall Down, to be the sax player in the band.

I just played with them once.

ROD GORDON: Steve wanted to come up with a gimmick to sell us. We were trying to think of something everybody knows: spoon, fork, wallet. So we said, "Wallets." And then he started this theme about money, and we did a song about a cash register. He started shouting about a cash register, and then he wanted to climb over the bar and take the cash register and rip it out. It was memorable!

JAY BERINE: The Wallets were eighty-sixed from the Longhorn for a while because, during their first show, Steve Kramer climbed over the bar, opened the cash register, and threw money into the crowd.

DAVE FOLEY: Steve Kramer's big idea was, we're going to play this song, "Cash Register," and the band is going to break down, then Steve is going to grab the cash register off the bar and open it up and throw all the money to the people. I'm supposed to quit right before and walk off, and then the horns are supposed to walk off, and Erik is supposed to be the last guy onstage, playing drums. We get to the point where Steve is going to grab the cash register, but it's bolted down. I don't know if he got money out of it. But the people who are running the place see he is trying to do something really crazy, so he runs down the hallway, and they grab him. I go, "Oh, they're going to beat him up."

They start beating him up in the hallway. Erik and I go and stop the fight, and he runs away. Steve had his jaw wired together at the time, from falling off a building in New York.

He still sang, but he was healing himself. He got into a fight once someplace in town, and we took him to the hospital. They had to operate on him again to set his jaw back because he got hit in the face pretty hard.

I liked Steve; he was cool. The guy was a good piano player. He straightened his life out.

JACQUE HORSCH: I think I was there that night Steve Kramer tried to pull out a cash register drawer. He really was crazy! The Wallets were truly great, they were one of my favorites, but they didn't play that much at the Longhorn. I remember seeing them more at Duffy's.

ROD GORDON: We did unique stuff. A favorite performance was when we all dressed as nuns; we did a few shows that way. We even toured around the Midwest dressed up as nuns. Steve put on body paint, all black, and had himself decorated with a bunch of white Xs. We came out and started playing, and then he would make a grand entrance and start jumping around and run through the audience.

MAX RAY: One of my favorite stories is when we dressed as nuns in Cleveland, colder than snot, at the Agora Ballroom. There was a room called the Pop Shop in the basement. So we're in a cold basement and we're doing the nuns and "Aboriginal Steve," the black body paint with the loincloth and feathers. We're chasing Steve around this basement labyrinth with the spray adhesive. It was cold and he didn't want to—we had to catch him to spray the adhesive and then get the feathers on him.

So there's eight people, we're putting on a good show. All of a sudden, flames and smoke—I'm not kidding you—are leaping out of the amp rack for the PA. All the sound goes off. The soundman wasn't running sound; he was in the dressing room getting intimate with his girlfriend. We interrupted them and said, "Hey man, there's smoke and flames...." And he said, "Oh, shit!" That Pop Shop in Cleveland is definitely my favorite Steve story.

We also got carded at that gig. Only time I've ever been carded. We were loading in and the guy said, "Can I see your union card?" I'd been a union member since '78. I handed him my union card, and you could just see his face fall. "Oh, shit. The fucking punks have a union card." He was absolutely crestfallen.

ADAM LEVY: The Wallets were in their own class. They were musicologists. That band, you felt like you were listening to people that had studied so many different styles of music and older American music. That was about the same time I started looking into lounge records. So there was this sophistication of the Wallets music more than any other band in this area, I thought.

ROD GORDON: There's a lot more jazz and stuff in there than maybe we wanted people to be aware of. *[laughs]* But I'm really more of a jazz person, and I still play jazz. That sort of came through in the music, I think. I used to see jazz at the Longhorn. That was a little bit before they opened the rock bar on the main floor, they had a jazz bar upstairs.

We played at a nice little auditorium in San Francisco, part of the Kool Jazz Festival. I really liked that because we really didn't play jazz festivals. But somehow, we got hired to do the Kool Jazz Festival. We were followed later that evening by Dave Brubeck. So that felt like a big step for me, to be part of that.

For *Take It*, we went down to New Orleans, lived there for at least a month, found a house where we could stay. We were out in the suburbs and came in to the city to record. Allen Toussaint was somebody Steve Kramer knew, I think, in New York. Allen listened to some recordings and said he'd like to produce us. He came to Minneapolis, we went out to dinner, and we decided it would be good. It was a great experience working with Allen Toussaint.

MAX RAY: We had a '68 straight-roof ambulance that we bought from Erik's friend, the Flying Dutchman, who was a mechanic/dealer. We used that when we went to New Orleans in early '86 to record *Take It*. It had a trailer, and we kept all the stuff in the trailer. Then Jim got a Framus, an upright electric bass, and it wouldn't fit in the trailer, so Steve made a coffin for it. We'd put the coffin on top and strap it on. We had to be resourceful. We never had a budget.

We replaced that with a '70 high-top Cadillac ambulance. People always associated it with *Ghostbusters*, which was a '59, a much more exciting body style. But the '70 was an unbelievable car. The thing just would never die. Ten miles to the gallon—winter, summer, trailer, no trailer, cold, hot, didn't matter. And that was your main travel expense of course. We took everything out of the back and just put a mattress, so four people could ride back there, with two in the front seat. A five-piece band and a sound person. A lot of trips from Kirby's in Moorhead to the Mad Hatter in Iowa City, a little circuit.

ROD GORDON: I know the ambulance well. We spent many, many hours in that thing. All over the country. We went back and forth a little bit, between Minneapolis and New York. We used to sleep in the ambulance. It was a tight squeeze. And we're together 24-7 on the road, sleeping in the same rooms and driving. So a lot of it was maybe not pleasant, but we made the most of it. People had a good sense of humor, and we got on okay for quite a few years.

We probably played through maybe 1988, '89. We were in New York. I think Steve just was in too deep, and he came back to Minneapolis to clean up a little bit. And then the band just kind of stopped for a while. They basically all came back here, except for me. I stayed in New York for a while. I didn't do much, except wait tables and bartend to pay the rent. I played a couple of goofy little gigs. I had a little portable organ. Finally, I got a call from Steve, and he was like, "Why are you still in New York?" "I don't know. It's a nice town." [laughs] He wanted me to come back to Minneapolis and play some gigs.

We had a reunion, maybe at Duffy's. We hadn't played for maybe a year or two. I sort of got talked into staying here. We played for quite a few years after that.

The Longhorn didn't really seem to want to pay us too much, but there was a time when we were bringing in pretty good crowds. We had a pretty serious following that was faithful. I think we were a big draw partly because we were coming in from New York. We had more people after being in New York for a while.

MAX RAY: You always wanna be the first on your block to have the newest thing, so those who were able to think forwardly like that, like Leslie and Dan Johnson at Duffy's, were the ones who were booking us. The real stars are Steve McClellan and Jay Berine. Hartley Frank was such an odd duck.

You didn't want to go up to the office. If you're getting paid, you didn't really sit down.

ROD GORDON: Steve McClellan booked us. He was a good guy. I liked that place. We did some wild stuff at First Avenue, where we were up on stilts, and everything was raised up. We had a bunch of live chickens onstage, which was a little bizarre. Then we didn't know what to do with them after the show. I wound up taking the chickens to my place. The landlady who lived upstairs was calling, asking us if we had chickens downstairs. We finally said, "Yeah," and we found some neighbors to take them. *[laughs]*

We played the Uptown Bar a lot. Maggie Macpherson was booking the Uptown. That was a fun bar to play. It was even smaller than the Longhorn. We pretty much carried the same following to the Uptown Bar. We got a few more people maybe.

The Wallets mostly did our own booking, but for a couple of years toward the end, we had a manager who was booking stuff, Bob Hest. We generally needed to have our own sound engineer. We're kind of a unique setup. Even on months-long road trips, we would try to get a soundman to come with us. We had a couple. Ann White ran sound with us; she'd come on the road. We had a guy named Skip Wasilowski. He runs sound at the Orpheum now.

CHARLIE LAWSON: The Wallets' first configuration had a three-piece horn section and three women singers from the West Bank Trackers. We warmed up Talking Heads. We also played with David Byrne as part of the Walker's New Music America series.

We played in front of Dayton's and there was a sign that said, "Steve Kramer and Friends, Rock Music!" Kramer took a pen, viciously scratched out "Rock Music," and then wrote "Disco" underneath.

MAX RAY: We played at noon and you could see the working people out for lunch walking down the Nicollet Mall, and as they got closer you'd see them crossing the street and walking up the other side, because Steve's jaw was wired shut and he had red shoe polish in his hair and Jimmy Engelbert was playing violin and he just scared the heck out of everybody.

A lot of the paring down was when the band moved to New York, I think, in January of '81. Suddenly it was a smaller band. Steve had been out there and had a lot going on out that way and wanted to go back. The accident brought him here to convalesce. As soon as he could, he wanted to go back. We lived in New York almost two years. It wasn't like Minneapolis. They had a real scene there.

Catch a Falling Star was an EP we recorded at Cookhouse Studios, at 26th and Nicollet, with Jerry Steckling in '83. That was really great. It has a black and white photo of the band and the other two albums are color photos. You just can't imitate that vibe you get from black and white.

The twelve-inch single was "Totally Nude" backed with "How to Keep Time to Music and Learn to Become a Better Dancer."

Max Ray on baritone sax with the Wallets at the Peppermint Lounge, spring 1982. Photo by Michael Markos

ROD GORDON: Erik Anderson was good to work with. He studied piano. Sometimes it seems like drummers make better piano players. They have a better percussive sense. Yeah, Erik took it very seriously. It showed. He did a great job. The Wallets was a hard band to play with. The expectations were pretty high. Stuff that maybe seems or sounds simple when you listen to it, really is not that simple.

CHARLIE LAWSON: Those Wallets parts were really difficult for me because if you play like four notes over and over again, like for ten minutes, it's very, very physical. So you had to get in this sort of Zen thing. The Wallets were really sticklers on extremely accurate timing.

MAX RAY: I remember in the rehearsal studio just playing parts for a half hour at a time while Steve tried different things to go with it—this was right before computerization, which Steven went to big time as it came out in the '80s. But all of those parts are from Steven. He would give us credit for arrangements because we would contribute parts. Or the way that we played the part he gave us would end up being a contribution to an arrangement. But he wrote all the songs and we played them.

It's unconventional. Like the bass player doesn't just play the bass line and the horn line isn't just a horn line, they kind of exchange rhythm and melody duties. So nobody could pigeonhole it, and so we never got anywhere with it. But it's very well remembered. Say, "the Wallets," to anyone who ever heard the band and their eyes light up, and that's nice.

MARTIN KELLER: The Wallets were great. They were similar to the Suburbs in that when they came through the door, nobody was sure what to make of them. Steve Kramer had a reputation as this New York guy who'd played with James Chance and got caught up in a pretty heavy drug cloud for a while. But he came back here and cleaned up. He put together this band that was a delightfully eclectic group of musicians that obviously all knew a lot of different music and threw it into the pot that Steve would stir.

I always thought of them more as a performance art rock band, because they would put on different costumes for different shows, or they'd have themes for the night. With the Wallets you knew you were gonna get a floor show, you just never knew what bag it was gonna jump out of. Kramer was kind of a maniac onstage. A lot of their stuff was visually comic, an inside joke or societal commentary.

The music was wonderful. I mean, if you could find *Catch a Falling Star*, their EP, or their version of "The Night Before Christmas" on the flip side of a 45—that stuff's just great. I don't think we'll ever see anything like the Wallets again. And they were pretty short-lived.

I don't think the Wallets appealed to as many people as the Commandos or the Suburbs or the Flamin' Oh's. It was a little more art-driven, almost like a rock burlesque show. It was really strange and a lot of fun. Kramer was totally unpredictable.

PETER JESPERSON: Steve Kramer was really one of the most talented people I've ever met. I lugged a big reel-to-reel recorder downtown and recorded him improvising for an hour. I still have the tape. It says "Live at Rod's Sister's Apartment." I thought he was a stone cold genius.

STEVE BRANTSEG: The Phones played some shows with the Wallets. I loved them. I'm a guitar freak, obviously, but I love the fact that they did not have a guitar player. That's what really made them stand out, along with everything else. I remember their release at First Avenue when he rode a horse into the club. It was pretty wild. Crazy antics.

MICHAEL MARKOS: Steve used to play with James Chance and the Contortions, and I think that's where his main inspiration came from. It was more of an art band. Steve's props and all his artwork were amazing, especially in his videos. They were very inventive and creative. The Wallets were more funk and R&B tradition. But they never really broke through.

Their shows were really excellent. Their shows in New York were really tight. Then their farewell show at the Guthrie, in '89, '90.

DAVID MOE: The Wallets were one of the biggest, most entertaining bands. I met Steve Kramer early on on the West Bank around Cedar Riverside. They were just starting the Wallets, but Steve had played there with other bands.

I met him before he had his fall. His face had reconstructive surgery. His kick in New York used to be he'd stand on the edge high up on a building and kind of play chicken with himself, check his balance, and just goof around. He fell and thankfully, as I understand it, he was able to get his arm around a fire escape and cling on, after four stories or whatever, and saved his life.

I don't know how you couldn't like the Wallets. They were unique, catchy; everybody had fun. I can't explain what that music was. I just know I liked it and it put a smile on my face.

DOUG ANDERSON: When I was moving to New York, I got to meet all these artists and filmmakers. For the first couple of years I lived in New York, people would say, "You must know Steve Kramer."

So Kramer was legendary in New York City. By the time I moved to New York, Steve had come back to Minnesota. I would run into him and I would say, "Hey, so-and-so asked about you." That's how Kramer and I got to be friends.

Because of Steve Kramer, I got to know a lot of really whacked-out people in New York. All the nightclubs people knew Kramer. Kramer was so wild, he was so entertaining, and when he was drinking he was a very funny guy. But when he drank, he was really unpredictable.

A lot of musicians from New York embraced Minneapolis because we had bars that would take them. Their memories of the place were so good.

ROD GORDON: I started in my early twenties, maybe late twenties. I think I was the oldest Wallet. I might have been around thirty or so when we were breaking up. But we played the Peppermint Lounge and other big-name places that you don't think you're ever going to play. The Guthrie always was a big deal in my life, and our final gig was the Guthrie Theater. Standing up on that stage, I remember thinking, "Wow! This is huge!" It was a full house. The last show at the Guthrie was a significant point in my life.

That was January '89, when we decided we were going to quit. Maybe five or six years before, during one of our trips across country in the ambulance, and the air conditioner isn't working—it was just hell—we decided: "If we're not rich and famous, if we don't make it in five years, we're going to break up." That was our decision, and that's what we did.

I never wanted to grow old being a struggling musician. It was sad, but I guess it felt right. We logically thought it through: "Are we going to keep struggling, forever? Or should we decide to just stop at a certain point?" We decided, "Let's just stop." It was kind of a struggle. It's a hard way to make a living.

But I'm very lucky that I did stuff like that and played certain places. That's not anything I even thought I was ever going to do. And hearing ourselves on the radio is always fun. It still happens every once in a while.

DAVID MOE: During this magical time, a million new bands and sounds were springing up. Many of the bands encompassed many influences to create their own sound. One of the more unique bands to do this was Things That Fall Down. They brought their own brand of jazz/funk/new/no wave to many dance-filled nights at the 7th Street Entry.

As the other, more popular bands like the Wallets or the Suburbs began to hone their sound into perhaps a more streamlined approach, TTFD seem to continue to push the limits of their avant-garde jams. They transcended other styles of music at the time.

New York transplant David Foley—a character looking to have come straight out of a Jim Jarmusch film—continued to hold a torch for that art-noise guitar, reminiscent of New York no wave bands like James Chance, Swans, DNA. His playing and attitude was very different than the other new guitarists in town. He seemed to do stuff that juxtaposed what the rest of the band was grooving on. But it added that necessary tension that would help push their hypnotic, pulsing art-funk over the edge. And to me, it put a smile on my face and it just worked. Foley's playing, and even the band, wasn't for everyone, especially at first, but that's why I was drawn to it. It wasn't that spoon-fed music for the trendy set, like a lot of avant-garde art: either you got it or you didn't. I think that's part of why they were so great and eventually seemed to be playing all the time in the Entry.

TTFD seemed to have a more stylized look onstage as well, even more of a fashionable element than most of the new crop of bands. When you walked into the Entry and saw them onstage, they had a visual presence all their own. Lead singer Scott Brooks had a '40s or '50s crooner look—short cropped hair, bowties, sharkskin pants—and charisma, and the rest of the band seemed to follow suit. Scott crooned his vocals, but they fit in like just another instrument. The band always came across first and foremost with their instrumentations and grooves. His lyrics seemed to ride along into their overall sound. Their bass player, Garrison White, was always styling some sort of new-looking pompadour haircut and played a contemporary-sounding, jazz-sounding bass.

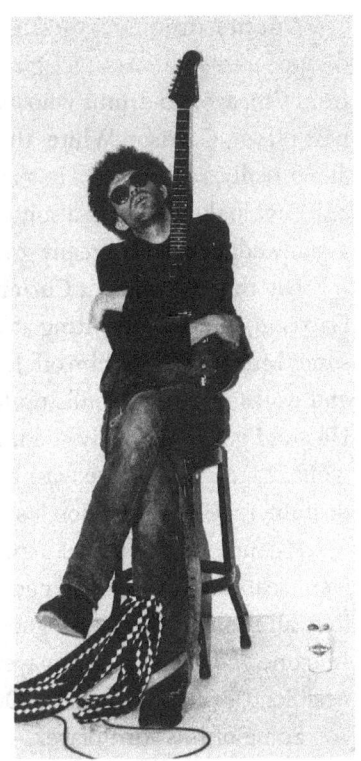

Dave Foley, circa 1977. PHOTO BY BAYARD MICHAEL

They seemed to be from somewhere other than Minneapolis. Their sound was infectious, very tight, and based on long, heavy rhythmic grooves that would eventually turn the dance floor into a frenzy of the hippy-jerkers [dancers leftover from the Longhorn] and other improv bouncing. They seemed to be happy testing the audience's stamina as their jams seemed to never end, one funky art groove right into the other. They stood out from other bands of the time, because they never gave in to the trends or genres that were starting to divide some of the local music scene.

DAVE FOLEY: Things That Fall Down's first gig was at the Longhorn bar. We wrote all of our songs in two rehearsals and we went out and got a gig.

Our first drummer, we don't know what happened to him. That guy just disappeared—he was a nice guy. We got Steve Foley. We had this guy, James, from Chicago, on drums who was so fucking good. He was friends with the bass player, Garrison White; they were both living in Chicago. He and I got along really, really well. He was into rap and all that kind of stuff. He was real cool looking, too, in a suit that looked like it was made for him. He was a really edgy person, a really great guy.

Dig this: We were at Curran's Restaurant on 42nd and Nicollet. James, Garrison, and I were sitting at a table eating breakfast, and Garrison does something that pisses him off. James gets up, says "Fuck this shit, I'm leavin'," and walks out. A bus pulls up to the bus stop, and I never saw him again. He and I got along really good. I thought he was going to play with us for a while; then suddenly he wasn't around anymore. He was probably the best drummer we ever had. Bob Joslyn was really good, too. That was at the end.

A couple of things that happened with Things That Fall Down I thought were really weird was, we couldn't find any horn players that were good; they all thought they were good, but they weren't, or they didn't practice. And one of our saxophone players died in South Dakota visiting his parents. And Scott Brooks went crazy. Our drummer Steve Foley died in 2008.

Some of the horn players were just difficult to deal with. You couldn't write new music with them, because there would be all these personality clashes. I would fire one horn player and get another one, and fire another one, get another one. We got Max Ray and Rochelle Becker to play horns. They're good; they're really cool, I like those guys.

We got good gigs. We opened for the Gang of Four for the "I Love a Man in Uniform" tour. We played with the Contortions, we played with the Plastics, we played with the Time. We were the first band to be hired by the Loring Alley Block Party to play outside.

DANN CARLSON: I remember playing with David Foley at the Longhorn, in the Avanti Jetsons, some free-form jazz punk—in other words, we were all over the place on purpose. Hartley Frank is up there going, "Get off!!" pulling cords. It was really funny!

DOUG ANDERSON: Dave Foley is a genius. Things That Fall Down is one of my favorite bands. I would go see Foley's band all the time. Honestly, given the choice of like Soul Asylum, Hüsker Dü, the Replacements, and Things That Fall Down, I would go to Things That Fall Down.

ROBERT WILKINSON: Têtes Noires were really cool, too. They came along later, they were all girls, they were kind of experimental. We didn't really hang with them too much, but I was kind of a fan of theirs. So I would go to the shows.

JENNIFER HOLT: I was in one of the very first female bands in Minneapolis, the Hug, in 1980. There were a couple other women in that band who went on to be in other female bands as well. Then I replaced Terri Poling [now Owens], the wife of Chan Poling at the time, in Fine Art. I played the violin and sang, began writing lyrics. We toured quite a bit. Colin Mansfield was absolutely brilliant. He's an amazing writer and technician of music. Everybody in the band was very talented.

I changed a song's lyrics so it was female to female, and Colin said, "We aren't having that in this band." So that was my cue to start Têtes Noires, because I was bisexual and I wanted that to be included. So I left the band and started my own performance art project.

CAMILLE GAGE: Most of us were in other bands. Polly was in Radio for Teens, Jennifer was in Fine Art, Cindy and I were in a band called My Five. Jennifer had had it with bands where men were telling her what to do. She saw a couple of us at a party and floated the idea: it would be fun to do all women, for the summer. Write some songs, play, and see what it would be like to do something, just women. It wasn't like, "Let's start a band." There wasn't any thought to long term.

ANGELA FRUCCI: My memory of Têtes Noires is that it was an experiment. And not with the intention that everyone was going to leave the bands they were in. But we really enjoyed playing and writing together, and we did indeed end up leaving our other bands.

JENNIFER HOLT: At first, Têtes Noires was just, "Hey, let's get together some of the women who are in other male-dominated bands and do our own performance-art thing where we don't care what the person plays." It was more about being creative and deconstructing the normal concept of what a band has to look like to perform onstage and be entertaining. We got a show at Walker Art Center, an art opening, in 1982. We did a cappella, we wore weird clothes, and there was a lot of standup comedy on the stage.

CAMILLE GAGE: Our music in Têtes Noires was very unusual. We played the Walker for some art opening by the person that had made seventeen thousand mission marks in a book, or wrote the numbers out, it took years to do. It might have been a Japanese artist, because we put on full white geisha face paint, and we took a grease pen and put numbers on our face. I loved whenever we played in costume. You're a little bit more removed from the audience.

ANGELA FRUCCI: It was like kids playacting. You get to become somebody else. That is the great thing about rock and roll.

We were nominated for a Minnesota Music Award, Best New Band in 1984.

CAMILLE GAGE: *PM Magazine* did a pretty long piece on us that aired the night of the music awards. Prince came to our teeny-weeny dressing room and said, "I hear you guys are going to be on TV tonight. Do you wanna watch it in my dressing room?" He didn't stay, though. That was a bummer, because we thought: "We get to hang around with Prince!" But he brought us to his dressing room and then left. We watched ourselves on TV.

We lost to Urban Guerillas. Back then it was all popular vote. We hadn't done anything to, like, gin up any votes, like we should have. But again, we costumed for that. We all wore wedding dresses.

ANGELA FRUCCI: We were covering Billy Idol's "White Wedding." We did our a cappella version. We got vintage wedding dresses, and we rented a fog machine. Then we appeared in these wedding dresses in a sea of fog. We totally punked out "Soldier Boy."

CAMILLE GAGE: That was a song with four-part harmony from the '60s. We did that like a punk song. And we did "White Wedding," a punk song, like a '50s song.

ANGELA FRUCCI: I remember looking out after our performance. There was just silence. Not a clap.

CAMILLE GAGE: Well, the guy who wrote for *City Pages* really liked it. He said one of the biggest moments of the night for him was our performance. And when we got done, the guy behind him was saying, "I don't know if I loved them or hated them. But I'll never forget them." I think that's our whole career, right there.

A lot of our songs were topical, and we got both fans and foes for that. Which is true yet today, I think, for bands. Then, we were a really melody-driven band, because we had four singers. I listen to our music now, and I'm kind of astounded by the complexity of some of the stuff that we did. We seemed so innocent, and naïve, and not self-serious. I think it's true, at least in the beginning. But you listen to the interweaving melodies and how the percussion played off the melodies and the singing. Cindy was a really good bass player. She came up with some really interesting percussive ways of playing. And so, not having a drummer I think made us more creative in a way, because we were doing something completely different for the first few years.

JENNIFER HOLT: We were very artistic. The Wallets were our friends. We got each other. They would put on these big performance pieces. They were very inventive and creative, and so were we, and so we liked them a lot. We did a lot of shows with them.

We played a lot with the Replacements and Hüsker Dü. We would do triple-headers with them, always as the opening act. We were never taken seriously. We were more the novelty band that would bring in a certain demographic.

CURT ALMSTED: I remember doing a gig with Têtes Noires at Duffy's. I tried to be supportive, and we got them up with our band to do "Iko Iko." I think they opened and then we played and then they came up as guests. I know we had fun.

CAMILLE GAGE: We went on after the strippers, stripping on the bar tops. They stopped, and we went out and sound checked. Curtiss A said to us, "So, this must be kind of weird for you guys, huh?"

Têtes Noires, in the First Avenue upstairs bathroom, circa 1984. PHOTO BY CATHERINE SETTANNI

TERRY KATZMAN: I guess you could call Têtes Noires the first female band. Were they a rock band? That could be an argument. Têtes Noires were very skilled musicians, but they weren't really a rock and roll band. They were doing something else, in my mind anyway, in presentation and art. There's a bookmark on them in the Minneapolis music scene for sure. They did something no one had tried before, and they were daring in what they did. You couldn't deny it.

JENNIFER HOLT: What I'm most proud of is that, despite the fact we didn't have a typical band set up, we were extremely popular, we did really well, and we made three products and got a record label deal and broke some barriers. I think when you create a band that's unusual and eccentric, you broaden people's minds to what's acceptable, enjoyable, and what is art and what is music. I think being able to be women onstage singing political lyrics that people took seriously in a very funny format was disarming and great in raising political awareness at the time, as well as creating greater acceptance of women of all sizes and sexuality to be onstage as viable performers.

14

NEW-NO-NOW WAVE: M-80 FESTIVAL

Marathon '80: New-No-Now Wave Festival—better known as M-80—was a two-day festival heralding the advent of new music heading into the 1980s. M-80 was organized by journalist Tim Carr, who was assistant to the director of performing arts at Walker Art Center, the host of the festival. M-80 took place on September 22 and 23, 1979, at the University of Minnesota's Field House. The first major rock music festival in Minneapolis, M-80 featured a who's who of no wave, punk, and art rock bands of the day, such as Devo (performing as Dove: The Music of Love), Chris Stamey and the dB's, Skafish, Tuxedo Moon, and the UK's Monochrome Set. New York City's no wave scene was represented by the Contortions featuring James Chance and Steve Kramer, Suicide, the Fleshtones, the Feelies, and Richard Lloyd of Television. Also appearing was the cream of the crop from the local scene, including the Suicide Commandos, the Suburbs, NNB, Curtiss A, the Overtones, Fingerprints, and members of the Wallets, the Hypstrz, the Pistons, and more. M-80 marked a turning point for the Minneapolis scene, both an explosion and a splintering.

CHRIS OSGOOD: M-80 was the brainchild of Tim Carr, who worked at the Walker Art Center. He made a deal with the University of Minnesota to host this festival at their Field House, featuring everybody from James White and the Blacks, some bands from Scotland, and Devo—except they couldn't call themselves Devo, so they were "Dove: The Band of Love." It was a cool two-day festival. That scene gave way to the new wave scene sweeping the nation.

The Walker was open to new music and theater. Tim was assistant to the director of performing arts, Nigel Redman. Tim was in charge of rock 'n' roll and music, because that's what he knew about. Nigel gave him the lead, and he did M-80. The following year Tim did *New Music America* there.

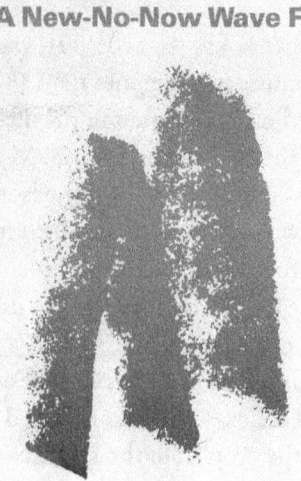

Poster and ticket stub from the M-80 festival, September 22–23, 1979. POSTER COURTESY OF DICK CHAMP, TICKET COURTESY OF JOHNNY REY

BRUCE ALLEN: Tim and I used to have a lot of fun late at night. We did illegal stuff. Back in those days, Tim Carr played a big role in Minneapolis music. He started writing about it. Tim Holmes did, too.

TIM HOLMES: Tim Carr had a really interesting music sensibility and made things happen. He had his finger on the pulse, because he was a hipster and music writer. He's someone I really miss. He wrote for the *Star Tribune* and I wrote for *City Pages* and the *Reader* and we knew the same people, but he had the situation at the Walker where he was working with Philip Glass and was instrumental in bringing people to town. It was another venue where bands could come from out of town.

CHRIS OSGOOD: It was really a fun scene, a good melding of the international pop scene, as Tim construed it, and our scene here—the new-no-now wave. In a lot of ways, M-80 was a watershed moment, because all these bands came to town. Whether it was Richard Lloyd or Devo—the list goes on and on. And suddenly all of them found out about us. I think that M-80 opened the door for Curtiss A to go to New York and get a great reception out there. It really helped the back and forth. The *Village Voice* was interested in M-80.

Thanks to Tim and thanks to the Walker, M-80 was another step in putting the Twin Cities on the map as a destination to play and as a place that bands knew was going to be receptive to new music and whatever we wanted to do.

TERRY KATZMAN: It was a really cool concert, but that place sucked. All the bands' sound was very challenged. Only a really good sound person could make it sound good in there. Devo sounded the best because they had an expert sound guy. It was like being in a coal mine. But Tim Carr deserves a page in history for making that come together. The organization of that was quite skillful. It was just a no wave festival of bands that were from small scenes from all over the country. It was built on the concept of M-80 welcoming 1980: the New-No-Now Wave festival.

ANDY SCHWARTZ: Tim Carr did an incredible job. He brought together bands and performers from across the US and even from England. For being held in a field house, I remember the sound being pretty good. There were

James Chance and the Contortions at M-80, September 23, 1979. Photo by Steve Madore

some really great sets. Devo, James Chance and the Contortions, Judy Nylon. The Fleshtones were pretty hot at that time. Minnesota bands.

JEFF BUSWELL: M-80 was very cold. The high I think was like thirty degrees. And the Field House had no heat in it. But it was warmer than outside. I think it had a sawdust floor. The amount of talent there was unbelievable. Most of it was local, because we had a lot a good talent here that was blossoming at that point. But to have Devo play there, and James Chance and the Contortions, and Tuxedo Moon—there were some really cool bands from around the country.

BRUCE ALLEN: The hottest band to my mind, definitely, was James White and the Blacks, who sometimes played as James Chance and the Contortions. And Devo was great. The bands were on the same page. Everybody got along.

STEVE ALMAAS: M-80 was pretty exciting. I think that was a month after I'd moved to New York. The Commandos got back together to play there. It was almost a year after we'd split up. They flew me out; we played this really fun gig. The whole thing was really interesting, a great scene of people. I got home and then I got my picture in the *Village Voice*. [laughs] It was nothing but fun.

CHRIS OSGOOD: We had to go down and break into the Longhorn to get our gear out to play at M-80. Hartley Frank, who was still asleep in the middle of the day, showed up in his bathrobe. All we had done is take the door off from the hinges and set off the alarm. But it swarmed with cops, and there was Hartley. He was going to send us all to jail. And we said, "Hartley, no, please observe that we didn't even go in. You just didn't pick up your phone. And we were trying to get your attention, because we needed our gear." So he let us off the hook, and we went and played M-80.

MARK FREEMAN: M-80 was going on and Hartley Frank, ever the mercenary—I can't say anything bad about Hartley Frank—he decided, "Well, if this is going on, then I've gotta get something out of the deal." So, before M-80, he had the bands that were playing M-80 play at the Longhorn. I think it was a two-nighter, and NNB played on the second night. M-80 was the next day and everybody got done playing and wanted to go get loaded and get out of there.

So we said, "Hey, can we leave our gear here? We'll come back tomorrow and pick it up." Hartley says, "No problem." Many bands left their gear at the Longhorn, and many bands had to be onstage at one o'clock, or thereabouts. So, I get to the Longhorn and there's like a dozen, maybe more musicians standing outside. Curt Almsted says, "The place is locked. We can't get in." I'm like, "Well, screw that." So, I can't swear to it, but I'm pretty sure Curt and I did this: took a screwdriver and took the hinges off the door of the Longhorn to get our gear, which set off the alarm. So we took the door off, and the cops showed up.

I had a bunch of warrants out for my arrest for parking tickets and crap like that. So when the cops showed up, I took off, because I didn't want to get arrested, because I had to play. So I backed up a little bit down the alley and then ran like hell. I get over to the Field House and everybody is coming up to me going, "Freeman, there's cops everywhere. They're looking for you. You're in big trouble." I'm like, "Just let me get through the set." Somebody told me, "If you even get onstage, they are going to arrest you." That same week we had done an interview for Bayard Michael's paper, *Minneapolis Incest*. Which *may* have involved alcohol and *definitely* involved me saying at least a dozen times that "Harley Frank is an asshole" in the interview.

So, I'm over there, the cops are looking for me. Hartley comes up to me and says, "I hear the cops are looking for you. Let's go get it taken care of."

So he drove me downtown; he paid all my fines. I was feeling pretty bad at the time. We get back into the car and he goes, "Not too bad for an asshole, huh?" I said, "Hartley, I am *so* sorry. There is no excuse for that. I am *so* sorry." He said, "Don't worry about it. I've heard worse." And I said, "I know, but I feel bad and you've been really nice about this." So then he drove me back down, and we played the gig, and the rest is history.

DANNY AMIS: The Overtones played M-80, and that was a surprise. I'd been bugging Tim Carr. I wanted to get on the M-80 show, but there just wasn't room for us. I think that the second day of the festival, somebody couldn't make it. Tim Carr called me that morning and said, "Hey, Danny. Can you guys be over at the Field House in a couple hours?"

I got the other guys together, and we got to play at M-80. That was really good for us. We made a lot of connections. I met a lot of my New York friends doing that show, like the dB's and the Fleshtones. So when I moved to New York a couple years later, I already had quite a few friends there.

HUGO KLAERS: We played at eight or nine in the morning or something. It was truly a marathon. There was music around the clock in the Field House. James Chance was there, and I remember Devo, Dove, played Chance's big single "Contort Yourself" last, because they played right before him. He was so pissed.

And speaking of pissed, I was just pissed the rest of the weekend after we played. There was a TV news program there. Bruce and I were hammered and we went up to their cameras. They were interviewing somebody else and were like, "Who are you guys?" And we went, "We're the fucking Beatles!" Bruce is saying, "Don't you know us? I'm George, he's Ringo." They were just like, "Turn the cameras off. Let's go."

CURT ALMSTED: Mark Goldstein, of Skogie, was at the rehearsals and at M-80. But then we couldn't find him for our set; he was asleep in his girlfriend's car. Frank Berry, who wasn't at the rehearsals, just showed up to play. It went okay, although the sound was cavernous. The second day I didn't play, but I did play as part of the finale, "Land of the Free," which was written by Mark Goldstein. He recorded it using the Suicide Commandos as his back-up band and he wanted me to sing it, but he needed some help on

The Minneapolis Rockestra at M-80, September 1979: *(left to right)* Dave Ahl (obscured), Steve Almaas, Curt Almsted, Bob Dunlap, Chris Osgood, and Chris Berry. PHOTO BY MICHAEL REITER

some of the lyrics. He had most of it down, and there were just a few things I helped with. I did enough evidently for him to give me writing credit as well.

We did a bunch of '50s and '60s rock songs. We did Chuck Berry's "Back in the USA," and a Rolling Stones song, "Citadel." We did "Gloria" by Them with Van Morrison. There were about a half dozen songs for the finale. There was a bunch of guys. I insisted Bongo [John Haga] play, and that's why he still likes me—because I stood up for him that day. Some of the Fingerprints guys were there: Steve Fjelstad played bass, and Jeff Waryan. It was like a big dumb-ass garage band jam. Chris Osgood called it a Rockestra.

CHRIS OSGOOD: I was the conductor of the Minneapolis Rockestra, where we got everybody up to play "Complicated Fun" and a couple of other songs. It was members of NNB, the Commandos, and the Pistons, and Jeff Waryan, Harvey Ginsberg, Steve Fjelstad—everybody was in that band.

JEFF WARYAN: I got to play at M-80, in the huge band, Rockestra, led by Chris Osgood, with Curtiss A. We got to play "Complicated Fun." I got to play with Fingerprints. It's a pretty good set, too. Got to do that, and the local jam band with Curt and Chris and everybody.

M-80 was so great for me. One of the high points was doing this very strange conglomeration with Devo. Chris Osgood was part of organizing Rockestra with the Mothersbaugh guys and putting together this big song with all of these people playing. Devo was going to write the song and they were going to be the main concept people. They came over to Blackberry Way and we rehearsed, and it was really fun. Here I am playing with Devo. I was like twenty years old. But I think the high point of that particular experience was I got to stand next to Richard Lloyd [of Television] and play. I had Chris Stamey [of the dB's] on one side of me and Richard Lloyd on the other. Television had disbanded, but still Richard Lloyd was a guitar hero of mine.

DANIEL MURPHY: I would've been seventeen or eighteen, and Karl Mueller was about a year and a half younger than me. We went to M-80 the day that Dove, the Band of Love played—it was Devo. I remember seeing some kind of weird act like Robin Crutchfield's Dark Day, some kind of goth stuff. The Suicide Commandos did "Saturday Night"— "S-A-T-U-R-D-A-Y"—that Bay City Rollers' song. That didn't go over so good.

There were only a few hundred people there. It was not well attended, which was kind of surprising. Dove was kind of the surprise band. I thought they sucked, but you know, I was a kid, so I just wasn't ready. I didn't get it at all. You're supposed to look a certain way and you weren't supposed to make fun of music. I grew up later to appreciate them, but at that age, you have a certain conception of what rock and roll should be, and that wasn't it.

I saw James Chance there. I saw him at Duffy's, too; he played a couple nights. Actually, Karl punched him because he started pulling Karl's hair at Duffy's. He was kind of being his character, you know? It was the "Contort Yourself" era. Karl had razor blades in his ears. He started pulling Karl's hair and Karl reached up and tagged him. It was par for the course. I liked James Chance; I thought it was cool. So, yeah, M-80 was a huge part of my life.

LORI BARBERO: M-80—that's something that no one else had done. Tim Carr took the chance and did that. He really pushed his boundaries and took risks on a lot of things that he believed in, because he had such passion for things that no one else had done before.

DICK CHAMP: Here in town, I would say there were probably about a couple dozen local bands at the time of M-80. The names that come to mind, like the ones that played the festival: the Psychonauts were really a very interesting group. I didn't have a chance to see them but a couple of times. It was clear they had a unique vision. Fingerprints was still going strong. The Suburbs were thriving. The best years of their tenure were ahead of them because they toured extensively. They went all over the country, made videos and stuff, major releases by way of the success with Twin/Tone.

But, honestly, for me personally, I thought that M-80 was kind of the end, which is really gonna irritate people who'll say, "My god, you've gotta be kidding! What about Hüsker Dü and the Replacements?" Well, you know, fine—but personally I couldn't wait to leave Minnesota. I always wanted to be in New York, going all the way back to my junior year in high school. Getting NNB back together so we could play 7th Street Entry, in many ways that was supposed to be the vehicle to get out of Minneapolis. I was already craving something different. The whole scene had grown enough that it could host something as big as M-80 with class, but in many ways it was still a very small group of people who called the shots. So it became very difficult to constantly make your personal changes in public.

I went through a lot of evolution and revolution in my mind around that time, and I began to feel Minneapolis was too—this is almost forty years ago, folks, believe me—it *was* small. I wanted to be lost in the anonymity of a place like New York. Did I have my friends? There was some loss there, sure. But god bless them, they're still my friends, the very same people from that same scene. But yeah, I wanted to bury myself in total anonymity, which is so different from today because now everybody is trying to connect, with all the tools the Internet has. I just totally embraced the idea of underground and still do, you know? Anyway, it wasn't underground anymore to me here.

15

NEW YORK CITY EXODUS: MINNEAPOLIS MUSICIANS MOVE TO THE BIG APPLE

By the early 1980s, some on the burgeoning Minneapolis scene began to feel restless, like they had reached the limits of what they could accomplish in the Twin Cities. While continuing to grow, the scene was still relatively small, a "Mini-Apple" compared to the Big Apple. These artists wanted to expand their horizons and explore a bigger and more established scene—the one that had inspired many of them in the first place. New York City was home to many small but thriving clubs: CBGB, Mudd Club, Peppermint Lounge, Hurrah, Tier 3, Max's Kansas City. These clubs had hosted touring Minneapolis bands as well as the groundbreaking New York acts. Soon, many key figures from the Twin Cities scene began moving to New York City, including journalists, tastemakers, and musicians. Some, like the Wallets, simply relocated; others hooked up with new acts: Steve Almaas, who formed the Crackers and then Beat Rodeo; Danny Amis, who joined the Raybeats; and Mark Freeman and Cindy Blum from NNB.

MARK FREEMAN: It was an exodus. Everyone we knew moved to New York. *[laughs]* We [NNB] were among the first of that generation, you know. Everybody goes to New York sooner or later. It was entirely inspired by what was going on out there in music at the time. The reason everybody moved out there was because right then, it was an amazing scene. There was so much going on. It was past the Ramones, past Television, although the Ramones obviously were still together, Television maybe. It was the peak of the no wave thing, when we first got out there.

CHRIS OSGOOD: One example of New York City connections is Jim Clifford from the Wallets playing in Marbles. So there was a Minneapolitan there. And Steve Kramer, we knew him from high school. A lot of ex-Minneapolitans. And that's how it happened.

STEVE ALMAAS: The Wallets were there a while. That's when I met those guys. Everybody used to hang around the Holiday Cocktail Lounge on St. Mark's Place. It became sort of a Minnesota ex-pat bar. It was just a great old East Village bar, an old Polish bar. I met a lot of people from Minneapolis, guys in the Wallets and artist Dick Jerome, a lot of people I hadn't even really known in Minneapolis. I met them because they all hung out in the Holiday Cocktail Lounge.

ANDY SCHWARTZ: I had lived in Minneapolis for five years and felt I had pretty much done what I wanted to do there. I felt the pull of what was happening in music in New York in this underground rock scene. I thought I could make it and find some kind of job in the music business or as a music journalist.

The *New York Rocker* was founded in the spring of '76 by a guy named Alan Betrock. He was ready to fold the publication; he had published I think ten issues in about a two-year period. I offered to buy him out and keep it going. So I took over at the end of '77 or the beginning of '78 as publisher and editor.

CHRIS OSGOOD: The Commandos helped Andy move back to New York. We hauled his whole apartment in a U-Haul trailer, which blew out the engine in our van going across the Allegheny Mountains in Pennsylvania. So, we kind of sacrificed a van to get Andy Schwartz back out to New York.

My contribution to the discussion about the exodus to New York would be that Tim Carr moved there. Tim said the greatest thing one time. Somebody asked him, "When was the most exciting time to live in New York City?" And Tim's response was, "Two weeks before I got there." I think that that's so charmingly accurate. And it says a lot about Tim, too.

Tim moved to New York City right after M-80, around 1980. I'd go out to see him at his apartment on the Lower East Side, and we would have a lot of fun. It would be about ten o'clock at night, and Tim would go, "Well, are we ready to go out and seek intelligent life?" And off we'd go into the Manhattan night. Oh my gosh, all these parties that would go until dawn—that was the no wave times of Talking Heads and their parties. Tim was in the thick of all of that.

Steve Almaas was already living out there. The Commandos split up so he could move out there. He really wanted to get a band going in New York. But I had the fight with Danny Fields, the Ramones manager. The Commandos weren't going to move out there, but before that, we were. That was our plan, to relocate and use the Ramones' studio in New York. We were going to pay a thousand bucks a month for a nice, big studio that we could make noise in. But Danny Fields wanted to charge us something called a fixture fee—the Ramones had put a shower in.

In New York, it's normal that when you improve a space, you pass the expense of that on to the next occupants. But I didn't know that. I thought Danny was trying to screw us. But for that, we all probably would have lived in New York. It was that close.

Steve by then knew that that's where he wanted to live, and that's where he wanted to make his music. So when we lost our recording contract in '78 and decided that we were going to play through our Thanksgiving shows, Steve was planning on moving right after that.

STEVE ALMAAS: I fell in love with New York the first time we went there with the Suicide Commandos. We must have gone back there four or five times to play. I loved being there and wanted to be a part of it.

KAREN HAGLOF: Steve and I met and I think he wanted to be more of a pop-based person at the time than the Commandos necessarily was going to be, and also he had visions of going to New York and getting out of the area here.

Twin/Tone was putting together *Big Hits of Mid-America Volume Three* and starting to record for that. Jan King and I wrote a song called "Chains," which we played out at the Longhorn under the band name the Wad with Dave Phelps on drums, Steve Almaas on bass, and Mark Goldstein on keyboards. I think we did the one gig and ended up getting "Chains" on *Big Hits of Mid-America*. I think that was the last thing we did before moving to New York.

The Crackers came out of Steve and me, with Mark Goldstein, and Jay Peck on drums. It was basically Steve's push that we all move to New York. We came to New York in the spring of 1979 just for a visit. It was like, "Yeah, this is where I want to be. This is the kind of place I want to live in." So we moved. We had a gig within a week.

MARK FREEMAN: It was a great time in New York, so everyone wanted to live there. It was still reasonably cheap, I mean, under a thousand bucks for a decent apartment.

CINDY BLUM: Our apartment was $235 a month in the East Village, and it was a really horrible apartment. But it was an apartment in the East Village, you know. You could lay a pencil down and it would roll across the whole apartment. You come in the front door and there is the bathtub, and there is the stove across the room from the bathtub. There was a little closet with a toilet in it, and it was really awful. The guy next door would drill holes through the wall right above the bathtub.

Handbill for NNB's last Minneapolis performances, at the 7th Street Entry, before the band moved to New York, August 1980. COURTESY OF DICK CHAMP

MARK FREEMAN: And I would poke him in the eye with a straw. Yeah, it was terrible. It was cheap. Steve Almaas lived in the same building.

We all went to New York because the Minneapolis music scene—everybody who went there just wanted more. We wanted to be part of a bigger scene, a crazier scene.

The first time I ever went to New York City, Dick Champ and I drove out there together. We went up to the top of the Empire State Building to take a look at where we were, get the lay of the land, see the territory that we needed to conquer. Dick said, "Look at that, man. You look at all that and you just think, 'What's the point?'" I said, "Are you fucking kidding me? I look at that and I think, 'That's the battlefield.'"

It was a great trip. It was such a crazy time then. There was so much stuff going on. Yeah, no doubt about it, it was more vibrant than the Minneapolis scene. I've lived in a lot of music scenes, and every scene has its own kind of flavor. The Minneapolis scene was sort of a small pond kind of thing, where there were a lot of good bands around, but you saw the same people all the time. It had a predictable feel to it on some level. When I'd go see a band or we would go out in New York, you would always come away going, "What the hell?" It was like every time you saw something, they were out to wreck stuff. It was on a level of shattering the world. There were so many people who moved there. Tim Holmes, Tim Carr.

We were at Maxwell's [club in Hoboken, New Jersey] talking with Jody Kurilla. The drummer from the Jon Spencer Blues Explosion was there, and I'm a drummer at heart, and you put a guy like that in the room with me, I'm speechless. He was there and Jody Kurilla was there. We were talking to Jody and somebody came in and said, "Ms. Kurilla, your car is here." She says, "Oh, I gotta go." So she left and got into this freakin' limousine. It was gigantic. I turned to Steve or somebody and said, "What the hell does she do for a living?"

STEVE ALMAAS: Jody Kurilla was pretty large and in charge in New York. She ended up booking bands at a lot of different places, and opening a few. She booked bands at Danceteria and she started a club called Siberia. She DJ'd at the Pyramid Club, and I think she booked bands there, too. She booked a lot of shows I played on. She booked Beat Rodeo a lot. Later she became an A&R person at Geffen and was on the ground floor of the whole grunge thing. She had quite a bit going on.

JODY KURILLA: The Crackers, the Wallets, the Suburbs—all those bands were playing at Danceteria when I was DJ'ing and working there. It was *really* fun seeing those bands there. Some bands I may have helped get gigs in New York at that time.

We had this little area we all lived in called the Mini-Apple. We all had the same landlord, and that's how we got our apartments, down on Ludlow Street below Houston. We stayed very connected.

What happened, for me personally, is I was sitting in Minneapolis and watching a lot of my friends move to New York City. One of my friends and fellow Twin Cities scenester Henry Norton said, "My roommate moved out, and I'm taking over this apartment. Why don't you move here and be my roommate?" And Lori Newstrom, one of my roommates in Minneapolis and a good friend, had already moved out to New York. Steve Almaas was already there. Erik Hanson, who used to DJ at the Longhorn, he was gone. All these people were already gone from Minneapolis. And then my little house got robbed twice. I thought, "Heck, I've been broken into twice in Minneapolis. What can happen in New York?" Tony Peil and I hit the road with my records and my ironing board.

It was around Halloween, and we thought, "Let's go to Studio 54." We got picked out of the crowd right away, and went in. Tony had the mod haircut. I was wearing a '60s black cocktail dress. I remember we were doing the twist. Bianca Jagger and Andy Warhol were watching us. It was really funny. We're like, "I guess we're here! We're in New York! We're in Studio 54, and look who our audience is!" Literally, that was the second night we were there, October 31, 1981.

It was much harder being there. Minneapolis is easy. But for me, what I wanted to do was book bands and venues. I didn't feel like I could do that in Minneapolis. It was done. So I went to New York.

Danceteria had just opened. I walked in, and the owner came up to me and says, "What are you doing here?" I said, "I want to work in music, and I really want to book bands. I want to work in a club." And he said, "Come back tomorrow." So I got a job in the office, and I started right away—answering phones, writing all the press releases.

I DJ'd a lot of the clubs in New York at the time—Area, Tunnel, Pyramid, Danceteria, King Tut's Wah Wah Hut—and one-off parties, too. I did the Limelight once in a while for fashion shows, but I wasn't a fan of that club; it was creepy.

Then I started promoting shows and ran a club way ahead of its time because of what we were booking and its location, in the meatpacking district before anything other than Florent was there. I had a company called Off World Productions and booked so many bands in the late '80s and early '90s. I was booking the Pyramid, the R.A.P.P. Arts Center. I was the music director of a big music festival in New York called the New Music Festival for a couple years. It was the biggest festival in the world at the time.

I was working with a lot of bands from Sub Pop, Amphetamine Reptile, Touch and Go Records, Twin/Tone, K Records, and more—so many great small labels! The first time Mudhoney came to New York, it was my show at the Pyramid. I worked with so many bands during that time. I booked the first Nirvana show; it was a disaster!

MICHAEL MARKOS: Danceteria, Peppermint Lounge, Pyramid Club, Kamikaze, Palladium were some of the main clubs I went to after I moved to

New York City. Some clubs like the Mudd Club and Palladium and Club 53 were trying to be more exclusive, but I had some celebrity status because I ran a gallery in the East Village. The gallery would have an opening and then have an after party at one of these clubs.

The Minneapolis group sort of centered around Megan Williams, who is originally from San Francisco. She sort of was the den mother for all the Minnesota people. She dated Minnesota boys heavily: the artist James Crosby, Steve Kramer, and Dick Jerome, another artist from Minneapolis. You would have these different groups you could hang out with. Having the gallery, I met people internationally.

It was very diverse, and I think as an artist or musician or anything you chose to do, it would be vastly accelerated from what you could do here in Minnesota. What would take years here could happen in a few months there, with the connections you made and the input you got and the stimulation. There seems to be a ceiling here for artists in general. And people are still moving there—the Hold Steady moved out there, and a lot of Minnesota bands still go out there.

KAREN HAGLOF: We got to New York and Mark Goldstein had a psychotic break within a week or two. So we [the Crackers] never ended up playing that first gig because we were busy dealing with Mark's breakdown and getting him back to Minnesota.

I think the first gig we did have was at Tier 3. We played there several times as a trio. Then we got Mitch Easter [producer of R.E.M.'s early albums and front man for Let's Active] on guitar. Mitch came up from North Carolina. He had some idea he was going to start a recording studio in New York, which was far too expensive to do in New York. Now he has a great studio down in North Carolina, where I go do my mixing.

The Crackers went a year and a half or so before it all splintered apart. We made one EP, down at Mitch's Drive-In Studio in North Carolina after he had effectively left the band. It was called *Sir Crackers*.

STEVE ALMAAS: The whole mid-'70s CBGB and Max's scene was really appealing to me, but by the time I got there, it was changing. But the Mudd Club was happening. This club called Tier 3 was really good. And then Hurrah uptown. From 1979, when I got there, through 1986, '87, it was a real

Promotional photo of the Crackers—Steve Almaas, Karen Haglof, Jay Peck, and Mitch Easter—shortly before the release of *Sir Crackers* on Twin/Tone, 1981. PHOTO BY MICHAEL MARKOS

golden age to be in a band in New York. There were a lot of good gigs and good places to play.

MARK FREEMAN: Mars, Tier 3 was the scene then. Tier 3 was a great tiny, tiny, tiny little club down in Tribeca. I saw so many really great bands that I completely hated that club, because it was back when the New York noise stuff was happening—I wasn't that much into it. I just liked hanging out in that scene. It was so crazy.

Ruth Polsky booked at Hurrah. Hurrah was an amazing club. She was this beautiful person who took us in when we moved there. She was amazing. She was standing on the sidewalk out front of the Limelight club, and a cab jumped the curb and killed her in 1986.

DICK CHAMP: NNB played so many shows at Hurrah, where bands of the time were playing on a regular basis. Ira Kaplan [later of Yo La Tengo] was DJ'ing there. Maxwell's was Steve Fallon's club. He loved NNB. The club was very cush and very crowded.

CINDY BLUM: Mudd Club was big.

MARK FREEMAN: Steve Almaas and I went down there one night, and Chuck Hultquist went down there, but I don't think we got in. I think they turned us away. Some guy like Calvin Klein or something got Steve in. But he wouldn't get us in. I'm serious, it was like *he* can come in but *you* cannot come in. I guess he was wearing a polo shirt or something, I don't know.

DOUG ANDERSON: You meet people and you realize maybe 75 percent of them aren't as smart as you hoped they were. But 25 percent are great. So those people I looked up to, a lot left and went to New York. People like Duncan Hannah, a great painter and a really brilliant guy. Tim Holmes left pretty early. Tim Carr was a pretty big part of it, too. Tim went to New York City and ran the Kitchen for a while.

You inevitably drift toward a larger and a more interesting city, and the stimulation is much greater in a place like New York, right? I think all these people were intrepid and they really loved the *new*. That's what made everybody leave. You exhaust the resources in a small town.

But at that time you could go to First Avenue. What it became was modeled largely on Danceteria. It was important. You go to the Longhorn one night. Everybody sort of informed everybody else. Then once you went through the pool here, which was about a quarter of an inch deep, then you wanted to go to New York, where you would see people from uptown, the beginnings of hip hop. And the no wave bands and what was left of punk.

I think most of us left Minneapolis sort of as fans, but New York also is very provincial, so you would end up knowing those people. You would help to further their career by buying records or getting them shows or pushing people to like them. It was this weird symbiotic thing. I'm sure it happens with other cities, but somehow it seemed like in Minneapolis, that kind of music popped here really fast. The speed in which people left and went to New York developed this bridge. Jody ran Danceteria, right? That was *the* club that McClellan loved and everybody would go to when they would go visit New York. They would come back with all this exciting stuff and that would inspire another wave of people that were desperate for something new to leave and go there.

PART 03

16

NEW DAY RISING: HÜSKER DÜ

A hard-driving three piece consisting of guitarist Bob Mould, drummer Grant Hart, and bassist Greg Norton, Hüsker Dü was one of the most innovative, hard-working, and influential bands to come out of the Twin Cities. Vanguards of the DIY movement, they set up their own tours and handled booking, promotion, and merchandising while performing hundreds of shows annually and garnering attention from punkers around the nation. The band's first records were released on their own label, Reflex Records, and they went on to sign with national labels SST Records and then Warner Bros., before breaking up in 1987. Hüsker Dü's uniquely layered melodies within loud and extremely fast music combined with personal, poetic, and often wry socio-political lyrics as the band's style evolved rapidly from

Hüsker Dü—Grant Hart, Greg Norton, and Bob Mould—at Jay's Longhorn, circa 1980.
Photo by Kathy Chapman

post-punk to hardcore leanings and then various directions beyond. One of the first of a new generation of bands to follow the first wave of the punk and original rockers, Hüsker Dü set off in their own direction and took Minneapolis punk and hard rock to a wider national audience.

JODY KURILLA: I was getting band information for this newspaper calendar I was working for. I went down to the Longhorn, and Greg Norton came up and said, "We've got this band! You gotta come see our band." I said, "Well, what's it called?" He said, "Hüsker Dü!" And I, being bad with Swedish said, "What does *that* mean?" He said, "*Exactly!*"

JOHN KASS: I met Grant Hart at M-80. He's like, "I got this new band you should come see, Hüsker Dü. We're playing our second show ever, at Christiansen's." I went to go see the show. I think their first official show was at the Randolph Inn. I think they did a Macalester show when they had a keyboardist, Charlie Pine, in Hüsker Dü. He did a couple of gigs.

LORI BARBERO: I probably saw Hüsker Dü's first show at the Longhorn, because I was working there in '79. They were pretty sludgy. But I loved it. The music was really cool. You just stood there and went into this cathartic kind of "Ahhh." I think of the song "Statues." As soon as that bass line would start, this guitar is feeding back, and it was just so pure.

I love them and I was friends with them and we all hung out. When they put out their first single, that was pretty great. I bought a couple of them because I was so proud of the guys.

Bob Mould is one of my favorite singers. His voice makes tears come to my eyes. He has unbelievable talents. But in the early days it was a little rough. That is one of the great things about seeing a band before they're big or famous. I wish bands would start a little bit earlier, when they're not a polished turd, because there's nothing better than seeing a band start from scratch and just get better and better and better.

PETER JESPERSON: Hüsker Dü was a band I saw play a lot because they became one of the biggest draws at the Longhorn. For me, they were a little different, and what they were doing wasn't exactly my cup of tea. It was more hardcore than it was punk, I thought. And for a while it seemed like one of their main objectives was to play as fast as possible. Hence, *Land*

Handbill for Hüsker Dü concert at Jay's Longhorn, circa 1979, artwork by Grant Hart.
MINNESOTA HISTORICAL SOCIETY COLLECTIONS

Speed Record, for god's sake. I liked some of what they were doing, but it was a little out of my wheelhouse, and frankly a little beyond my understanding. I didn't really ever understand hardcore music, I guess. That's really not a criticism as much as an observation and possibly a faulty wiring in my own head or something.

But I loved the guys from Hüsker Dü, and all the guys were good friends and they hung out at Oar Folk. They gave me a tape of "Statues" and "Amusement"—it definitely had a lot of piss and vinegar. I remember thinking that it was good and had potential, but I also sort of made a decision that it wouldn't work for Twin/Tone because I felt it would put Charley Hallman on the spot, the third partner at Twin/Tone who was a dear man and a great friend of mine at the time. I thought Charley was a bit more old-fashioned. He was a record hound, but his favorite band was the Beach Boys, and I just thought he would not get Hüsker Dü. To discuss bringing Hüsker Dü into the Twin/Tone fold, I thought would make him uncomfortable. And so I passed on it. I just didn't think it was the right thing for Twin/Tone at the time.

The other thing I believe I said to Grant when I passed on bringing them to Twin/Tone was that I didn't think Hüsker Dü was a very good name. I can't deny it and it's sort of funny to look back on now. There's a lot of groups that have names that sounded silly when they began that we all embrace later. You think about somebody naming their group the Beatles in an era when the Crickets were a huge band. That's kind of dopey seeming in a way.

TERRY KATZMAN: The Suicide Commandos had just ended. And there I was, in trouble again. This would be worse, though. Hüsker Dü would take up more of my energies and my attention. Commandos were just a little party. But this was a band I would end up working with, and working for, and so it was different.

My first impression of Hüsker Dü was the same as the Commandos but more intense. The energy came from a different spot than the Commandos, maybe not quite as friendly. Chris Osgood is the one who told me about them. He'd been instructing Bob on guitar. I think he took like three lessons from Chris. Chris told him, "I think you're going to be okay."

Chris knew I loved Johnny Thunders's music, and he said, "You should go see this band. They do a couple of Thunders covers." That became a bonding link between Bob and me, because we both loved Thunders. Bob's playing is very much influenced by Thunders, to this day. Some of the ways he slides the strings are very Thunders-like.

I was scared when I met Bob the first time, because he seemed so mean. He wasn't, though. We got off on music right away, because we had a lot of similar musical tastes.

At that point they were just really a pop band. It wasn't like *Land Speed Record*. That was kind of the beauty of those days: they were fast, but they didn't play breakneck like they did later on, when some of the stuff got lost in the blur of speed. It was interesting to be part of those early songs that they wrote, all very simple pop songs, really, not with a lot of flourishes. They just kept moving at warp speed, both figuratively and realistically. From all of 1980 to part of '81, just in those two years, they progressed from that to *Land Speed Record*. They only had one single out. It was pretty fresh. They didn't have the canon of material they did later on.

MIKE MADDEN: Suicide Commandos were fast, and Hüsker Dü were faster. Just the whole punk aesthetic: get to the point, fast, there's no reason to repeat yourself. One chorus and one verse is enough, and three choruses is maybe too many. It just seemed like a natural evolution, you know? You really can't get any faster than Hüsker Dü, so you've gotta go some other direction with your music.

DAVE PIRNER: I felt really lucky to have seen Hüsker Dü before they decided to play everything incredibly fucking fast! It was before they moved into *Land Speed Record*. Their single was "Statues."

I remember there was a purple Mosrite guitar at Knut Koupeé. I thought it was the coolest guitar ever. It was the kind of guitar the Ventures play. I was one of those kids that looked at guitars in guitar stores and got all starry-eyed. I thought, "Oh my god, if I had that, I'd be really fucking rocking out." Lo and behold, I get to the Entry and Bob Mould is playing that guitar. That was kind of cool.

Handbill for Hüsker Dü concert with the Suburbs at Duffy's, circa 1982, artwork by Grant Hart. COURTESY OF MIKE MADDEN

JOHN KASS: Hüsker Dü was amazing. We couldn't believe how fast they were. In fact, the first article ever written about them was in *Trouser Press* magazine. It might've been Terry Katzman who was doing a Minneapolis scene report, and he writes, "The guys in Hüsker Dü, all they're trying to do is be the fastest band in the world, even faster than the Dickies."

The thing about Hüsker Dü that I don't think a lot of people realize is, even in their early days, they did two very distinct sets. They would do the fast set and then they would do the more arty, slow, Public Image Limited, Killing Joke kind of set. Their first 45 is more toward the latter stuff. Both "Statues" and "Amusement" is more the arty end of Hüsker Dü, whereas the first album, *Land Speed Record*, is total hardcore thrash.

Land Speed Record is one of the best records ever made by anybody ever. I still listen to that record and get goose bumps every time I hear it. That record changed my life so much.

TERRY KATZMAN: "Statues" and "Amusement" was the first single. "Statues" was recorded at Blackberry Way, and "Amusement" I recorded live. They were going to put in a studio track on the other side. I got the Duffy's tape home one night, and Bob went, "Oh, we kind of like this. Let's listen to it again." So we listened to it a couple of times. After they finished recording "Statues," we took the cassette over to Blackberry Way and snipped the song off.

I wrote an article called "Hüsker Dü" about seeing them play and that their first mini EP was coming out, which they never really released. That was the original plan for "Statues": it was going to be a ten-inch record, but the economics got in the way. They did four studio songs and then the one live thing. They added "Writer's Cramp," "Do You Remember," and "Let's Go Die," which had been previously released. But they didn't want to spend the money and they wanted to get the record out quickly, so that's why it got reduced to a seven-inch single. They wanted to have something to sell on the road and get in record stores. They were already looking at getting out of Minneapolis very quickly. They knew that they had to leave to make a real statement, and they couldn't just be hometown heroes.

Once *Land Speed Record* came out [January 1982], they were gone. There was really only one year, from the summer of '80 to the summer of '81, that they were homebodies. After that they started going to Kansas City or Madison or Chicago, and then it was Madison, Chicago, and New York, then it was Madison, Chicago, Boston. By the time they recorded *Zen Arcade* [1984], they were on the move.

Then I was relegated to be the Hüsker Dü gofer. Getting the mail up on 31st and Lake Street, where we had our PO box. My duty was to funnel out the chit-chat and make sure I didn't lose any checks. After *Zen* came out, you couldn't even get into the mailbox, it was so stuffed with mail. So I'd bring the mail back to the office, see if there was anything addressed to any of them individually and make sure it went on their desk, and then I waited for them to call and tell me to do something else.

I was a huge fan and went along for the ride. I never had a thought that I would ever manage them. They never really did have a manager until they got David Savoy later on. They were self-managed. But I did some little crap that they would have had to worry about; I just took care of it.

DAVE AHL: Hüsker Dü were pretty self-sufficient. They were pretty much creating their own tour support, their whole scene.

JOHN HAGA: The first time Hüsker Dü played at the Longhorn, I was standing on the side of the stage going, "What is this?" It was just so bombastic and over the top, but Bob was Bob even back then. Grant was Grant. They played enough that they got a following. You have to hop in a van, you have to give up your life, you have to eat dog food, you have to put up with shit attitudes if you want to make it.

MIKE MADDEN: I felt really lucky they picked me to go on the *Children's Crusade* tour in 1981 with them. I was a college student and had summers off. Maybe they just felt like, "Every band has a roadie; we need a roadie." I didn't know how to plug stuff in, even. I was more of a babysitter. I was there to help carry stuff, and there are some pretty volatile personalities. Maybe I was a calming influence or something. I was just a grunt and kind of kept the peace.

The most memorable date we had was at the Calgarian Hotel in Calgary. Grant and I had a room together in this hotel, Greg and Bob shared a room, and the bar was on the first floor. It was a dive bar in the daytime, a bunch of regulars who just stared straight ahead and nursed their drinks. Then the rock and roll show would start at eight or nine at night, and you could tell they were really irritated. They didn't like this intrusion on their place. The crowds were pretty small, but there was a band in Calgary that had heard of Hüsker Dü and contacted us and probably set up the gig, too. We hung out with them, and they brought their friends to all the shows. But it was still under twenty or twenty-five people at the show. There was a stabbing in the bathroom during the show. We met people on the stairway going up to our room that you'd rather avoid. It was a real dive.

By the time we got to Vancouver, we had pretty well-attended theater-type shows with maybe fifteen hundred people. In Vancouver we hooked up with DOA. They brought a lot of people to the show, and we became fast friends with the guys in DOA. They had this house they were squatting in. We went to food distribution places and stole food. That's how they got most of their food.

The tour was then Seattle and down the West Coast. They played with Dead Kennedys on that tour. That's when Bob met Jello Biafra, and boy, they hit it off. They were really fast friends. Bob was probably driving, Jello in the passenger seat. But they were in their own world.

DICK MADDEN: We were just following Hüsker Dü around all the time and living with Bob. Mike did the first half of the *Children's Crusade* tour.

We switched off in Seattle and then I took over. The *Children's Crusade* tour ended with the show at the Entry. They had the set completely down by then.

MIKE MADDEN: There was nothing like it at the time. They would run through fifteen to eighteen songs in thirty-five minutes. The song would end and Grant would count down and—bam!—the next song would start. It blew your hair back.

DICK MADDEN: The audience response on the tour was enthusiastic. It was the dawn of hardcore, so they had plenty of audiences every place. They were well received.

By the end of the tour, it was just spectacular sound. Plus it was their flirt with hardcore, right? They ultimately rejected it, I think for ideological reasons or something. They were really good at it and other bands were doing it, too. The Minutemen would do quick little snippets. It was sort of a political thing to do at the time, short and fast.

MIKE MADDEN: I remember an uptick in attendance when they got back from that tour. They had that triumphant return show at the 7th Street Entry. I wasn't there, but I heard it was jam-packed.

Bob was definitely the one with the ambition. I couldn't see how their music was ever gonna have mass appeal. Personally I loved it, but I remember one time he said, "I can't wait to sell out." I said, "What are you gonna sell? Nobody's gonna buy this." How wrong was I?

I loaned them a few hundred dollars to get *Land Speed Record* out, and they acknowledged that on the catch track. Etched in there is "Baby Warbucks." That was the good-natured nickname they gave me for lending them some money.

ERIC PIERSON: At first Hüsker Dü reminded me of a tribal kind of Public Image Limited. They had some poppier songs, some things that later they played much, much faster, but a lot of their early stuff, like "Statues," was a lot more post-punk. I always loved when they played their pop songs, but man, when they came back from their *Children's Crusade* tour you could tell that, not just their lives, our lives were different. All of a sudden they came back so over the top and so focused, like, "No, here's what you're in for." They were insane. It was like watching an explosion, especially in the early days when their gear was always breaking and Grant's drum set always looked like a washing machine that was coming apart.

DAVID MOE: But he had that great sound *because* it sounded like a broken washing machine.

I had seen almost every show early on in the Entry and was there for the recording of *Land Speed Record*, of course—both shows. They played two nights, and I remember, you didn't talk about it, but you sensed something was really happening, like it was really a happening thing.

TERRY KATZMAN: The only record I had a hand in personally, outside of the single, was I helped record *Land Speed Record* at 7th Street Entry when they completed their first tour. I was the running sound engineer between downstairs and the upstairs soundboard. They were frazzled. They got back into town on Thursday and recorded the thing on Saturday. So it was a very hastily arranged thing.

I think the last time I did sound for them was probably early 1984, in the Entry. The last thing I really worked on was the *Spin Radio Concert* taping at First Avenue. That was sort of my swan song. That was August '85. It ended up being my last audio connection with the Hüskers. By then they were going on the road. That life is not for me.

Lou Giordano took over doing sound right before *Zen Arcade* came out.

MARK TREHUS: I'll never forget taking LSD and laying in front of Mould's amplifier at the church in St. Paul [where Grant Hart lived] when the Hüskers were rehearsing the material that was to become *Zen Arcade*. "Recurring Dreams" seemed to get more and more daring and probing with each passing guitar phrase. In my blotter-splattered haze, I was convinced that Bob applied each and every twist and turn in his arsenal just to please my psychedelicized nodules. The absurdity of my arrogance, in retrospect, does little to diminish the impact I remember to this day. This was important stuff, and I knew it. At that moment there was no doubt in my mind that Hüsker Dü was the greatest rock band in the world.

MARTIN KELLER: When *Zen Arcade* came out, I didn't know what to think about it. I remember writing a lame-ass review that had a line in it like, "transitional at best." Then I started reading these national reviews, and I'm going, "Oops." Bob Mould xeroxed that review, put my name under it, and put flyers around Oar Folk. I went, "Yeah, I get it. I totally missed this fucking record." I should've waited a month to write it and lived with the record more. I totally missed what they were doing.

I loved *New Day Rising*. If I didn't write about it, I should have. I still think that's a really powerful record and song.

I wasn't as crazy about Hüsker Dü as I was the Replacements. I always felt they were a rapid work in progress that had the potential to self-destruct. It was so much craziness in that group, too. I went to see them a lot of times just trying to figure out, "What are they trying to do?" I think early on it seemed like they were practicing onstage or learning to play onstage. They evolved so quickly.

TERRY KATZMAN: They were one of the hardest working and most prolific bands, almost to their undoing in a way. As soon as a record came out, they'd be already playing songs from the next one. When *New Day Rising* came out, they were already doing songs from *Flip Your Wig*. That confused some people, because you're laying so much on them and they haven't even caught up with the other record. They were writing, music was coming out of them, and what are you gonna do about it?

I think they were actively playing outside of Minneapolis quicker than any other bands were. Again, they had a very strict work ethic they adhered to, and it included playing shows, recording, and running their business affairs, and that took up all the time.

That was one of the things that kept them pretty disciplined. There was some drinking and some drug taking, sure. We all heard about it, but they never let it interfere with what they were doing, what they were trying to prove, the music they were trying to make. I think Grant gets unfairly lumped into the drug issue. Mould wasn't a boy scout, trust me. When he knew he was drinking too much, Bob just stopped completely, and that was the end of it. A lot of people aren't able to do that. But Bob likes to be in control of things, and that's one reason he doesn't like to be diverted with unnecessary chemicals or anything else. His mind is always working on what the next thing's gonna be.

I like both Grant Hart and Bob Mould's music, in different ways. I can never *not* be a fan of either of them now. Their music is part of me after all these years. I like the power and the attack of Mould, but I also like the way Grant writes songs, and his voice. Neither is better than the other; they're both good in their own way.

Mould's stuff I like a lot just because I like what he does with a song within the context. Whenever he's in angst, he makes great records. It's always been that way. Too bad he has to pay the price for it, but we get great music out of it.

Grant's approach is a little different. The different approaches that they have are what made Hüsker Dü special, because they had two different ways of looking at things and brought it together in the music they made.

MIKE MADDEN: Grant had a real pop sensibility about him, whereas Bob was all about the wall of sound and the rage. But it all worked for about five years.

Grant also did all the artwork, and they were not your typical handbills. There were all these cut-and-paste things. A lot of religious iconography and booze bottles, and some ignominious historical figures—maybe Chairman Mao or people like that—would make it into his handbills, anything controversial. Always done artistically with those voice bubbles. He would put words in various characters' mouths. Of course they all loved Hüsker Dü in the voice bubbles. They made demands for the reader to be there. I really think he did it for the benefit of the fans, because we all got a great laugh out of it. Grant was the first that I was aware of doing flyers like that, and it was a style that caught on. Grant's were pretty sophisticated.

PAUL DICKINSON: To us, Hüsker Dü were like the anti–rock stars, because, no offense, they were kind of like slobs. We thought, "Wow, these guys are playing so fast." That was impressive how fast they were playing. That was a big deal.

MARK ENGEBRETSON: My favorite memories of the Entry are when I got to know the Man Sized Action guys and Bob Mould and those guys. The best show was probably our last one as the MORs, and I thought Tippy [guitarist for Man Sized Action] and those guys hated us. It was a full house; the Hüsker Dü Veggies—who later became Man Sized Action—were there. People were throwing stuff at us, I think because they liked us, but at the time I didn't know. This was January 29, 1981, and at the end of the night, we had an encore and I was singing that song that I first sang with the Hypstrz, "Just Like Me" by Paul Revere and the Raiders. Before I was done, the Veggies picked me up by the legs and I fell back on the stage and they carried me off while I was still singing.

We turned into the greatest friends. We started hanging out at parties. I was hanging out with them almost every week, but it seemed like almost every night at the Entry. And they really *were* the Veggies. They'd stand at the bar the whole time until Hüsker Dü would start, then they'd be right up front and we'd end up slam dancing together.

When I first heard Hüsker Dü, I probably wasn't that impressed. But after meeting the Veggies, I started to go see the band more often. I was totally blown away by how great they were.

There's a lot of people who were like, you're either a Hüsker Dü fan or a Replacements fan. You couldn't be both. I wasn't one of those guys. In fact, one time I was visiting Tippy when he was living with Bob Mould, and Tippy had to go to work. I hung out a while; Bob wanted to play some records for me. He started putting on Replacement records and talking about how great they were. I was surprised because I thought everybody who was associated with Hüsker Dü hated the Replacements. But no, he liked them.

MIKE MADDEN: I think the thing that got people to the shows was just word of mouth. Back then it was a phone tree. Sometimes we were fortunate and the show had been scheduled for weeks in advance and you could plan, and other times you would just get a call from Grant or Bob saying, "Hey, so-and-so cancelled at the Longhorn and we're filling in tonight," so we'd get all the Veggies down there to support them.

We were called the Veggies because we acted so stupid all the time. We acted like we were All-Star wrestlers on the dance floor. My former roommate, Tony Pucci, is the drummer in Man Sized Action and was one of the original Veggies. All those guys in Man Sized Action were Veggies. There were about fifteen of us, I'd say. We were mostly focused on Hüsker Dü, and other than that we all had dispersed interests.

It was different, though, in later years when it really got aggressive out there. The last thing you wanted to do when you were dancing at Hüsker Dü was hurt anybody else. If you were falling with somebody, you wanted them to fall on you, you didn't want to pile on them. Later on it got really aggressive and elbows would fly and people didn't care if others got hurt.

PAT WOODS: Tippy and I were from Minneapolis. Kelly Linehan, Tony Pucci, and a couple other guys were from St. Paul, and we would see them across the room at Hüsker Dü shows. We would point at them and make fun of them, and they did the same to us. We eventually would get drunk and end up standing in front of Hüsker Dü and bump into each other. We started talking and found out that we were all wrestling fans, and we started having fake wrestling matches on the stage when Hüsker Dü was playing.

EVA MOZEY ETOLL: I ended up going to almost all of the Hüsker Dü shows. It was when they first started playing, and there were only a few people who were fans: me, my dorm roommate Chrissy, the guys who formed Man Sized Action, and a few other people. Early on, Lori Barbero started coming to the shows. We became almost inseparable. To me, those people were my punk rock gang! It was a small group of people they called "the Veggies." I was a "Veggette." When they first started, Hüsker Dü used to play at the Longhorn, and then they would play the same night at the Entry. They'd carry all their gear from the Longhorn to the Entry; we would help.

DAVE PIRNER: It's hard for me to imagine something like the Hüsker Veggies around now. The first time I saw that I was pretty stunned. It was right around the time that *Land Speed Record* was coming out. It was a bunch of dudes in leather jackets slam dancing and beating the shit out of each other, but it was the *fun* kind of beating the shit out of each other. *[laughs]* I was like, "Holy shit! What on *earth* is going on here?" I don't know how much sobriety or not was involved with that thing.

ERNIE BATSON: The Hüsker Veggies—they were a group of other musicians. Man Sized Action and about four or five others. I think they called themselves that. Or maybe they got that from the doorman or something. *[laughs]*

BILL BATSON: We did some shows with Man Sized Action, Hypstrz (without Ernie), and Hüsker Dü in the First Avenue Mainroom on a Monday night. Those were just punk rock things. Three hundred people were there.

PAT WOODS: Tippy and I would sing doo-wop with Grant in the stairway to the 7th Street Entry. That was always fun. Bob gave me a pile driver on the floor in the dressing room. That kind of hurt. They were just good guys all the way around.

There was this weird change that happened with the crowds around that time. Was it when [the documentary film] *Decline of Western Civilization* had come out? A lot of idiots saw the slam dancing in that film and decided they could come to the Entry and try to hurt people.

TONY PUCCI: Before that it had been a lot of horsing around and a lot of fun and now this new element appeared and started throwing elbows and being real nasty. That was too bad. And once the Hüskers got more popular, the rooms were crowded all the time. The days of twenty-five, thirty friends watching their favorite band was over forever. You want them to be successful, obviously, but there is a little sense of, "Oh crap, now we lost our *thing*."

It was probably a matter of months until they caught on, and they caught on real fast because they were amazing. We were at the *Land Speed Record* live show. It was really crowded.

I thought Home Rock was awesome. They did it a couple of times [at the Longhorn], but it was too expensive. They would get all this second-hand furniture and an old TV and lamps and set the stage like a living room. Good idea, not sustainable. And they would never take the stuff with them when they left. Obviously the club's management was strongly opposed to Home Rock.

KEVIN BOWE: I remember once—a good Longhorn story—I don't know if the Dads were opening for Hüsker Dü or if I was just watching, but right from the beginning there was this incredible tension between Bob and Grant. So many great bands have that, whether it's Mick and Keith, or Daltrey and Townshend, or Lennon and McCartney. They were arguing in the dressing room heatedly; they had a TV and they were going to smash the TV onstage during their set, and they were arguing, like it was the most important thing in the world, over at what point in the set were they gonna bust up the TV. I was like, "Who gives a shit? You guys have such great songs. Bust up the TV right now, who cares?"

But the power—that three people could make such a big noise was incredible. That's the thing about Hüsker Dü, the majesty and the power and the physicality—they could sit there on the First Avenue Mainroom stage and fill up the whole room. And then the great songwriting, the polarized

Handbill for Hüsker Dü concert with Red Meat at Goofy's Upper Deck, March 13, 1982, artwork by Grant Hart. MINNESOTA HISTORICAL SOCIETY COLLECTIONS

Handbill for Hüsker Dü concert with the Hypstrz at the 7th Street Entry, December 13, 1980, artwork by Grant Hart. MINNESOTA HISTORICAL SOCIETY COLLECTIONS

songwriting between Grant's Beatles-y lovey-dovey things, in a way, and Bob's more muscular, angular things—both so great. From the beginning I knew they wouldn't last because a) I could tell they wanted to kill each other and b) they were just so different. But what a great thing they had when they managed to keep it together. It must've been hard. I always wondered what it was like for Greg.

PHILIP HARDER: I was living in Eau Claire and in a band who were obviously inspired by Hüsker Dü: you could hear that from just one note of our music. A bandmate and I drove to Minneapolis, to Twin/Tone Records on Nicollet Avenue, which also housed a recording studio and band offices. We walked the hallways to find someone to listen to our first cassette. It was a rough mix EP. We found Bob Mould, who also had Reflex Records. He was really nice and said he'd give it a listen. We thought we would just leave it for him, but he put the tape in right there and intently listened to all three songs on side A. I was thinking, "Wow! Bob Mould is listening to our tape." He flipped the cassette over and listened to the three songs on side B. There was no doubt he knew we were completely influenced by the Hüskers. He gave some comments, said good luck, and we said our good-byes.

But when we left he called after us and invited us to his house to listen to music and grill some food. We were like, "Of course!" We drank beers and Bob grilled steak. After a while Bob rather politely asked, almost as if he were putting us out: "Hüskers are mixing a new record. Would you care to give it a listen?" I thought, "Are you kidding!" Bob Mould was like our Bob Dylan. So just like when he listened to our crappy little cassette, we sat intently listening to every song, at full volume. The songs were recorded that week, and he seemed eager to play it and get some reactions. It was a very raw, rough mix, but it was probably the best recording I'd ever heard, considering the setting. The whole time he was looking at us, perhaps feeling out if this new music direction would work with a couple fans from Wisconsin. I'm not sure if I was very helpful because I thought every song was amazing. We got to hear *New Day Rising* in its early stages. The whole time we acted super cool like it was no big deal to listen to a rough mix of our favorite band in the home of one of our favorite musicians (the other being Grant Hart). After we left we went to our car, closed the doors, looked at each other, and just screamed. For me Bob Mould was a rock star, but he didn't fit the typical bullshit of mainstream stardom. That's why this music mattered.

KEVIN COLE: Hüsker Dü took the scene by storm and bulldozed it. They were ferocious—louder, faster, and more intense than any of the other bands at the time. They also seemed like three of the most unlikely guys to be in the same band. Bob was vicious, a whirlwind of pent-up energy, unleashing on the guitar, the music, and the crowd. He looked like he could explode at any moment. Grant, also intense, was so much more earthy— long hair, frequently barefoot, brilliant, wild, and loose on the drums, like Keith Moon with jazz chops. And a sweetheart of a vocalist, perfect counterpoint to Bob. Greg, frequently flying through the air, looked like he was actually having fun, which was an awesome juxtaposition to Bob's fury. They also had a strong DIY approach, and after an initial rejection from Twin/Tone, they released their first single on their own Reflex Records, inspiring other up-and-coming bands.

DAVE PIRNER: Hüsker Dü had their office right across the hallway from Twin/Tone when Soul Asylum was doing its Twin/Tone shit. They were real champions of the do-it-yourself aesthetic, DIY. You don't sit around and wait for somebody else to grant you permission to play music. You fucking do it.

I remember crossing the street heading toward Oar Folk and seeing Bob Mould. He said, "I heard you're going to make a record for Twin/Tone," and I said, "Yep," and he said, "I want to produce it," and I laughed. I didn't know what that meant. Nobody said, "That is a bad idea." Nobody said anything. We just went into the studio with Bob and that's the way it was. That's how I started to learn how things work in the studio. People say stuff like that. You think they're joking, and they're dead serious.

It was a great example, as far as Hüsker Dü was a band that went after it. "We don't give a fuck what anybody thinks; we're going to do *this*. Either you're in, or you're out. Get on the bus, or get the fuck out of the way."

17

THE SCENE GOES ON: DUFFY'S, GOOFY'S UPPER DECK, AND 7TH STREET ENTRY

Within a few years of the Longhorn opening its doors to original punk and indie rock, the scene was spreading fast. The number of bands was exploding in more and more genres: punk, post-punk, hardcore, new wave, art rock, experimental, and others. At the tail end of the heyday of Jay's Longhorn (then called Zoogie's), other venues began welcoming these acts, whether local, national, or international. Duffy's (at 26th Avenue and 26th Street in south Minneapolis) and Goofy's Upper Deck (at 654 2nd Avenue North in downtown Minneapolis), among others, picked up the rock 'n' roll and punk baton, and although those two venues were short-lived, Sam's—soon to be rechristened First Avenue—and the 7th Street Entry were staking claims as the Twin Cities' premier venues heading into the 1980s. The influx of new locally grown and imported bands was supported and encouraged by the more established acts from the first wave, and by the mid-'80s, Minneapolis was firmly established as a vibrant center of musical activity and creativity.

KEVIN COLE: By the early '80s, there were so many great local bands playing. The Warheads were an exceptional band, and Don the Baptist [Holzschuh], who was their lead singer, was just outrageous, a confrontational, in-your-face, rant-style performer. You had bands like Rifle Sport, Fine Art, and the Overtones. I loved the Overtones, a Minneapolis-based surf band. Safety Last was an incredible rockabilly band. Safety Last spun off Gary Louris, who went on to do the Jayhawks with Mark Olson. There were a bunch of cool rockabilly groups like Stagger Lee. So there was no shortage of local bands.

PD LARSON: The number of bands exploded after the Longhorn closed. By 1980, it was the new-band-a-week thing. You're like, "Huh? Who are *they*?"

On a lot of those early '80s tours, people were sleeping on couches of other musicians, writers, and venue dudes. It was an underground circuit all done on the telephone and US mail. It was the birth of indie rock as we know it. The whole concept of booking tours and tour managing and record distribution had its birth then. At the beginning of the '80s, a lot of people didn't know what they were doing, and by the late '80s, it had become a full-blown billion-dollar industry.

PETER JESPERSON: When a scene is growing, nobody would begrudge other rooms opening up. I guess I was a little worried if it was going to challenge my favorite home club, the Longhorn, but mostly it was like, the more the merrier. Duffy's really couldn't compete with the Longhorn. They overlapped for a while, but there was the 7th Street Entry, which was kind of the natural next favorite place after the Longhorn. Goofy's Upper Deck had its share of great shows. It had more hardcore stuff. I like punk rock and all kinds of music, but hardcore was not one of my favorites. Duffy's was more like the Longhorn, all kinds of different stuff. The people who ran Duffy's were nice people, but they weren't really rock savvy. Still, I saw lots and lots of good shows at Duffy's.

TERRY KATZMAN: All four of them—the Longhorn, Duffy's, Goofy's, 7th Street Entry—maybe were open for a very brief time together. I don't think Goofy's really started booking bands until later on, in '81, maybe? So it was close.

CHRIS OSGOOD: By the time of Goofy's Upper Deck, the scene had already, as far as I'm concerned, shifted away from what I consider myself a bigger part of. By that time we were playing First Avenue and Duffy's. And then Goofy's came along. Curt [Almsted] played Goofy's. Man Sized Action was there, and Hüsker Dü and the more hardcore things. Mosh pits were happening by that time. That just wasn't our scene. The Hüskers were the leading edge of it, and certainly bands like Black Flag, other LA bands, and Butthole Surfers. Dead Kennedys I think of as being sort of precursors to that scene, too. But it wasn't ours anymore. It had moved on.

ROBERT WILKINSON: The Longhorn became Zoogie's and we kept playing there for a while. There was a gay bar called Sutton's, and we played there. Wherever the major bars were in town, we'd play. We played First Avenue; I

Advertisement announcing Duffy's opening as a rock club, with Flamingo the opening act, July 12–14, 1979.
COURTESY OF CHRISSIE DUNLAP

don't think we played too often. Flamin' Oh's played the Union Bar at Central and Hennepin in Minneapolis. It was one of our last shows. We did the Cabooze every now and again, too. That was always fun. I think the Cabooze was just more established and wasn't known for being cutting edge.

Duffy's and the Longhorn/Zoogie's were offering the newer punk, new wave. Duffy's was awesome. The staff was always great to us. It became a real hot spot. Those guys were bringing in all kinds of cool people: [reads list on T-shirt] Bauhaus, Iggy Pop, the Cramps, the Damned, Bruce Cockburn, the Fleshtones, Nina Hagen, Plasmatics, the Jets, Joan Jett, the Psychedelic Furs, Jools Holland, Circle Jerks, Curtiss A.

JODY KURILLA: Duffy's was a strip club, and then, "We've got rock bands!" That place was hilarious. There was nothing *special* about any of those places. There was Goofy's, too. The same thing: nothing. It was just a bar. There were no hip bartenders. There was no attitude, no hipster décor. The people behind the bar thought we were weird and funny.

It wasn't like, "We're building a scene; we have to have this brand or concept." It was like, "We have a venue. Boom. We're going to go in and do our thing." Nobody was building nightclubs so that we could have a *cool* venue. Like, "If it's a cool venue, they must have really cool bands." We didn't do that. We went into some funky place with longhorns on the carpet.

Danceteria and those places in New York were building a scene and what they wanted the clubs to be like. But in Minneapolis, that wasn't happening. It was too early for that and, frankly, the New York money wasn't there, and it just wasn't part of what we were doing.

TOM HAZELMYER: I was a transplant kid from Michigan and trying to get a sense of what was going on in general and in Minnesota. The whole punk and new wave thing was a hidden underground spread across the Twin

Cities. Through a series of masonic handshakes and cloaked questions you might figure out where to go. No such thing as all-ages shows back then. Weird shows like Iggy at the Leamington Hotel would pop up. Hours and hours spent hanging around Oar Folkjokeopus and Harpo's and Hot Licks.

I started going to Duffy's in 1979 or '80. My older brother had joined the Marine Corps, and as a parting gift he gave me his ID, so my fifteen-year-old ass had a way in! Got to see some great shows until my mom found the ID. The Dead Boys was a particular highlight. Goofy's was like two lifetimes later, in '82.

STEVE ALMAAS: My band Beat Rodeo played at Duffy's. I remember doing sound check in the afternoon, and there were strippers on the bar. The Beat Rodeo people were all East Coast people. And we got quite a kick out of that, that those were just the most wholesome-looking strippers they'd ever seen.

STEVE BRANTSEG: The Phones started playing in Minneapolis in '78, '79. We were one of the first, as far as I know, to play at Duffy's, when it was still kind of an Irish bar. The owners liked us and we played there a lot.

We opened for the Psychedelic Furs on their first American tour. The way the Furs got booked in Duffy's was the Phones were playing there, and our soundman had a mix tape playing during the breaks. The guy booking the place said, "Wow, that's really cool music. Who's playing that?" My wife, Meera—who was my girlfriend at the time—said, "I made this tape. These are the Psychedelic Furs, and you should get them in here because they're a hot, up-and-coming band from England." So

The Phones: *(left to right)* Rick Taves, Jim Riley, Jeff Cerise (on the floor), Steve Brantseg, and Brad Mattson (obscured, on drums). PHOTO BY SHERYL MARQUARDT

she was kind of instrumental in getting them booked into that club. When they came to Duffy's we opened for them. Iggy Pop did two nights there. The Replacements opened one night and the Phones opened another night.

That was great, really raw and raucous. Iggy's new record at the time was *Soldier*. We opened his Friday night show and went to a party with him afterwards. Let's just say it was the crazy days!

JOHNNY REY: Johnny Rey and the Reaction played Duffy's. The Flamin' Oh's played there a *lot*—even then they would play three or four nights in a row, with different bands.

Duffy's was a great place to play. Nothing was ever as cool as the Longhorn, but that was like second place.

JAY BERINE: I did the booking and managed the room at Duffy's for two years, maybe '80, '81. I booked a ton of national stuff there, like Duran Duran. I did a bunch of shows with David Johansen, who also had played the Longhorn. After the show at Duffy's, about twenty people from the bar ended up in David's tiny hotel room. We started smoking Nepalese Temple Ball hash, which is laced with opium. David couldn't remember what we were smoking and kept asking if it was Japanese Camel's Balls. We laughed and laughed. He was a great guy.

LORI BARBERO: Duffy's had a lot more diversity, and the bigger acts. I saw the Replacements there a lot. The Damned played there. They were great. It wasn't packed.

DOUG ANDERSON: My favorite shows at Duffy's are super easy: Bauhaus, certainly Wall of Voodoo. The Replacements used to play every Tuesday for free. That was always fun. All the English bands would go to Duffy's. I've seen OMD. I've seen a million of them. I could start dropping names. All the rockabilly guys would come and play. Duffy's did kind of function more like a rock and roll club in my mind than First Avenue did, because First Avenue would have disco, too, and would alternate. Duffy's was fully on board.

MICHAEL REITER: There was a period when Duffy's was a cooler venue than First Avenue. They were getting more interesting shows because First Avenue was still Sam's and they were still wrestling with dance nights. So they weren't going to book some band that would draw a few hundred people on a Friday or Saturday if they could fill the whole place with dancing.

Duffy's was a fun venue. I played there a handful of times with local bills. Civil Defense played with Loud Fast Rules a lot. We were compared to the Buzzcocks sometimes.

DANIEL MURPHY: The first time [Loud Fast Rules] played Duffy's, we probably opened for the Replacements in maybe '82 or '83. I was nineteen or twenty and I was alarmed, and not at all bummed out, to learn that they had strippers for happy hour in the front room. Dave [Pirner] was still in high school. We figured that was maybe just a perk of being in a rock and roll band. But they weren't terribly nice at Duffy's to the bands. I remember the sound guy, we nicknamed him "Feedback Frank." He hated punk rock, so whenever we'd play there with the Replacements, he'd just turn the faders up and walk away from the sound booth. He thought it was just noise. Duffy's was notoriously bad sounding.

DICK MADDEN: Those early shows were sparsely attended. It took a long time for them [Loud Fast Rules] to catch on. At the time they were pretty much a hardcore punk rock band.

ADAM LEVY: My band Go Borneo played Duffy's and Goofy's Upper Deck, too. Duffy's would have an afternoon stripper. I was sixteen years old and I'd never seen anything like this, so we'd try not to look at these women onstage as we're bringing our gear in. We played with the Suburbs, the Wallets, the Replacements, Flamin' Oh's.

DAVID MOE: The early shows that I went to at Duffy's, I'd go there for the cute girls. But I also saw the Phones, and I was a big Wallets fan. We could easily go from the Wallets to Black Flag and not miss a beat. We'd totally be happy, great music, but it was more new wavey bands at Duffy's, and so when you heard Black Flag it kind of cracked me up.

MIKE MADDEN: Duffy's was really close to my house; it was walking distance. I've got six tapes I made at Duffy's. The XTC tape is fantastic. Sun Ra was like outer space. The banter was way out there.

My transition was from the Longhorn to 7th Street Entry. I liked twenty-five-cent beer night at the Entry, and Hüsker Dü was regular there, so I was there a lot. I grew to like it as much as I liked the Longhorn.

CHUCK STATLER: I liked going to shows at Duffy's. They had a good roster of touring artists. Sue McLean was booking there; she went from there to the Guthrie, and then from the Guthrie to Sue McLean and Associates. It's unfortunate that she left when she did because she was great. She was in a guy's business and it's tough for a woman, but she certainly made a mark.

I would prefer to go to Duffy's or the Longhorn over First Avenue or the Entry. Probably most of my time was spent at the Longhorn. Goofy's Upper Deck, I think that was kind of the last wave that came through. I know they might have all been operating at the same time, but my recollection is it was really kind of the tail end because I think it was Fred Gardner's [the bouncer at Duffy's] idea to open this upper deck at Goofy's.

BILL BATSON: By the time the 7th Street Entry opened, we were almost out of the Longhorn. The Entry was such a cool place, and the payoff was more honest. It was what everything was moving toward. We were also doing Duffy's and a couple other places that opened and died within six months. Goofy's Upper Deck started after that. Duffy's was below a strip joint, and the Upper Deck was empty office spaces they put a stage in. I did sound there several times.

Duffy's was run by Dan and Leslie Johnson and they were assholes, on the same level as Hartley Frank. They were star fuckers. They were just out for the thrill of having big names in their place so they could be seen with them. If you didn't have an English accent, then she didn't want to talk to you. And he wanted to get anything besides his wife. And they wouldn't pay and they were pricks about it. They didn't care. We were just a piece of meat to them. A lot of bar owners were like that, most of them. They're not all Steve McClellans.

Duffy's was such a pain in the ass. It was a lousy-sounding room. It was hard to hear anything, because there was a dome over the stage and the dance floor. It was like an atrium. It would just swirl around in there. And the sound guys weren't people I recognized. Those guys didn't want to be there.

Fred Gardner, who was a bouncer at Duffy's, became the booker at the Upper Deck, or at least that's who we dealt with. We played with the Trashmen there. That was weird. It was the '70s still for them, for all of us I guess, and they did their ballroom thing. That's where the Trashmen met the Hypstrz for the first time. Every time we talk to them since, they remember that show because it was so weird they're playing downtown Minneapolis. At that time they were playing out in the 'burbs, making real good money, but they did this one show.

ERNIE BATSON: It would get kind of wild and frenetic up there at Goofy's. There was potential for fights. I think I had left the band when you guys did a whole bunch of stuff there. You graciously let me join the band again the one night opening for the Trashmen. I saw the Effigies a couple of times. The Three O'Clock were fun.

TONY PUCCI: Goofy's had those damn steep stairs. It was really hard loading in, and it was harder loading out. If you'd had a couple of cocktails, that was brutal.

DANIEL MURPHY: I rarely went to Goofy's. I think I saw Hüsker Dü there once, and I saw the Salvation Army, and then they turned into the Three O'Clock, an LA kind of hippie-core, punk band, and they were really cool. Bands like Final Conflict had a scene there.

There was a big guy who used to bounce at Duffy's who kind of ran and booked Goofy's. He was like "Fred, the friendly bouncer." He was much nicer to the bands. But that place was a dump. And the load out was a nightmare. It was at the top of the place, and you had to load all your Marshall cabinets on the rickety old stairs. You'd get out of there about 1:30 AM and you'd be ready to go have a couple beers, and then you had to load all your crap down this staircase. It was real bad.

The Upper Deck was always unorganized, and we could only draw like thirty, forty, fifty people. We'd play with, like, the Magnolias and Jim Walsh's band, the REMs, but no real advertising. There was a fanzine called *Your Flesh* that wrote about all the bands that played the Upper Deck, but they wouldn't do advertising. Shows at the Upper Deck were totally word of mouth.

TERRY KATZMAN: Goofy's was more off the beaten path. That was a select punk rock club. Except no one could make any money. Hüsker Dü couldn't make any damn money playing there because the place was crooked. It was a whorehouse really, to be completely blunt. It was a bar downstairs and an escort service upstairs. All around the stage were these escort rooms.

Goofy's is where we recorded *Kitten: A Compilation* for Reflex Records in '82, in one of the escort rooms. We did that to document the Upper Deck, because we knew it'd probably be one of the few things recorded there. The Hüskers didn't really want to play that night, and we kind of had to twist their arms to do it. Mecht Mensch played. They were from Madison, just smoking little youngsters that had these crazy fast songs that gave the Hüskers a run for their money.

It was two nights, Friday and Saturday. We ran cords from the back of the stage into one of the back dressing rooms and recorded. We had each band play a short set for the sound check—like it really mattered. The second set was the "keeper." But everybody knew we were only gonna use a couple selections in the end.

Handbill for Reflex Records Benefit Concert at Goofy's Upper Deck, October 8–9, 1982, for the recording of *Kitten: A Compilation*. COURTESY OF DALE T. NELSON

Each band submitted a page of artwork, and we xeroxed it off, stapled them all together, and slid them into the bags. Bands on *Kitten* included Man Sized Action, Rifle Sport, Exmo-6-Desmo, which is this Zappaesque, free-form band that featured Mike Etoll. And then we had Todlachen, the earliest version of Otto's Chemical Lounge when Tom Hazelmyer was in the band. Then you had Willful Neglect, which was our straight hardcore-type aficionados, and Radio for Teens, which had Polly Alexander, who went on to be in Têtes Noires.

DANIEL MURPHY: We recorded the *Kitten* compilation at the Upper Deck under the name Proud Crass Fools. That show didn't go well for us at all. We were the first band that played because we were just starting out. All those other bands were way bigger and had more fans. I think every band probably played twenty or twenty-five minutes. We opened with a Creedence Clearwater Revival song, "Bad Moon Rising," just to test the sound levels. That was the thing they ended up using, that's how bad that show was.

TONY PUCCI: Back in 1980, we had been in New York City for spring break. We saw somebody at CBGB every night. When we were at Peppermint Lounge, this little guy dancing, smashes into Kel [Kelly Linehan]. Kel's gonna yell at the guy, and the guy turns around and it's Billy Idol! *[laughs]*

So we're walking to the hotel, we're lost. We're sitting in front of a gay porno theater, trying to get our bearings. There's a poster of a movie called *Pump Number Nine*, and in big letters across the poster, it says "Man Sized Action." And I say to Kel, "That would be a good name for a band!"

PAT WOODS: Summer of '81, Hüsker Dü left on their *Children's Crusade* tour, and we were bored, going, "What the hell are we going to do?" Somebody came up with the idea, "Let's start a band." Tony was like, "I can drum." Tippy said, "I'll play guitar." We spent the summer learning seven songs. We couldn't play any covers, so we had to do our own.

TONY PUCCI: Steve McClellan goes, "All right. You can open for Hüsker Dü on this night. What's your name?" And I just say it. "We're Man Sized Action!" And I tell the guys, "Guess who we are?!" [laughs] And it stuck.

PAT WOODS: We played one of the first "punk" shows at Goofy's Upper Deck, on New Year's Eve going into 1982, with the Replacements and the Hüskers, Dead Lemmings, Blue Hippos. It was funny because the backdrop of the stage was a huge reproduction of a Jefferson Starship album.

Somebody booked a show for us, Red Meat, and Articles of Faith from Chicago at the Upper Deck. We got there and there was no PA. So somebody got the bright idea of calling Gérard Boissy and Pete Conway, because they had a PA. Rifle Sport didn't come along until a little later, but we had seen Pete and Gérard around. So we went to their apartment and schlepped their PA to the Upper Deck. That became the house PA. It eventually got trashed when they had the last two shows at that club.

LORI BARBERO: I was booking the Upper Deck. I got Black Flag, the Minutemen, and Hüsker Dü. Grant Hart was friends with Black Flag and did the poster. Hüsker Dü was on SST Records with them.

The Goofy's stage was probably only about ten inches high, so it was really intimate. There's a lot of wood we painted black. I painted it with a couple other people. I think Bill Batson might have been one of the sound engineers there. I kind of made it into a punk rock club. Not all the shows were big, but some of them were *really* big! It was pretty fun. I'd say Goofy's Upper Deck bar was probably about one-fifty capacity.

ED ACKERSON: The atmosphere at some of the big hardcore shows at the Upper Deck is something I'll never forget. Shows like the Black Flag show were *soooo* intense. Kids were incredibly psyched to be in the middle of all the energy. It felt like a new type of culture or sound was being created, and in very real ways that was true.

Another real highlight show to me was the Three O'Clock (formerly Salvation Army) show with Otto's Chemical Lounge opening in about July '83 at the Upper Deck. That show was a sort of coming-out event for the psych/garage/'60s scene that my friends and I were to play a large part in over the next few years.

TOM HAZELMYER: Me and guitarist Paul Osby were on a big Blue Cheer/MC5 kick with a bunch of psychedelia thrown in. We were all growing tired of how formulaic hardcore had become by '82 and decided to dissolve our hardcore band and start up Otto's Chemical Lounge. We were both still in high school at the time. Paul and I were each writing material as well as writing together. I was only around for the first year of the band, so the dust hadn't really settled on who the main songwriter would be.

STEVE BRANTSEG: We'd see Otto's Chemical Lounge at Goofy's Upper Deck. They were a favorite band! Dale T. Nelson was the most entertaining guy. Man, he was *so* funny. Paul Osby was so young at the time. Dale looked like he looks now. Paul looked about twelve. We were like, "What the hell? Is this a father and son band, or what is this?" But the energy and enthusiasm was just fantastic.

PETER JESPERSON: I loved Otto's Chemical Lounge. Dale was a stalwart of the Minneapolis music scene before he was ever in a band. He was an obsessed record hound like the rest of us. I love Dale.

DALE T. NELSON: Jello Biafra [Dead Kennedys] said once, "Otto's Chemical Lounge sounds like James Brown meets Blue Cheer on acid." Pretty much hit it right there! He said it at a show and on a *Maximum Rocknroll* record review. Of course, hearing it from Jello Biafra's mouth is enough for me.

We played a show with Dead Kennedys—oh boy! When I first got there, I was so scared because we'd never played in front of two thousand punk rockers before. When I saw all these mohawks and leather jackets and skulls, I was like, "Holy shit!" I got really nervous. We opened up the first song. Next thing I know, somebody grabbed me by my foot and pulled me out and started passing me around like a joint. I thought, "This is gonna be crazy." I was really scared, but at the same time I was excited. It was like, "God, this is great. I can't believe it." And they gently put me back up, guy hands me my mic, and I started singing—perfect timing, too. It's like they knew how my entry was gonna be. I've never had so much fun. That was one of my favorite rock shows ever.

Hüsker Dü took Otto's Chemical Lounge under their wing, right away. We played twenty or so shows with Hüsker Dü. And like two shows with the Replacements. That's a drunken memory.

We played Duffy's and Goofy's with Hüsker Dü, and Duffy's with Loud Fast Rules right before they changed their name to Soul Asylum. I always got to play with them and we got to be friends real quick because they liked us, and we liked them. The camaraderie was really good. I mean, back then, the bands were almost like a family. You all played together and you all dug other bands. Even if you didn't like their music, you liked them. It didn't matter, because you liked the attitude and it was a punk thing, you know? It was real punk.

TOM HAZELMYER: Todlachen, being part of the just-starting hardcore scene, was playing largely to crowds as wet behind the ears as we were. Certainly a large chunk of the original punk crowd had no time for us newcomers.

PAUL DICKINSON: Adam Levy had a ska band called Go Borneo, and he got Manifest Destiny our first real live show, at Goofy's Upper Deck. We played some house parties before that, but it was the first legit gig. Exciting story about that is loading in my drum set and some drunk homeless guy stole my snare drum. So I run down the street after him and we get into a tug of war over this snare drum, and I won. It was like, "Welcome to Minneapolis." Playing Goofy's was fun, and a little terrifying. It was hilarious. I saw a lot of shows there and we played all-ages shows. Manifest Destiny played at Duffy's a couple times. We played with the Urban Guerillas a lot. The thing is, we did play a lot because there weren't so many bands back then. Now there's so many bands. Also, you didn't have to be that good. *[laughs]*

Manifest Destiny was me and my friends. I was sixteen years old. I was the drummer. Russ Mazion was the singer. Mike Prichard—my best friend who I grew up with—played bass. Erick Volden played guitar. He was the driving creative force. He was like the first punk rocker at my high school, but we were more like a new wave band. What you have to understand about that era is that we were all freaks together: new wave, punk. We would just practice after school because we were losers. We had nothing else to do, nowhere else to go. Might as well go into the basement and make a bunch of noise for four or five hours straight.

When I was a kid, either you played covers or you were a freak—learn the side of this album note for note, or forget about it. That's part of what we were rebelling against. We played our own music. And punk told us, you don't have to write some stupid love song; you can write a song about anything you want. That's what was liberating about the whole DIY thing.

JOHN KASS: Willful Neglect played a few shows at the Entry and at the Upper Deck. They were part of the last show at the Upper Deck. Played a bunch at McCafferty's in St. Paul, Duffy's a couple times, notably with the Circle Jerks.

I wasn't as good a musician as the other guys, and it was Rory Schoenheider of Willful Neglect who pulled me aside and said, "John, you should be our manager." That's how I ended up getting in the record business. I was kind of sad that I was kind of being kicked out of the band, but I also knew these other guys were much better musicians than me—Rory and especially Roger DeBace, a fantastic guitar player.

Willful Neglect put out a record in 1982. I remember saying to them, "How are you gonna get this distributed and promoted?" They looked at me like, "I don't know. We just made the record." I decided to help them. I learned the business by making mistakes and getting advice from Grant Hart and Bob Mould. I remember going over to Twin/Tone, and Jill Fonaas was totally open: "Here's our radio station list, our magazine list, and if we get any updates we'll let you know." I would mail copies of the Willful Neglect record to radio stations, magazines, and fanzines. We actually used to take out ads in the fanzines and in just about every issue of *Your Flesh*.

DAVID MOE: I had this hardcore band with Bill Devlin called Church Picnic. The reason it was called Church Picnic is we started practicing in a church that his brother owned and we ended up crashing. We played there, Hüsker Dü rehearsed there with us, and we did a lot of impromptu shows. We put up a lot of bands, we put up DOA once, we put up Dead Kennedys. A friend of ours has a Dead Kennedys album autographed by Jello Biafra: "You guys live in the coolest place ever."

One infamous show was the band Scream from DC. Grant Hart put it on with Dale T. Nelson. I caught word that this was going on and I go, "Huh, well, I might want to go see that." When I showed up there are all these people at the door at the top of the church steps, which nobody ever went through. So I was asking, "Well, who opened this door?" There were all these people I never knew, and they're gonna charge me ten bucks to get into my own place! I just pushed in and I hear this music playing and I'm thinking, "Well, we set up a stage with a PA and they're probably using our gear," so another reason I'm not gonna pay. I got down there and long story short, Dave Grohl was playing drums with Scream and there he was, hammering away on Bill Devlin's drum kit, unannounced, unasked. There was a couple hundred kids there. But it wasn't until years later I found out who Dave Grohl was. He had really long hair at the time.

ERIC PIERSON: He wasn't in Nirvana yet; this was much earlier. It was '83, '84 maybe. We played one gig with Hüsker Dü in the church. It was pretty wild. In '82, '83 when they were getting the material for *Zen Arcade* worked up, it was in that church that Davey had.

DOUG ANDERSON: My band for a good year and a half was a hardcore band, Red Meat. But we were more interested in Motörhead, Aerosmith maybe. Red Meat would play at Duffy's, Goofy's, a lot of VFW halls and house parties. We could not play First Avenue. I didn't play First Avenue until like '84, when I was playing bass with Caleb Palmiter's band, A Single Love.

Caleb's music was so good. He was so square that he was cool. We all loved Caleb. Caleb was a big part of this town's music thing, too. He taught and encouraged a lot of people to play. He started the Jayhawks with Mark Olson. I think he gave him the name the Jayhawks.

ED ACKERSON: I had done some weird little shows from age fourteen onward out in the Stillwater area, and I'd been to many punk shows, so by the time Mr. Slate finally played the Upper Deck I felt comfortable and ready to join the party. Mr. Slate was me on guitar, Paul Harsha on bass, and Jed Mayer on drums. We were all about sixteen or seventeen and extremely limited in our abilities, but we had a ton of energy and were determined to get noticed. We did shows with a range of bands, including Ground Zero, Red Meat, Todlachen, Church Picnic, Irenic Regime, Neglecters, Outcry, Skull Fuck, Urban Guerillas, and others.

JOHN KASS: The Urban Guerillas were the band that a lot of the class of '84, '85 opened for. They were the band that was playing the most and everybody had to open for them. They were super fun. They didn't take themselves very seriously, and when the whole label thing happened, they weren't really a part of it because I think they all moved to LA or something. They were as important a part of the scene at one point as Hüsker Dü and the Replacements in terms of going out on a weekend.

DOUG ANDERSON: Audiences were changing a little bit. There was a thing about where your allegiance was, what club you were really with. There was a good year or two where I was going to Duffy's all the time. They were bringing in cooler shit. Hardcore was all Goofy's was booking. When hardcore happened, you had to stop seeing *everything* because it was real hardcore, right? It was so homophobic and so masculine and so boring and ugly and sweaty and gross.

That kind of killed a lot of the extravagance of the Minneapolis scene, because in the early days, it had a huge gay contingent. There would be these great hairdressers, these great drag queens. It was much more tolerated back then, I think, than in the '80s. The '80s were really dark and hardcore. I helped in a way by facilitating a lot of what was going on at Goofy's, but I wasn't that way. I could care less what anybody did. I was there so I could see bands like Discharge or PDH. The American hardcore stuff really didn't interest me much. I loved Rifle Sport, and Final Conflict was really good. Those bands I thought were great, but a lot of the surrounding stuff was so boring.

It totally changed artistically. Rifle Sport was exceptional in that way, because they were smart guys. Gérard-Jean Boissy also loved all that geeky old music. Gérard and I would secretly love Kraftwerk or Devo or Sparks when you weren't supposed to. That was outside of what was allowed by hardcore.

TERRY KATZMAN: I thought Rifle Sport was like an avant-garde rock band that had some punk rock going on. Gérard was more of a technical guitar player, not really a punk rock guitar player. He paid a lot of attention to technique, to his style, though he rocks really hard.

They were part of the cognoscenti. They warmed up Hüskers, Man Sized Action. They were the satellite band of Hüsker Dü at that point. They were more than that, but that's what brought them to greater prominence, I think.

Man Sized Action reminded me a lot of my heroes of punk rock: more studied Wire, Joy Division, Buzzcocks. They also had another thing that was very much their own. They had a kind of tenderness to some of the things they did, and a real compassion to their sound I think some people missed.

JOHN KASS: I'd go see the Man Sized Action and Rifle Sport guys all the time. At one point there was kind of a rivalry because I would try to get gigs for Willful Neglect, and those guys would get gigs, and they ended up putting records on Hüsker Dü's label. But it was a friendly rivalry. It wasn't anything bad. We would go to their shows. I would see all those guys at Willful Neglect shows, too.

TIM PIOTROWSKI: We went and saw Rifle Sport, Man Sized Action, and Hüsker Dü probably every time they played, and you had to. That was part of paying your dues. Not only that, you'd go to all the punk shows. You went to *every* fucking one. There were nights when we'd cross town to go see Hüsker Dü at McCready's in St. Paul and try and make it back to the Uptown to catch Man Sized Action and then go to the Entry after that, or an after party for the show at the Entry.

TONY PUCCI: We played as much as we possibly could. Our friends that knew what we were doing would show up. The usual suspects: the Rifle Sport guys were there, as we were there for them when they played. We were tagging along on the coattails of Hüsker Dü and the Hypstrz and those guys. So that's how people saw us: we happened to open for actual popular bands. The Hypstrz let us open for them whenever we wanted. We played

Man Sized Action, performing in First Avenue's Mainroom, 1982. Left to right: Pat Woods, Kelly Linehan, Tippy, and Tony Pucci. PHOTO BY TOM CANNON, COURTESY OF TONY PUCCI

a lot of shows with the Whole Lotta Loves. The first year, most shows were with them and Rifle Sport and Hüsker Dü. Then we formed a lifelong partnership with Rifle Sport and they played with us forever and ever and ever. We played a hundred shows together in town and on the road. We'd open for each other. It didn't matter.

Rifle Sport was pretty self-sufficient, pretty quickly. Chris [J. Christopher] was a real driven leader and really industrious. He had been in Vendetta, so he had been around the scene. Pete and Gérard played in bands in college in Wisconsin, so they knew what they were doing. We did a lot of shows together and would take turns headlining. We would rather open and then drink beer and watch the other guys play. It was an opportunity to have fun and goof around and get a couple of bucks and get a couple of beers and see all your friends.

PAT WOODS: We had an incredible group of supportive friends—the Whole Lotta Loves, the Hypstrz, the Hüskers, all were more than happy to put us on their bills. People liked what we were doing, at least liked the effort we were putting into it. Steve McClellan supported us, too. He liked what we were doing, so he would throw us on with national acts from time to time.

TONY PUCCI: We played with Richard Hell. We got to open for R.E.M. Playing with Wayne Kramer and MC5 was pretty cool. I felt very young and inexperienced. He was cool because we were in sound check and I was banging the drums and we were doing some typical thing we would do, and he was into the beat, walking in front of the stage. It was like, "All right, we are okay!"

The people were great and the scene was really cool. We would always open for everybody with the full intent of playing harder and doing everything we could to leave a lasting impression. There were some bands that weren't as friendly with each other as others. But for the most part you could borrow gear from anybody and people would help each other out. People would put you on their bill if you needed a show.

When we started, to be a headliner you had to be able to play two forty-five minute sets. There were never three bands on the bill. It was two bands, so I think you had to work harder, certainly have more material.

PAT WOODS: It was a community definitely. As we started to develop and began headlining sets, we would try to help other bands come along, to kind of grow the community that way. I felt like it was an obligation. People like the Hypstrz and Hüsker Dü took us under their wing, and that was the least we could do, whether it was for Tiltawhirl, which became Arcwelder, or Exmo-6-Desmo, or Ground Zero.

TONY PUCCI: Tiltawhirl—great guys, really good players, really interesting band. Scott Macdonald had drummed with 2i and was really accomplished and a fun guy. I was always drawn to the Arcwelder guys. They're fun to hang out with. Those guys took off and flew and are still tremendous.

JOHN KASS: There were East Side St. Paul bands, the Minneapolis bands, and then there were the ones in the middle like Lindberg's Baby, the Odd, Pax Americana and Manifest Destiny, Tiltawhirl. That's like Midway punks, right? Paul Dickinson put out a cassette, *Hypnotic Tornado*, a compilation album of Midway-area St. Paul bands around '84. It is one of the coolest unknown records in Minnesota history.

Scott Macdonald of Arcwelder was part of that whole scene. 2i is some of the guys that worked at TCI [Twin City Imports]. TCI was in the Midway neighborhood, too.

SCOTT MACDONALD: I played drums with teenage cover bands at first, but was recruited in 1979 by a fellow student, Murat Konar, to join a Minneapolis band called the Situation. In my mind, this was a step up as they played their own music. I was sixteen years old. I played my first show with them at an after-hours party that a six-month-old Hüsker Dü played at as well. I got kicked out of the band when I couldn't make a gig because I had a prior high school concert band commitment. Which is too bad because the gig I missed was with NNB.

Before Tiltawhirl we were called Velvet Elvis. Paul Dickinson was playing drums, I was playing bass, and Rob and Bill Graber were playing guitars. A year later, maybe less, we started Tiltawhirl. We officially call it '87 but I think it was more like '86, just as 2i was breaking up. The first single came out in '87.

Tiltawhirl was a whole new thing. It was inspired by the Replacements and Soul Asylum. I loved Tommy Stinson jumping around on the stage and I would take the Grabers to see those shows, so they could see Tommy jumping on the stage. So a lot of the Minneapolis stuff I absorbed and I kind of downloaded on Rob and Bill.

I remember being in Los Angeles once and seeing all the hardcore kids and thinking, "I don't think I could approach those guys or even go to a show." In Minneapolis it was friendly.

SHARON KANIESS: At the Entry there would be a lot of hardcore at that time. Dan [Kaniess] and I weren't about to try and replicate it, but we liked it. The philosophy was different in other places that had hardcore, it seems to me—different being exclusive, whereas in the Twin Cities it seemed fairly inclusive.

TOM HAZELMYER: The hardcore scene was mind blowing to a teenager. In retrospect, you could barely call fifty folks strong a "scene," but it was all you could hope for in the sense of camaraderie and being united in the face of a completely apathetic world towards what we were up to. The lessons learned in rolling up our collective sleeves and making shit happen have never been lost on me.

It was such a new, raw, revolutionary sound that it was impossible to get your fill through the media or live. So each event was just that, an event.

I think this phenomenon occurs regularly throughout documented art/music movements that collide or have crossover elements. The newcomers are viewed with disdain by the hardened "vets" and haven't "paid their dues." The up-and-comers are usually bringing in change or evolution, which is resisted by even those most ardent individualists. It was a bit confusing to us younger lot at the time, as we certainly loved the music and movement that preceded us—New York punk and UK punk and post-punk—but as kids are wont to do, we had different ideas of where this should evolve. Back then, that three- to six-year age difference was a fucking chasm. At Discharge or Black Flag's first Minneapolis shows the crowds were solidly under twenty-two, I'd guess. I still know folks from the preceding punk generation that will go on about how much they hate hardcore.

TONY PUCCI: It seemed like the scene kind of started to compartmentalize, which was sad. When I first got into it, I'd go see music three, four, five, six nights a week; it didn't matter who it was or where it was, just so it was something new. And everybody was mutually supportive. If a band was willing to give it a shot, everybody was receptive. The scene was so hungry, just starving for stuff. And then after a couple of years, it seemed to kind of splinter. "*I* only go to hardcore bands, and *I* only hear new romantic bands, and *I* only listen to rockabilly, and *I* only. . . ." And that was sad.

LORI BARBERO: Goofy's was around for maybe a year, not very long, around '82 to '84, maybe, and then it shut down because a riot happened. They unplugged the band Final Conflict. You can't just unplug the band; people paid money to get in there. Chairs were flying out the window. It was just crazy. I was slamming a microphone against a beam on the stage. One of the bouncers or security guards picked me up by my throat and lifted me. I was in the air, strangled, I couldn't even breathe, and Bill Batson pretty much saved me. People were arrested, cops came in squad cars. I remember people singing, "What are we gonna do about the boys in blue? What are you gonna do?" because it was like a punk rock anthem. It was just chaos. It made the front cover of *Sweet Potato*.

TOM HAZELMYER: I think I was at Goofy's during the riot. Anything I could do to add to the confusion! I recall that Goofy's being scheduled to shut down played a part in the event.

STEPHEN McCLELLAN: Goofy's was hardly anything. Those were all the people who thought we were making a bundle [at First Avenue and 7th Street Entry], and they were going to get a piece of the action. Bands were leaving, saying, "Well, Steve you're only giving us 75 percent, and we get 100 percent of the door at Goofy's." I went over and I watched one night what their 100 percent was. It was 100 percent *after* they paid all their expenses; they paid the sound man; I don't know how much they paid themselves. So it was 100 percent *after* expenses. Well, I was giving bands 75 percent right off the top. Bands didn't understand that.

That was also when I realized I was pissing Hartley [Frank] off, because he never told the musicians how much they made. He would say, "Ah, pretty good night, I'll give you this." I would sit down with anybody in the band that wanted to see how I was doing it.

DICK CHAMP: The Longhorn thing had fizzled, I think it was even gone by then. Then you had places like Duffy's—oh my *god*. Personally, that was the end for me. I wound up leaving anyway, but places like that drove me right out of town. But not the 7th Street Entry. No way.

I get back to the Twin Cities around February 1980, and the next thing I knew, 7th Street Entry opened. No sentient musician could walk into that place and say to himself, "I'm not interested in this bar." That stage, that room, and the tremendous excitement the place offered as a new place to hang out. The Entry really was where the excitement was, certainly in my estimation. And Steve McClellan, besides being an absolutely decent person, was very generous. We thought we were compensated phenomenally. As a matter of fact, we bankrolled the purchase of the Econoline van we used to move ourselves to New York later that year on the strength of those Entry shows in 1980, after NNB re-formed, and a few other things that were going on.

The Wallets really deserve the credit for that club. I never read anything about that, which is a total joke, but that's the way it goes, folks. But they were drawing crowds and a craziness similar to that at the Longhorn. It was when Steve Kramer had just had his surgeries. He had his jaw and mouth rigged up in such a way that he actually sang without being able to open his mouth. And it was a funk band in the James Chance tradition, really something. All credit to those guys for launching that club.

LORI BARBERO: Chrissie Dunlap and Steve McClellan built that empire. There were a lot of other people, but those two are the two. There was also Danny Flies, Jack Meyers.

DANNY FLIES: It was May 1980 when all hell broke loose for the 7th Street Entry. Eric Lindbom from the *Minnesota Daily* wrote a fantastic story on the 7th Street Entry. With that story and what he wrote about NNB, we had about six hundred people in the bar that night—the Entry had about a one-twenty capacity, I think. That was the first night we had that kind of crowd. And from that night on, we had people coming religiously to the bar. We were bringing heavy national stuff that was really good.

7th Street Entry concert calendar, May 1980. COURTESY OF DICK CHAMP

KEVIN COLE: R.E.M. was scheduled to play the 7th Street Entry Thanksgiving week, 1981. At the last minute, Steve McClellan moved them into the Mainroom to do a full set, as part of the Mainroom dance night. I was DJ'ing dance music. Then R.E.M. played. Because it wasn't an official band night, we used the soundboard that was up in the DJ booth, which meant I mixed their sound. That was incredibly exciting! And they only had one 45 out at the time, which their manager Jefferson Holt had dropped off on consignment earlier that day at the Hot Licks record store I managed.

There was this network of people who worked at stores and fanzines where you'd hear about these bands ahead of time. There was a buzz on R.E.M., at least with a small group of people. It's such a different world than it is now. There was no social networking that would allow people to easily check out a band ahead of time. People had no idea what they sounded like, other than a blurb they might have seen in a fanzine, or perhaps a phone call that they'd gotten from somebody who had seen them in Georgia or somewhere.

So maybe a hundred people showed up to see R.E.M. in the Entry. And there'd be another four hundred people in the Mainroom for dance night. And people instantly embraced them, even though they hadn't heard their songs before. There was an openness and an excitement, an expectation that was like, "What do you got? Let's hear what you have. Bring it," not expecting to hear songs you necessarily knew yet.

BILL BATSON: It was the same audience at First Avenue and the Entry, but it was growing, and we were a part of that, watching it grow. The DJs in the Mainroom especially were pushing toward getting the dance people to understand why real music and new music were important.

The dance people didn't gravitate toward the punk rock at first. They voted with their feet, out of the club. When we [Hypstrz] did the first cameo in the Mainroom, there were 750 people in there, and we went on at 11 or 10:30 PM. It was a ten-minute set and 250 people left immediately. "We are never coming back here." Then there were 250 people who *hated* us and threw things at us and spit at us, and 250 people who danced and liked it.

The Wallets did the same thing and they got a better reaction. The Suburbs definitely had the same reaction. Flamin' Oh's did one of those dance night cameos.

It took several years for audiences to gravitate toward the punk and live music at First Avenue. But, with a touring band, it didn't matter, because the Ramones sold out First Avenue. And Prince sold it out. That was the live music; that was where it was at.

ERNIE BATSON: The Hüskers sold out shows and the Replacements sold out shows, but it took a long time. Of course people weren't going to like it; this was Minneapolis, late '70s, early '80s. It was going to take a while for people to decide that it was all right.

TONY PUCCI: September 1981, a seven-song set, was the first show for us [Man Sized Action] and for the Whole Lotta Loves. We opened for Hüsker Dü in the Entry. Our second show was four days later, on a bill with the Ramones, and it was *insane*. The Ramones were headlining in the Mainroom, and there were a dozen alternating bands in the Entry and the Mainroom.

So we get there early for sound check, I'm alone in the Mainroom, and the Ramones are sound checking. I can't believe that I'm there. This is the coolest thing in the world. And then they stop in the middle of the song, and Joey Ramone points at me and goes, "You, motherfucker. Get out of the room." *[laughs]* I'm like, "Okay." I left. But it was a great, great night.

DANIEL MURPHY: Once we got used to playing the Mainroom and got good at it, it was really fun. When you're playing and the place is packed and everybody is pogoing, there's not a stronger feeling. Sometimes you just look out—the way that room is set up and the sightlines, it can be amazing. It's just so powerful, you go, "Holy shit." The whole place is just drenched in sweat because they're packed in there.

BEEJ CHANEY: The Suburbs moved on to First Avenue when the Longhorn lost its license. Different people, but we still drew a decent crowd, so we started building that scene and then we got on national record labels and sort of became mini-big shots. *[laughs]*

Duffy's and the Cabooze and the Longhorn to me were some of my favorite shows, because those were stripped down, raw. By the time we got to First Avenue, we were kind of stars. We could hold a night and that was really cool, but it was scary. The stage was bigger and the amplifiers were farther away—we had to deal with a bunch of stuff. But it could hold a lot more people, and the sound system is ten times as good. Still, I crave our old shit.

PETER JESPERSON: I've been going to that building [First Avenue and 7th Street Entry] since I was fifteen, since it was the Depot. A big portion of my life was spent under that roof. Steve McClellan was very generous. I'd never met him before the Entry was opening. Before it opened he actually called me up and said, "Look, we're not trying to compete with the Longhorn or take anything away from it; we just think there should be a place for another room in this music community, and I'd like you to see the club before it opens." I went and he showed me the room and we had a lovely talk and we've been close friends ever since. He's one of my favorite human beings of all time.

Steve was a guy who really cared about people, and so I think he was— to a fault almost—maybe too generous in paying bands more than other clubs and maybe even more than he needed to. It might've been one of those things that made his position a little dodgy there with some of the financiers of First Avenue, that he paid well and made sure that bands were taken care of in all respects.

You can't say enough good about Steve. He's just one of the great people of Minneapolis music and one of my dearest friends. We're fifteen hundred miles apart, but it doesn't change the fact that I love the man dearly and I have so much respect for him. Everybody in Minneapolis music and beyond owes a debt to Steve and the work he did there.

STEPHEN McCLELLAN: Going back to the early days it was kind of like a madhouse. I didn't know what I was doing. I tell people about the early days, I was throwing stuff up against the wall. I had no credibility. The Kevin Coles, the Peter Jespersons, the Chris Osgoods, the Jimmy Jams—they were the music people to me. My basic scheme was long range, but we didn't have much time. It was imminent: the disco era has crashed.

When it was Uncle Sam's, they had nights to fill, so obviously we were already doing some live music when I walked in. All I did was, instead of exclusively going with Marsh Productions [booking agency], I started booking other things. This is where I learned that being number one on Billboard doesn't necessarily make it a success. Being on Billboard and getting radio play don't necessarily bring a crowd.

I hooked up with an agent in New York at Premiere called George, who was not happy working with whoever he was working with locally, and he threw me the Ramones on a Wednesday and Pat Benatar on a Thursday. We did them back to back. It was a KQRS-sponsored Pat Benatar concert when her first album came out, and the Ramones sold out, not even charting in Billboard.

I didn't know what I was doing. That's why I went to people. Kevin was working at Hot Licks with other music tastemakers that would help me. I still remember walking into stores and saying, "Hey, do you think I should book the Pretenders?" Of course it sold out, and the record store clerks all told me it would. There was no doubt. It was all me learning what the hell I was doing. I think my basic concept was more, "There's an audience we don't have; let's book it." So, booking diversity was just trying to get in new audiences—not realizing that downtown had strict guidelines as to what audiences the police wanted downtown. I didn't know. It was a matter of keeping the club open.

I didn't know if we booked bands that had somebody in the band that meant something and it would sell out. The first time Alex Chilton played the Entry, he didn't sell out probably, but he did better than most just because of Big Star. I didn't know, but the record store clerks knew, and I had people in the office—Chrissie Dunlap, primarily, in the early days—that would give me information, and my DJs of course. So a lot of the stuff I get credit for I shouldn't. I just didn't know what I was doing. So I did it differently.

I learned how to book by hook or crook. If the club was going to stay open, I had to make decisions that were financially solid, and oftentimes I didn't. I didn't follow any rules because I didn't go to any "how to book" training school. The rules were explained to me by the people that I always trusted. I started the all-ages nights because Sundays were either closed or I had too many nights to fill. So I wanted to program. My goal was to keep it open seven days a week, try to build a regular audience.

That's where I met Peter Jesperson, because I was filling the Entry with the bands that couldn't get into the Longhorn. It was like I was taking the rejects from the Longhorn. Newer bands that couldn't headline played the Entry. The big bands like the Suburbs and Flamingo would stay on the Longhorn schedule. Fingerprints—I'm trying to remember all the bands that wouldn't play the Entry, because they were too big for the Entry. A lot of them played both rooms. Curt [Almsted] played both rooms.

Well, the Entry filled up no matter who played. It was an immediate success; it packed out. In two years, we had to fix it better because we hadn't put much into it to get it open, because we had no money. Bands would complain we didn't have a bathroom in the dressing room. It was just a downtown dive, not near the stature it has presently.

The funnest it was, was the early days. There was no script to follow. The more you had to play the game, the more the fun went out of it.

LORI BARBERO: It took a long time for the music to catch on. There were a lot of intimate shows. I look at my ticket stubs and I don't remember most of those shows, because it was every night. Missy [Mozey] and I would dance and dance and dance. We danced every day, all the time. People went out all the time to support music. People liked music with a passion. It's different now.

18

RAISED IN THE CITY: THE REPLACEMENTS

An electrifying quartet renowned for their raucous live shows, the Replacements were pioneers in the indie rock movement and were highly influential, in particular to the later grunge scene. Singer Paul Westerberg joined brothers Bob and Tommy Stinson (guitar and bass, respectively) and drummer Chris Mars in 1979. When Westerberg brought a four-song demo tape to Peter Jesperson at Oar Folk in hopes of getting a Longhorn gig, Jesperson told them he'd also like to record them. The Replacements' first show at the Longhorn was July 2, 1980, and Twin/Tone signed them right away. They released *Sorry Ma, Forgot to Take Out the Trash* in 1981. Their fourth record, 1984's *Let It Be*, became Twin/Tone's biggest selling album of all time. Catching the attention of major labels, the Replacements signed to Sire/Warner Bros. in 1985. After Bob Stinson left the band, Bob Dunlap, nicknamed "Slim," joined in 1987. Notorious for their unpredictable shows and excellent songwriting—at times irreverent, other times poignant, sometimes both—the Replacements shook up the nation and the idea of what punk music was and could be.

PETER JESPERSON: I think when the Replacements came along they were polarizing. Some people loved them and some people did not love them. I think for the people who loved them, like me for instance, they were the best band in town, hands down. And then there were the people who didn't think the band was good, who either scratched their heads or were a little angry about it.

It was a pivotal time when they came in. I think that happened a little bit, too, with Hüsker Dü and some of the other new bands. It maybe threw a little scare into some of the established bands. Where the Commandos were able to get themselves out of town and have some kind of a career outside of

Twin/Tone promo photo for the Replacements. COURTESY OF DALE T. NELSON

Minneapolis/St. Paul, some of the other bands that weren't able to do that got defensive about it. The same thing happened when the Replacements came along.

There were bands that were saying they didn't think the Replacements were any good, and yet the Replacements were making headway, real fast. They built an audience real fast. When I first met them, Paul had written just a few songs. Then, once they got going and there was a record deal on the table and real gigs at real clubs—that weren't ballrooms in the suburbs or kegger parties—suddenly he exploded and wrote forty or fifty songs in that first year. I think that intimidated people, and some people who didn't want to admit that the band was great or that Westerberg was great somehow still knew it inside and were sort of threatened by it.

TERRY KATZMAN: The first time I heard the Replacements was the tape at Oar Folk that Peter played of the four-song demo that they did. Clearly you could hear that it was something exciting, and from there, things started to move really fast. You're talking within a six- to eight-month period. They were in the store all the time, and recording sessions started. You've got the energy of Peter behind you—it's gonna go someplace. Obviously they were talented on their own, but were it not for Peter, the acceleration wouldn't have happened nearly as fast for them. He had a huge impact on touting them to the locals and making sure that people paid attention to them.

The first Replacements show I saw was at the Longhorn, and it reminded me of everything you liked about rock and roll. They had almost a New York Dolls flavor to them, mixed with the Stones. It was raw and nothing you'd ever really seen before. Paul had a lot of charisma and stage presence. It was a different sonic experience than Hüsker Dü.

I went to just about all of the Replacements shows. It was mandatory.

RYAN CAMERON: Peter was maybe four or five years older than me, a little like my guru, and just knowing that he was involved with the Replacements made me take notice of them. I saw some of the shows at the Longhorn. I was a little late on Hüsker Dü because when the first single came out, I didn't quite get it. I was more of a melody and pop kind of a guy. That wasn't necessarily very noticeable in the first Hüsker's records. I grew to love those records much later. I was more of a fan of the Replacements when they first started out.

JODY KURILLA: When the Replacements first started playing, I remember them rehearsing in the basement of Oar Folk. Jesperson was *so* excited about them and how great they were. They were a little too pop for my taste at that time. But, I remember hearing them down there, and being like, "Yeah, whatever. Okay." *[laughs]* I never was a big fan of theirs until later. I saw them a lot in New York at CBGB. And they were a brilliant train wreck!

ERIC PIERSON: One time I was at Northern Lights records, and Grady Linehan said, "Here, you should listen to this; you'll like this." I'm getting blown away and I'm freaking out because it's really raw and really fast and I'm going, "What is this?" He goes, "It's a rough mix. A new band." This was the fall of '80 or something. I was like, "I've gotta get a copy of this." He's like, "No way; this is just a rough mix. It won't be out for like seven months." It turned out it was the first Replacements record. It really blew my mind. I liked my KISS and I liked my Ted Nugent, but that record kind of stole from everything.

JOHNNY REY: When we moved back from LA, I went down to the Longhorn and ran into Peter Jesperson. The first thing he says to me is, "The Replacements! Oh my god, Johnny, you've gotta see this band." Not, "Hi. How you been? How was it out there?" But, "The Replacements! Oh my god." *[laughs]*

JACQUE HORSCH: I was working at the Longhorn the first night the Replacements played. I remember that night clearly because Peter Jesperson was so excited. He was an excitable guy anyway, but that night he was off his head, he was so excited. I remember him looking at me and going, "I'm signing this band." Of course he did.

While I was setting up the room, Hartley Frank dragged me over and goes, "That kid [Tommy Stinson], there's a kid in here. He's twelve. Don't let him drink!" Then they were up there playing and I'm like, "Oh my god!" It was crazy noise. It was sort of chaotic. But there was so much energy, and you were drawn to it. Peter saw it and felt it. He knew it. This was early, must have been '78 or '79. I didn't have a clue what was going to happen in the future. I didn't realize I was at this center of things to come. This was an education for a girl from the suburbs of Minneapolis.

I recall the Replacements playing the Longhorn maybe twice. I think Peter just got a hold of them and that was the end. He took them away. Then I didn't see them for like eight years. It felt like a really long time.

Peter Jesperson was an essential part of the whole thing, for sure. He had great enthusiasm. He couldn't not get excited about what he was excited about.

DAVE AHL: I may well have been there the first show the Replacements played at the Longhorn. There was nobody there. Tommy was this little boy, and they are all bouncing around the stage. They had to grow into their persona. It was good, really interesting. Neat to see them that early on.

COLLEEN FOLEY: I remember when the Replacements first played at the Longhorn and seeing Tommy, I'm like, "How did you get in here?" But they let him in and they let him play. It was huge. Groundbreaking. They were crazy, but everybody loved them. You didn't know what to expect. For my brother Stephen to eventually play with them was just so cool.

MARK FREEMAN: Seeing the Replacements for the first time was mayhem. I think Tommy was like twelve or thirteen years old. They were amazing. I thought the whole playing half a song and quitting shtick got old after a while, but I also thought they wrote great songs. Westerberg was writing really great lyrics.

We saw them at the Cabooze one night, too. Peter and I were talking and Bob Stinson came up with a handful of change, and he goes, "Peter, Peter! Look! Seventy-eight cents!" and Peter looks at him and goes, "Yeah, that's great Bob, congratulations." He was not joking. He was really excited about the change they had thrown at him. And, yeah, he'd wear the tutu onstage.

DALE T. NELSON: The first time I saw the Replacements, I was like, "Oh shit! These guys are different than any other band." They were like rock and roll radio meets punk rock. Real clever hooks, and they had the potential to be on the radio, but nobody would touch 'em. A little too edgy for the radio at that time.

JIM WALSH: I knew Chris Mars from high school. He was a couple years younger than me and his brother Jim was a friend of mine. I saw Chris on the bus one day and he told me his band had a gig at the Longhorn coming up. Me and my band [REMs] were practicing at Podany's, and I said, "I know this band playing. You guys want to go?" Our guitar player was seventeen and our drummer was sixteen and we just walked in the back door of the Longhorn. It was wide open in those days.

I thought they were like a force of nature, pure rock and roll and loud as hell. I loved that they went song to song to song, very much like the Ramones. And Tommy yelling, "Fuck you!" into the mic. There weren't many people in the bar, so it was really funny. Paul and Bob were ripping it. They did great covers of Johnny Thunders. It was before they had recorded.

That idea of young kids going from a practice space to a club to see another band is very romantic to me. We're all casting about trying to find our songs and our sounds. When I start connecting the dots from seeing the Commandos at Regina High School, seeing Flamingo at the Longhorn, starting my band, going to see the 'Mats, it feels magical and mythical.

MICHAEL HALLIDAY: I remember Tommy Stinson said to me, "Michael, why are you turning into this funk player when you're white?" I'm going,

"Because it moves me." Tommy was just thirteen at the time, playing in bars. He was really cool. I'm looking at him now, he's great. Just great.

DAVID MOE: We saw Tommy play when he was fourteen years old. His bass was as tall as he was. So it was like, "What's this kid doing?" Really good bass player even at a very early age.

I'll never forget, I was excited, "Hey, we're gonna play in the Entry with the Replacements." The Replacements already kind of had a name. They'd put out the first album. I thought, "I should just go say 'hi' to these guys." Whatever.

Tommy Stinson was sitting in a booth at Duffy's. I was excited we're gonna play this new place, and I said to him, "I'm David Moe. I'm a singer in Johnny Quest, and we're gonna play with you guys in the Entry."

Tommy stopped. "Wait, who are you? Nobody told me you're gonna play." Paul was sitting there. "Do you know these guys?"

I thought, "That's when you see the line being drawn. There used to be camaraderie, even though people played different genres and stuff. This is a new thing." And Tom at a young age was like, "Well, you gotta run it by my …" I thought that was funny.

This was the beginning of when certain bands were getting recognized by bigger, influential music folks, and now it was looking like a career for folks like Hüskers or the Replacements. So, they were starting to align themselves with proper support bands. Things were quickly changing for them and others, and we were still in it to just rock and be young.

MIKE MADDEN: I didn't feel the division. I had more time for Hüsker Dü. I went to *every* Hüsker Dü show. But I'd go to a Replacements show. I remember one of those infamous Replacements shows at Duffy's, where they were *so* drunk. Bob Stinson was in a dress. And they were trying to do a Jackson Five song that they never played before, probably. I think it was "I'll Be There." I thought it was great. I thought, "This is rock and roll."

PAUL STARK: I did not work with the Replacements a whole lot. For their first album, *Sorry Ma, Forgot to Take Out the Trash*, Peter went into Blackberry Way with Steve Fjelstad and recorded. I did the original demos with the band when they came in.

Basically, Peter would go out and see the bands, and if he wanted to sign a band, the best way for me to judge them was to see how much trouble they would be in the studio. So I wanted to see them under studio conditions. We had to record albums at a reasonable cost. If it was going to take forever to record, then it wasn't really worth putting the money in. The Replacements came in to do the demo, and I thought that they could record an album reasonably quickly and well. And they were a great live band. Peter liked them already from that point of view.

When it came time for recording *Hootenanny*, I had recently sold my Dinkytown studio, p. david studios, to the Blackberry Way people and had bought a mobile recording unit. It had a twenty-four-track machine in it. Blackberry had an eight-track machine. We thought we'd do *Hootenanny* with the twenty-four-track mobile unit, recording at the warehouse where I kept it. I ended up being the engineer on that. And that was more, from my point of view, experimental. Other than a few odd tracks from time to time, that was really my main involvement with the band as far as recording goes.

MONTY LEE WILKES: The Replacements were one of the coolest bands on the face of the earth. Getting to listen to my favorite music every night and how I wanted it to sound was just a blast. I was recommended to Peter Jesperson by Michael McKern, and they liked me and the way I mixed, and there you have it. I did [front-of-house live sound] for *Tim* and *Pleased to Meet Me*.

You could always count on Bob Stinson being loud. They never failed to deliver. When they hit the stage it was "Go!"—a true hallmark of any great entertainer.

I did play bass for them one night, and no, it really wasn't any fun at all, no, it wasn't cool, and no, I don't think I'm swell because of it. You do what you gotta do to do the gig, and right then, I didn't have any choice in the matter. "You're gonna go up there and do it or we're gonna come here and grab you like a roll of carpet and haul you up to the stage."

The Replacements were the first major label client that I ever had. They taught me that there's a lot of different ways to make big sound. I also learned how to deal with extremely high stage volumes.

PETER JESPERSON: Monty Lee Wilkes came in when we needed a sound guy and did an amazing job. He's another person I couldn't love more. He did great sound for the band, really brought the production of a Replacements show up a few notches. Of course, he had to battle with all the other variables: their volume, level of inebriation, or whatever.

Monty and I got very close. We found him when we were in a pinch. Our then soundman, Mike Bosley, decided to take an apprenticeship at a studio in London, and it was two, three weeks before a tour was scheduled. I had to scramble to find somebody. I believe it was John Shanderuk, the soundman for Flamingo, who said, "You should talk to this kid who works at a record store in Duluth, Monty Lee Wilkes." I called him at the record store and I said, "I work with a band and we need a soundman for a tour coming up quick, and we're wondering if it's something you'd be interested in talking about." I don't know if he was playing catty with me or hard to get, but he was like, "Well, maybe. What band are you talking about?" I said, "The Replacements." He said, "I'll be right there," and he drove to Minneapolis probably as fast as he could.

We sat at the CC Club and had a nice conversation, and I thought, "This is the guy." I just hired him and never looked back, never regretted it. He was a wonderful guy to travel with. Most of the time I'd be driving the band in the van, and we had a second vehicle for equipment. Often that was Monty and Bill Sullivan or Casey Macpherson, but there were times Bill would drive the band van and I would catch a ride with Monty. Those were some of my favorite times. We'd listen to music and talk. He had a Fuzzbuster, so we could zoom ahead and were in the next city ahead of the band. I remember many times pulling in and I'd have dinner with Monty before the band showed up and all hell broke loose again. I love him. I think about him every day and I miss him.

MARTIN KELLER: Paul Westerberg lived in an apartment a couple blocks from the first apartment I lived in in Minneapolis. I interviewed him over there. I heard Ricky Nelson playing when I went in. I go, "This doesn't seem to be your speed." He goes, "I really like Ricky Nelson." He was serious.

I always loved the 'Mats. They just had great songs, great bad attitudes. Their impact on rock music was huge. I don't think there would've been the Seattle scene without them and the Hüskers.

BRUCE PAVITT: I was really impressed by the Replacements' early stuff. Paul Westerberg had such an amazing voice. It was just a classic rock voice, on par with John Fogerty of Creedence or something like that. You could tell that even though conceptually the band wasn't particularly interesting, the songs were good.

PETER JESPERSON: The Replacements started really touring in '83. We did our first tour out to the East Coast and New York, and I think that's when they really started to make an impact nationally. Their very first show in New York, for instance, they're playing this little place called Folk City. It was a weekly series called Music for Dozens put on by Ira Kaplan, later from Yo La Tengo, and Michael Hill, who was a journalist and went on to work with Seymour Stein at Sire Records and became the Replacements' A&R guy there.

The idea was to have rock bands come and play semi-unplugged or turned down a bit. Of course, the Replacements didn't do that, and I remember seeing one guy right up in front of the stage while they played this incredibly explosive set. I was thinking he must be deaf. They were so loud, but he was right there from the time they walked on until the moment they were done. Afterwards I went up and introduced myself. I said, "Looks like you really enjoyed the band. I just wanted to say 'Hello,' my name's Peter, I manage the group." He said, "My name's Glenn Morrow." I recognized his name as the guitar player/singer of the band the Individuals, and he went on to form the label Bar/None. So you think about somebody like that—Bar/None is still operating and making great records—and the Replacements had a big impact on him. That's just one example of dozens and dozens.

They definitely made their impact, but as far as major labels starting to sniff around, we were shocked that it took four albums before somebody signed them to another deal outside of Twin/Tone. It was something we strived for and felt the band deserved, and as we had many times, Twin/Tone was quite content to sort of be a farm team for the major labels. That's part of what we saw as our role. It wasn't like we were upset the band was leaving Twin/Tone. We thought they deserved to be on a bigger label earlier. But that's the way the world works sometimes.

CRAIG FINN: I was turned on to the Replacements by a guy I was playing tennis with. I went out and got *Hootenanny*. *Let It Be* was the first record I really remember waiting for to come out. I couldn't get to Oar Folk until Saturday, and it was killing me all week.

I'd gotten in with some skateboarders, and they weren't really music people, and I wasn't a very good skateboarder. But hard, fast music would get played around skateboarding, so I was friendly with them. One of those kids started going to shows and bringing back flyers. So I figured, "I wanna go to a show." I don't think I got to a real show until the summer after eighth grade—the Violent Femmes in the Mainroom. And that September, I went to the Replacements' *Tim* album release party.

That was my first time in the Entry. It was an all-ages show; it started at four in the afternoon. But it wasn't like a concert I'd seen before where you'd try to be really awesome. They were giving up in the middle of songs and they're kind of in shambles. I was like, "I don't understand what's happening here. It doesn't seem like they're trying to be kick ass." So that was a weird thing, but I loved it. It was fun and crazy and people were throwing things and jumping onstage.

DANIEL MURPHY: The Replacements were really special. I knew Bob Stinson a little bit. I didn't see him much after he got famously fired. He was troubled and he wasn't super bright, but he was really the person that was actually crazy in that band, and so he kind of defined how the show was gonna go that night. Paul would get pissed off if Bob was really drunk, and then after he left they all kind of realized that was part of what people expected out of them. So they took turns kind of riffing on Bob Stinson's crazy, fucked up, demonic persona.

Bob was a great guitar player. I'd go see him and he had this guitar made by Silvertone, a music company that Sears had. He had this whole PA system for his guitar amp, and then on the top there were these little LED lights for how loud it was gonna be, and they'd be green, yellow, and red. He'd be playing these solos and it'd just be red, red, red.

Tommy Stinson, the first time I heard about him, was from this girl named Jenny Roth, who produces movies now. Her brother was Dave Roth—who had a fanzine called *Ferret Comix* back in the day—and she's like, "My brother's got this little friend and he jumps up and down and his hair looks really funny. He's in this band called the Replacements. They're really fucking good." Tommy was like in eighth grade at this point. I went and saw them, and I just flipped out. I'd never seen anything like that. They were really rambunctious and really focused where we weren't at that point.

I probably saw those guys fifty or a hundred times over those years. They took Soul Asylum on one tour and then our van broke down, so we only made, like, the first two shows and that was enough for them.

PETER JESPERSON: The first time I saw the Replacements was after Paul dropped a cassette off for me at Oar Folk, and I loved the recording, so I wanted to see them live. When I went to see them that night at the place on 26th and Chicago—at a chemical-free coffeehouse—the very first person I see is Chris Mars. He was sitting on the steps looking kind of dejected, and he said, "You must be Pete. I'm Chris. I'm the drummer and we just got kicked out, so we ain't gonna play." So my first in-person memory of those guys is of Chris. He was always such a great person. There were lots of times when there was a whole lot of craziness going on and Chris was the anchor and held down the fort. He was probably the most consistently good in terms of performance, as well, though he certainly had his off nights, too, or his bouts with the bottle or whatever it was. I enjoyed his company always. We had sort of an intellectual bond. He was very artistic, and though I wasn't artistic myself in a painting sort of way, I always appreciated it. I watched what he was doing when he was sketching in the van or hotel rooms. I have several early drawings that he had given me.

Bob Stinson was just a teddy bear of a guy. One of the strangest guys I've ever known, but a very inspiring guy to be around. In those early days, there were as many people who came to see Bob Stinson as came to see Paul Westerberg. Bob was a big part of the show. He and I had a great relationship that was marred only by the fact that he felt I was one of the people that was responsible for the band falling out of his jurisdiction and into Westerberg's. It wasn't anything intentional on my part or disrespectful to Bob, but to me

Handbill for a Replacements concert at 7th Street Entry, January 23, 1981. MINNESOTA HISTORICAL SOCIETY COLLECTIONS

Paul was the final piece and unquestionably the biggest piece of the puzzle that made it a very special band, and so I maybe took care of Paul a little more than Bob thought should've been necessary. So that affected our friendship to some degree, but for the most part we were great friends, and we remained good friends until the end. I saw him a few days before he died, and he brought his new girlfriend in to introduce me at the Twin/Tone building.

Bob was extremely funny. I remember our first tour going to New York in April of '83, and we were driving through Ohio and we hit the time zone change. I made a joke, "Okay, everybody set your watches ahead an hour. We're in eastern time now." None of those guys had watches, and I was just kidding, but Bob said, "What do you mean?" And I said, "Well, we're in eastern time now. It's an hour later." And he said, "They can't do that." I remember it struck me as *so* Bob. One of his favorite sayings, we'd be stuck in traffic, and Bob would say, "Just close your eyes and floor it."

Tommy and I got close really fast in those early days. He was like a little brother to me. I've always loved to share music that I love with people, and he was all ears. He would hang around at the Modesto or the record store and was always open to hearing stuff. He didn't always like everything, but he liked a lot of it and it certainly had an effect on him. I'm very proud of having been a part of his musical education. He also was an incredibly fast learner when Bob encouraged him to pick up the bass guitar. He grew to be, as many have said, one of the best rock bass players of all time. He was always super fun to be around in the early days. There was a time when things got a little bit tough on the road and everybody was maybe drinking too much and not getting enough sleep and having to move from one city to another at such a rapid pace. Our tempers could flare, and Tommy and I grew apart at a certain point. After I stopped working with the band in '86, he and I really grew apart, and that made me very sad. But we resurrected our friendship in the early '90s when I started working in LA. We're close friends again, and he was the best man in my wedding, so he's a very important person in my life.

Of course Paul is a difficult guy, but we formed a very strong bond in those early days, and we spent so much time together. One of the things that I reflect on periodically is how intense our relationship was, especially making the records. I was there for the recording with Steve Fjelstad or Paul Stark, whoever the engineer was on the particular project. When the basic tracks were done, Chris and Tommy and Bob split, and Paul and I and the engineer would finish the records and put them into album form. That's something that I treasure, that we worked very closely together. Again, we didn't always agree on things, but we always found someplace where we had a meeting of the minds. Sometimes it was me giving in to him and other times he gave in to me and respected my wisdom on certain things. Sequencing the records was something he always trusted me with, and helping with the song selection. I would encourage him to choose certain songs and discourage him from choosing others that I didn't think were as strong.

So it was a very strong relationship for many years, but again, when things got tense on the road and Paul was expecting more to be happening with the band and it didn't happen, I was one of the people he blamed. That was hard for me, because I don't think I always deserved the blame, though sometimes I probably did. So obviously that created some difficulty between us.

There are few people I think are more talented than Paul Westerberg, and I still expect great things from him in the future. I've known just a handful of people in my life that I would say without batting an eye are geniuses, and he's one of them.

EPILOGUE

KIDS DO FOLLOW: NATIONAL ACCLAIM AND A NEW NEXT GENERATION

The year 1984 marked a milestone and a turning point for the Twin Cities music scene. Hüsker Dü signed on with a national label, SST out of California, and released the landmark double album *Zen Arcade* in July; two years later the Hüskers made the switch to Warner Bros. for what would be their final record, *Warehouse: Songs and Stories*. The Replacements, meanwhile, came out with their final Twin/Tone release, *Let It Be*, in October of 1984 before signing on with Sire Records, which would produce the band's final four albums, beginning with 1985's *Tim*, and bring the band further renown, and notoriety, throughout the world. And Prince, already established as one of the most innovative and talented musicians anywhere, rocketed to international acclaim with *Purple Rain* and with it brought Minneapolis and its up-and-coming club, First Avenue, into the limelight. That also was in 1984.

By this time, Minneapolis had firmly stomped its boot print on the landscape as one of the most creative, prolific, and powerful music scenes in the nation. Major labels were seeking and signing local artists, and critics lauded the scene in major newspapers and magazines. The Suburbs were already working with a national label, and Soul Asylum wasn't far behind the Hüskers and the Replacements—bands that had inspired them and cultivated their musical output. More and more Minneapolis bands were building audiences through extensive touring and ambitious recording.

To this day, artists from the Twin Cities and beyond can trace the path of success back to the pioneering punk and indie rock acts that begin taking shape in Minneapolis in the late 1970s. New young punk, original rock, and experimental bands are continually forming, performing, recording, and touring, and many are embracing the DIY approach and aesthetic that allowed the scene to rise in the first place.

CHRIS OSGOOD: By 1984, Terry Katzman and Jim Peterson were at Oar Folk, and that was raging. The Hüskers were writing *Zen Arcade*. It was just such a creative period for that band and that scene. The Replacements and the Hüskers were the two top bands. There were all these other bands, not to mention Loud Fast Rules coming up, and everybody coming along in their wake. So they were the tip of a much bigger iceberg.

STEVE BRANTSEG: All three of those bands—Hüsker Dü, the Replacements, Loud Fast Rules—I remember just being amazed, in a good way, at how popular they got and how fast they got *so* popular, not just in Minneapolis but all around the country. That was another thing about timing. It was really catching on where independent labels were more acceptable and major labels were copying what independent labels were doing. And the Minneapolis scene happened to be a kind of hotbed. Those three bands captured that moment and became internationally popular. But it just happened so fast, and they all put out a lot of records, really fast. That's what it took: bands being persistent and consistent and playing. I remember watching Hüsker Dü recording and they would go in there and whip out these songs and go, "Does that sound good?" "Yeah, that sounds good." And that was it. They'd do a really quick mix and capture it right there at Cookhouse Studios on Nicollet.

DANIEL MURPHY: We [Soul Asylum] opened for the Replacements a lot and that was always fun. Paul Westerberg took a liking to us. Then we started playing some shows with Hüsker Dü. Bob Mould produced a couple of our records, and they took us on a six-week tour when their record *Flip Your Wig* came out. These were hardcore shows. You'd play two of them a day: the all-ages show and the drunk show at night.

Bob really showed us that scene, because the Replacements never had the work ethic that Hüsker Dü had. I don't think they went on tour nearly as much, either. Hüsker Dü would buy a panel truck, they brought a monitor guy out, they did their own driving, they stayed at budget hotels, and they'd come back from tour and they'd have $5,000 to split up. That was totally Bob Mould, like, "Here's what we do." He was always very intense about

Soul Asylum during their European tour in support of their 1988 release, *Hang Time*. PHOTO BY DANIEL CORRIGAN, COURTESY OF DANIEL MURPHY

everything. They didn't do drugs as much as we were around then, so that was a good thing to see. We used to drive after a show with a bunch of blow and popcorn, get to the next show, and not sleep for four days. You can do that when you're twenty, but it's lucky we're still alive, actually, for how many bad decisions we made as kids.

We decided early on that we were gonna be a touring band; we toured a lot. We didn't really go to Europe or Japan or places like that until we got big. It was such a whirlwind. We had this crew over in Europe. They were from Holland and they'd drive us around to all these little punk rock clubs. We played all over Germany, Holland, Denmark. There's a huge festival in Denmark called the Roskilde Festival, and they had us play their biggest stage. There's like 55,000 people there. We never played a stage this big—Dave keeps walking out with his eyes closed and he pulls his guitar plug out of the amp because it's such a big stage. I have no idea why they wanted us to play. This was 1988, before we were even on A&M; we're still on Twin/Tone. We'd got written up in *Spin* magazine and it was this cool underground thing. We were so surprised that they asked us to play.

DAVE PIRNER: At that point we were pretty much trying to figure out what the fuck Soul Asylum was going to do. They set up a deal where our record would be on Twin/Tone/A&M, and we were able to bring our people, primarily Dave Ayers, along with us and keep the relationship between Twin/Tone and us alive, but then also have A&M on the other end distributing to a wider swath than Twin/Tone was able to.

I think there was a lot of trepidation about signing to a major label, as far as not wanting to leave the nest. We were very wary of being anywhere other than Twin/Tone. We had been watching Hüsker Dü and the Replacements try to adapt and understand it. We had that thing where, "Let's watch these guys fuck it up, and then try not to do that." There wasn't that much to glean from the other bands' experiences with major labels, though, other than seeing how it was different than making a record for Twin/Tone or SST or whatever.

STEVE BRANTSEG: Minneapolis was very much a major music stage. What made it that? It feels like it was serendipity and timing. I think being right in the middle of the country made for a cross-cultural thing and diversity of musical styles—they all sort of blended into each other, but it's still a small enough town where everybody was aware of each other. I mean, Prince came out to watch us play a number of times at First Avenue, both the Phones and Figures. In fact, the Phones did our first single at MoonSound, where Prince had just finished his first record, a little tiny studio. I'd barely heard of him: "I guess I read a little bit about this guy." *[laughs]* We were all influenced by a lot of the same things. All the genres would bleed into each other.

PETER JESPERSON: Another thing that made Minneapolis different was that a lot of other punk/new wave scenes at the time were much more myopic. We never believed that was the way you listened to music. To me that was one of the reasons Minneapolis had such a broad range of bands across different genres that were so strong.

CHRIS OSGOOD: Prince wasn't so different from us that we didn't get what was going on. We understood he was blending R&B and rock 'n' roll. I saw about four Prince shows. We would find out late in the afternoon on Friday that he was playing that night. Steve McClellan will tell you that he always knew for days ahead but he didn't tell anybody about it so that it wouldn't be overcrowded. You got a phone call. Then you called three or four people and everybody piled down to First Avenue. Even with only a phone tree and word of mouth, you had to get down there early just to get in. It was absolutely packed.

Those shows were fantastic and all of us knew how special they were. To this day, they are among the most memorable shows I have ever seen. The other thing is, no white kids from the suburbs had ever seen choreography like that. I remember his whole band dancing in time and I'm going, "What is this?" It was so mesmerizing and energetic. It was just otherworldly.

CURT ALMSTED: Opening for Prince the first time he played First Avenue is one of my most cherished and sacred memories. He performed the entire *Dirty Mind* album with a couple songs from *Controversy* and a couple songs from his first two. It was splendiferous.

When he did the benefit for the Nancy Hauser Dance Company, I walked in a couple minutes before he walked in and we were both wearing fuchsia head to toe. He took one look at me and gave a little haughty laugh and went and changed immediately. The song he chose for sound check was one he'd never done before, and I don't believe he did since. It was Jerry Lee Lewis's "Whole Lotta Shakin' Going On." It was choreographed and executed like a Broadway number and funkified.

I think Prince was this generation's Sammy Davis Jr., Little Richard, Jimi Hendrix, James Brown, and Sly Stone in one amazing package. The absolute best, most focused performer and entertainer I've ever witnessed. And I've seen them all.

CHUCK STATLER: I did the Prince concert film, which had a component of interstitial material that by some accounts were the seeds of *Purple Rain*, because it was this biographical take on Prince's history. That was the end of the *Controversy* tour, I think the spring of '80.

Steven Fargnoli, Prince's rep, was talking to me about doing a video with the Time. I went out to Eden Prairie and they were rehearsing in a warehouse there. Prince was there, didn't say a word. We did the Time video and Prince really liked that. Then he hired me to do a concert video. He liked the concert footage and decided he was going to put a little storyline in with it. Once we shot that, the record company and the management started talking about, "We're going to do more shooting and make a feature film." But then he lost interest and stepped away. That was the end of that.

Without question, Prince was iconoclastic. Bob Dylan is one of the best poets; what he says strikes a chord with people and it endures. It's universal and timeless. And the same with Prince. That's rarified air. He had this stature and yet he stayed here and stayed connected. It's admirable. Fifty years from now people will still listen to Prince.

KEVIN COLE: Prince for me was an incredible transcendent experience—he just blew me, and everyone, away. A musical genius and virtuoso. To watch him play was insane, and that period of time where he really responded to the crowd at First Avenue was amazing. He would usually do an unannounced show before a tour, where he'd test-drive the new material. Then he would do a show at the end of the tour that was a party. "The tour's over: let's have some fun!" All of them were phenomenal extended blowouts.

He would bring down new material for me to spin on Friday and Saturday nights. He would have me play new songs so he could test-drive these recordings with the Mainroom audience. One night, I was DJ'ing in the Mainroom and felt someone tap me on the shoulder. I looked behind me and Prince was standing there holding a twelve-inch single. He said, "Hey, will you play my record?" It was "Erotic City." Word is, he had seen George Clinton the night before and had been so inspired that he went back to the studio, wrote and laid down the tracks for "Erotic City," all within less than a day, then brought it down to the club for me to play. It was a really amazing moment for me, and kind of scary.

I was hyper-aware of the fact that Prince was sitting in this little VIP area we set up for him. I wanted to take him by surprise so he wouldn't know when I was going to play the song. It was like an hour later. And when the song came on, he ran down to the dance floor and stood in the middle, with people dancing all around him, listening to how it sounded on the main speakers.

When the song was over, he went back upstairs and sat down and watched, like he did all the time. At the end of the night, I walked over to where he was sitting in the VIP space, and he asked me what I thought of it, which was amazing. "What did you think of my song?" To which I responded, "It's great!" There wasn't any constructive criticism I could give him because it was amazing. And he was like, "Thanks." I asked him if he'd sign it. I figured that was a way for him to say "I'll take it back" or I could keep it. He signed it, and I have an acetate of "Erotic City."

Prince was an artist with a capital A: one of the greatest guitar players of all time, a brilliant songwriter, amazing singer, and dynamic performer who was also a champion of personal freedom and individualism. He was fearless—singing about sex, God, gender, race, sometimes all in the same song. He could move your ass and stir your soul simultaneously. He was deeply spiritual, even in a g-string and leg warmers. Prince was principled and fully committed to his artistry. And as serious as he was about his art, Prince was also unbelievably funny and charming in a sly and quiet way. He just gave and gave and gave, and in the end, he really just wanted to bring people together, which he did through his music and artistry.

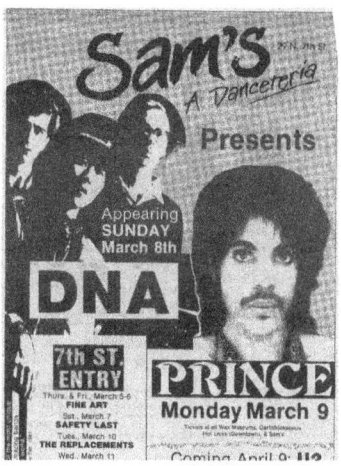

Advertisement for Prince concert at Sam's (First Avenue) in March 1981, along with other local notables playing in the 7th Street Entry that month. COURTESY OF KEVIN COLE

I can't think of anyone who's more of a musical genius than Prince. He was so much more than a pop star; he was one of the greatest artists of all time. Nothing compares to Prince. He changed our lives, First Avenue, and Minneapolis, forever.

STEPHEN McCLELLAN: Uncle Sam's to Sam's to First Avenue when Chrissie Dunlap was there was to me the golden era. It ended when *Purple Rain* came out. The movie came out in '84. Then even the William Morris Agency noticed us: "Oh, we can actually do shows there." I could tell them, "Hey, we just did Tina Turner," or "Hey, we just did U2," but they didn't care. That's the way of the world. When bands like Sonic Youth left little agents to go with big major agents, when they signed with William Morris, that was the first sign of decline.

DOUG ANDERSON: What was great about back then was all of us were kids and we were living here, right? Mostly the Nicollet area, and then there were some Northeast kids like Paul Osby from Otto's Chemical Lounge, a phenomenal guitar player.

I remember guys like Chris Osgood and Don Holzschuh were really open to us hanging around. Regardless of how smart you think you are, you're sixteen. They would buy you a soda, hang out with you and tell you about cool shit. We all got to learn a lot from those guys. Dale Nelson also had a great reputation. We all loved Dale. Maybe he was ten years older than us, but it was a lifetime then.

CURT ALMSTED: I think that of our crop of new wave bands, I'm pretty sure the Replacements will be in the Rock and Roll Hall of Fame, and possibly Hüsker Dü. I don't know if they have as much legend around them, but they probably had more impact musically. Part of me is proud of the Replacements, Jayhawks, Soul Asylum, Babes in Toyland, and others who may have seen me when they were at a formative stage, being influenced by me. [*laughs*]. I just happened to be around and met them and, I imagine, I got a tad osmosis-ized. The world would've been fine without me, but I'm glad I'm in it.

PETER JESPERSON: There certainly was a connect between the first and second waves in that Chris Osgood was a guitar teacher and gave lessons to both Bob Mould and Dave Pirner, among many others. That's pretty significant. We might've had a little bit less of the "fuck the old" attitude. Maybe there was a little more respect for what had come before, more than what is the clichéd vision of what punk rock did, like Joe Strummer singing, "No Elvis, Beatles, or the Rolling Stones" in 1977. We didn't really think that way. There were certainly people in the scene that probably bought into that, but we were always very respectful of our elders. We loved Elvis Presley, Buddy Holly, Muddy Waters, Howlin' Wolf. We didn't have any problem with that stuff or the Beatles or the Rolling Stones. We thought all that stuff was cool, and it was just a continuation. That's what happens with rock and roll. The beat goes on.

CHRIS OSGOOD: Bob Mould and Dave Pirner were my guitar students. I taught Bob in my apartment. My girlfriend at the time would hide in the closet, and Bob would come in for his lessons. He would take the bus from Macalester College and get off the bus—I remember this so clearly—at 24th

Ad for Chris Osgood, "Guitar Teacher Extraordinaire," at Knut-Koupeé Music Store, December 1979. COURTESY OF DOLORES CHAMP

and Pillsbury with his flying V guitar case and come upstairs. We would needle drop, and I showed him some stuff.

I was calling my apartment the New Wave Academy of Applied Guitar Sciences. I went and put flyers up in grocery stores: "Come get lessons at the New Wave Academy of Applied Guitar Sciences." I got so busy that I went to Knut Koupeé. They didn't have a lesson program. I said, "Hey you guys, may I do lessons? Is there a room I could use?"

Pirner was one of my first students at Knut Koupeé. It was concurrent with Loud Fast Rules. Dave told me a few years ago that he carries around the shredded-up yellow piece of notepaper where I wrote the pentatonic scale for him. I gave Beej a couple of guitar lessons, too, back in the day. So, yeah: One generation teaching the next. I loved the new generation.

DAVE PIRNER: I was trying to emulate Ramones songs on the guitar without really knowing what I was doing. From fucking around with it, I was like, "Shit, I can do this. This is music I understand."

I went to Knut Koupeé, across the street from my high school, and I took a couple of lessons from Chris Osgood. To this day I look to him as a bit of a mentor. He took me to see Speed Wiener, his band at the time. Hüsker Dü was opening for them. That was the first time I stepped foot in 7th Street Entry, and because I was underage, I wasn't allowed to go all the way into the bar. Once I was standing in the Entry, though, I knew that was where I needed to be.

CRAIG FINN: When I was in seventh grade I got an electric guitar, must've been 1984. This kid at school told me about Knut Koupeé at 28th and Hennepin. My parents called and asked about lessons. I ended up lucking into getting lessons with Chris Osgood. I had started listening to the Ramones a lot, so the first lesson I brought in a Ramones record. When I brought it in, Chris was like, "Yeah man, I haven't seen Joey in a while." I was like, "What?! You know Joey Ramone?" I learned Chris had been in this band, the Suicide Commandos.

Chris was really a lifeline to cool information. He was like, "If you're gonna get really cool records, you're gonna go to Oar Folk." He taught me a lot about bands. He turned me on to punk stuff, the Stooges, and ZZ Top, which were huge influences on him. He mentioned he had students that were in Soul Asylum and Hüsker Dü. He'd show me flyers and say, "The Entry does all-ages shows if you wanna check out some bands." He had a lot of tips on how to be cool.

The first time I went to Oar Folk, I got the Suicide Commandos' record, shortly after Chris told me about it. It was amazing. I loved the songs. It's still one of my favorite records. His guitar playing is better than 99 percent of punk rockers. He's a monster of guitar.

The lessons stopped because the Replacements' *Let It Be* did really well and Chris went to work over at Twin/Tone. It's funny because that's my favorite album of all time, and that's why the lessons stopped.

CHRIS OSGOOD: I can't really answer the question about the Commandos' impact, because I'm a Commando. I naturally see things skewed. But I have heard from enough other people that we were able to show a lot of other bands that it could be done. They saw us play and thought: "Well, wow. If those guys can do it, we can do it." That's what happened to me when I saw the New York Dolls.

I have to mention, even though it's not a good reflection on me, it's disconcerting when you see your fans look away from you to embrace the new thing. That's a part of growing up and that's a part of the whole scene maturing and moving on, but I would be disingenuous if I didn't say that I was a little wistful about that. The Suburbs came up right behind us and became the rage, followed by the Replacements, followed closely by Hüsker Dü. And then suddenly that was the scene, in the mid-'80s.

And what a scene it was. It was so productive. There was so much good music being written and recorded. By that time, the scene was all set up. The infrastructure was there for the bands to record and to tour, too.

DANNY AMIS: I think the international impact that groups like the Replacements and Hüsker Dü had is unmistakable. Neither one of those bands, or me for that matter, would have happened if the Suicide Commandos and the Suburbs hadn't been around. There's no question about that.

Starting out playing music in that scene was such a positive thing for me. I owe my whole career to that. I would probably be working a sales or a banker job or something if I hadn't been in the middle of such an inspiring scene of creative people. There was a lot of camaraderie. It was not competitive, like I've seen in other places. We all supported each other's bands. Sure, there was a little friendly competition—there always is—but it was great to be part of that scene where all the bands were fans of each other.

ROBERT WILKINSON: The music scene has evolved, and I always try to stay positive. I'm not one to say, "Oh, it was better back then." I don't wanna be one of those guys, but there's a truth there that it was *different*. It did change and it was the birth of alternative/indie music and punk and new wave.

The whole business has changed so much, and especially the past five years. The landscape has totally fractured. It's more of an Internet-driven business now. I think it's a more artist-driven business, too, and I think that's a good thing for the artists, cutting out the middle man. Record labels have gone down. Bands are becoming more do-it-yourself all the time.

If it had been this way back when we were playing, in that heyday, it might have been more beneficial to us to a certain extent. But we had to rely on people in record companies. There were artists and bands who got signed to major labels, but it didn't really do anything for them because the

A&R person who signed them was fired the next week. A&R people and record labels back then had a high turnover. So if the guy who signed a band was fired a month later, then the band was forgotten about.

Now you can put stuff out there yourself and have a million people hear it. The downside of it is, anybody can make a CD in their bedroom, which can sometimes sound tepid and amateurish. The one thing that a lot of us bands had back then is that experience of touring and playing. I'm going to brag a little here and say a lot of us bands used to go out and play three, four nights a week and play four sets a night. That's how you created your musical identity. That's how you got your chops and how you learned. You toured and played all the crappy bars, but you got tight and developed this band identity. I'm very grateful that I did get to play all those crappy shows and play three and four and five sets a night. I think more bands should do that. That's really important, to play as much as you can when you're younger, when you're developing your musical identity.

So yeah, the landscape's different. In some ways it's better for the artist, but in some ways not so good for the audience. There's not much mystery left in bands anymore. Part of the excitement of when a band came to town was seeing them for the first time. Now you can see them play live on YouTube. I'm just amazed and very grateful that I'm still playing these days. At this stage in the game, we're just enjoying playing music. I still believe in trying to get out there and put out a good show. And you do it because—in my case, I have an awesome fucking band; they're such amazing musicians to play with. And we're doing new stuff. I don't even think in terms of, how long can it go? It's just day by day. We're gigging, had a new release. Everything is good.

That time we all went through, some of us made it and some of us didn't. It was amazing to be a part of that whole musical history of the Twin Cities, and it's not lost on a lot of us who were a part of that that it was definitely a change that was needed. I consider myself very lucky to have been a part of it. I don't think anything like it has been witnessed since.

JODY KURILLA: A friend of mine in the early '80s was a dressmaker and traveled all over the country. Inevitably the question that would come up was: "How were you guys able to make the scene happen?" Her answer was: "We weren't branding anything." Now everybody brands everything before they even do anything. Then, we just did it. You could live fairly inexpensively, and you could do what you wanted to do. That's really hard to do now in some of the bigger cities. And from that, everything just happened. It just blossomed!

When you're young, your experiences are new; you are new to the world pretty much. A long time ago, I went to this Lord Byron birthday party in London. It was period costumes. This woman had been doing this party forever. She was in her eighties, I think. She said to me, "You kids don't know anything. Back in our day, heroin was legal. Cocaine was legal." We always think that we're the ones that experienced everything: "This is new." "This is exciting." "We did it first." I think of what that lady said to me. She was talking about the 1920s. So everybody has their time. I tend to think ours was kind of special, and I'm sure she thought her time was special, too.

JEFF BUSWELL: We really did create a cool music scene here. I got to take a peek into other ones when we were out touring, and this was one of the more progressive music scenes. At the time it was happening, we were running around the country, trying to display what we had. You don't really realize what you're doing until you do it. Then all of a sudden everybody starts patting you on the back, saying, "You guys have got a really great scene there." Then of course Prince jumped into the middle of it, and made it even cooler to a lot of people around the country.

STEVE BRANTSEG: I believe Minneapolis becoming a scene was because of a number of factors. I think during the long, cold winters people get bored. Being a teenager and you love music and you have all this energy and angst and aggravation, and you've gotta get it out somehow. A lot of times people would be in their basements learning to play instruments or having fun with their friends. Most of the bands started out as friends hanging out liking music. As everybody got a little older it was like, "God, let's get out of the basement, out of the garage, and if we only had a place that we could play, another venue, more public." There'd be high school dances, whatever. All of a sudden the Longhorn starting to have local music and also encouraging people to play original music.

That's another thing: if you were out of town and playing in bars, you usually had to play all cover songs, maybe a few originals. But in Minneapolis you were encouraged to do original music, especially after the Suicide Commandos got signed to a major label in 1977—that really helped put things on the map.

PAUL DICKINSON: People other than me have made the point that, in the cold winters, you've just gotta keep busy. With my band Frances Gumm, a couple winters ago when it was a terrible winter and it was just so brutal, we decided we were gonna get together and totally woodshed this material, you know? I think that's what Minnesota's all about. And it is a demanding scene, because the fans here are very demanding. They're really spoiled. They want to see blood. It's got ups and downs, if you think about it. You see bands come and go. But the thing about a band is, there's every reason in the world for you to give up. That's why it doesn't make sense. It's not for logical people. It's a lark, but you have to believe in your own delusions to make it work.

There was a lot more mystery back then. That's what I think is lacking today. Everything's explained, everything's all lined up. Before it was more mystery, which I'd like to bring back on the scene.

PHILIP HARDER: I started visiting Minneapolis in 1984 to see my favorite bands in the Entry and Uptown Bar, around the time Hüsker Dü's *Zen Arcade* came out—it was a masterpiece double record that didn't fit the typical punk/hardcore sound. It was epic in both sound and story, like the soundtrack to the entire life of a punk. Of course I saw several Hüsker Dü and Replacements shows. Hüsker's were always great. Replacements usually sucked and played covers or forgot their songs, but I loved them anyway. Both bands changed everything for me.

A couple years earlier I was living in small-town Wisconsin and there was no way to hear this music. I was torn by the thought of getting some typical mainstream job for some boring materialist lifestyle.

There was something screaming in my head that I didn't yet have the vocabulary for. A guy named Doc from my hometown returned after working a few years at Goofy's. He played me Replacements *Sorry Ma* and *Stink* and Hüsker's *Everything Falls Apart*. When I discovered this music I knew that was it. As a small-town kid I'm so lucky I happened upon this music.

Doc informed me that everyone in Minneapolis writes their own music, puts out their own records, and hits the road. From that point on I felt like I had a mission. It was all very new and very exciting. This DIY attitude, along with the political and social awareness, was my education, and it stayed with me as I transitioned from bands to being a filmmaker and is still with me today. It was punk rock. I identified with it.

ED ACKERSON: Coming into Minneapolis and seeing bands like the Replacements and Hüsker Dü at close range was an amazing experience. These bands were as good as any national or international touring band I had seen, and their songs were the equal of anything I was hearing in my record collection. I was massively inspired, and I decided to start my own band and see if I could somehow swing in the same league.

EMILY "BEE" (DUNLAP) BOIGENZAHN: I had the great fortune of growing up in a rock 'n' roll household. As young as age five I got to dance to Curtiss A and my dad [Bob Dunlap] playing together at an outdoor concert; as a preteen I remember dancing to Prince while we cleaned the house—my mom's enthusiasm was infectious. All through the '80s my mom [Chrissie Dunlap] worked at First Avenue. I went to my first all-ages show in the Mainroom in 1984 when I was thirteen. It was the Replacements, and I was hooked. I loved them and discovering all the great music coming out of Minneapolis. I think I was at every all-ages show during those years. I got to see Loud Fast Rules before they were Soul Asylum, and I loved Hüsker Dü, Trip Shakespeare, Run Westy Run, the Gear Daddies, and on and on.

Then something strange happened: Bob Stinson left the Replacements. I was so upset. I thought it was all over for my favorite band. But shortly afterward my mom announced, "Bee, you'll never believe this: Dad is the new Replacement!" That was so surreal—and I was thrilled.

I didn't start playing music myself until I was in my thirties. As a teen I asked my dad to show me how to play guitar. He said if I wanted to be original I had to just figure it out myself like he did. That was the end of that for a while. But in 2007 when my girlfriends and I formed RuDeGiRL, a female tribute band to the Clash, he set me up with his Telecaster and a Rat box, helping me find the right tone and working through learning the songs. Later, when I wanted to start writing my own songs, he promised to help me with some "song starters," songs he had started but hadn't finished. He thought I could add lyrics and finish them to get the feel for songwriting. As it turns out, the day we planned to work on those songs was the day of his massive stroke in 2012. I never got to hear those "song starters," but the emotional turmoil of the stroke, followed by the incredible response from the music community, ended up triggering a flood of songwriting for me. I was playing music with a group of close friends for fun, but suddenly writing songs became a way of coping with what was happening in my life, helping me get through it.

DANIEL MURPHY: I had no idea what Minneapolis was on to; it was a revolution. Like the first time I saw the Jayhawks, I couldn't believe how good they were. I'd go to the Uptown and see them all the time, and the Replacements. Sometimes they'd be great and sometimes they'd be not so great, but it was always interesting. While it's going on, you have no realization of how special it is, that there's all this great music that doesn't sound all the same, and there's a scene going on. The music scene totally consumed my life. All I did, 24-7, was play shows, organize shows, go see my friends' bands. It was really special in hindsight. Some bands that were great didn't make it; some bands people still talk about.

BRUCE PAVITT: Of course in the early '80s Prince was blowing up, but it wasn't really until [Hüsker Dü's] *Metal Circus* and [the Replacements'] *Sorry Ma, Forgot to Take Out the Trash* caught my ear. I remember the track by Grant Hart called "Diane" I played on my Sub Pop USA radio show. It was possibly the most intense song I'd heard come out of the underground to that point. Not only the subject matter, but Grant Hart's vocals, and the arrangement of it. I was very, very moved by that.

In the early '80s there was definitely a coming together of the North American hardcore scene and the culture of hardcore. Although I appreciated its spirit, it was ultimately pretty generic, and the energy really went against the grain of late '70s punk rock, which had more to do with creating a unique style. Hardcore was a call to arms for young people to express themselves in a high-energy way, but a lot of the music was really generic.

I was happy to see Hüsker Dü break out of that and step into their own sound. I do think in retrospect they, in particular with their melding of pop sensibility with the emotional intensity of punk, totally laid the groundwork for Nirvana and *Nevermind*. I feel *Candy Apple Grey*, with its huge production and its incredible songs, was an obvious predecessor to *Nevermind*.

DAVE PIRNER: By the time Hüsker Dü decided to play everything eight million miles an hour, a new generation of bands had begun. That's when hardcore started to take over a little bit. I didn't even know it was a movement. When I wrote a song and thought to myself or said to the band, "Let's play this thing as absolutely fast as we can," I didn't know that was a *thing*. But sure enough, it fit right in to what was happening. *[laughs]*

To a degree, I didn't really know any other music scene than my own. There was an amazing amount of innovation going on here, and a lot of the "necessity is the mother of invention," when you don't know how to play your instrument and you take your wrench to it and make noise. It was a real concerted effort to be different. You had to bring something no one had never heard before; it couldn't be like any of the other local bands.

In this little microcosm, there were real artists in there. It was another way to be creative. The music scene was influenced by people who ended up going to MCAD [Minneapolis College of Art and Design]. I didn't know that they were creative artists, that they weren't just musicians. They were painters and writers and whatnot. I've always been a fan of Mike Etoll [of Exmo-6-Desmo]. He is one of the most creative people I have ever met. All of those people are still in the arts community, if they are not in a band. That part of it is really pure, I think.

There was a flair for performance art. Sometimes attitude was more pronounced than the music. Or the sound of somebody smashing something was as interesting as the sound of somebody trying to play something. All these creative people are at a certain age, and the natural thing to do is find your three best friends and start making noise and it doesn't matter if it sounds like music to anyone else. You're doing it for your own amusement.

LORI BARBERO: I think bands supported each other more then than they do now. People are disconnected a lot now. It's more about *them*. You're more successful if you're willing to be open and support each other. That's life, not just the music business.

Music really changed my life. Living in New York during high school, I got to see it in its heyday, kind of, with CBGB. Then I came to Minneapolis in '79 or '80, and there was the Longhorn. I was involved in that. I saw the first Hüsker Dü show there. And I saw the development of all the music over time: Prince, Jimmy Jam and Terry Lewis, and the Replacements and Hüsker Dü and Soul Asylum, and then the ones underground, the Cows and stuff like that. I got to see everything. The Suicide Commandos, the Hypstrz, everything that made this city. And the Suburbs and the Wallets, all those guys. You plant the seed and the tree grows. All the music I saw, the bands I heard, every drummer I watched, every musician I saw perform, made me who I am today.

People say, "Oh, New York. Oh, LA. Oh, whatever." I think besides the UK, Minneapolis has the best music that was created.

ADAM LEVY: I think just the accessibility of the scene inspired me as a musician. Most of the things I was listening to were from across the Atlantic. I was a big Elvis Costello fan and the Clash and earlier British invasion stuff. I also liked Talking Heads and a lot of the new wave American stuff, the New York things, but here it felt like, "Wow, this is something you can actually do. You can start a band, you can tour, you can make records and you don't have to go to London, you don't have to go to New York." Everything was here. There was this vibrant club scene, there were these amazing record stores and the folks that worked in the stores were always willing to share things and chat about music. I remember submitting our [Go Borneo] tape to Chrissie Dunlap at First Avenue and how nervous I was walking in there. For a sixteen-, seventeen-year-old kid, I was so scared of those folks, and Steve McClellan. Knowing them now, you know, they're so sweet. That was a stage in my life where I was a sponge. It's like, "Who am I? What am I? How do I find some sort of musical identity?"

TERRY KATZMAN: At the same time that Oar Folk was thriving, the Longhorn was rising. It was a confluence of those elements, one feeding off the other. Peter Jesperson was really the central point of that, because he was getting bands booked at the Longhorn, and he was managing Oar Folk. So it was a two-fisted attack. And we were pulled into the tidal wave. We had a lot of things coming together at the same time. You had a really cool record store that was selling the music. You had a really cool scene that was featuring live local bands and all these bands coming in from out of town. One thing just helped the other. The Longhorn helped Oar Folk, Oar Folk helped Twin/Tone, Twin/Tone helped Oar Folk, Twin/Tone helped the Longhorn.

KEVIN COLE: Minneapolis became a music hotbed in part because it was isolated, and it was a cultural mecca for art- and music-loving misfits from the surrounding suburbs, cities, and states. In a way it was provincial. We created a scene we loved, for ourselves. We didn't do it for validation or recognition or to be like somewhere else. 1984 was the turning point, the year that all changed, when the spotlight turned on Minneapolis. In 1984, the Replacements, Hüsker Dü, and Prince all had albums in the Top 10 of

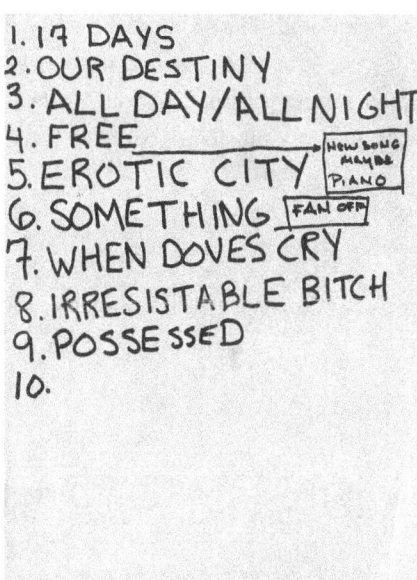

Set list from Prince concert at First Avenue, June 7, 1984. COURTESY OF CHRISSIE DUNLAP

Promo postcard for the Replacements' *Let It Be*, the band's final album with Twin/Tone, released October 1984. MINNESOTA HISTORICAL SOCIETY COLLECTIONS

Concert handbill for Hüsker Dü's *Zen Arcade* tour, July 7, 1984. COURTESY OF DALE T. NELSON

the esteemed *Village Voice*'s Pazz & Jop Critics' Poll. The scene that had been developing for a decade had "arrived." Minnesota music owned the world. With that attention came expectation, self-sabotage, superstardom, and the seeds of inspiration that would impact Minnesota musicians forever. That's for another book.

CAST OF CHARACTERS

ED ACKERSON: Guitarist, vocalist for Mr. Slate, the Dig, 27 Various, Polara, and BNLX. Producer. Owner of Flowers Studio, a recording facility housing his Susstones label.

DAVE AHL: Drummer, vocalist, songwriter for the Suicide Commandos; also L7-3, Boys Life, Dave "Snaker" Ray, and more. Ahl Inc. recording studio designer, builder, and consultant.

BRUCE ALLEN: Guitar, vocalist, songwriter for the Suburbs; also Seth, Tsetse Flies, X-Boys, and more. Graphic design artist for Campbell Mithun and Twin/Tone Records. Died 2009.

STEVE ALMAAS: Bassist, vocalist, songwriter for the Suicide Commandos; also the Crackers, Jonny III, Beat Rodeo, the Raybeats, the Del-Lords, and solo. Record producer.

CURT ALMSTED (CURTISS A): Singer, guitarist for the Wire, Thumbs Up, Spooks; also the Jerks of Fate, the Dark Click, and Long Gone Daddies and the Cold Cold Hearts. Visual artist.

DANNY AMIS: Guitarist, composer, producer for the Overtones; also the Raybeats, Los Straitjackets, Lost Acapulco and Los Twin Tones.

DOUG ANDERSON: Guitarist, vocalist for Red Meat. Music promoter.

LORI BARBERO: Drummer, singer, songwriter for Babes in Toyland; also Eggtwist. Server at Jay's Longhorn. Booker for various venues. Owner of Spanish Fly Records. SXSW assistant production manager and booker. DJ.

BILL BATSON: Lead singer for King Kustom and the Cruisers, Hypstrz, the Mighty Mofos. Professional soundman and speaker service technician. Cofounder of Bogus Records.

ERNEST "ERNIE" BATSON: Guitarist for King Kustom and the Cruisers, Hypstrz, the Mighty Mofos; also the Whole Lotta Loves, the Leeds. Cofounder of Bogus Records. Former librarian.

JAY BERINE: Owner of Jay's Longhorn. Booker and manager at Duffy's. Entrepreneur.

CINDY BLUM: Drummer for NNB and Red House. Former staff photographer for *Connie's Insider* and *Sweet Potato*.

EMILY "BEE" (DUNLAP) BOIGENZAHN: Singer, songwriter, guitarist for Whale in the Thames; singer and guitarist for the 99ers; guitarist for RuDeGiRL.

KEVIN BOWE: Musician, songwriter, engineer, producer. Lead guitarist for the Dads, Summer of Love; front man for the Revelators and the Okemah Prophets. Program chair at IPR College of Creative Arts.

STEVE BRANTSEG: Guitarist, vocalist for the Phones and Figures; also Chan Poling Band, Bash & Pop, the Jerks of Fate, the John Ewing Band, Hillbilly Voodoo Dolls, and the Suburbs.

JEFF BUSWELL: Crew and tour/production manager for the Suburbs.

RYAN CAMERON: Record store clerk and manager for Musicland, Hot Licks, Northern Lights. Owner of Let It Be Records.

DANN "DC" CARLSON: Promoter, artist, musician. Produced and hosted independent shows in warehouses, barns, and bars. Lead vocalist, songwriter for the Ironics, the Generics, the Bleeding Hearts. KFAI DJ and host, Dr. Dann Placebo.

JEFF CERISE: Vocalist, saxophonist, and percussionist for the Phones and Stickman. Founder of Secret Agent Man Inc. creative services company.

DICK CHAMP: Guitarist for NNB and the Scene Is Now. Musician, archivist.

BEEJ CHANEY: Front man, lead singer, guitarist for the Suburbs; also solo.

JON CLIFFORD: Owner of HiFi Hair and Records. Lifelong Twin Cities music junkie.

KEVIN COLE: DJ, journalist, Longhorn regular, record collector, diehard music lover. Former in-house DJ at First Avenue and 7th Street Entry, manager of Hot Licks and Platters record stores, radio DJ at KJ104, cofounder and program director of REV105. Chief content officer and host of the *Afternoon Show* at KEXP in Seattle.

DANIEL CORRIGAN: Music photographer and First Avenue staff. Shot concert and promo photos for many bands and cover images for numerous album covers.

BOB DeBOER: Singer for Entropy; trumpeter, singer for Eleganza, Chooglin', GST, BrassZilla.

PAUL D. DICKINSON: Musician, drummer, guitarist for Manifest Destiny, Pax Americana, Poetry Grenade, Frances Gumm. Founder of Speedboat Gallery. Poet, promoter, actor.

LORNA DOONE: Visual artist, writer, Longhorn regular, local music supporter. Co-owner of Rock-It-Cards shop and art gallery. Host of punk art shows.

CHRISSIE DUNLAP: Assistant promotions manager for Sam's/First Avenue. Wife of Bob Dunlap.

BOB "SLIM" DUNLAP: Guitarist for Thumbs Up, the Spooks, Curtiss A, the Replacements; also solo artist and singer-songwriter.

MARK ENGEBRETSON: Vocalist for the MORs, the Whole Lotta Loves, Go Van Gogh, the Silverteens. Developing a documentary on Jay's Longhorn bar and the early Minneapolis punk rock scene.

EVA MOZEY ETOLL (MISSY MOZEY): Live music attendee, punk rocker. Currently a veterinarian and haunted house producer.

JIM FENN: DJ at the Longhorn. Lighting production and road manager for Flamingo/Flamin' Oh's.

CRAIG FINN: Singer, songwriter, guitarist for Lifter Puller, the Hold Steady; also, solo.

DANNY FLIES: First music booker for 7th Street Entry.

COLLEEN FOLEY: Longhorn regular. Sister of musicians Kevin and Steve Foley.

DAVE FOLEY: Musician, painter, creative type with an entrepreneurial bent. Guitarist for Things That Fall Down; also Kindergarten, Hypo. Bartender, cabdriver. Owner of the Record Spot record store.

MARK FREEMAN: Musician, songwriter, engineer, producer. Guitarist for NNB and Red House.

ANGELA FRUCCI: Farfisa, keyboards, backup vocals for Têtes Noires.

CAMILLE GAGE: Songwriter, vocals, keyboards, percussion for Têtes Noires; also Radio Kings, Daughters of Invention.

ELLIOT GORDON: Bassist, keyboardist, guitarist, drummer for Danger Boy and the Road Vultures, Tornado, Mary Allen and the Percolators, Neon Dirt. Son of Cam Gordon and nephew of Rod Gordon, both of the New Psychonauts.

ROD GORDON: Keyboardist for the Wallets, the New Psychonauts, Gondwana.

JOHN "BONGO" HAGA: Drummer, vocals for King Kustom and the Cruisers, the Hypstrz, Soda, the Rock-a-Dots, the Jerks of Fate, Gini Dodds and the Dahlias, Hip Bone; also substitute drummer for several bands. Former Knut Koupeé staff. Owner of Bongo's and Bud's Music Center.

KAREN HAGLOF: Visual artist. Singer, songwriter, guitarist for Spitfire, the Wad, the Crackers, Band of Susans; also solo artist.

MICHAEL HALLIDAY: Bassist for the Suburbs.

GRAHAM HALLMAN: Archivist, son of Twin/Tone cofounder Charley Hallman.

PHILIP HARDER: Award-winning film and video director. Produced music videos for Foo Fighters, Incubus, CSS, Low, Prince, Cornershop, Pulp, Har Mar Superstar, the Afghan Whigs; also commercials and feature films.

WAYNE HASTI: Bassist for NNB; also founder, guitarist, songwriter for Ben Day Dots; bassist, organ player for Red Eye Blue. Wax Museum staff.

TOM HAZELMYER: Musician, visual artist and printmaker, record label executive. Founded Amphetamine Reptile Records. Worked at Reflex Records. Co-owner of Grumpy's Bar. Front man for Todlachen; bassist, vocalist for Otto's Chemical Lounge; guitarist, vocalist, front man for Halo of Flies.

ROBB HENRY: Guitarist for Fingerprints, Inside Straight (Duffy's house band); also Sweet Thing, Big Daddy Kinsey and the Kinsey Report, Parisota Hot Club.

DEBORAH HOUGH HEWITT: Waitress at Sutton's. Longhorn regular.

SPRAGUE HOLLANDER: Guitarist for Safety Last, Curtiss A, the Jerks of Fate, the Dark Click, Long Gone Daddies and the Cold Cold Hearts, Certain General, John Cale, Erik Koskinen.

TIM HOLMES: Journalist, musician. Former performing arts curator at Walker Art Center, publicist for Columbia Records.

JENNIFER HOLT: Cofounder, violinist, singer, songwriter for Têtes Noires; also singer for the Hug, violinist and singer for Fine Art, solo artist.

JACQUE HORSCH: Posed as waitress at Jay's Longhorn. Worked for Schon Productions. Coiffeur to Paul Westerberg, Tommy Stinson, and Steve Foley on the Replacements 1990 tour.

LINDA HULTQUIST: Lighting and FX for the Suicide Commandos; lighting for the Suburbs.

PETER JESPERSON: Cofounder of Twin/Tone Records. Manager of Oar Folkjokeopus record store. Booking advisor for Jay's Longhorn. Manager and co-producer for the Replacements. Record producer, A&R man, radio and club DJ. Vice president of New West Records. Lifelong music hound.

JERRY JOHNSON: Drummer for Cribdeath; bassist, drummer, and vocalist for Mezzo Fist, the Silverteens.

RUSTY JONES: Bassist and cofounder of NNB; also bassist for the Regenerates, Ben Day Dots, Safety Last, the Jerks of Fate. Wax Museum staff.

SHARON KANIESS: Guitar, keyboard, vocals for 2i, BLACKi; also vocals for Poetry Grenade.

JOHN KASS: Record store owner, record manufacturer, radio DJ, guitarist, venue booker. Cofounder of Susstones record label. Owner of Prospective Records and GoJohnnyGo Records. A&R at Twin/Tone. Staff and/or owner at Music 2, Northern Lights, Roadrunner, Dead Media, HiFi Hair and Records, Flashlight Vinyl.

TERRY KATZMAN: Assistant manager at Oar Folkjokeopus. Sonic archivist of early Longhorn and 7th Street Entry shows. House soundman for 7th Street Entry. Producer for Rifle Sport, Hüsker Dü, and more. Co-owner Reflex Records. Owner-operator of

Garage D'Or Records, Garage D'Or Recording Company. Merchandise sales for Suicide Commandos.

MARTIN KELLER: Journalist, author, music editor, publicist, pop culture critic for *City Pages* and the *Twin Cities Reader*. Appeared in *Rolling Stone, Billboard, Pioneer Press, Star Tribune, Washington Post,* and more.

LU ANN KINZER: Fashion designer. Longhorn regular, local music supporter.

HUGO KLAERS: Drummer, vocalist, songwriter for the Suburbs.

JODY KURILLA: Host of house parties and after parties, local music supporter, promoter. DJ and music booker and promoter in New York. A&R for Geffen Records.

PD LARSON: Journalist, manager of the Jayhawks, press officer for Susstones Records.

CHARLIE LAWSON: Bassist for Crazy Legs Blues Band, the Wallets, Charles and Ed, Swamp Twisters, Charlie's Combo.

ADAM LEVY: Singer-songwriter, activist, producer, educator. Founder, lead singer, lead guitar for the Honeydogs; also numerous collaborative projects and solo work.

GRADY LINEHAN: Twin/Tone staff. Northern Lights staff. Various distribution companies and independent promotions.

SCOTT MACDONALD: Singer, drummer, songwriter, arranger for Arcwelder; also drummer for Blaze of Glory, Red Letter Day, 2i, Ringout!

DICK MADDEN: Saxophonist for 2i, BLACKi. Roadie for second half of Hüsker Dü's *Children's Crusade* tour.

MIKE MADDEN: Fan, babysitter, record collector, archivist.

MICHAEL MARKOS: Music attendee, performance and fine art photographer, art gallery owner and director in New York and Arizona. Performer in the Pilots Club Dance Troupe's "Swan Lake MN" and more.

STEPHEN McCLELLAN: General manager and main talent buyer for Uncle Sam's/Sam's/First Avenue (1975–2004). Teacher at McNally Smith College of Music. Researcher for Minnesota Music Museum. Director and booker for the Diverse Emerging Music Organization (DEMO). Independent music booker.

BONNI McCONNELL: Partner of Bruce C. Allen.

MICHAEL McKERN: Audio and mastering engineer, producer, studio owner. Owner-operator of six Twin Cities recording studios. Recording facility design and installation. Music production instructor at McNally Smith College of Music. Drummer for Johnny Rey and the Reaction, Curtiss A.

DAVID MOE: Bassist for Johnny Quest; also Ankle Chop, Church Picnic, Tangent, the Silverteens. Minneapolis commercial director and filmmaker.

DANIEL MURPHY: Lead guitarist and songwriter for Soul Asylum; also guitarist for Golden Smog. Founder and co-owner of Grapefruit Moon Gallery.

DALE T. NELSON: Singer for Otto's Chemical Lounge; also Noble Mice, the Hearsemen, Sheepherders, and Piston Wrist. Former co-owner of Records on the Nile and of Otto's Record Lounge. Record collector, DJ.

KURT NELSON: Lead singer, songwriter, guitarist for the Pistons, Simba, Rock-a-Dots, and the Mell-O-Tones; guitarist for Jets (of Valdosta, GA) and various collaborations in the Twin Cities. Organizer and promoter of Peas on Earth food shelf benefit and of barn parties.

CHRIS OSGOOD: Guitarist, singer, songwriter, composer for the seminal punk rock band the Suicide Commandos; also guitarist and singer for L7-3, Boys Life, 55401, the X-Boys. Label manager and producer at Twin/Tone records. Vice-president of community relations at McNally Smith College of Music and executive director of McNally Smith College of Music Foundation. Board member for the American Composers Forum.

MICHAEL OWENS: Guitarist for Fingerprints; also the Idle Strand. Cofounder of Blackberry Way Recording Studios and Blackberry Way Records.

BRUCE PAVITT: Entrepreneur, music historian, author, DJ. Founder of Sub Pop Records label with Jon Poneman. Creator of and music reviewer for *Sub Pop* 'zine. Creative director at 8Stem.

LESLIE CARLSON PERKINS: Waitress, bartender, fashion buyer/liquidator/model, Longhorn regular, local music supporter.

ERIC PIERSON: Guitarist for Johnny Quest, Motorhome, the Silverteens; drummer for Halo of Flies. Touring sound engineer for Soul Asylum. Recording engineer for Zuzu's Petals, Arcwelder, and more. FOH sound engineer for Gear Daddies. Northern Lights staff.

TIMOTHY G. PIOTROWSKI: Artist, poet, filmmaker, guitarist, singer/songwriter, photographer. Bands include Duck Kicking Vulture, Mommy Log Balls, and Yanomamo.

DAVE PIRNER: Lead singer, guitarist for Loud Fast Rules, Soul Asylum. Solo recording artist. Record producer.

CHAN POLING: Cofounder, singer, keyboardist for the Suburbs; also the New Standards. Composer and lyricist for stage musicals, including the award-winning *Glensheen*. Produces scores for television, film, and commercials.

TONY PUCCI: Drummer for Man Sized Action, Breaking Circus.

JODY RAY: Bassist for Flamingo, Flamin' Oh's.

MAX RAY: Saxophonist for the Suburbs and the Wallets; also Frank Noise and the Logs of Wood, Parade, Explodo Boys, Crazy Legs Blues Band, Volunteers of the Blue Knights, Gondwana, Willie Murphy and the Angel Headed Hipsters, X-Boys, Rich Lewis Band, Mr. Rowles Band, the New Standards Holiday Show, and countless one-offs.

MICHAEL REITER: Drummer for Civil Defense/Propaganda, the Dig, the Mighty Mofos, the 27 Various, Bob Stinson, and more. Photographer and e-commerce specialist.

JOHNNY REY: Guitarist, founding member of Flamingo; founder, guitarist, singer-songwriter for Johnny Rey and the Reaction.

SHARON SAMELS: Longhorn regular. Wife of Johnny Rey.

ANDY SCHWARTZ: Writer, music critic, musician. Guitarist and singer for cover bands Fast Buck and Rock-Ola. Writer (as Seth Schwartz) for *City Pages*. Staffer and columnist for alt-weekly *Metropolis*. Oar Folkjokeopus Records staff. Publisher and editor-in-chief for *New York Rocker*. Director of editorial services for the publicity department of Epic Records, a division of Sony Music.

PAUL STARK: Photographer, sound engineer, producer, president and cofounder of Twin/Tone Records.

CHUCK STATLER: Film and video producer-director. Produced music videos for Devo, the Suicide Commandos, Flamin' Oh's, Tiny Tim, Madness, James Chance, Prince, Elvis Costello, and more. Also many television commercials and corporate promotional videos.

JIM TOLLEFSRUD: Drummer for the Regenerates, Ben Day Dots, Rock-Ola, NNB, Rockin' Pinecones, the Front Porch Swingin' Liquor Pigs, Wasteband; founder/drummer of Twa Corbies/The Tanglewoods. Keyboardist for Safety Last.

MARK TREHUS: DJ and regular at Jay's Longhorn. Manager of Oar Folkjokeopus, owner of Treehouse Records, manager of Treehouse Records label, owner of Nero's Neptune record label. All-around music and record fanatic.

JIM WALSH: Author, journalist, songwriter. Front man of Jim Walsh and the Dog Day Cicadas; also REMs, the Mad Ripple. Ringleader of the Mad Ripple Hootenanny showcase.

JEFF WARYAN: Guitarist, singer, songwriter for Fingerprints, Figures; also 55401, Curtiss A, the Meadows.

MONTY LEE WILKES: FOH sound engineer for Johnny Rey and the Reaction, the Suburbs, the Replacements, Soul Asylum, Prince, Babes in Toyland, Redd Kross, Beastie Boys, and more. FOH sound engineer at First Avenue. Tour manager for Nirvana. Recording engineer for Curtiss A, Sonic Bouquet, and more. Musician. Died 2016.

ROBERT WILKINSON: Singer, songwriter, guitarist for Prodigy, Flamingo, Flamin' Oh's; also the Snaps, the Robert Wilkinson Band, and solo.

AL WODTKE: Booker at Jay's Longhorn. Singer for Badfinger, Kyx.

PAT WOODS: Singer, songwriter for Man Sized Action; also Tangent, the Let Downs, and Va-VOOM!

ACKNOWLEDGMENTS

So many people were supportive and encouraging through the process of bringing this book into existence. I would like to express my thanks to the following:

To the Minnesota Historical Society Press staff for all their work and support. To my editor, Josh Leventhal, huge thanks for your belief in this project, for your patience and support and tremendous, excellent work editing throughout this project. Thanks to production and design manager Daniel Leary, Pam McClanahan, designer Ryan Scheife (Mayfly Design), managing editor Shannon Pennefeather, copyeditor Mary Russell, and reference associate Jackie Beckey of the MNHS Gale Family Library for all your help.

A special thanks to transcribers Mary Benner, Anna Mataczynski, and Dana Morrison for tirelessly transcribing over a hundred interviews. I deeply appreciate all your patient work.

Thank you to all the people I interviewed. You led adventurous, inspiring lives, creating our great music scene. I appreciate your sharing and trusting your stories with me. To the people whose stories didn't make it into this book, please know they were essential to my understanding of the early music scene.

To Danny Amis, Kathy Chapman, Tom Cannon, Daniel Corrigan, Paul Lundgren, Steve Madore, Michael Markos, Sheryl Marquardt, Bayard Michael, Michael Reiter, Catherine Settanni, John Tollefsrud, and Michael Weiler for contributing photography.

To Dann Carlson, Dick Champ, Kevin Cole, Lorna Doone, Chrissie Dunlap, Colleen Foley, Denise Halverson, Peter Jesperson, Martin Keller, Mike Madden, Tony Pucci, Johnny Rey, the Suicide Commandos, Howie Wilkes, Robert Wilkinson, and more, for graciously contributing photos and memorabilia, and time in your homes interviewing and hearing stories about your collections. Special thanks to Dale T. Nelson, who generously provided access to his rich collection of photos and memorabilia, which was tragically lost in a house fire a few months before publication of this book; I am grateful to be able to share a few of those now-lost but precious items.

To Mark Engebretson for providing numerous image scans from collections of the Suicide Commandos, Danny Amis, the Hypstrz, and more.

To Monty Lee Wilkes, my deepest gratitude for sharing your stories, humor, and passion for the musicians you worked with, and your support. You enriched so many lives and our experience of live music, throughout your life as a friend, family member, and extraordinary FOH sound engineer. Thank you so much for all you brought to us. You are sorely missed by many.

To Bruce C. Allen, of the Suburbs, I am lucky to have known you and to be able to share your stories.

Thanks to the Suicide Commandos for graciously allowing me to use your song title "Complicated Fun" as the book title.

To my early readers and supportive friends who made editing recommendations, essential to bringing this book to completion: Andrew Donaldson, Maureen Higgins, Peter Jesperson, Michelle Leon, Miki Mosman, Paul Pirner, Sam Ridenour, Dana Thompson, Mark Wojahn, and Brad Zellar.

To Katy Ryan Levin, for your beautiful author photograph.

To Mary Beth Mueller, for your networking and connecting me with people essential to this book.

To fellow KFAI DJs and staff, for providing me a space to share independent music with the community and keep it going strong on the airwaves.

To the music community including the staff of Grumpy's, First Avenue/7th Street Entry, and the Turf Club.

To Birchwood Café owner Tracy Singleton and staff; Masu Sushi and Robata staff; Ramen Kazama owner Matthew Kazama; Moto-i; the Draft Horse owners, Luke and Katie Kyle, Anne Saxton and staff; and Food Building owner Kieran Folliard—thank you for all the sustenance and encouragement.

To my friends who have been so supportive and encouraging while researching and during the writing of this book: Jill Seifert Thiele, Louie Dunlap, Patrick Dwyer, Angela Behrends, Brian Vanderwerf, Lola Lesheim, Matt Panschar, Jane Minton, Holly Matzke, Danny Sigelman, Joan Vorderbruggen, Tom Siler, Ryan Bouchey, Alissa Barthel, Jon Clifford, Charlie Mueller, Lori Hoffman, Liz Alvarado, Mark Moffa, Chad and Ben Erickson, Sho Nikaido, Geri Casler, Matt and Kristin Werner, Tony Zaccardi, Alexander Walsh, Marlon James, Steve Barone, Patti Walsh, John Adams, and more.

Most of all, thanks to my family for their love, support, and encouragement. My love and gratitude to Mom and Dad, Paulena and Vern, and to my brother Guy, my sister Leslie, and my extended family. In loving memory of my late brother Toby, who continues to inspire me and whom I'll always miss.

INDEX

Bold page numbers indicate speaker; *italicized* page numbers indicate photo/illustration.

2i (band), 5, 231, 305–6, 350–51
7th Street Entry: bands at, 59, 165–66, 229, 234, 244–45, *263*, 278–79, 281–84, *285*, 289, 293, 300, 303, 308–10, 313, *333*; beginnings of, 149, 288; as gathering place, 5, 294, 308–9; influence of, 336; staff, 348, 349–50
8 Eyed Spy, 131
9:30 Club, 4, 59, 200
10cc, 75
27 Various, 347, 353
99ers, 347
1980–1990 (Spooks), 211, *216*
55401 (band), 352–53
"6654321" (Hypstrz), 62

A&M Records, 6, 204, 209, 226, 329, 330
Ackerman, Dougie, 111–12
Ackerson, Ed, **70**, 229, **298**, **302**, **341**, 347
"Action Woman" (Hypstrz), 66
Adverts, 69
Aerosmith, 301
Agora Ballroom, 237
Ahl, Dave: gathering places and parties, **34**, 73, **176**; music scene and, 184, 215; in other bands, 48, 146, 149, 200, 225; on other musicians, 10, **13–14**, 29, **143–44**, **276**, **317**; others on, xi, xiii, 198; Suicide Commandos and, 23, **24–27**, 31, **33**, **40–41**, **48**, 347; venues and, *30*, *51*, *133*, *146*, *257*
Aldridge Arena, 90
Alexander, Polly, 296
Alexander, Willie "Loco," 70
All the Young Dudes (Mott the Hoople), 104
Allen, Bruce: as designer, **187**, 215–16; gathering places and parties, *173*, *179*; loss of, xii, 205–6, 210; M-80 and, **254**, 256; other musicians and, 24, **52**, 152, 184–85, **254**; style of, 190, 192–93, *192*; Suburbs and, *54*, 184–87, *188*, 196–98, 201, 203, 207–8, 347;

351; Tsetse Flies and, 173, 185; Twin/Tone and, 215; venues and, *130*, *147*, *189*, *206*
Allen, Mary, and the Percolators, 349
Allman Brothers, 90
Almaas, Steve: gathering places and parties, **32**, **75–76**, 96; on M-80, **254**; New York and, 260, **261–62**, *263–64*, **266–67**, 268; in other bands, 152, 168, 221, 260, 262, *267*, **291**; other musicians and, **19–20**, 90–91, **184–85**, **264**; others on, xiii, 198; Suicide Commandos and, 23, **24**, 25, **28**, *37*, **38**, **41**, **50**, 347; venues and, *36*, *124–25*, *128*, *135*, *257*
Almsted, Curt (Curtiss A): about, 87, 96; career of, xii, 2–3, 5, 17, 20, **101**, 218, 221, 341, 347, 348, 350–51, 353; gathering places and parties, 21–22, **74–75**, 76, 178, 180; influences of, **89–90**; Lennon Tribute and, **99–100**; M-80 and, 251, 253, 255, **256–57**, *257*; on music scene, **334**; in other bands, 91; on other musicians, 13, **42**, **92–94**, 109, **214**, **220**, **249**, **331**; others on, x–xi, 19, 93–95; Spooks and, 211; Thumbs Up and, 12, **97**; Twin/Tone and, 213, 225; venues and, 44, 46, 78, *91*, *93*, *98*, 123, 126, 132, 212, *257*, 289, 290, 313
Alpha Productions, 27, 49
Alstad, Roy, 10, 152
Amboy Dukes, 25
American Dream (Têtes Noires), 225
American Recordings, 6
Amis, Danny: career of, 347; gathering places and parties, **77**, *176*; on M-80, **256**; on music scene, **337**; on other musicians, 29, **64**, **96**; others on, 135; in Raybeats, 96, 260; venues and, *135*, **148**
Amphetamine Reptile Records, 229, 265, 350
"Amusement" (Hüsker Dü), 273, 275
Anderson, Al "Big Al," 94, 101
Anderson, Danny, 25

Index

Anderson, Doug: career of, 347; gathering places and parties, **78–79, 178–79, 181**; on music scene, **333–34**; on New York, **268**; on other musicians, **96–97, 170, 208, 243, 246–47, 301–3**; others on, 142; venues and, **292**
Anderson, Erik, 231, 237–38, 241
Anderson, Larry, 84
Anderson, Laurie, 83
Anderson, Randy, 104
Anderson, Scott, 64
Animals, 57
Ankle Chop, 351
Anthology (record company), 35
Arcwelder, x, 305–6, 351–52
Area (venue), 265
Articles of Faith, 228–29, 297
Asheton, Ron, 53
Astronauts, 57
"Attacking the Beat" (Suicide Commandos), 38
Aviator (venue), 37
Ayers, Dave, 83, 225–27
Aztex, 90

B-52s, 3, 70, 130, 136, 137, 140, 142
Babes in Toyland, ix, 6, 211, 334, 347, 353
"Baby Heartbeat" (Suburbs), 197
Babys, 51
"Back in the USA" (Chuck Berry), 257
"Bad Moon Rising" (Creedence Clearwater Revival), 296
Badfinger, 353
Ballard, Hank, 88
Band of Susans, 349
Barbero, Lori: career of, 347; on M-80, **258**; on music scene, **343–44**; on Oar Folkjokeopus, **79**; on other musicians, **135, 169, 181, 272, 283**; venues and, **130–31, 292, 297–98, 307, 309, 313**
Bar/None, 322
Bash & Pop, 348
Bators, Stiv, 142–43
Batson, Bill: career of, **62–63**, 347; gathering places and parties, 172; Hypstrz and, 55, **56–57, 59, 61, 64**; influence of, 66; in other bands, **55**; on other musicians, 18, 64, **160, 198, 283**; others on, 56, 65; on venues, **294–95**; venues and, **49–50, 53, 60–61, 130, 143, 297, 307, 310**

Batson, Ernie: career, **62–63**, 347; gathering places and parties, **60, 172, 174–75**; Hypstrz and, **55–57, 59, 64**; on other musicians, 18, 61, 97, **142, 160**; others on, 65; on Veggies, **283**; venues and, **48–50, 132, 143, 295, 310**
Bauhaus, 290, 292
Beach Boys, 57, 212
Beastie Boys, 353
Beat Rodeo, 76, 260, 264, 291, 347
Beatles, 9–10, 68, 88–90, 99, 101–2, 159, 195, 334
Beatles for Sale, 91, 93, 98–99
Becker, Rochelle, 246
Behrend, Joseph, 102, 106, 111, 114–15
Ben Day Dots, 145, 350, 353
Benatar, Pat, 312
Berine, Jay: on Duffy's, **292**; Longhorn and, 2, **123–25**, 127, 129, 130, **136**, 151, 347; on music scene, **45, 84, 145**; musicians and, 22, **107, 137, 139, 147, 191, 236**, 239
Berlin, 29
Bernstein, Cliff, 212
Berry, Chris, 257
Berry, Chuck, 49, 257
Berry, Frank, 95, 223, 256
Betrock, Alan, 261
Biafra, Jello, 277, 298–99, 301
Big Daddy Kinsey, 350
Big Hits of Mid-America Volume Three, 62, 142, 149, 152, 161–62, 164, 170, 211, 219, 221–23
Big Money Records, 229
Big Star, 76, 313
Bingenheimer, Rodney, 37
Bingham, Charlie, 152–53
Bishop, Elvin, 44
Black Flag, 289, 293, 297–98, 307
Blackberry Way, 26, 141, 149, **162**, 196, 213–14, 218, 226, 230, 258, 275–76, 319–20, 352
Blackburn, Sean, 9
BLACKi, 350–51
Blam Bar, 181
Blank Records, 34–35, 37–38, 212, 221
Blaze of Glory, 149, 351
Bleeding Hearts, 348
Blessing, Dave, 152, 162
Blitz Bar, 19, 26–27, 44–47, 47, 105
Blondie, 2–3, 29, 36, 70, 123, 126, 128, 130, 136, 137, 141
Blue Cheer, 298

Blue Earth (Jayhawks), 6
Blue Hippos, 297
Blum, Cindy: career of, 347; gathering places and parties, **33**, **84**; in New York, 260, **263**; NNB and, 152, **155**, 158, 165, **167–69**; in other bands, 100, 162–63, **166**, 235, **236**; other musicians and, 51, **99**, **178**; in Red House, 64, 160; venues and, **46**, **267**
Blumenthals, 123–24
BNLX, 347
Bogus Records, 62, 347
Boigenzahn, Emily "Bee" (Dunlap), **341–42**, 347
Boissy, Gérard-Jean, 297, 302–3, 304
Bomp Records, 36, 62
Bon Jovi, 209
"Bongo Rock" (Suburbs), 187, 197
Bongos, 96
Bonham, John, 168
Bonzo Dog Doo-Dah Band, 24–25, 232
Bookie's Club 870, 37
Bosley, Mike, 321
Bowe, Kevin, **42**, **169**, **284–85**, 348
Bowie, David: albums at Oar Folk, 74, 76; bands covering, 104, 117; influence of, 1, 11, 15–17, 20, 77, 106, 185, 195–96; legend of, 101
Boys Life, 347, 352
Brantseg, Steve: career of, 348; on Duffy's, **291–92**; on music scene, **328**, **330**, **339**; on musicians, **95**, **98**, **207**, **210**, **242–43**, **298**; Phones and, **224**, *291*; on Twin/Tone, **225**
BrassZilla, 348
Breaking Circus, 352
Bream, Jon, 177
British rock, 11, 77
Bronx Zoo, 111
Brooks, Scott, 245, 246
Brown, James, 56, 88–89, 97, 298, 331
"Brown Sugar" (Rolling Stones), 223
Brubeck, Dave, 238
Bryant, Eloise, 179
Buck, Peter, 64
Bunky's, 59
Burdon, Eric, 54
"Burn It Down" (Suicide Commandos), 33–34
Burnsville Bowl, 57
Buswell, Jeff: career of, 348; on M-80, **254**; on music scene, **20**, **52**, **339**; on Podany's, **174**; on Suburbs, **189**, **191**, **193**, **200–202**, **205**, **209**
Butch Greaser and the Hoods, 55

Butthole Surfers, 289
Buzzcocks, 123, 126, 130, 293, 303
Byrne, David, 35, *71*, 72, 138, 141, 177, 234, 240

Cabooze, 10, 44, 189, 193, 209, 290, 311, 318
Cain, 185
Cale, John, 350
Calgarian Hotel, 277
"Calhoun Surf" (Danny Amis), 135
Cameron, Ryan, **80–81**, **86**, **159**, **316**, 348
Candy Apple Grey (Hüsker Dü), 342
"Can't You Hear Me Knocking" (Rolling Stones), 223
Caplan, Zippy, 56
Carlson, Dann, 52, 53–54, 191, **199–200**, **246**, 348
Carlson, Mike, 135
Carr, Tim, 108, 180, 251–53, 256, 258, 261–62, 264, 268
Cars, 109, 113–14
"Cash Register" (Wallets), 236–37
Catch a Falling Star (Wallets), 241, 242
CBGB: bands at, 4, 33, 35–36, 163, 316; influence of, 16, 21, 23, 260, 266, 297, 343; Longhorn similar to, 128, 136, 149
CC Club/Tap, 3, 78, 87–88, 90, 100, 215, 321
Cedar Inn, 51, 52
Cerise, Jeff, **148**, *291*, 348
Certain General, 350
"Chains" (Wad), 262
Champ, Dick: career of, 348; gathering places and parties, 12, **21–22**, **32–33**, 73, **74**, 84, **172–75**; on M-80, **258–59**; New York and, 263, **267**; NNB and, 152, **153–54**, 156, 161–62, **164–66**, 170–71; on others, **16**, **17**, **31**; others on, xi; "Slack," 156, **157–59**, **164**, **218–19**; studios and, *162*; venues and, **45**, **125**, **127–28**, **151**, **155**, **308–9**
Chan Poling Band, 205, 210, 348
Chance, James, 232, 242–44, 251, *254*, 256–57, 309
Chance, James, and the Contortions, 196, 243, 251, 254
Chaney, Beej: gathering places and parties, 173, 181; in other bands, 148, 186; on other musicians, **141**, **144**, **205**, 335; Suburbs and, ix, *4*, *54*, 176, 184–85, **186**, 188–90, 192–95, 197–98, **202**, 204, 207, 209, 348; venues and, 54, **146–47**, 311

Index

Chapel, Neil, 100
Chappell Music, 165
Charles, Ray, 102
Charles and Ed, 351
Charlie's Combo, 351
Cheap Trick, 26, 28, 178
Cheapo Records, 82–83
"Chemistry Set" (Suburbs), 147, 187, 195
Chicago Fest, 202
Children's Crusade tour, 277–78, 297, 351
Chilton, Alex, 313
Chooglin', 348
Christgau, Robert, 224
Christiansen's, 272
Christopher, J., 304
Chrome, Cheetah, 35, 143
Church, 179
Church Picnic, 301–2, 351
Cinderella, 209
Circle Jerks, 290, 300
"Citadel" (Rolling Stones), 257
City Hall, 68
City Pages, 166, 249, 253, 351, 353
Civil Defense, 293, 353
Clark, Gene, 80
Clash: bands covering, 150, 341; influence of, 20, 344; at Longhorn, 130; musicians on, 14, 53; Oar Folk and, 2, 76, 79; Peter Jesperson on, 126
Claustrophobia (Man Sized Action), 228
Clegg, John "JC," 83
Clifford, George, 172
Clifford, Jim, 231, 235, 260
Clifford, Jon, **65**, **142**, 238, 348
Clinton, George, 332
"Closer to the Stars" (Soul Asylum), 225
Clown Lounge, 140
Club 53, 266
Cobblestone Ballroom, 51
Cochran, Eddie, 49, 57, 126
Cockburn, Bruce, 290
Coffeehouse Extemporé folk music, 9
Coffman Union, 28
Cold Party, 182
Cole, Kevin: career of, 348; Longhorn and, **126–27**, 127, **134**; music scene and, **17–18**, 126, 312, **344**, 346; music stores and, **73**, 81, **86**; on musicians, **23**, **43**, 81–82, 152, 171, **286**, **288**, **309–10**, **332–33**

Columbia Records, 350
Comic City, 93, 178
Commandos. *See* Suicide Commandos
The Commandos Commit Suicide Dance Concert, 80, 133, 142, 211–12, 221
Commodore, 114
"Complicated Fun" (Suicide Commandos), xiii, 5, 221, 257
Connie's Insider, 347
"Contort Yourself" (James Chance), 256, 258
Contortions, 246, 251
Controversy (Prince), 331
Conway, Pete, 297
Cooke, Sam, 88
Cookhouse Studios, 225, 241, 328
Cooper, Alice, 161
Cooper, Dale, 34
Corrigan, Daniel, **134**, **143**, **233**, 348
Costello, Elvis, 3, 33–34, 80, 109, 123, 136–40, 344
County, Wayne, 36
Courtesy (Curtiss A), 94–95, 97, 142
Cows, x, 343
Crabs of Culture, 200
Crackers, 260, 262, 264, 266, 267, 347, 349
Crackpot Records, 229
Cramps, 136, 290
Crash Street Kids, 111, 115
Crazy Legs Blues Band, 351, 352
Cream, 103
Creation Audio, 225
Credit in Heaven (Suburbs), 196, 204, 209, 223
Cribdeath, 350
Crosby, Bing, 126
Crosby, James, 266
Cryan' Shames, 87–88
Cubby Bear, 160
Cunningham, Jack, 28
Curran's Restaurant, 246
Curtiss A. *See* Almsted, Curt (Curtiss A)

Dads, 217, 284, 348
Dahlias, 349
The Daily. See Minnesota Daily
Damage is Done (Curtiss A), 94, 98
Damned, 2, 58, 75, 76, 82, 144, 290, 292
Danceteria, 96, 264–65, 268, 290
Danger Boy and the Road Vultures, 349
Dark Click, 347, 350

Daughters of Invention, 349
Dave Clark Five, 57
Davis, Michael, 53
Davis, Sammy, Jr., 331
dB's, 251, 256
Dead Boys: music scene and, 2, 69, 72, 116, 200; venues of, 3, 35–36, 123, 130, 137, 138, 143, 147, 291
Dead Kennedys, 277, 289, 299, 301
Dead Lemmings, 297
Dead Media, 350
DeBace, Roger, 300
DeBoer, Bob, **27–28**, 348
Decline of Western Civilization (film), 284
Del Counts, 1, 57
Del-Lords, 347
Depeche Mode, 194
Depot, 90, 311. *See also* First Avenue
Destri, Jimmy, 141
Destroy All Monsters, 53
Detroit, 2, 9
Devlin, Bill, 301
Devo, 33–34, 79, 114, 126, 140, 176, 184, 191, 200, 251–54, 256–57, 302
Diamondbacks, 148, 200
"Diane" (Hüsker Dü), 342
Dickies, 275
Dickinson, Paul, **83**, **281**, **299–300**, 305–6, **340**, 348
Dictators, 31, 142
Dig, 347, 353
Dirty Mind (Prince), 331
Discharge, 302, 307
Disco Duck, 82
"Dish It Up" (Suburbs), 197
DNA, 244
"Do You Remember" (Hüsker Dü), 276
DOA, 277, 301
Dodds, Gini, and the Dahlias, 349
Don the Baptist, 288
Doone, Lorna, **131**, **176–77**, **192**, 348
Doors, 24, 232
Doug Maynard Band, 9
Dove: The Music of Love, 251, 256. *See also* Devo
Dr. Feelgood, 75
Dream Hog (Suburbs), 204
Duck Kicking Vulture, 352
Duffy's: bands at, 98, 102, 109, 234, 237, 239, 249, 258, *275*, 288–89, 291–93, 299, 301, 311, 319; as gathering place, 5, 230, 290, 294, 295, 302, 308; Jay Berine and, 347
Dunlap, Bob "Slim": career of, 341–42, 348; Curt Almsted and, **91–92**, 93, 95; Lennon Tribute and, 99; on music scene, **10**; Paul Stark on, 91; on Peter Jesperson, **220**; in Replacements, 314, 341; Thumbs Up and, 87–89, **88**, 100; venues and, **93**, 97, **132**, *257*
Dunlap, Chrissie: career of, 348; Lennon Tribute and, 99; music scene and, 313; on musicians, **42**, **100**; on Peter Jesperson, **86**; venues and, 309, 333, 341, 344
Dupay, Joe, 55–59
Duran Duran, 81, 84, 292
Dutch East India, 228–29
Duvall, Margaret, 129, 130, 139, 146
Dwight Twilley Band, 28, 54
Dylan, Bob, 95, 126, 141, 202, 332

Easter, Mitch, 266, *267*
Eddie & the Hot Rods, 58, 75
Eddie Hurricane, 57
The Edge, 100
Effigies, 295
Eggtwist, 347
E.I.E.I.O., 25
Elbow Room, 90
Electric Fetus, 2, 67, 74
Eleganza, 348
Elioff, Richard, 80
Elko Speedway show, 53–54
"Emission Control" (Suicide Commandos), 41
Engebretson, Mark, **97**, **166**, **170**, **281–82**, 349
Engelbert, Jimmy, 240
England's Newest Hit Makers (Rolling Stones), 103
Eno, Brian, 73, 76, 195
Entropy, 348
Entry. *See* 7th Street Entry
Epic Records, 353
"Erotic City" (Prince), 332–33
Etoll, Eva Mozey, **283**, 313, 349
Etoll, Mike, 296, 343
"Everybody Stomp" (NRBQ), 90
Everything Falls Apart (Hüsker Dü), 228, 340
Exile on Main Street (Rolling Stones), 11
Exmo-6-Desmo, 296, 305, 343
Explodo Boys, 48, 352

Faces, 103, 116
Fall, 80
Fallon, Steve, 267
"Faraway Eyes" (Rolling Stones), 223
Farfisa, 349
Fargnoli, Steven, 331
Farrell, David, 112–13, 115
Fast Buck, 353
Fat City Records, 113, 115
Faust, 156
Feelies, 251
Fenn, Jim, **108–9**, 111, **115**, 172, 349
Ferret Comix, 323
Ferry, Bryan, 195
Fields, Danny, 262
Figures, 98, 330, 348, 353
Figures (Jeff Waryan), 98, 224
Final Conflict, 295, 302, 307
"Final Solution" (Pere Ubu), 160
Fine Art, 5, 231, 247, 288, 350
Fine Young Cannibals, 112
"Fingerprint File" (Rolling Stones), 217
Fingerprints: career, 2, 20, 52, 217–18, 350, 352–53; at M-80, 251, 256–57; Twin/Tone and, 3, 213–16, 218; venues and, 52, 126, 132, 141, 313
Fingerprints, 211, *216*
Finn, Craig, **78**, **322–23**, **336**, 349
"Fire" (Arthur Brown), 31
First Avenue: audiences at, 145, 310; bands at, 44, 55, 60, 63–64, 99, 168, 207, 209, 240, 243, 284, 289, 292, 301, 323, 327, 330–32, *345*; beginnings of, 136, 288, 292; as gathering place, 5, 130; Kevin Cole at, 73, 81, 127, 348; as music scene, 114, 230, 268; popularity of, 294; staff, 348, 351, 353; Steve McClellan and, 308, 333
Five Story Garage (Man Sized Action), 229
Fjelstad, Steve: in bands, 98, 149, 217–18, 257; as sound engineer, 127, 133, 140, 214, 225–26, 319, 325
Flaig, Carol, 25, 48
Flame, 10
Flamette, 50
Flamin' Groovies, 110
Flamin' Oh's: beginnings of, 109–11; career, 102, 112–13, 200, 216, 242, 293, 349, 352, 353; gathering places and parties, 60; others on, ix–x; venues and, 50, 212, 290–91, 310

Flamingo: beginnings of, 2, 17, 106; career, 5, 20, 34, 102, 113, *117*, 218, 352, 353; covers performed by, 74, 106; gathering places and parties, 21, 60, **74**; influence of, 198; others on, 118–19; people involved with, 321, 349; playing original music, 12, 106–7, 109; Twin/Tone and, 211, 217; venues and, 2, 44, 46, 54, 102, 107–9, 116–17, 123–25, 126–28, 131–32, 198, 212–13, 313, 318. *See also* Prodigy
Flash Cadillac and the Continental Kids, 48
Flash Tuesday, 103
Flashlight Vinyl, 350
Fleshtones, 85, 251, 254, 256, 290
Flies, Danny, **166**, 309, **309**, 349
Flight 581 (Pistons), 223
Flip Your Wig (Hüsker Dü), 280, 328
Flock of Seagulls, 84
Florent, 265
Flowers Studio, 347
Flyte Tyme Studios, 209
Fogerty, John, 322
Foley, Colleen, **317**, 349
Foley, Dave: career of, 349; on music scene, **44**, **179**; on musicians, **13**, **162–63**, **236–37**; in other bands, 162, **236**; talent of, 170, 178; Things That Fall Down and, 244, **245–46**, 247
Foley, Kevin, 96
Foley, Steve, 96, 99, 135, 246, 317
Folk City, 322
Fonaas, Jill, 226, 300
Foreigner, 9, 190
Frances Gumm, 340, 348
Frank, Hartley, 139, 144, 145–48, 151, 180, 234, 239, 246, 255–56, 294, 308, 317
Frantix, 80
Frantz, Chris, 35, 71, 72
Freedom, Roy, 127
Freeman, Mark: career of, **152–53**, 155, 170, 349; gathering places and parties, 33, **84–85**; on M-80, **255–56**; New York and, **260**, **263–64**, **268**; NNB and, 17, 152, **154**, **156**, 159–60, **160–62**, **164**, **171**; in other bands, 64, 160, 162–63, **166**, **235–36**; on other musicians, **15**, **19**, 99, **138**, 155, **167–69**, **178**, **318**; others on, 153, 160–61; "Slack," 156, **158–59**, **165**; studios and, **157**, *162*, **167**; venues and, **46**, **147**, 163, 166, **268**; Wave 7 and, 219

Freiseis, Mark, 64
Friars Club, 55
Front End, 106
Front Porch Swingin' Liquor Pigs, 158, 353
Frucci, Angela, 247, **248–49**, 349
Fults, Dan, *71*, 77
Fury Things, xiii, 353

Gage, Camille, **247–49**, 349
Gang of Four, 63, 123, 130, 177, 246
Garage D'Or Records, 67, 85, 206, 350
Gardner, Fred, 294–95
Gargoyles, 200
Gay Pirates, 200
Gear Daddies, 341, 352
Geffen Records, 264, 351
Gehring, Greg, 129
Generics, 348
George's in the Park, 90
Giordano, Lou, 279
"Girlfriend" (Suburbs), 186, 197
Give Thanks (Articles of Faith), 229
Glass, Philip, 185
Glensheen, 352
"Gloria," 95, 257
Glynn, Kevin, 11, 12, 213, 217
"Go" (Suburbs), 186
Go Borneo, 293, 299, 344
Go Van Gogh, 349
GoJohnnyGo Records, 350
Golden Earring, 70
Golden Smog, 352
Goldstein, Mark, 153, 256, 262, 266
Gondwana, 349, 352
Goofy's Upper Deck: about, 307–8, 340; bands at, 94, 99, 234, *285*, 288–89, 291, 293, 295–96, 297–302; beginnings of, 294–95; as gathering place, 5
Gordon, Cam, 349
Gordon, Elliot, **232–33**, 349
Gordon, Jon, 235
Gordon, Robert, 70
Gordon, Rod, **225**, **231–32**, *233*, **234–41**, 244, 349
Graber, Bill, 306
Graber, Rob, 306
Grand Funk Railroad, 25
Grant, Peter, 112
Grapefruit Moon Gallery, 352
Greenberg, Steven, 209

Griffin, Mitch, 78, 90
Grohl, Dave, 301
Ground Zero, 228–29, 302, 305
Grumpy's Bar, 350
GST, 348
Gumprecht, Blake, 223, 227
Gun Club, 181
Guthrie Theater, 24, 232, 243–44
Guy, Buddy, 89
Gypsy, 90

Haga, John "Bongo," **53**, **56–59**, 61, **62**, 64–65, 92, **93–94**, 133, 257, **276–77**, 349
Hagen, Nina, 290
Haglof, Karen, **22**, **45–46**, **95**, **178**, 221, **262–63**, **266**, *267*, 349
Haley, Bill, 57, 196
Haley, Bill, and His Comets, 57
Halliday, Michael: music scene and, **10**, 24, 152; in other bands, 173, **185**, 209, **235**; on other musicians, **185**, **192**, **318–19**; others on, 184–85; at Podany's, 173; Suburbs and, *54*, 184–86, **187**, *188*, **190**, 193, 196, **197**, 199, **201**, **203–5**, 210, 349; venues and, **147**
Hallman, Charley, 3, 31, 112, 141, 211–12, 218, 220, 228, 273
Hallman, Graham, **31**, 349
Halo of Flies, 350, 352
Hammond, John, 90
Hammond, Stefan, 134
Hampshire College, 36
"Hanging on the Telephone" (Jack Lee), 109
Hannah, Duncan, 36, 268
Hanson, Erik, 264
Harder, Philip, **285–86**, **340**, 349
Harpo's, 67, 80, 291
Harrison, Jerry, *71*, 72, 145
Harry, Debbie, 141
Harsha, Paul, 302
Hart, Grant: as designer, 215, 281, 297; gathering places and parties, 78, 181–82; in Hüsker Dü, 61, 148, **271**, 272–73, 277, 279–86, 297, 342; as influence, 82, 300; in other bands, 301; Reflex Records and, 229
Harvey, Alex, 41
Harvey, John, 34
Hasti, Wayne, **10–11**, **145**, 152–53, 155, **160–61**, *162*, 221, 350
"Hawaii Five-O," 135

Hayes brothers, 10
Hazelmyer, Tom, **229**, **290–91**, 296, **298–99**, **306–7**, 350
Hazlett, Buck, 135, 214
Hazlett, Johnny, 96, 214
Hazlett, Kevin, 76, 214
Head Blues Band, 25. *See also* Suicide Commandos
Hearsemen, 352
Helgeson, Robin, 22
Hell, Richard, 72, 305
Hendrix, Jimi, 103, 232, 331
Henry, Robb: career of, 350; Fingerprints and, 141, **217**; gathering places and parties, **72**, **179–80**; as influence, 152–53; music scene and, 185; Peter Jesperson and, **11**, 12; on venues, **134–35**
Henry Cow, 156
"Heroes" (David Bowie), 74, 117
Hest, Bob, 240
Hewitt, Deborah Hough, **193–94**, 350
HiFi Hair and Records, 348, 350
High Fidelity Boys Live 1979, 206
Hill, Michael, 322
Hillbilly Voodoo Dolls, 348
Hinding, Chris, 157
Hines, Jim, 217
Hinkley, Bill, 9
Hip Bone, 349
Hitchcock, Robyn, 227
Hold Steady, 266, 349
Holiday Cocktail Lounge, 261
Holland, Jools, 290
Hollander, Sprague, **100**, 350
Hollies, 88
Holly, Buddy, 334
Holme, Cliff, 103
Holmes, Tim: career of, 350; on Longhorn, **132–33**, **136**, **146**; music scene and, 15, **16**, **21**, 22, **71**, **253**; musicians and, **18–19**, **26**, 29, **35**, **159**, **195**; in New York, 264, 268
Holt, Jefferson, 309
Holt, Jennifer, **247–50**, 350
Holzschuh, Don, 28, 143, 288, 334
Home Rock, 284
Honeydogs, 351
Hootenanny (Replacements), 215, 320, 322
Horsch, Jacque, **96**, **129–30**, **140**, **144–45**, 207, **237**, **317**, 350

Horses (Patti Smith), 15–16, 75
Horseshoe Lake Ballroom, 49
Hot Licks, 2, 67, 73, 78, 80–81, 84–86, 166, 291, 309, 348
House of Breakfast, 114
"How to Keep Time to Music and Learn to Become a Better Dancer" (Wallets), 241
Howlin' Wolf, 334
Hug, 247, 350
Hull, Dakota Dave, 9
Hultquist, Chuck, 31–32, 152, 155, 165, 268
Hultquist, Linda, 24, **31–32**, **48**, **50–51**, 350
Human League, 209
Hunter, Ian, 134
Hurrah, 260, 266–67
Hüsker Dü: beginnings of, 83, 148, 271–72, 336; career, 6, 61, 109, 224, 289, 297, 316, 319, 328–29, 334, 340–44, 350–51; DIY aesthetic of, 271, 286–87; gathering places and parties, 81, 83, 181–82; impact of, 43, 321; others on, xiii, 247, 259, 337; playing fast, 66, 275, 281; playing with other musicians, 181, 249, 282, 299, 303–6, 336; popularity of, 206, 207, 302, 314; record labels and, 5, 217, 228–29, 273, 327, 330; Veggies, 281–83; venues and, 3, *271*, *273*, *275*, 289, 293, 295, 297, 301, 310, *345*
Hypnotic Tornado, 305
Hypo, 349
Hypstrization! (Hypstrz), 55, *63*, 65
Hypstrz: beginnings of, 2, 57–58; career, 3, 5, 43, 55, *61*, *63–64*, 200, 251, 343, 347, 349; gathering places and parties, 174–75, 182; influence of, 65–66, 198, 232; musicians playing with, 282–83, 303–5; on other musicians, 18, 61, 132; others on, x, 60, 150; Twin/Tone and, 219; venues and, 44, 48–50, 53–54, *58*, 64, 141, 294, 310
Hypstrz Live (Hypstrz), 62–63

"I Need a Torch" (Suicide Commandos), 38
"I Remember Romance" (Flamin' Oh's), 102, 114
"I Wanna Meet You" (Cryan' Shames), 87–88
"I Want to Hold Your Hand" (Beatles), 10
"I Will Dare" (Replacements), *345*
Ice Stars, 214
Idle Strand, 352
Idol, Billy, 297
Iggy and the Stooges, 25. *See also* Pop, Iggy

"Iko Iko," 249
"I'll Be There" (Jackson Five), 319
"I'll Wait" (Suicide Commandos), 38
"I'm on Fire" (Dwight Twilley Band), 28
"In a Free Land" (Hüsker Dü), 229
In Combo (Suburbs), 141, 197, 208, 211
"In the Beginning Was the End" (Devo), 34
Individuals, 322
Infinity Art Unit, 152
Information (band), 163
Inhofer, Gregg, 104
Inside Straight, 350
Insider, 218
"Instant Karma" (John Lennon), 99
Irenic Regime, 302
Ironics, 348
It's Only Rock and Roll (Rolling Stones), 217
Ivers, Robert, 214

Jackson, Janet, 209
Jackson Five, 319
Jacox, Maurice, 101
Jagger, Bianca, 265
Jagger, Mick, 202
Jam, 79, 150
Jam, Jimmy, 312, 343
James, Brian, 144
James from Chicago, 246
Jayhawks, ix, 6, 211, 220, 288, 301, 334, 342, 351
JEM Records, 68–69
Jerks of Fate, 347, 348, 349, 350
Jerome, Dick, 261, 266
Jesperson, Peter: career of, 350; on First Avenue, **311–12**; gathering places and parties, **180–81**; Longhorn and, **126**, 129, **136**, 137–38, **151**; on music scene, **289**, **330**, **334**; on musicians, **11–12**, **42**, **87–89**, **118**, 152, **159–60**, 184, **190–91**, **242**, **272–74**, **298**, **320–21**; Oar Folkjokeopus and, **67–69**, 70–71, **73**, 85, 90; record-listening parties and, 11, 172; Replacements and, **314**, 315–20, **321–26**; as tastemaker, 15–16, 20, 73–80, 83, 86, 98, 117, 220, 312–13, 344; Twin/Tone and, 3, 112, **211–16**, 218, **219**, 220, 223–28
Jet-A-Way Lounge, 44
Jets, 290, 352
Jett, Joan, 290
Joel, Billy, 63
Johansen, David, 13–14, 70–72, 130, 136, 292

John Ewing Band, 348
Johnny Quest, 150, 319, 351–52
Johnson, Dan, 239, 294
Johnson, Jerry, **65–66**, 350
Johnson, Leslie, 239, 294
Johnson, Prudence, 101
Joint (venue), 10
Jon Spencer Blues Explosion, 264
Jones, Grace, 3, 139, 145
Jones, Rusty, 12, 16–17, 75, 99, 152–53, **156**, 158, 161, 172, 350
Jonny III, 37, 135, 347
Joplin, Janis, 232
Joslyn, Bob, 246
Journey, 104
Joy Division, 303
"Jumpin' Jack Flash" (Rolling Stones), 117
"Just Like Me" (Paul Revere and the Raiders), 282

K Records, 265
Kamikaze, 265
Kane, Abbie, 226
Kaniess, Dan, 306
Kaniess, Sharon, **306**, 350
Kaplan, Ira, 267, 322
Kass, John: career of, 350; on musicians, **62**, 66, 96, 106, 144, 161, 221, 272, 275, 300, 302–3, 305–6; on Oar Folkjokeopus, **79**; on parties, **181–82**; on record labels, **217**, 219, 227, 229–30
Katzman, Terry: career of, 350–51; gathering places and parties, **174**, 180–81; on M-80, **253**; on music scene, **20**, **344**; on musicians, 40, 41, 160, **169–70**, 190, **205–6**, 218, 250, 274–76, 279–81, 303, 315–16; Oar Folkjokeopus and, **69–70**, 72, 75, 85, 90, 328; on record labels, **228–29**; as tastemaker, 76–79, 83; venues and, **127**, **134**, 148–49, 289, 295–96
Kaye, Lenny, 117
KBEM, 20
Keillor, Garrison, 199
Keith, Mike, 118
Keller, Martin, **9–10**, 20, 79, 113–14, 136, 170, 242, 279–80, 321, 351
Kelly's Pub, 1, 9, 18, 29–31, *88*
KFAI, x, 2, 20, 86, 199, 348
"Kids Don't Follow" (Replacements), 180–81
Killing Joke, 275

Kindergarten, 349
King, Albert, 10, 44
King, Freddie, 10
King, Jan, 22, 221, 262
King, John, 36
King Kustom and the Cruisers, 55–57, 60, 347, 349. *See also* Hypstrz
King Tut's Wah Wah Hut, 265
Kinks, 104, 106
Kinsey Report, 350
Kinzer, Lu Ann, **108**, **175**, **209**, **231**, 351
KISS, 82, 161, 316
Kitchen, 268
Kitten: A Compilation, 296
Klaers, Hugo: gathering places and parties, **53**, 173, **175–76**; on M-80, **256**; in other bands, 148, **185**, 210; on other musicians, **60**, 107, **189**, **195–96**, **203**; Suburbs and, 54, 184–85, **186–87**, 188, **190**, **192**, 193, 196, **197–98**, **201–2**, **204**, 208, **216**, 351; venues and, **132**, **146**, **200**
Klemz, Steve, 180
KMOJ, 20
Knut Koupeé, 56, 178, 275, 335–36, 349
Kolath, Arpad, 181
Konar, Murat, 306
Kool Jazz Festival, 238
Koskinen, Erik, 350
Kraftwerk, 302
Kral, Ivan, 144
Kramer, Steve, 36, 231–37, 239–43, 251, 261, 266, 308
Kramer, Wayne, 103, 305
Krauss, Scott, 168
Kristal, Hilly, 21, 23, 35, 163
Krocus, 202
Kurilla, Jody: career of, 351; on music scene, **337–38**; on musicians, **18**, **143**, **169**, **208**, **272**, **316**; New York and, **264–65**; parties and, **52**, 172, 175, **176–77**; on venues, **134**, **290**
Kyx, 353

L7-3, 146, 149, 347, 352
Lack, Pete, 96, 99
Ladies and Gentlemen, the Suburbs Have Left the Building, 189
Lake Street Stink Band, 10
Lamont Cranston Band, 9–10, 47, 109

"Land of the Free" (Mark Goldstein), 256
Land Speed Record (Hüsker Dü), 272–76, 278–79, 283–84
Landau, Jon, 15
Landmark Center, 114
Larson, Judy, 9
Larson, PD, **288–89**, 351
Lawson, Charlie, **235**, **240–41**, 351
Leamington Hotel, 291
Led Zeppelin, 9, 60, 112
Lee, Jack, 109, 110
Leeds, 347
Lennon Tribute, 87, 96, 99–101
Let Downs, 353
Let It Be (Replacements), 6, 215, 224, 226, 314, 322, 327, 336, *345*
Let It Be Records, 67, 80, 85, 348
Let's Active, 266
"Let's Go Die" (Hüsker Dü), 276
Levy, Adam, **207**, **238**, **293**, 299, **344**, 351
Levy, Randy, 27–28, 136, 192
Lewis, Gary, and the Playboys, 57
Lewis, Jerry Lee, 100, 102
Lewis, Terry, 343
Li, Erik, 235
"Life Is Like" (Suburbs), 204
Lifter Puller, 349
Limelight (venue), 265, 267
Lindberg's Baby, 305
Lindbom, Eric, 309
Lindsay, Mark, 56
Linehan, Grady, 77, **83**, **223–24**, 316, 351
Linehan, Kelly, 83, 283, 297, *304*
"Listen" (NNB), 161
Litter, 1, 26, 56, 66, 185
Little Richard, 57, 89, 97, 331
Live at the Longhorn (Hypstrz), 62–63
Lloyd, Richard, 36, 163, 251–52, 258
Long Gone Daddies and the Cold Cold Hearts, 347, 350
Long John Baldry, 185
Longhorn (bar): beginnings of, 2–3, 10, 22, 84, 123–30, 238, 344; compared to CBGB, 136, 149; end of, 5, 180, 288–89, 293–94, 308; as gathering place, x, 131–35, 175–76; musicians at, 4, 55, *58*, *63*, 97–98, 102, 107–9, 112, 116–17, 137–40, *143*, 160, 191, 193, 198, 200, 203, 211, 214, 216–17, 230, 234, 236–37, 239, 245–46, 262, 271–73,

283–84, 290, 311, 313–14, 316–18, 343–44; Peter Jesperson and, 86, 289; popularity of, 291, 294, 339; staff, 347, 349–50, 353
Loring Alley Block Party, 246
Loring Park, 149, 189
Los Straitjackets, 347
Los Twin Tones, 347
Lost Acapulco, 347
Lothar and the Hand People, 90
Loud Fast Rules, 5, 224, 293, 299, 328, 335, 341, 352. *See also* Soul Asylum
Lounge Lizards, 195
Louris, Gary, 288
"Love Is the Law" (Suburbs), 209
Love Is the Law (Suburbs), 187, 189, 204
Luers, Mark, 163
Lunch, Lydia, 130
Lundeen, Mark "Bucky," 26
"Lust for Life" (Iggy Pop), 52
Lynyrd Skynyrd, 18

M-80 New-No-Now Wave Festival, xii, 4, 165, 232, 251–54, 257, 258
Macdonald, Scott, **149**, **306**, 351
Macpherson, Casey, 200, 321
Macpherson, Maggie, 240
Mad Ripple, 353
Madden, Dick, **277–78**, **293**, 351
Madden, Mike, 77, **144**, **198**, **274**, **277–78**, **281–82**, **293**, **319**, 351
Magnolias, 295
Man Sized Action, 65, 83, 182, 228–29, 281–83, 289, 296–97, 303, 310, 352–53
Manifest Destiny, 299–300, 305, 348
"Mannequins Drink 3.2" (New Psychonauts), 233
Mansfield, Colin, 247
Manske, Scott, 103, 105
Marathon '80. *See* M-80 New-No-Now Wave Festival
Marbles, 235, 260
March 4th (store), 3
Margolis, Barry, 74
"Mark, He's a Terror" (Suicide Commandos), 41
Markos, Michael, **138–39**, **243**, **265–66**, 351
Marquee Moon (Television), 169
Mars, 267
Mars, Chris, 314, 318, 324–25
Marsh Productions, 27, 49, 312
Martin, Bill, 236

Masterman, Gerry, 108
Mattson, Brad, *291*
Mauseth, Tim, 172
Maverick, 101
Maximum Rocknroll, 298
Max's Kansas City, 4, 33, 36, 116, 260, 266
Maxwell, Dennis, 156
Maxwell's, 164, 264, 267
Mayer, Jed, 302
Maynard, Doug, 9
Mazion, Russ, 300
MC5, 2, 25, 83, 89, 94, 103–4, 298, 305
McCafferty's, 300
McClellan, Steve: career of, **312–13**, 351; decency of, 294, 305, **308**, 308–9, 311–12, 344; musicians and, 60–63, 99, 163, 239–40, 297, 330–31, **333**; parties and, 179; venues and, **149**, 268
McConnell, Bonni, **187**, **189–90**, **193**, **205**, 351
McCready's, 303
McGowan, Dave, 135
McKean, Tom, 99
McKern, Mike, 111, **157–58**, 320, 351
McLean, Sue, 27–28, 136, 232, 294
McNally Smith College of Music, 351–52
Meadows, 353
Mecht Mensch, 296
Meide, Bob, 102–5, 107, 115, 116, 118–19
Mell-O-Tones, 352
Melody Maker, 11, 73
Melton, Bill, 77, 85
Mensch, Peter, 37
Mercury, 204
Merlyn's, 225
Met Center, 203
Metal Circus (Hüsker Dü), 342
Meyers, Jack, 309
Mezzo Fist, 350
Michael, Bayard, 255
Mighty Mofos, x, 55, 64–65, 97, 347, 353. *See also* Hypstrz
Mink DeVille, 128, 136–38
Minneapolis College of Art and Design (MCAD), 189, 343
Minneapolis Incest, 255
Minneapolis Star, 129
Minnesota Barking Ducks, 26
Minnesota Daily, 75, 99, 145, 189, 227, 309
Minutemen, 181, 278, 297

"Misery" (Pistons), 223
Mission of Burma, 181
Mod Girls, 176
Modern Corduroy, 162–63
Modern Lovers, 16, 80
Modesto, 86, 172, 180–81, 325
Moe, David, **65–66, 84, 150–51, 243–44, 279, 293, 301, 319,** 351
Mofungo, 163
MOJO, 219
Mommy Log Balls, 352
Money, Eddie, 136
Monochrome Set, 251
"Monster Au Go Go" (Suicide Commandos), 41
Moon, Keith, 103, 118–19
MoonSound, 330
Moore, Rick, 104, 153
More Songs About Building and Food (Talking Heads), 196
Morgan, Ellen, 176
Morris, Mike, *71*
Morrow, Glenn, 322
MORs, 60, 166, 281, 349
Mothersbaugh, Mark, 114
Motörhead, 301
Motorhome, 352
Mott the Hoople, 1, 17, 74, 104
Mould, Bob: Chris Osgood and, 274, 334–35; gathering places and parties, 78, 83, 181; in Hüsker Dü, 41, 61, 148, *271*, 277–86, 328–29; in other bands, 228; others on, xiii, 272, 300; as producer, 226; Reflex Records and, 229; venues and, 275
Mozey, Missy, **283**, 313, 349
Mr. Rowles Band, 352
Mr. Slate, 302, 347
MTV, 34, 102, 114–15
Mud Pie (restaurant), 78
Mudd Club, 260, 266
Muddy Waters, 100, 334
Mudhoney, 265
Mueller, Karl, 226, 258
Murphy, Daniel: career of, 352; on M-80, **258**; on music scene, **342**; on other musicians, **207, 296, 323, 328–29**; on record stores, **77**; Soul Asylum and, **226**, 328; on Twin/Tone, **225–28**; venues and, **149–50, 293, 295, 311**
Murphy, Willie, 9–10, 48, 89, 95, 101, 352
Murray, Tom, 26

Music 2, 350
"Music for Boys" (Suburbs), 197, 209
Music for Dozens, 322
Musician's Insider, *159*, 166
Musicland, 82, 348
My Five, 247

Naked Raygun, 160
Nancy Hauser Dance Company, 331
Natural Life, 127
Neglecters, 302
Neils, Henry, 25, 48
Nelson, Chris, 162
Nelson, Dale T., xi, *75*, **226, 298–99**, 301, **318,** 334, 352
Nelson, Kurt, **53–54, 148, 202–3, 223,** 352
Nelson, Ricky, 321
Neon Dirt, 349
Nero's Neptune, 353
Nerves, 110
Nevermind (Nirvana), 342
New Alliance, 229
New Day Rising (Hüsker Dü), 280, 286
New Music America, 240, 251
New Music Festival, 265
New Musical Express (NME), 11, 67, 73, 77
New Psychonauts, 231–34, 258, 349
New Romantics, 194
New Standards, 352
New Values (Iggy Pop), 144
New West Records, 350
"New World" (NNB), 156, 158
New York Dolls: albums of, 72, 74; David Johansen and, 136; influence of, 2, *14*, 17, 41, 107, 161, 316, 336; at Minnesota State Fair, 1, 9, 13, 20, 25; others on, xi, 14–15
New York Rocker, 73, 75, 95–96, 163, 261, 353
Newstrom, Lori, 264
Nicollet Studios, 225
"The Night Before Christmas" (Wallets), 242
Nino's Steakhouse, 123–24
Nirvana, 265, 342, 353
NME. See New Musical Express (NME)
NNB: beginnings of, 2, 17, 153–57, 159; career, 5, 20, 152, *154*, *159*, *162*, 165, 169, 218–19, 260, 308, 347–50, 353; influence of, 198; at M-80, 251, 256; musicians playing with, 64, 306; others on, xi; venues and, 125, 132, 147, 161, *166*, 255, 259, *263*, 267, 309

NO Magazine, 162, 164
Noble Mice, 352
Noise, Frank, and the Logs of Wood, 352
North Country Music, 67–68, 75. *See also* Oar Folkjokeopus
Northern Lights, 2, 67, 72, 73, 78, 80–81, 83–85, 316, 348, 350–52
Northrup Auditorium, 139, 234
Norton, Greg, 61, 83, *271*, 277, 285–86
Norton, Henry, 264
NRBQ, 90, 94
Nugent, Ted, 316
Nylon, Judy, 254

Oar Folkjokeopus: hangout for musicians and fans, 3, 12, 19, 60, 67–68, 72–79, 83, 90, 273, 280, 291, 314, 328, 336, 344; musicians at, 29, 38, *39*, *69*, 315–16, 324; Peter Jesperson at, 181, 211–12, 350; staff, 85, 350, 353; tastemakers at, 1, 2, 17, 81, 86, 117, 322
Odd, 305
Oedipus, 163–64
Off World Productions, 265
Oh! (Flamin' Oh's), 112
Okemah Prophets, 348
Olson, Mark, 288
OMD, 292
"Once Bitten, Twice Shy" (Ian Hunter), 134
One Groveland, 90–91, 104, 153
O'Neill, Michael, 177
Only Ones, 3, 80, 123, 130, 137–38
Ono, Yoko, 99
Orpheum, 82, 240
Osby, Paul, 298, 334
Osgood, Chris: gathering places and parties, 32–34, **76**, 80, **173, 176, 180**; as guitar teacher, **334–35**, 336; M-80 and, **251–54**, 257; music scene and, 184, **230, 328**, 334; on New York, **260–62**; in other bands, 149; on other musicians, **10, 13–15, 48**, 274, **330–31**; others on, xi, xiii, 26, 43, 135, 185–86, 198, 312; Suicide Commandos and, 16, 19, **23–28, 31, 35, 37–38, 40–41, 51, 336–37**, 352; Twin/Tone and, **212, 221, 224–25, 226–27**; venues and, **28, 35–37, 46–47, 50–52,** *98,* **133–34, 146, 147, 257, 289**
Otto's Chemical Lounge, 229, 296, 298–99, 334, 350, 352
Oulman, Jon, 179

Outcry, 302
Overtones, 3, 64, 135, 148, 251, 256, 288, 347
Owens, Michael, 12, **141**, 213–14, **214**, 217, **218**, 352

p. david studios, 26, 211, 214, 320
Palladium, 266
Palmiter, Caleb, 64, 99, 301
Paquin, Mark, 55
Parade, 352
Parisota Hot Club, 350
Parker, Graham, 70
Patti Smith Group, 144
Pavitt, Bruce, **38, 321–22, 342**, 352
Pax Americana, 305, 348
PDH, 302
Peak Productions, 49
Peck, Jay, 90–91, 98, 185, 262, *267*
"Peggy Sue" (Buddy Holly), 57
Peil, Anne, 176
Peil, Tony, 265
Peltier, Carol, 217
Pepper Fog, 104
Peppermint Lounge, 4, 116, *233*, 244, 260, 265, 297
Pere Ubu, 15, 36–38, 136, 138, 141, 160, 168, 170, 196, 227
Perkins, Leslie Carlson, **191–92**, 352
"Personality Crisis" (New York Dolls), 15
Pete, John, 111, 115
Peterson, Jim, 76, 78, 83, 85, 90, 328
Peterson, Terry, 83
Pezzati, Jeff, 160
Pharoahs, 58
Phelps, Dave, 262
Philadelphia Story, 72
Phones, ix, 98, 111, 148, 207, 224–25, 242, 291–93, 330, 348
Pickett, Wilson, 88–89, 93
Pierson, Eric, **82–83, 151**, 278–79, **301, 316**, 352
Pine, Charlie, 272
Pink (Ground Zero), 229
Pink Floyd, 11
Pioneer Press, 145
Piotrowski, Tim, **303**, 352
Pirate's Cove, 36
Pirner, Dave: Chris Osgood and, 334–35, **336**; gathering places and parties, **78, 182–83**; on music scene, **283, 342–43**; on other

musicians, **97**, **161**, **208**, **275**, **287**; Soul Asylum and, **226**, 329, **330**, 352; venues and, **149**, 293
Piston Wrist, 352
Pistons, 202, 212, 223, 251, 257, 352
Placebo, Dr. Dann, 199, 348
Plasmatics, 3, 130, 290
Plastics, 246
Platters, 348
"Please Please Please" (James Brown), 97
Pleased to Meet Me (Replacements), 320
Plimsouls, 110
Pluta, Bill, 49
PM Magazine, 248
Podany's, 147, 172–75, 186, 192, 318
Poetry Grenade, 348, 350
Polara, 347
Police, 130, 136, 138, 140, 141, 145
Poling, Chan: gathering places and parties, 73, **76**, 173, 181; on music scene, **9**, **15–16**; in other bands, 186, 205, 210; on other musicians, **141**, **196**, **198–99**, **202**, **210**; others on, 91; Suburbs and, 4, 184, **185–87**, *188*, **189–90**, 193, **194–97**, 198–99, 203, **204**, 207, 215, 352; venues and, **131–32**, **146**
Poling Owens, Terri, 247
Polsky, Ruth, 267
PolyGram, 187, 201, 203, 209
Poneman, Jon, 352
Pop, Iggy: Beej Chaney compared to, 193, 195; influence of, 2, 17, 25, 41, 52; at Oar Folkjokeopus, 79; other musicians and, 28, 35, *37*, 202; venues and, 3, 123, 136, 141, 144–45, 290, 291–92. *See also* Iggy and the Stooges
Pop Shop, 237
Possum Road, *52*
Powell, George, 166
Powell, Mark, 166
"Prehistoric Jaws" (Suburbs), 195
Presley, Elvis, 100, 102, 126, 334
Pretenders, 312
Prichard, Mike, 300
Prince: career, 6, 209, 327, 342, 344, *345*, 353; at First Avenue, 310, 330–31; gathering places and parties, 82, 178, 202; legend of, 101, 331–33; loss of, xii–xiii; music scene and, 207, 339; Têtes Noires and, 248
Prior Place, 28, 50

Proch's Popular Ballroom, 48
Procol Harum, 11, 68
Prodigy: beginnings of, 2, 102–4; at Blitz Bar, 19, 46; career, *105*, 112, 353; playing original music, 17, 104, 107. *See also* Flamingo
Propaganda, 353
Prospective Records, 350
Proud Crass Fools, 296
Psychedelic Furs, 81, 290–91
"Psycho" (Sonics), 56
Public Image Limited, 228, 275, 278
Pucci, Tony: career of, 352; Hüsker Veggies and, 282–83; on music scene, **83–84**, **182**, **307**; on musicians, **42–43**, **65**, **208**, **284**, **297**, **303–5**; in New York, **297**; venues and, **295**, *304*, **310–11**
Purple Rain (Prince), 6, 327, 331, 333
Pyramid Club, 264–65

Quast, Matt, 33–34

Radio Birdman, 79
Radio for Teens, 247, 296
Radio Kings, 349
Raitt, Bonnie, 178
Ramone, Joey, 311, 336
Ramones: career, 2, 16, 128, 196–97, 262; gathering places and parties, 69, 70, 72; influence of, 16, 18, 20, 58–59, 79, 161, 169, 260, 318, 335–36; others on, 18, 28–29, 137; venues and, 1, 9, 18–19, 29, 36, 55, 60–61, 123, 310–12
Randall, John "J. R.," 115
Randolph Inn, 272
R.A.P.P. Arts Center, 265
Rat (venue), 4, 36, 163
Rathskeller, 172–73
Ratt, 209
"Rattle My Bones" (Suburbs), 205
Raw Power (Iggy Pop), 17, 79
Ray, Dave "Snaker," 8, 347
Ray, Jody, **22**, 102, **105–6**, 111, **114**, **118–19**, 352
Ray, Max, **132**, **196**, 200, 231, **234**, **237–41**, *241*, 246, 352
Raybeats, 96, 260, 347
Reader, 136, 145, 253
"Rebel, Rebel" (David Bowie), 117
Record Spot, 349
Records Limited, 68

Records on the Nile, 352
"Recurring Dreams" (Hüsker Dü), 279
Red Eye Blue, 350
Red House, 64, 160, 171, 347, 349
Red Letter Day, 351
Red Meat, 297, 301, 302, 347
Redd Kross, 353
Redman, Nigel, 251
Reflex Records, 228–29, 271, 285–86, 296, 350
Regenerates, 350, 353
Reiter, Michael, 66, **78, 97–98, 207–8, 292–93,** 352
Reller, Rick, 57–59
R.E.M., 63–64, 181, 204, 266, 305, 309–10
REMs, 295, 318, 353
REO Speedwagon, 9, 190
Replacements: career, ix, xii, 6, 86, 180–82, 204, 224, 314, 320, 322, 325, 327–28, 334, 340–41, 344, *345*, 348, 350, 353; influence of, 306, 337, 341; influenced by, 43; musicians performing with, 225, 249, 293, 299; others on, 247, 259, 315–16; popularity of, 207, 280, 282, 302, 314–15; record labels and, 3, 5, 215, 220, 223, 225, 227, *315*, 330; venues and, 3, 98, 145, 207, 291–93, 297, 310, 314, 317, 318, 319, 323, 342
Reprise Records, 6
Residents, 156
REV105, 348
Revelators, 348
Revere, Paul, and the Raiders, 56, 57
Rey, Johnny: Flamingo and, 102, **106–8,** 109–10, 353; gathering places and parties, 22; music scene and, **103–6, 119,** 137; in other bands, **110**; on other musicians, 17, **116–17, 138, 198, 317**; others on, xi; and the Reaction, xii, 99, 111, 292, 351, 353; venues and, **48, 128, 292**
Rey, Renaldo, 93
Rey, Tommy, 64, 182
Rezillos, 82
Rich Lewis Band, 352
Richards, Keith, 96, 103, 104, 119, 152, 223
Riff Raff, 214
Rifle Sport, 228, 288, 296, 297, 302–3, 304, 350
Riley, Jim, *291*
Riley, Terry, 185
Ringout!, 351
Riviera, Jake, 140

Rivkin, David, 112
Roadrunner, 350
Roamin' Catholics, 200
Rock World (television show), 115
Rock-a-Dots, 349, 352
Rockestra, 257–58
Rockin' Pinecones, 353
Rock-It Cards, 3, 177, 348
Rock-Ola, 353
Rockpile, 137
Rolling Stone, 40, 101, 209, 219
Rolling Stones, 11, 88–90, 102–4, 106, 109, 113, 119, 131, 159, 185, 217, 223, 257, 316, 334
Roskilde Festival, 329
Roth, Dave, 78, 323
Roth, Jenny, 323
Rotten, Johnny, 16, 89, 94
"Roxanne" (Police), 140
Roxy, 110
Roxy Music, 1, 17, 20, 26, 73, 76, 106, 208
Rubin, Rick, 6
RuDeGiRL, 341, 347
Rue, Gary, 99
Run Westy Run, ix, 341
Rundgren, Todd, 20, 110
Runyon, Paul, 179
Runyun's, 179
Rush, 60
Ryder, Mitch, 53, 88

Safety Last, 224, 288, 350, 353
St. Croix Boom Company, 64, 209
Saints, 69
Salvation Army, 295, 298
Sam the Sham, 58
Samels, Sharon, **107, 110, 119, 128–29, 137–38,** 353
Sam's, 73, 111, 288, *333*, 348, 351. *See also* First Avenue; Uncle Sam's
Sanden, Vern, 67–68, 70, *71*, 74, 85
"Saturday Night" (Bay City Rollers), 258
Savoy, David, 276
Say What You Will (Soul Asylum), 226
A Scarlet Letter (Curtiss A), 94
Scene Is Now, 162, 348
Schitz, 150
Schoenheider, Rory, 300
Schon Productions, 22, 27, 136, 350
Schwartz, Andy: career of, 353; gathering

places and parties, 21, 22, **70**, 90; on M-80, **253–54**; music scene and, 2, 75, 95; musicians and, 19, **169**, 187; on New York, **261**; as tastemaker, 15, 75–77, 80; venues and, 125, 163
Scream, 301
Seconds, 172
Secret Agent Man Inc., 348
Seth, 152, 347
"Seven Deadly Finns" (Brian Eno), 73
Sex Pistols, 2, 14, 16, 20, 58, 75, 76, 80, 84, 126, 185
Sham 69, 79
Shanderuk, John, 111, 321
Shaw, Greg, 36–37, 62
"She Got Sex" (Pistons), 223
Sheepherders, 352
Sheet Music (10cc), 75
Shinders, 60
Shoes, 75
"Shooting Pistols" (Suburbs), 197
Si Sauvage (Suburbs), 210
Siberia, 264
Silverteens, 65–66, 349, 350–52
Simba, 54, 148, 200, 202, 352
Sir Crackers (Crackers), 266
Sire Records, 72, 101, 112–13, 322
Sire/Warner Bros., 314
Situation, 306
Skafish, 251
Skogie and the Flaming Pachucos, 1, *12*, 21, 40, 47, 104, 153, 256
Skull Fuck, 302
Sky King, 152
"Slack" (NNB), xi, 132, 152, 156–61, 163–65, 170, 218–19
Slickee Boys, 59
Small Faces, 88
Smart Alex, 20
Smith, Patti, 2, 9, 15–16, 21, 28, 70, 116, 144
Snail Lake Supper Club, 56–57
Snaps, 353
Soda, 349
Soft Machine, 152
Soldier (Iggy Pop), 292
"Soldier Boy," 248
Soma, 57, 221
Sonic Bouquet, 353
Sonic Youth, 333

Sonics, 56
Sorry Ma, Forgot to Take Out the Trash (Replacements), 215, 223–24, 314, 319, 340, 342
Soul Asylum: career, xii, 5, 299, 324, 328, *329*, 336, 341, 343, 352–53; impact of, 43; others on, ix, 247, 306, 334; record labels and, 6, 211, 220, 225, 327
Sound 80 Studio, 112
"Sounds of Silence" (Simon and Garfunkel), 150
Spanish Fly Records, 347
Sparks, 302
Speed Wiener, 336
Speedboat Gallery, 348
Spin magazine, 329
Spin Radio Concert, 279
Spin with Cyn, x, xiii
Spitfire, 22, 169, 349
Spooks, 2, 87, 92, 95, 214–16, 218, 220, 223, 347, 348
"Spring Came" (Suburbs), 186
Springsteen, Bruce, 130, 202–3
SRC, 25
SST Records, 6, 271, 297, 327
Stabstock, 28
Stagger Lee, 288
Stamey, Chris, 163
Stamey, Chris, and the dB's, 251, 258
Stang, Tommy, 145
Star Tribune, 108, 145, 177, 253
Starfish (Church), 179
Stark, Paul: other musicians and, **26**, 36, 62–63, 91, 133, 140, **196**, 205, **215**, **319–20**, 325; stores and studios, **73**, 85, 211, 214; Twin/Tone and, 3, 112, 211–13, 216, 218–20, 224, 226–28, 353
State Theatre, 28, 116
Statler, Chuck: career of, 353; musicians and, 33, **34–35**, 114, **115**, 145, **192**, **209**, **331**; venues and, **131**, **140**, **294**
"Statues" (Hüsker Dü), 81, 228, 272–73, 275–76, 278
Steckling, Jerry, 225, 241
Steeples, Bruce, 64
Stein, Seymour, 322
Stenshoel, David, 152
Stenshoel, Peter, 152
"Stereo" (Suburbs), 186
Steve Miller Band, 24

Stewart, Rod, 116
Stickman, 348
Stiff Records, 140
Sting, 140
Stink (Replacements), 180, 182, 215, 223, 224, 340
Stinson, Bob, 78, 181–82, 314, 318–20, 323–25, 341, 353
Stinson, Tommy, 78, 306, 314, 317–19, 323, 325
Stipe, Michael, 64
Stone, Sly, 331
Stooges, 16, 79, 161, 195, 336
"Stop" (Flamin' Oh's), 114
Straight Up, 26, 29, 91
Stranglers, 79, 143, *151*
Stray Cats, 141
Strength, Bob and Dale, 104
Strummer, Joe, 94–95, 334
Studio 54, 265
Sub Pop Records, 265, 352
Suburbs: beginnings of, 2, 17; career, ix, xii, 5, 20, 34, 43, 53, 82, 109–10, 150, 172, 184, *188*, 190, 196–200, 204–9, 211–12, *216*, 242, 244, 327, 343, 347–53; gathering places and parties, 60, 173–74; impact of, 337; at M-80, 251, 258; musicians playing with, 55, 202–3, 234, 293; others on, ix–x, 242; Twin/Tone and, 3, 214–15, 218, 220, 223–25, 227; venues and, 2, 4, *54*, 128, 131–32, 146, 147, 149, 189, *199*, 201, 264, *275*, 310–11, 313
Sue Veneer and the Mementos, 25, 48, 225
Suicide, 251
Suicide Commandos: beginnings of, 2, 17, 19; career, 5, 13, 31–38, 41, *47*, 75, 109, 113, 119, 164, 166, 171, 184–85, 190, 196, 200, 208, 212, 218, 221, 242, 261–62, 274, 336, 339, 343, 347, 350, 352; gathering places and parties, 21–22, 32–33, *39*, 60, 73, 173, 178; impact of, 198, 337; at M-80, 251, 254, 257–58; with other musicians, 55, 105–6, 116, 133, 149; others on, x–xi, xiii, 16, 66; as pioneers, 20, 23, 42–43; playing original music, 12, 17, 21, 26–27, 190; Twin/Tone and, 3, 211–13; venues and, 2, 29–30, 35–36, *40*, 44–46, 123, 126, 128, 133–34, 149, 318
Suicide Commandos Make a Record, 38, 40, 221
Sullivan, Bill, 321
Summer, Donna, 126
Summer of Love, 348

Summers, Andy, 138
Sun Ra, 293
Supernaturals, 100
Susstones Records, 229–30, 347, 350, 351
Sutton's, 289, 350
Swamp Twisters, 351
Swans, 244
Sweden House Smorgasbord, 123
Sweet Potato, 26, 129, 136, 145, 166, 307, 347
Sweet Thing, 217, 350
Sylvain Sylvain, *14*
Sylvester, Paul, 12
System, 90

Take It (Wallets), 225, 238
Talking Heads, 2–3, 16, 29, 35, 69–72, 116, 123, 130, 136–41, 145, 176–77, 184, 196–97, 234, 240, 262, 344
Tangent, 351, 353
Taste, 69
Taves, Rick, *291*
Technocats, 186
Television: at CBGB, 21, 128; influence of, 15–16, 70, 154, 196–97, 260; NNB similar to, 159–60, 169–71; Richard Lloyd of, 163, 251, 258
"Tell Her No" (Zombies), 87
Tempo Bar, 88
Ten Years After, 11
Têtes Noires, 5, 225, 231, 247–49, *250*, 296, 349–50
Them, 256
Thielges, Steve "Tilly," 92–93, 100
Things That Fall Down, 5, 175, 231, 236, 244–46, 349
Third Stone Music, 69, 77
"This Is It" (NRBQ), 90
Thorgrimson, Neil, 230
Three O'Clock, 81, 83, 295, 298
Throne, Mark, 217
Thumbs Up, 12, 17, 19, 46, 87–93, 100, 123, 213–14, 347–48
Thunders, Johnny, 13, 29, 36, 81–82, 274, 318
Tier 3, 260, 266, 267
Tiger Night, 148, 149, 151
Tiltawhirl, 305–6
Tilton Ballroom, 49
Tim (Replacements), 225, 320, 323, 327
Time, 246, 331

Tippy, 281–83, 297, *304*
Todlachen, 296, 299, 302, 350
Tollefsrud, Jim: career of, 353; music scene and, 12, 16, 22, **160**, *162*; NNB and, 17, 152–53, **155–56**, **163–64**, 165, 168
Top O' Utopia, 32. *See also* Utopia House
Tornado, 349
"Totally Nude" (Wallets), 241
Touch and Go Records, 265
Tour-Spiel (Minutemen), 229
Toussaint, Allen, 225, 238
Tower Records, 224
Tracks on 5th, 157
Trashmen, 1, 10, 48, 57, 294–95
Treehouse Records, 67, 85, 229, 353. *See also* Oar Folkjokeopus
Trehus, Mark, **15**, **31**, **43**, **80**, **85**, **130**, **279**, 353
Triangle Bar, 10
Trip Shakespeare, 211, 341
Trollhaugen, 49
Troubadour, 110
Trouser Press magazine, 275
Tsetse Flies, 173, 185–86, 347
Tucker, Moe, 169
Tuff Darts, 84
"Tumbling Dice" (Rolling Stones), 104
Tunnel (venue), 265
Turner, Tina, 63, 333
Tuxedo Moon, 251, 254
Twa Corbies/The Tanglewoods, 353
Twilley, Dwight, 54
Twin Cities Reader, 351
Twin City Imports (TCI), 80, 306
Twin/Tone record label: career, 6, 215, 219, 220–21, 223–28, 344; founding of, 3, 86, 211–14, 216; musicians and, 62, 112, 158, 184, 196, 218–19, 262, 265, 273, 285–87, 300, 314, 322, 329–30, *345*, 347; staff, 336, 350–53
Tyler, Steven, 37

U2, 100, 202, 333
Uncle Sam's, 28, 55, 60, 62, 73, 312, 333, 351. *See also* First Avenue
Union Bar, 107, 290
University of Minnesota Field House, 98, 251, 256
Upper Deck. *See* Goofy's Upper Deck
Uptown Bar, *98*, 240, 303, 342

Urban Guerillas, 5, 81, 231, 248, 299, 302
"Uruguay 1983" (NNB), 161
Utopia House, xi, *14*, 25, 32–35, 105

Van der Graaf Generator, 69
Van Morrison, 257
Va-VOOM! 353
Vee, Bobby, 90
Veggies, Hüsker Dü, 281–83
Velline, Bill, 90
Velvet Elvis, 306
Velvet Underground, 16, 79, 169
Vendetta, 304
Ventures, 275
Vertebrats, 80
Vibrators, 136
Vicious, Sid, 16
Village Voice, 97, 224, 227, 253–54, 346
Vincent, Gene, 57
Violent Femmes, 81, 323
Vixen, *88*
Voice of Reason (Rifle Sport), 228
Volden, Erick, 300
Volunteers of the Blue Knights, 352

Wad, 22, 221, 262, 349
Wagner, Pop, 9
"Waiting" (Suburbs), 197, 209
"Walk on Water" (New Psychonauts), 233–34
Walker Art Center, 106, 149, 161, 185, 189, 248, 251, 253, 350
Wall of Voodoo, 292
Wallets: career, 6, 231–32, 235, 238–41, 244, 343, 349, 351–52; in New York, 260–61; playing with other musicians, 196, 234, 249, 251, 293; theatrics of, 5, 237, 242; Twin/Tone and, 211, 225; venues and, 132, 166, 175, 234, 237, 240, 244, 264, 293, 308–9, 310
Walsh, Jim, **109**, 138, **318**, 353
Walsh, Joe, 152
Warehouse: Songs and Stories (Hüsker Dü), 225, 327
Warheads, 5, 143, 175, 231, 288
Warhol, Andy, 15–16, 265
Warner Bros., 271, 327
Waryan, Jeff, 24, **90–91**, **95–96**, 98, **137**, **140–41**, 152–53, 185, 257, 353
Wasilowski, Skip, 240
Wasteband, 353

Watts, Charlie, 119
Wave 7, 152, 157, 219
Wax Museum, 2, 67, 73–75, 78–80, 84, 154–55, 159, 350
Weaver, Jay, 172
Weaver, Tom, 172
"Weekend Warrior" (Suicide Commandos), 221
Weirdos, 37
Weiss, Randy, 55, 58–59, 64
"Well, Oh Well" (NNB), 162
Werstein, Kyle, 353
West, Julian, 99
West Bank Boogie (Collins), x
West Bank Trackers, 47, 240
Westerberg, Paul, 78, 180–82, 223, 314–16, 318–19, 321, 323–26, 328
Weymouth, Tina, 35, *71*, 72, 138, 139, 145
Whale in the Thames, 347
While You Were Out (Soul Asylum), 225
"Whip It" (Devo), 114
Whiskey a Go Go, 37, 110
White, Ann, 240
White, Garrison, 245–46
White, James, and the Blacks, 251, 253
White Castle Party. *See* Cold Party
"White Wedding" (Billy Idol), 248
Who, 88–89, 103–4, 232
Whole Lotta Loves, 304, 310, 347, 349
"Whole Lotta Shakin' Going On" (Jerry Lee Lewis), 331
Wilkes, Monty Lee, xii, **64, 94, 111, 198–99, 320,** 321, 353
Wilkinson, Robert: career of, 17, **102–3,** 106–7, **114–16,** 118, 133, 353; Flamin' Oh's and, **109, 111–13, 118–19;** Flamingo and, 102, 108; gathering places and parties, 22, **33,** 74, 76; on music scene, **21, 337–38;** on other musicians, **117–18, 247;** others on, 19; Prodigy and, **104,** 105–6; venues and, **46, 48, 127, 137, 289–90**
Willful Neglect, 296, 300, 303

William Morris Agency, 333
Williams, Megan, 266
Williams North (venue), 50
Willkomm, Jeff, 99
Wilma and the Wilbers, 20, 64
Wilson, Jim, 152
Winchester, Jesse, 80
"Wipe Out" (Surfaris), 57
Wire, 87, 90, 303, 347. *See also* Thumbs Up
"The Witch" (Sonics), 56
Wodtke, Al, 84, **107, 129,** 136, 353
Wood, Ronnie, 116
Woods, Pat, **43, 65, 83, 182, 283–84, 297, 304–5,** 353
Wray, Link, 70
"Writer's Cramp" (Hüsker Dü), 276

X-Boys, 347, 352
Xeno, 26
XTC, 293

Yanomamo, 352
Yardbirds, 106
Yes, 104
Yo La Tengo, 267, 322
You and Whose Army, 223
Young, Neil, 9, 11, 152
Your Flesh, 295, 300
"Your Phone" (Suburbs), 186
"You're Not the First One" (Suicide Commandos), 221

Z, David, 112
Zappa, Frank, 232
Zen Arcade (Hüsker Dü), 6, 276, 279–80, 301, 327, 340, *345*
Zombies, 87–88
Zoogie's, 5, 142, 146–50, 288–90. *See also* Longhorn (bar)
Zuzu's Petals, 352
ZZ Top, 25, 336

ABOUT THE AUTHOR

Cyn Collins is the DJ/host of KFAI Community Radio's *Spin with Cyn* program and a radio documentary producer for KFAI and Ampers.org. She is the author of *West Bank Boogie: Music, Mayhem and Memories* (2006) and a freelance music, arts, and culture journalist whose work has been published in *City Pages*, the *Star Tribune*, Twin Cities Daily Planet, *Twin Cities Metro*, *Pulse of the Twin Cities*, RIFT magazine, *Southside Pride*, and more. She lives in Minneapolis with her two cats.

www.ingramcontent.com/pod-product-compliance
Lightning Source LLC
Chambersburg PA
CBHW071648160426
43195CB00012B/1390